A PINNACLE OF FEELING

20|21

A PINNACLE OF FEELING

American Literature and

Presidential Government

Sean McCann

PRINCETON UNIVERSITY PRESS

PRINCETON AND OXFORD

Published by Princeton University Press, 41 William Street,
Princeton, New Jersey 08540
In the United Kingdom: Princeton University Press, 6 Oxford Street,
Woodstock, Oxfordshire OX20 1TW

Library of Congress Cataloging-in-Publication Data

McCann, Sean, 1962–
A pinnacle of feeling : American literature and presidential government / Sean McCann.
p.   cm. — (Princeton University Press series ; 20/21)
Includes bibliographical references and index.
ISBN 978-0-691-13695-0 (cloth : acid-free paper)
1. American literature—20th century—History and criticism. 2. Politics and literature—
United States—History—20th century 3. Executive power in literature. 4. Presidents
in literature. 5. Executive power—Philosophy. 6. Authors, American—20th century—
Political and social views. I. Title.
PS228.P6M39   2008
810.9′35873—dc22   2008012782

British Library Cataloging-in-Publication Data is available

This book has been composed in

Printed on acid-free paper. ∞

press.princeton.edu

Printed in the United States of America

10 9 8 7 6 5 4 3 2 1

For Dexter

CONTENTS

PREFACE

L IKE MOST NINETEENTH-CENTURY AMERICANS, Walt Whitman had few expectations for the presidency before the Civil War. Although he revered Washington as a founder of the republic and celebrated Jefferson and Jackson as champions of democracy, Whitman saw little in the recent history of the United States to make the power of the chief executive appealing. Indeed both conviction and experience made him suspicious of the popular leaders he dismissed as "hero presidents."[1] As a radical Democrat, the young Whitman felt an intuitive distrust toward centralized power and political eminence. "Men must be 'masters unto themselves,' and not look to Presidents and legislative bodies for aid," he declared in 1847.[2] As an opponent of slavery, he found himself increasingly disgusted in the decade leading up to the Civil War by every feature of American government, but he expressed particular revulsion at the "scum" that had "floated into the Presidency."[3] In his poem "To a President," Whitman cast the office of the chief executive as the epitome of an entirely corrupt system out of tune with "the politics of Nature." "All you are doing and saying," he lamented, "is to America dangled mirages."[4]

By the end of the Civil War, however, Whitman's views had undergone a significant transformation. His fury at Secession led him to drop his former commitment to the states rights he had once viewed as "impregnable" and to embrace a new appreciation for the coercive arm of the federal government and its "conquering march" over the rebellious forces of the Confederacy.[5] His fascination with the heroism and suffering of the Union army led him likewise to shift his attention away from the radical individualism he had celebrated before the war and toward a new emphasis on the collective purpose of the American people. *Leaves of Grass* had been "the song of a great composite *democratic individual*," Whitman explained in 1872. The writing he did after the War would be dedicated to a new "electric *democratic nationality*."[6]

Above all, Whitman's encounter with Abraham Lincoln led him to change his views of executive leadership. Even before the war, his growing disdain for the corrupt system of party competition had led Whitman to imagine a "Redeemer President" who would share his own commitment to the Union and his own dedication to the democratic purposes enshrined in the Declaration of Independence.[7] During the war, as his admiration and sympathy for the president grew, Whitman found in Lincoln a realization of that unlikely hope and a political leader he could imagine as an intimate companion. "Lincoln is particularly my man" and "by the same token, I am Lincoln's man," Whitman told his friend Horace Traubel.[8] In his diary, he confided, "I love the President personally."[9]

Several decades after he made that remark, Whitman's view of presidential leadership would be taken up by a cohort of reformist intellectuals and Progressive politicians who had similarly grown frustrated with a decentralized political system built on representative government and party competition. Like Whitman, those new advocates of presidential power saw in the existing political order merely corruption, arrogance, and inequality. Like him, they contended that the United States had "outgrown parties" and that only robust executive leadership could make government responsive to "the real America."[10] Following Whitman's lead, they worked toward the creation of a new political system in which American voters would abandon their party affiliations to embrace a personal relationship with the president. In their view, as in Whitman's, the chief executive would ideally serve as a national redeemer who could restore the sovereignty of the people and return America to its democratic mission. The vision of presidential leadership they fostered would go on to form the core justification for a new constitutional order in which the power of the federal government and of the chief executive in particular would expand to an unanticipated degree. As Peri E. Arnold and L. John Roos explained looking back over the history of that growth in executive power, in the modern theory of the presidency, "all the Presidents were to be Lincolns."[11]

The main contention of this book is that this political history was matched by a comparable literary history. The theorists of the modern presidency followed Whitman in casting Lincoln as the founder of a new model of executive leadership, one suited to a political system that gave increasing emphasis to national identity and to the power of the federal government in realizing it. So, too, would a number of twentieth-century American writers follow Whitman in seeing their efforts as intimately bound up with the figure of the president. Even before Lincoln assumed office, Whitman imagined "a Dialogue" between himself and the new chief executive in which the poet would provide "Lessons for a President elect."[12] Though less evidently, many later writers would similarly see themselves as engaged in an implicit dialogue with the chief executive, so much so that the presidency often would become in effect a model and rival for the aims of their own work.

In drawing attention to this pattern, I hope this book will achieve two goals. Most fundamentally, I hope that seeing the importance of the presidency to the writers I discuss below will help to identity what is at issue in their work and will clarify the extent to which, like Whitman, they often were preoccupied with the relations among democracy, nationality, and executive power. More generally, I hope that seeing the way these writers conceived that problem will help to illuminate some of the assumptions of twentieth-century American political culture—assumptions that are outlined in Whitman's veneration of Lincoln and that were implicitly taken up by later American writers, but that are only rarely made explicit features of political discourse.

What Whitman most admired about Lincoln, of course, was the fact that "under" his presidency "was saved the Union of these States."[13] But two features of Lincoln's leadership assumed particular significance for Whitman in this light. The first emphasized Lincoln's "firm hand" and the "mighty powers" he wielded—"with more sway than any king in history"—in leading the Union and its army to victory over the rebellious states of the Confederacy.[14] In this guise, that is, Lincoln impressed Whitman as a commander-in-chief who used the occasion of war to transcend the pettiness of official Washington and to vastly expand the power that could be exercised by the chief executive. In keeping with that admiration, Whitman imagined himself as a comparably commanding voice, "rousing the land with breath of flame" and urging the Union soldiers on to victory. But this martial image was importantly answered by another view of Lincoln, as a man who suffered greatly and in solitude. In this latter guise, the president was important to Whitman for the sympathy and reverence that he, like the poet, displayed for the soldiers injured and killed in the war, and still more importantly, for the comparable sympathy that he occasioned in his own death. Against the image of the president as commander, in short, Whitman placed a differing image of the president as martyr—"the sweetest, wisest soul of all my days and lands"—and he cast himself no longer as the poet of democratic conquest, but as a voice of national mourning (467).[15]

It would be tempting to view these two images of Lincoln as offering two alternative visions of the presidency and of two analogously different poetic voices, and it would be tempting to suggest, as several critics have, that, in trading bellicosity for sorrow, Whitman matured as a poet and political thinker. But that view would be misleading. Despite the mourning he voiced on the death of Lincoln and despite the anguish and sympathy he expressed in response to the mass suffering created by the war, Whitman never lost his enthusiasm for "the absolute triumph of the National Union arms" or his admiration for Lincoln's "indomitable firmness" in directing them. Indeed in a poem like "Over the Carnage Rose a Prophetic Voice," Whitman imagined himself as an agent of "manly affection," binding the soldiers of the North and South in a new, irrevocable compact.[16] In his very title, however, Whitman also made clear that there would be no occasion for that sympathetic binding without the carnage that enabled the poet to speak for the fallen soldiers across the nation in the first place. Without "the conquering march," and the suffering that accompanied it, there could be no affectionate prophecy to follow.

Rather than seeing Whitman's two visions of Lincoln as inconsistent alternatives, then, it would make more sense to see them as aspects of a single dynamic pattern, each of which emphasizes the capacity of executive power to create, through both coercion and sympathy, an otherwise unrealized national community. In the logic implicitly bringing these two images together, the president's power is counterbalanced by his personal suffering, his role as commander answered by his martyrdom. If, on the one hand, Whitman envisioned the president standing at the head of a massive army and exercising powers that dwarfed those of any king, on the other hand, he shielded the president from the charge of tyranny by emphasizing Lincoln's willingness, like that of his soldiers, to surrender his life to the cause he served. Thus it was that Whitman described "the splendor" of Lincoln's death "purging" the tensions that surrounded his presidency.[17] Lincoln himself reportedly suggested that the president could remain a democratic leader only by leaving himself open to the constant threat of assassination. "It would never do for a President to have guards with drawn sabers at his door, as if he fancied he were . . . an emperor," Lincoln is said to have commented. "Where our habits are simple, and must be, assassination is always possible."[18] Whitman's own sense of personal connection to Lincoln was partly enabled, as the poet noted, by the president's demonstrations of public vulnerability, and he would go on to give a poetic elaboration to the understanding implicit in Lincoln's words. In his unwavering praise for the Union army, Whitman depicted a democratic nation that conquered its rebellious factions in the name of popular rule. In the martyrdom of Lincoln, Whitman complemented that image with a vision of a people joined by sorrow and fortified by the men who gave up their personal lives so that the nation might live. "He was assassinated—but the Union is not assassinated . . . . Death does its work, obliterates a hundred, a thousand—President, general, captain, private—but the Nation is immortal."[19]

Imagining a democratic nation whose immortal life was proven by the death of its soldiers and leaders, Whitman advanced a rhetoric that he may well have learned from Lincoln himself. (The poet reportedly tacked a copy of the Gettysburg Address to his wall during the war.)[20] In doing so, he also implicitly articulated a theory of democratic legitimacy that, although it would fit only awkwardly with the existing constitutional design of American government, would go on to become a significant, tacit justification for the rise of presidential power in the twentieth century. In the theory implicit in Whitman's two images of Lincoln, the president was justified in the exercise of awesome, even extraconstitutional, powers not by legislative authorization or even, strictly speaking, by the consent of the governed. Rather, presidential rule appeared legitimate so long as it served to bring forth a better, more democratic national community, and so long as the president demonstrated his commitment to that ambition in his willingness to sacrifice his own gratification, and in the limit case, his life, to the cause.

As Whitman recognized, those tacit assumptions about presidential leadership amounted to the core elements of a new civil religion for the new nation that had emerged from the Civil War. "There is a cement to the whole people, subtler, more underlying, than any thing in written constitution, or courts or armies," Whitman wrote in his celebrated address on Lincoln's death, "Namely, the cement of a death identified thoroughly with that people, at its head, and for its sake." For Whitman, as for many of his successors, the president was less politician than a quasi-monarch, at once a divinely sanctioned commander and a mere temporary vehicle for the popular will, a figure of awesome power and humbling vulnerability—in Whitman's tellingly paradoxical phrase a "martyr chief."[21] Though it was only rarely put in explicit terms, in various ways that sacral image of presidential leadership would exercise great influence over American political life in the twentieth century. As this book will attempt to explain, it would also be important for many of the era's most important writers.

I was lucky in writing this book to receive the support of generous institutions and the kind attention of valued colleagues. I wish in particular to thank the American Council of Learned Societies, whose Burkhardt Fellowship for Recently Tenured Scholars made it possible for me to begin research, and the National Humanities Center, where I spent a very happy year working on the early stages of the project. I am still more grateful to the many friends who read or listened to sections of the book as it was being composed or who talked with me about its ideas. Special thanks to Rachel Adams, Jenna Alden, Jennifer Ashton, Sally Bachner, Chuck Baraw, Dan Born, Wini Breines, Kate Brown, Abigail Cheever, Mary Esteve, J. D. Conner, Deborah Cohen, Christina Crosby, Jonathan Cutler, Ann duCille, Maria Farland, Malachi Hacohen, Michael Halberstam, Andy Hoberek, Tom Huhn, Amy Hungerford, Nick Jenkins, Indira Karamcheti, Natasha Korda, Pericles Lewis, Maureen Mahon, Louis Menand, Walter Benn Michaels, Deak Nabers, Debbie Nelson, Richard Ohmann, John Plotz, Joel Pfister, Carlo Rotella, Ashraf Rushdy, Matthew Schwarzfeld, Matt Sharpe, Richard Slotkin, William Stowe, Michael Szalay, Khachig Tölölyan, Katie Thorpe, Betsy Traube, Stephanie Kuduk Weiner, Mark Weiner, David Weisberg, and Nick Zebb.

My deepest debt as always is to my family, whose love and support made writing this book possible. I owe more to Bryan McCann, Jay McCann, Moira Moderelli, Helena Moraski, and Ray Moraski than I can say. I owe most to Minou Roufail and Dexter McCann, who made the years I spent working on this book not only endurable, but joyful.

A PINNACLE OF FEELING

The Executive Disease: Presidential Power
and Literary Imagination

In the United States the executive power is as limited and
exceptional as the sovereignty in whose name it acts.
　　　　　　—*Alexis de Tocqueville,* Democracy in America

My ambition is to be president.
　　　　　　　　　　　—*Allen Ginsberg, "America"*

I N THE THIRD BOOK of Richard Wright's *Native Son*, Bigger Thomas undergoes
a disturbing encounter with a madman whose manic energy both terrifies and
compels him. Arrested for the murder of Mary Dalton, Bigger awaits trial in the
Chicago jail, where he finds himself bewildered by the mix of intense emotion occasioned by his crime. He is frightened by the ruthlessness of the district attorney
and by the bloodthirstiness of the press and the white public; shamed by the humiliation of his family and friends; angered by the manipulation of his mother's minis-
ter; and unnerved by the friendship extended to him by his leftwing lawyer Boris
Max and by Mary's bereaved Communist lover Jan. Above all, he is overwhelmed
by the complete estrangement from ordinary society that his actions have confirmed and by his resulting "urge to talk, to tell, to try to make his feelings known."
In the depths of Bigger's confusion, Wright provides a comparison figure, whose
frenzy mirrors Bigger's own desperate "impulsion to try to tell."[1] As Bigger learns

from a fellow prisoner, the "insane man" is a former student driven to lunacy by the effort to write "a book on how colored people live." He has been found in his underwear in the post office, raving about his determination to deliver his report to the president and by the nefarious designs of "the professor" who has stolen his work. "I'll tell the President," the man now continues to scream as prison guards try to restrain him.

> "You're afraid of me!" the man shouted. "That's why you put me in here! But I'll tell the President anyhow! I'll tell him you make us live in such crowded conditions on the South Side that one out of every ten of us is insane! I'll tell 'im that you dump all the stale foods into the Black Belt and sell them for more than you can get anywhere else! I'll tell 'im you tax us, but you won't build hospitals! I'll tell 'im the schools are so crowded that they breed perverts! I'll tell 'im you hire us last and fire us first! I'll tell the president and the League of Nations" (397–98)

The scene is brief, but it is among the most vivid in the long, discursive last book of *Native Son*, and in its dramatic compression it effectively clarifies the main concerns of Wright's novel—and in this fashion speaks more broadly as well to a set of literary and political attitudes that characterize a wide range of twentieth-century American literature. In both contexts, what stands out about the moment is its deep ambivalence. On the one hand, Wright's madman suitably captures the author's distance from the reformist liberalism that dominated U.S. politics during the 1930s. Both as a member of the Communist Party and as an African American well aware of the racial injustice at the core of many New Deal reforms, Wright had little interest in the era's cult of the sympathetic president.[2] Casting that faith as a cruel delusion, Wright also neatly skewers the ineffectuality of U.S. political institutions—credible as the League of Nations—and implicitly the Negro leaders who sought to work within the system and to take advantage of the New Deal to pursue civil rights advances. In his madness, in his delusional eagerness to personalize the political (and in so doing to match the exaggerated figure of the president with the comically misplaced nemesis of the professor), and in his obsession with the material facts of segregation that reflect but do not fully plumb the depths of the oppression registered by Bigger, the "insane man" indicts what Wright thus portrays as the cruel inadequacy of mainstream liberalism.

Yet, however misguided this troubled man may be, Wright emphasizes that the impulses that drive him are not trivial and that indeed they render him a mirror for Bigger's own stifled yearnings for understanding and self-expression. Bigger himself, after all, has imagined taking the role of the chief executive. At the culmination of the game of "play[ing] white" he has earlier acted out with his friend Gus, Bigger imagines himself as a president solely concerned to enforce the repression of African Americans, a fancy that takes Bigger's longing for power and freedom to the limit of his imagination while simultaneously crystallizing the depth of his oppression (18). When he encounters the insane man in jail, then, he suitably recognizes a kindred spirit. Confronting the madman, Bigger has "the sensation that the man was too emotionally wrought up over whatever it was that he had lost. Yet the man's emotions seemed real; they affected him, compelling sympathy. . . . Bigger had the queer feeling that his own exhaustion formed a hair-line upon which his feelings were poised, and that the man's driving frenzy would suck him into its hot whirlpool" (397–98). Indeed, as a near double to Bigger, the insane man resembles no one so much as Wright himself.[3] Both in his attempt to draft a structural account of the effects of racial segregation and in his grandiose expectations, the madman's effort to write the book on the oppression of African Americans echoes the mission that Wright assumed with *Native Son*—so much so that the brief episode in which he appears can be taken to illuminate a crucial point of connection between Wright's ambitions and the very political attitudes he appears to scorn.

In his determination to address the president, Wright's madman picks up on and subtly mocks a central element of the politics of the New Deal: the hope that the grandeur of the presidency might provide a means to transcend the corruption, indifference, and inadequacy of local political and civil institutions. *Native Son*, it might be noted, outlines a directly comparable agenda—using Bigger Thomas's anger and suffering to deliver a report on racism not to local authorities or community leaders, nor to similarly frustrated African Americans, nor even to Wright's fellow radicals or Communist Party members, but directly to the vast American public invoked by Max when he explains that Bigger's case "touches the destiny of an entire nation" (444). As the title of Wright's novel indicates, *Native Son* casts its address toward an emphatically national audience, aiming not only to depict the incidental cruelty of segregation or bigotry, but to reveal racism as the core issue of American history—"the key to our future, that rare vantage point upon which every man and woman in this nation can stand and view how inextricably our hopes and fears of today create the exultation and doom of tomorrow" (444). In the process it casts itself as rising, symbolically as well as intellectually, above the many habits and institutions that conspire to obscure and localize the injustice. On one level, then, the madman's lunatic aim of reaching the deaf ear of the president amounts to the most fundamental demonstration that the American public still ignores that key vantage, remaining mired in deliberate ignorance and convenient parochialism. But for that very reason, the figure of the president remains the most direct representation of the sovereign perspective that both Max and his creator seek.[4] All through *Native Son*, it is often noted, Bigger Thomas seeks out elevation, yearning for "a pinnacle of feeling upon which he could stand and see vague relations that he had never dreamed of" (418).[5] Apart from the historical and political vantage proposed by Max—which Wright ultimately appears to reject—and apart from Bigger himself, the madman's president is the novel's sole concrete embodiment of that transcendent perspective. As he later suggested when he remarked that Roosevelt was the man "who really gave me a chance to write books," Wright's literary ambitions virtually mimic the image of the liberal presidency that his novel also mocked.[6]

In this fashion, *Native Son* can be seen to take part in a larger discourse on executive power that was a central feature of the New Deal and, more generally, of U.S. politics over the whole course of the twentieth century. What is striking, for instance, about Wright's retrospective account of the origins of his literary career is not just that by 1945 he downplayed the role of the Communist Party in his development, but that, as an alternative, he mentioned neither the Federal Writer's Project nor even the New Deal, but Roosevelt the man, casting the relation between the president and himself in just the directly personal terms that moved other members of the New Deal coalition. "We are stunned," Wright confided to his journal on FDR's death, "as though someone we know or who is related to us is dead."[7] That tendency—to view policies and political action almost wholly in executive terms and, further, to see the executive branch itself as embodied in the intimate person of the president—was in good part a legacy of Roosevelt's celebrated political genius. But more fundamentally still it was a consequence of some of the main structural reforms pursued during the New Deal, whose combined action pointed toward the establishment of a virtually new constitutional order, aptly summarized by Theodore Lowi as "presidential government." Reshaping to varying degrees nearly every structural feature of U.S. politics—the relations between federal and state governments, between the three branches of the federal government, and among voters, officials, and parties—the "Roosevelt Revolution" laid the groundwork for what Lowi sees as an "entirely new" political system best characterized as "a plebiscitary republic with a personal presidency."[8] In the regime inaugurated by the New Deal, the president would stand at the head of a system of executive administration, acting in theory as the active voice of the nation as a whole; overcoming the resistance and narrow partisanship of other political institutions; and in so doing working to create a more intimate and democratic relation between the nation and its government. As Harold Laski explained in the same year Wright's novel was published, by exercising the "great power [that] alone makes great leadership possible," the president could seize "the unique chance of restoring America to its people."[9]

While Wright composed *Native Son* in 1938 and 1939, the Roosevelt administration was in the midst of the effort to forge that new constitutional order, and both the personality of FDR and the power of his office stood at the forefront of popular awareness and public debate. During those years, while domestic concern about the growth of Fascist and Communist tyrannies on the continent was rapidly growing, a good part of political discussion in the U.S. was preoccupied with the fate of the Roosevelt administration's Executive Reorganization Act, a signal event in the making of the distinctly American style of presidential government and an unexpected source of intense controversy about the proper role of the federal government and the executive branch in political life.[10] In popular memory, the seemingly dry topic of executive reorganization has been overshadowed by the high drama of the contemporaneous court-packing struggle, but during the later thirties, the former was equally controversial, and it may have been more central to the ambitions of New Dealers and more consequential for the long-term development of the U.S. political system. For, in their plan to create a bureaucratically streamlined and robust executive office, Roosevelt and his advisers acted out of a long-standing progressive desire to strengthen the president's control of the federal administration and in so doing to also expand the power of the president at the expense of Congress and of state and local governments.

In this respect, the Roosevelt administration's plan for executive reorganization was far more significant than the "apparently routine" proposal for reformed management that FDR himself cast the bill as being.[11] In public, FDR described the reorganization plan by referring merely to "efficient and economical conduct of governmental operations."[12] In private, he suggested that a robust reorganization bill would amount to the nearest possible approximation of a new "Constitutional convention"—a restructuring of the nation's political institutions legitimized by the mandate Roosevelt and the New Deal had received in the landslide 1936 election.[13] The academic advisers who pushed the plan forward were more direct and still more emphatic. Operating on the conviction that "the development of executive leadership" amounted to "one of the great contributions of modern democracy to government," they viewed the creation of a powerful, independent executive office as "an epoch making event in the history of American institutions."[14] As Louis Brownlow, chair of the presidential commission that drafted the necessary legislation explained, executive reorganization would concentrate power in the president's hands so that "the national will [might] be expressed not merely in a brief, exultant moment of electoral decision, but in a persistent, determined, completed day-by-day administration of what the nation has decided to do."[15] In short, the plan looked forward to a day when the president, because of his administrative powers and his popular legitimacy, could act independently of Congress and partisan or parochial interests on behalf of the collective will. The assumption, as another New Dealer said, was that "the President, and not either party, was now the instrument of the people as a whole."[16]

Despite FDR's extraordinary popularity, however, the administration's first Executive Reorganization bill went down to defeat in the spring of 1938, the victim of intense congressional and popular resistance. Opposition came not only from the committed enemies of the New Deal, who organized a demagogic public relations campaign, but from liberal members of the press and from a surprisingly large number of voters who worried, as one man put it, that the bill would "give the

President [the] powers of a Julius Caesar."[17] In response, FDR backed away from the bill and in a rare moment of defensiveness assured the American people that he had "no inclination to be a dictator."[18] The moment marked a turning point for the New Deal. Though the administration eventually got a much watered down version of the bill through Congress in 1939, the weakness of the revised plan indicated both the wide resistance to the grandest ambitious of the Roosevelt men and the "political torpor" that had befallen the reform agenda they supported.[19]

The ambivalence of *Native Son* is perhaps fitting in this context. While Wright composed his novel, progressive hopes in the ability of the president to rise above ordinary politicking and lead a unified nation toward a new era of democratic reform had been raised to a historic peak and, in but a short time, shown to be badly exaggerated. *Native Son* all but directly addresses that situation. Appealing subtly to the transcendent authority of a sovereign president, Wright's novel also under-cuts that appeal by envisioning the presidency as but one more element of an unresponsive political system. In the process, *Native Son* takes up the two most potent impressions of executive power that circulated in public debate during the late thirties. The Roosevelt administration and its intellectual champions defended an unchained president as an instrument of democratic community, the simultane-ous expression and servant of a popular will otherwise hindered by corrupt institu-tions and needless division. Its critics cast the executive branch as a secretive cabal driven by an illegitimate appetite for power. Those two, structurally counter-poised images of the presidency echo throughout American literature of the twenti-eth century, providing the basic terms for what can be read as an extended medita-tion on the relation of executive power to democratic government. In this fashion, as we will see more fully below, they also combine to build the symbolic drama at the heart of *Native Son*.

Principles, Parties, and Persons: The Political Culture of the Nineteenth-Century Presidency

The controversy surrounding the Executive Reorganization bill during the late thirties was, of course, but one moment in a far longer history of presidential power in U.S. politics—one, however, that dramatized structural trans-formations in the institutions and culture of government that only rarely became the subject of explicit public dispute. The Roosevelt administration was unsuc-cessful in bringing about the thorough constitutional reconstruction that some of its most enthusiastic proponents advocated. But by nearly all accounts the New Deal did contribute substantially to a long-term reordering of political institutions exemplified by the shift toward the plebiscitary, president-centered regime described by Lowi. Over the course of the twentieth century, as the administrative and security capacities of the federal government expanded, the' authority and prominence of the president likewise grew, and American politics increasingly became a national drama focused on the personality of the president.[20] Precisely because the executive office never gained the full powers that some New Dealers sought, moreover, the ideal of presidential leadership remained a continually appealing vision. When political failures or frustrations needed to be explained, the weakness of the president or of his office could be called on to account for the problem. Time and again, therefore, intellectuals, policy makers, and politicians invoked the image of the president as a popular statesman capable of rising above the limitations imposed by other institutions and able therefore to call American citizens to a more complete national destiny. In Clinton Rossiter's paradigmatic formulation, the president would be frequently invoked during the postwar decades as "the one-man distillation of the American people."[21]

But, while most historians and political scientists agree that the New Deal was a pivotal era in the reshaping of American politics, the history of presidential government reaches back well before the 1930s. In their view of the president as an engine of democratic reform, FDR and his allies drew on theories of government that had been first popularized during the Progressive Era, especially by Teddy Roosevelt and Woodrow Wilson—each of whom not only shaped aspects of the reform agenda that culminated in the New Deal, but sought, in theory as well as practice, to justify new models of presidential leadership to carry out that agenda. The vision of executive leadership TR and Wilson helped create displays in turn an exceedingly complex relation to American political history, both drawing on possibilities latent in the nation's constitutional design and fundamentally rewriting some of the prevailing customs of governance.

As one feature of the complex system of federalized and divided powers devised by the framers, the presidency has always been, among the most distinctive features of American government and a source of dispute and conflicting expectations from the first. During the Constitutional Convention of 1787 and the intense period of debate that led up to ratification in 1789, the presidency was one of the most heated topics of disagreement—with anti-Federalists denouncing the office, in Edmund Randolph's famous words as "the foetus of Monarchy" and Federalists defending, in Hamilton's equally celebrated phrase, an effective government's reliance on "energy in the executive."[22] Their conflicting views testify to differing interests and convictions that would remain fundamental sources of political conflict in the United States throughout the nineteenth century and beyond. But in this manner they also speak to a dynamism incorporated by design and compromise into the new constitutional order. For, in creating an office that combined the head of state and the head of government in a single person, and in setting it at odds with an independent legislature and judiciary, the framers knowingly experimented with a novel political system that differed both from parliamentary and monarchical governments and from classical republican ones as well. The resulting institutional tensions would become defining features of American political life. Indeed, in the view of political theorist Harvey Mansfield, the signal innovation of the American Constitution lay less in the fact that it codified the legitimate powers of government in a written document, then in the way it created in the separation of powers a unique institutional framework for containing the inherent conflict between republican government (deliberative, law bound, and prey to faction and stagnation) and executive power (antinomian, unitary, prey to the abuse of prerogative), making it a dynamic but relatively stable engine of American government.[23]

A case can be made following Mansfield that a profound ambivalence about executive power has been built into American politics since the earliest days of the republic and that the various recurring caricatures of the president—as the leader of the nation or as an institution bound "clerk"; as prototyrant or feeble figurehead—are alternative, partial views of the complex relations at the core of American government, each possibility rising to the fore depending on context and the interest of the viewer. The predominant understanding of American constitutionalism through the nineteenth century held that the popular will was expressed primarily through the legislative action of Congress.[24] From this perspective, the concentration of executive power in the hands of a single person always implied the threat of tyranny and abuse. But one important consequence of the doctrine of popular sovereignty and of the long-standing distrust of public power has been an equally prevalent dissatisfaction with congressional preeminence and party competition.[25] From this vantage, the frustrations presented by representative democracy—in calcification, or corruption, or parochialism—could easily make executive power, and its promised capacity to invoke prerogative and burst the shackles of law, seem an appealing, alternative means for articulating an otherwise neglected popular will.[26]

In the words of its most devoted literary antagonist, Gore Vidal, this was "the executive disease" that infected the United States from its origins, driving the republic toward the imperial decline Vidal relentlessly indicts.[27] Seen by its light, the vision of presidential leadership advanced during the Progressive era and institutionalized by the New Deal may appear less a radical innovation than a resurrection of an ideal of the president as a "patriot king" long latent in political mores.[28] That was certainly the way that Teddy Roosevelt and Wilson, both enthusiastic imperialists, cast their own contributions to the twentieth century's model of presidential leadership. Rebuking conventional partisan politics and claiming to act beyond narrow legalism and hidebound institutions, each cast himself as an innovator who reinvigorated the civic ideals that flourished among the Revolutionary generation. Praising TR, Woodrow Wilson imagined his future rival to be recreating the "the spirit of civic duty" that had prevailed in the early days of the Republic. "The scale of our thought is national again," Wilson claimed. "Once more our presidents are our leaders."[29]

Whatever long-term continuities exist, however, most political scientists and historians agree that the "modern" presidency differs markedly from anything anticipated by the founding fathers or familiar in the nineteenth century. The framers did sometimes speak of the executive as a nonpartisan guardian of the general interest, but they meant by that role something quite different from what Laski imagined when he cast the president as the proto-Socialist hero of a reunified people or even from what FDR invoked when he claimed that he bore "the duty of analyzing and setting forth national needs and ideals which transcend and cut across all party affiliation."[30] In the philosophy of the framers, the president's stature as head of state was never joined to the thought that he might be a spearhead of democracy or the moving spirit behind any partisan or domestic policy agenda, and there was certainly no suggestion, of the type made by the Brownlow commission, that the executive might use administrative.powers to outflank Congress and state governments. The most energetic Federalist defenders of the early presidency were the least democratic of the framers, and they typically viewed the executive not as an advocate of the popular will or as the initiator of innovation, but as a figure whose wisdom and prestige would enable him "to withstand the temporary delusions" of "the people" and to recognize when their "interests" were "at variance with their inclinations."[31] The presidency from this perspective was to be not, as New Dealers would suggest, "the instrument of the people as a whole," but, an institutional rival to the democratic enthusiasms of the legislative branch and therefore but one, crucial player in the system of antagonistic powers that the framers thought necessary to check democratic passions.

As Wilson and TR rightly suggested, moreover, even this early view of the president as a nonpartisan shield of the national interest did not survive the first generation of American leaders. With the rise of Jacksonian democracy and the creation of the first mass party system, and with the increasing intensity of regional as well as factional division, the notion that the president should rise above partisanship and act through the federal government to protect the common good quickly faded.[32] In Andrew Jackson's mass popularity, Americans witnessed the creation of a new model of the democratic presidency, in which the president aspired to act, in Jackson's words, as "the direct representative of the American people." (The stance occasioned, in Moby Dick's apostrophe to Jackson, one of the rare invocations of the sovereign presidency by a major nineteenth-century American writer.)[33] But, the Jacksonian presidency would little resemble the idea of presidential government that developed during the twentieth century. Both by philosophy and by policy, Jackson and his allies acted less to strengthen than to disperse the powers of the federal government and the executive branch. Unlike the Federalists, who had envisioned the federal government as an elite guardian of the common good, Jackson spoke tellingly of plural "public interests" rather than a singular "public interest," and he suggested that Washington should leave "individuals and States as much as possible to themselves."[34]

As antistatists and party builders, Jacksonian democrats likewise influenced the development of a political culture that would long shape the understanding of the presidency and its relation to the parties, even among their political opponents. Viewing the president's authority as stemming less from the Constitution than from popular opinion, Jacksonians, along with their Whig contemporaries, accordingly celebrated the executive not for its capacity to rise above partisan passion, but mainly for its ability to articulate popular preferences through party organization.[35] The Jacksonian president was thus less national statesman than party representative and ultimate distributor of spoils. Elevating the platforms cobbled together out of the party's diverse interests above any pretense to virtuous, character-driven rule, the nineteenth-century Democrats claimed to value "principles rather than persons."[36] The consequence, as Alexis de Tocqueville recognized at the time, was to encourage the creation of a decentralized political regime where power was distributed among the states, Congress, and the parties. Intense party conflict—built in large part around patronage and loyalty—and provincial jealousies thus dominated political life during the nineteenth century. With the exception of the Jackson and, of course, Lincoln administrations, presidential politics often seemed no more significant, and drew only slightly more voter participation, than the factional rivalries that dominated Congress and local governments. Prevailing constitutional doctrine also emphasized the restrictions on presidential action and on the reach of the federal government. Not only did structural restraints limit the chances for presidents to wield significant power; political customs, rooted in deference to long-established constitutional attitudes, also limited the occasions when presidents might speak directly to the public or even to Congress. Until Woodrow Wilson revived the practice in 1914, for example, no president since Jefferson had delivered a State of the Union address in person and none could, without finding creative ways to disavow the practice, express his policy preferences or personal attitudes directly to a popular audience. Even as candidates, aspirants for presidential office during the nineteenth century were expected to bow to party platforms, leave campaigning to party leaders, and comport themselves as dutiful public servants reluctant to assume the heavy burdens of office. Few opportunities thus existed for presidents to distinguish themselves from their parties or to establish themselves as symbolic figures in the popular mind.[37]

In cultural stature as well as political power, therefore, the nineteenth-century presidency was rivaled by the prominence enjoyed by other political officials, and the role of the office in the significant literature of the era was a comparatively minor one. With the exception of Jackson and Lincoln, the nineteenth-century presidents acted, in the words of one historian, "as little more than chief clerks of personnel."[38]

They received less attention from the press overall than congressional politicians and were often less prominent public figures than celebrated senators and governors. [39] Even a poet like Whitman, who would prove vital to the creation of the image of the "Redeemer President," frequently portrayed the chief executive as something much less grand and powerful than later writers would envision. Memorializing Lincoln as the savior of the Union, for example, Whitman praised the slain president not as the type of boldly energetic, agenda-setting statesman that later figures like Teddy Roosevelt would popularize, but, in terms then widely used to praise presidential probity, as a leader distinguished for his "cautious hand."[40] More generally, before the Civil War, Whitman like his contemporaries downplayed the significance of the presidency, casting the chief executive not only as the democratic equal of the citizens he was compelled to serve, but as only one of a whole panoply of comparably situated public servants: "President, Mayor, Governor and what not." In "Song of the Answerer," for example, the poet speaks equally to "the President at his levee" and to "Cudge that hoes in the sugar-field," but he also "walks among the Congress, and one Representative says to another, Here is our equal appearing and new."[41]

By the early decades of the twentieth century, the political culture that nurtured these perceptions had begun the slow decline that would reach a definitive point with the New Deal. With the expansion of the nation's state apparatus, the presidency would accrue previously unanticipated governmental powers and begin a long term battle for leverage with Congress and state and local governments. Over the same period, the party and patronage systems came under growing criticism from intellectuals and Progressive reformers, who fostered institutional and cultural changes that increasingly undercut the power of party organizations. As they receded in prominence and effectiveness, and as their once primary role in binding voters emotionally and ideologically to the political process declined, a new political mode built around the charismatic personalities of presidential candidates came increasingly to the fore—a development further nurtured by the growth of the mass media and by constitutional and economic transformations that lessened the significance of regional differences and gave increasing primacy to the national political arena.[42] In Woodrow Wilson's influential vision, the twentieth-century president was neither to be one governmental figure among others, nor one member of a party organization, but a uniquely positioned national leader burdened and distinguished by his "extraordinary isolation."[43]

The first crucial moment in this transformation came with the Civil War and the Lincoln presidency. In his stewardship of the Union through the Civil War, Lincoln became for Progressive intellectuals a paragon of vigorous presidential leadership. "For a little while," Woodrow Wilson enthused, "the executive seemed . . . to become by sheer stress of circumstances the whole government."[44] But Lincoln was in certain respects as influential on his presidential successors for what he symbolized, and for the eloquence of his rhetoric, as for his actions in office. In his own self-depictions, Lincoln rarely claimed to be either the nonpartisan voice of the popular will or the boldly extraconstitutional executive that later presidents would often invoke, and, in fact, he seems to have assumed a view of the presidency that more closely resembled the predominant attitudes of his contemporaries.[45]

For later admirers like Wilson and TR, however, Lincoln's presidency would seem a watershed both for the expanded scope for executive power his administration seemed to portend and still more for his role in inaugurating "a second American revolution" that would ultimately transform the United States from a union of sovereign states and conflicting regions to a continental nation.[46] Voicing a new sentiment that spread among Union supporters during the war, Emerson expressed satisfaction that, because of the conflict, "We are coming . . . to a nationality."[47] In the postbellum decades, and especially during the first years of the new century, Emerson's hope would become a watchword among Progressive reformers, who saw a still unconsolidated sense of national citizenship as the crucial ingredient for the achievement of meaningful democracy. For many, as for Emerson, Lincoln became the shining hero of that promise, but his significance in the role had importantly as much to do with the power of his rhetoric and the image of his person as with what later admirers called his "magnificent operationalism."[48] Particularly in the Gettysburg Address, but throughout much of his writing, Lincoln famously envisioned a "new birth of freedom" secured by the lives of the fallen soldiers whose sacrifice testified to the sovereign power they willingly served and whose martyrdom consecrated a new national compact. In Robert Lowell's acute description, Lincoln's rhetoric joined "Jefferson's ideals of freedom and equality . . . to the Christian sacrificial act of death and rebirth." Following his assassination, that language took on a fateful resonance with Lincoln's own example, so that for his mourners and celebrants, Lincoln could become a spiritual symbol for the refounding of American democracy—a martyr whose seemingly self-chosen death established the prepolitical ground for a new order. "The blood of the martyrs was the seed of the church," a Philadelphia newspaper declared shortly after the assassination. "So the blood of the noble martyr to the cause of freedom will be the seed that will fructify to the great blessing of this nation."[49]

That sacrificial mythology would become a central element in the rhetoric of modern presidentialism, and it would prove enormously appealing to ambitious literary writers over the course of the twentieth century, particularly in two related implications. Invoking national identity as a profound origin underlying the confusion and fragmentation of liberal society, Lincoln's sacrificial symbolism envisioned national solidarity as the product of a complex drama of executive power—in which the president's power to command both evoked and was ultimately surpassed by his people's, or his own, willingness to suffer and die. Celebrating that sacrifice,

Lincoln similarly cast the nation as both the inspiration for and implicitly as the product of the president's distinctive capacity to speak (rather than, say, to act or legislate) for the American people. The combination not only made the presidency, nationality, and literary genius seem part of one inextricable package; by joining oratory to sacrifice, it suggested that the president transcended a political realm characterized at its most essential by conquest and force when, by assuming a willingness to suffer and die, he transcended the role of commander-in-chief to assume that of national poet. In this light, as Whitman contended, Lincoln's most important achievement could seem "neither military" nor "political," but ultimately "imaginative and artistic."[50]

In various ways, the appeal of that imaginative and artistic vision would exercise a powerful hold over both the political and literary imaginations of the twentieth-century United States, but perhaps because Lincoln's presidential example was so distinctly rhetorical, its influence during the latter decades of the twentieth century turned out to be notoriously insubstantial. After the Civil War, American politics returned to the regime of courts and parties. Indeed the prevailing constitutional orthodoxy, affirmed by the Supreme Court in *Texas v. White* (1869) reemphasized the understanding of the United States as a compact of sovereign states that the Civil War had supposedly begun to dispatch—"an indestructible Union, composed of indestructible states."[51] Beginning with the impeachment of Andrew Johnson (who among other crimes, was charged as a constitutional "usurper" for his effort to go over the heads of Congress and appeal directly to the American people), Congress entered into an extended period of institutional dominance, and both the power and prestige of the executive branch sunk to a historical nadir. The predominant understanding of the presidency during the era thus echoed Tocqueville's sense that the chief magistrate typically acted as little more than a feeble check on Congress. In the book that first brought him acclaim, Woodrow Wilson declared in 1885 that "unquestionably, the predominant and controlling force [in American politics], the center and source of all motive and of all regulative power, is Congress." Albert Bushnell Hart echoed the point and predicted that, "since the legislative department in every republic constantly tends to gain ground at the expense of the executive, the Speaker [of the House] is likely to become, and perhaps is already, more powerful, both for good and for evil, than the President of the United States."[52] So, too, did Henry Adams, whose 1880 satire *Democracy* envisioned an entirely corrupt federal government dominated by the "moral lunatic" of a senator—"the high-priest of American politics"—who placed party loyalty over a devotion to the public good. Viewing the president as a hopelessly impuissant party hack, Adams could find no alternative to the squalor of representative democracy apart from an air of resigned, aristocratic hauteur.[53]

This common assumption was put most forcefully, though, by the British observer James Bryce, whose widely read *American Commonwealth* (1888) famously considered "why great men are not chosen presidents." "Since the heroes of the Revolution died out," Bryce noted, "no President except Abraham Lincoln has displayed rare or striking qualities in the chair. Who now knows or cares to know anything about the personality of James K. Polk or Franklin Pierce?" In the course of his withering discussion Bryce both clarified the prevailing attitudes of American politics and, by implication, pointed as an alternative toward an emerging critical consensus that would recreate the image of executive power. Presidential mediocrity was a product of a nation that little valued statesmanship and of a political system that privileged party loyalty and regional competition, Bryce suggested, echoing Tocqueville. But still more serious was the influence of a constitutional order that limited executive power. So long as the president's "main duties are to be prompt and firm in securing the due execution of the laws and maintaining the public peace," Bryce noted, "eloquence, . . . imagination, profundity of thought or extent of knowledge" were "not necessary."[54] While he wrote, a rising generation of intellectuals and politicians was already beginning to imagine a reversal of this state of affairs.

His Position Takes the Imagination of the Country: Making a Modern Presidency

In fact, Woodrow Wilson, who would become one leading actor in bringing it about, predicted that reversal. Surveying the consequences of the Spanish American War, Wilson declared that the United States was now "in the very presence of forces which must make the politics of the twentieth century radically unlike the politics of the nineteenth."[55] To Wilson's mind, a fundamental feature of that transition would be the tandem rise of presidential power and national citizenship whose combined significance the war had appeared to clarify. As a young academic and journalist in the latter decades of the nineteenth century, Wilson had come to prominence especially for his celebrated complaint against a "Congressional government" that, like many reformers of the day, he saw as dominated by corrupt party machines, hidden power, and divisive self-interest. In response, he had worried about what he deplored as "leaderless government," and pleaded with his fellow citizens to adopt something on the order of the British model of cabinet government, believing that the executive was too institutionally weak ever to rival the powers of Congress.[56] The presidency appeared to the young Wilson a hopelessly trivial office. It "call[ed] rather for training than for constructive genius."[57] But then, impressed by Grover Cleveland and, more seriously still, by Roosevelt, Wilson reversed position and now looked to the presidency as the likely source of badly needed democratic leadership. "Power had somehow gone the length of the avenue," Wilson remarked with approval, "and settled in one man."[58]

Envisioning the possibilities for that newly concentrated power, Wilson would become, along with Teddy Roosevelt, one of the chief architects of an emerging model of presidential leadership. But, Wilson was just one of a cohort of Progressive intellectuals, activists, and politicians who shared his dissatisfaction with the prevailing system of federalized and divided government and who, looking in the decades around the turn of the century toward the expansion of executive power, outlined a political theory that would become the predominant account of American government over the whole course of the twentieth century.[59]

There were important political and philosophical differences among those various Progressives reformers, but nearly all of them shared a conviction that democratic politics in the United States had been disabled by the confluence of the new economic conditions of industrial concentration with an outmoded political system that encouraged fragmentation and venal partisanship rather than efficient collective action. Americans had been "denied a new order of statesmanship to suit the altered conditions" of modern society, Wilson complained. "The federal government lacks strength because its powers are divided, lacks promptness because its authorities are multiplied, . . . lacks efficiency because its responsibility is indistinct and its action without competent direction." Dominated as it was by the "petty barons" of party politics, Congress showed "no thought of acting in concert," no genuine debate, and no "real leadership."[60] The federal government remained a mere "collection of men representing each his neighborhood, each his local interest; . . . at best only a limping compromise between the conflicting interests of the innumerable localities represented."[61]

Against that factionalism, Wilson and his fellow Progressive reformers typically appealed to the power of executive leadership to discover the higher good of "national sentiment," and they consistently objected to the political institutions and constitutional orthodoxy that interfered with its power to act.[62] Objecting to "the theory of checks and balances," for example, Wilson dismissed the "Whig theory of political dynamics" that he perceived in the framer's Constitution: "The trouble with the theory is that government is not a machine, but a living thing," and "no living thing can have its organs offset against each other as checks, and live. On the contrary, its life is dependent on their quick cooperation, their ready response to the commands of instinct or intelligence." Effective leadership needed to break therefore with "the trammels of governmental forms."[63] Teddy Roosevelt was more direct. Identifying the president as the "steward of the public welfare," Roosevelt explained that he had had purposefully reversed the constitutional understanding summarized by Bryce—that, as Roosevelt dismissively phrased it, the president could act only with "some specific authorization"—and set out to expand the executive's freedom of action: "It was not only his right but his duty to do anything that the needs of the Nation demanded unless such action was forbidden by the Constitution or the laws."[64]

Implicit in such remarks, was a deep suspicion of constitutionalism and legalism, viewed by Progressives as effective guardians of reaction. But still more important was the tacit understanding that the president might evade such restrictions because he served as a vehicle of national sovereignty. It was common for Progressive thinkers to denounce the corruption of boss-driven political machines, the "selfishness" of party competition, and the disorganization and compromise of representative democracy. Against the seaminess of mundane politics, however, they frequently invoked the moments of Revolutionary and wartime history in which it seemed that national sovereignty was expressed, and they often pointed implicitly to the president as a leader who could reawaken and articulate its authority—who in effect could supercede or transform the Constitution by going directly to its sovereign origin in the people. In this manner, they proposed a significant reorientation of political doctrine. Since the Revolutionary era, the concept of popular sovereignty had been both central to American political thought and fundamentally contentious. Theoretically, whether the idea of sovereign rule should even apply to a democratic government was, as some anti-Federalists had emphasized, always questionable. Practically the Constitution rendered national sovereignty the origin of political institutions ("We the people . . ."), while simultaneously rendering its location problematic—making it, of course, a central element of the conflicts leading up the Civil War.[65]

Nineteenth-century constitutionalism, even after the Civil War, dealt with that problem by assuming the dual sovereignty of the states and the union and by emphasizing the Constitution, rather than the nation or the people, as the principle source of political authority. But, then as now, the fact that American political ideology simultaneously took the people to be ultimately sovereign and in practice ceded political authority to a diverse group of political institutions created an ever-present invitation for fruitful discontent. When combined with other sources of dissatisfaction, the fact that the people did not actually rule could always become a powerful motive for political transformation.[66] Much as Harold Laski would when he called on the president to return America to its people, the Progressive reformers who crafted a new vision of executive leadership went beyond calls for more efficient and organized government and effectively complained that economic transformation and a stagnant political system had combined to strip the citizenry of its rightful power. "While we have been shielding . . . [the Constitution] from criticism," Wilson lamented, "it has slipped away from us."[67] Proposing a sweeping new political theory, they cast the chief executive—in Wilson's words "that part of the government which is in most direct communication with the nation itself"—as the heroic voice of an otherwise fragmented people and a figure who could thereby act to restore popular rule.[68] Teddy Roosevelt made the connection directly, emphasizing the link between the wide berth he wished to give presidential prerogative and his assumption that the president was the vehicle of popular sovereignty. He acted, Roosevelt explained, on the conviction that "an inherent power rested in the nation, outside of the enumerated powers conferred upon . . . [government] by the Constitution."[69]

It was TR who, making bold use of the emerging powers of the executive branch, pioneered the new styles of leadership that would come to be associated with the modern presidency. Roosevelt was the first president to forge an intimate connection between the office and the national media, eliciting the creation of the White House press corps and inventing the techniques of public relations (the press conference, the backgrounder, the trial balloon, the deliberate leak) that would become central to the popular influence of the executive office. He was the first to successfully explore the possibility of using those avenues to achieve policy goals by reaching above the heads of Congress to address the American public directly; the first to establish a programmatic legislative agenda styled for popular consumption (the square deal); and, in asserting more emphatically than any other holder of the office that it was the president's role to call citizens to a national duty that surpassed their narrowly personal interests, he was the most influential figure in the creation of the belief that it was among the president's chief responsibilities to be a moral leader, and a spectacular public performer, for his nation.[70] In his own view, wisely expressed in private, the president could aspire to be an "elective King."[71]

But it was Woodrow Wilson who, inspired in part by his admiration for Roosevelt's example, articulated the most influential theoretical vision of the modern presidency. The president's "is the vital place of action in the system," Wilson declared, in a remarkable paean to the possibilities of executive leadership:

> The nation as a whole has chosen him, and is conscious that it has no other political spokesman. His is the only national voice in affairs. Let him once win the admiration and confidence of the country, and no other single force can withstand him, no combination of forces will easily overpower him. His position takes the imagination of the country. He is the representative of no constituency, but of the whole people. When he speaks in his true character, he speaks for no special interest. If he rightly interpret the national thought and boldly insist upon it, he is irresistible; and the country never feels the zest of action so much as when its president is of such insight and caliber. Its instinct is for unified action, and it craves a single leader.[72]

Though it would rarely be put in such enthusiastic language again, Wilson's view of the president as a nonpartisan embodiment of the national will would become the predominant understanding of the presidency for much of the twentieth century, only strengthened as the institutional reforms (including the primary nomination system) advanced by the Progressives to limit the power of parties became part of the ordinary working mechanics of American democracy. Time and again, Wilson's successors in office echoed his vision. Convinced that "the people of the Nation will have, more and more, a national point of view," FDR frequently reiterated his conviction that the chief executive "should speak as President of the whole people"—a mission that he emphasized, even more strongly than Wilson, contrasted to life on Capitol Hill, where "pests . . . swarm[ed] through the lobbies of the Congress."[73] John F. Kennedy, echoing the language of moral exhortation that ran strongly through the rhetoric of the Progressive presidents, likewise followed Wilson and Teddy Roosevelt in assuming that "only the President represents the national interest." So, too, did both LBJ, who defined the presidency as a "national and not partisan" office, and Jimmy Carter, who in his inaugural address informed the public of his "great responsibility—to stay close to you, to be worthy of you, and to exemplify what you are."[74]

Like FDR's scorn for lobbyists and congressmen, Carter's elevated rhetoric here captured a central presumption of the modern presidency. Against the failures of inherently parochial representative institutions—which might aggregate, or betray, the interests and preferences of different groups of voters—the presidency was consistently seen, by Republicans nearly as often as by Democrats, as an office that could soar above institutional restraints to exemplify or embody the national will.[75] In this manner, the modern presidency was typically envisioned not solely as a technique of more effective government, but as a solution to a philosophical and nearly spiritual problem lying near the heart of American liberalism. In the adoption of representative democracy as the republic's central political form, and in the creation of the system of federalized and divided powers, U.S. political philosophy historically had accepted a fundamental division between state and nation as the price for the restraint of governmental power.[76] In the twentieth century, that restraint often seemed to social democratic thinkers ever less valuable and ever more the obverse face of the powerlessness that individual citizens were fated to in their private lives as much as in their public status as citizens. In the vision of the modern presidency first advanced by Progressive reformers, however, that breach was to be healed by the person of the president, who not only in his actions or policies, but in his presence and voice was imagined as the suture that could bind together public opinion and political institutions and in so doing restore popular rule. The aim, Wilson later said, anticipating Laski, was to replace "organizations which do not represent the people," which operated by means that were "private and selfish," with a leader who, in "speak[ing] for that great voiceless multitude," could "bring the government back to the people."[77] Indeed, if on the one hand, the theory of the modern presidency frequently imagined the chief executive as a figure who could return governmental institutions to popular control, on the other, presidential rhetoric also typically imagined the president as a prophet or pedagogue who called citizens to their better selves, urging them to transcend the constraints of their private interests just as he drove popular government to evade the trammels of law. "What we have to determine now," Wilson wrote in his own campaign for the office, "is whether we are big enough, whether we are men enough, whether we are free enough, to take possession again of the government which is our own. . . . Only the emancipation, the freeing and heartening of the vital energies of all the people will redeem us."[78]

Alongside the rise in executive power that the theory helped justify, such attitudes would make the presidency the vastly predominant element of twentieth-century American politics. Over the course of the century, executive power would become the center of the most serious political struggles, the object of the most intense emotional and ideological investment, and the agent of the most consequential actions. Indeed both the sway of the presidency and the grandeur of its image would grow exponentially with increasing deference to the president's least contested authority—the power to act as commander-in-chief of the armed forces and the role of representing the United States in foreign relations. From the turn of the century, no observer failed to note that it was the United States's increasing prominence as an international power, and the federal government's growing tendency after World War II to assume a permanent war footing, that, as was first glimpsed during the Civil War, elevated the chief executive to unprecedented heights of power and prestige. From the Spanish American War, through the First and Second World Wars, the Cold War, and, most recently, the War on Terror, the modern presidency has always been the war presidency and the ability to command the use of force has been viewed consistently as both the epitome of executive prerogative and the prime justification for its expansion.[79]

But, in keeping with Carter's vision of the president as a figure who exemplifies his people and Woodrow Wilson's emphasis on imagination and interpretation, with Teddy Roosevelt's legendary invocation of the presidency as a bully pulpit, or his cousin Franklin's claim that a statesman's "greatest duty . . . is to educate," it should be noted that mirroring the modern view of the president as unrivalled commander-in-chief has long been the vision of the president as supreme orator—the ideal exemplar, in Bryce's terms, of eloquence, imagination, and profundity of thought.[80] During the nineteenth century, the American political order exercised strong constitutional and customary restraints on the ability of presidents either to command military action or to address the public. The modern presidency overturned both those conventions and rendered the president's power to direct the use of force and his ability to speak rhetorically to or for the nation seem like complementary faces of sovereign power. Indeed, since the Revolution, political ideology had sought to preserve a distinction between government as popular self-rule and the exercise of state power as coercion or conquest—between, in Woodrow Wilson's terms, the legitimate, and redemptive, expression of "sovereignty" and the illegitimate application of "physical force."[81] As commander-in-chief and national orator, the modern president could be seen to dramatize the dynamic interrelation of these two core political images. As in the foundational example of Lincoln, the president's power to command the use of force raised the specter of state coercion, while his ability to speak on behalf of a sovereign people legitimized the use of force as a transformative expression of popular will. In this fashion, the modern presidency from its first conception became a symbolic as much as a political office—not merely because the creation of the national media and the decline of the parties made imagery and rhetoric increasingly central, but also because in its therapeutic promise to overcome the problems of representation and to exemplify the ideal harmony of a people and its state, the modern presidency has seemed as important for what its occupants are and for the qualities they display as for the actions that they take or the policies they endorse.

The Imaginary Politician: Bigger and the Presidency

That such a vision would be as appealing to literary artists as to political thinkers comes as little surprise. Indeed, while it's nearly impossible to imagine a twentieth-century writer equating himself, as Whitman had, to a congressman, invocations of the presidency in the literature of the era are legion. The vastly expanded powers of the twentieth-century executive, and the pseudomonarchical stature with which they were invested, made presidents comparable to the tyrants and heroes that had long appealed, as Hazlitt famously noted, to the romantic imagination. Viewing the chief executive as a ruling figure whose democratic legitimacy was assured in his ability to interpret and articulate a latent popular will, Wilson and like-minded thinkers emphasized, beyond even managerial or political skills, a president's literary abilities. Casting the president as an embodiment of a people rather than as a representation of its wishes, they likewise echoed the late romantic critique of representation that would be central to the development of modernist and postmodernist literature.

More significantly perhaps, the theory of presidential government made the chief executive an extraordinarily resonant figure whose gifts might be seen not merely to resemble but to contend for the mission that modern artists often envisioned for themselves. In the rhetoric of its most devoted champions, the modern presidency appeared an invaluable supplement to representative democracy, able especially through the exercise of imagination and oratory, to cure the major ailments of liberal society and government—though crucially without requiring that liberal democracy itself be overthrown or abandoned. As a form of nearly pastoral care for the modern world, the idea of presidential government thus effectively competed with literature for a role that had long been near to the core of its modern self-definition. Whitman made the analogy explicit in the years immediately after the Civil War, as he searched for reassurance that the new national compact, sacralized by the sacrifice of soldiers and the death of Lincoln, would last. "To hold men together by paper and seal or by compulsion is no account, / That only holds men together which aggregates all in a living principle . . . Their Presidents shall not be their common referee so much as their / poets shall."[82] Poet and president are analogs and rivals here, as they are complements in Whitman's paeans to Lincoln, each aspiring to create a national solidarity independent of either legal form or political domination.

Though in more satiric tone, Allen Ginsberg echoed the point nearly a century later in the lines quoted as an epigraph above, explicitly invoking a Whitmanian mission overwhelmed amid the crass materialism of mid-century America. Casting himself as the embodiment of all those marginalized and excluded by a craven and repressive society, Ginsberg both mocked the trivial charade of democracy and gestured toward a new national compact to be formed around his person. Wilson and his Progressive contemporaries worried at the absence of popular sovereignty and at the powerlessness of a citizenry manipulated by parties, controlled by bosses, and deceived by a dominant, but dishonest press. Ginsberg ironically mimicked the complaint, envisioning a country of lost and alienated citizens and importuning, "America . . . I'm addressing you./ Are you going to let your emotional life be run by Time magazine?" Though less directly than in Wilson's or in Whitman's case, the suggestion here too was that the United States was a nation that suffered under domination because it lacked genuine sovereignty. Indeed, in the prophetic denunciations of Moloch ("soulless jailhouse and Congress of sorrows") that he issued in the contemporaneous "Howl," Ginsberg performed an imaginative operation comparable to that engaged in by his Progressive predecessors. First, depicting a continent of the scattered and lost, Ginsberg then envisioned his people unified by their common submission to a system of abuse, perceived whole only by himself, going on finally in his lamentation for the martyred Carl Solomons to gesture toward a nation reborn through the poet's ability to articulate popular desire.[83] If he was not really to become the president, Ginsberg envisioned himself serving a parallel role.

As it happens, Richard Wright drew an analogy similar to Whitman's and Ginsberg's in a lecture explaining his literary principles composed during the period he was working on *Native Son*. Already beginning to distance himself from the authority of the Communist Party, Wright used this lecture, titled "On Literature," to complain about what he viewed as the limits of the committed leftist writing of the thirties (too doctrinaire, too confident of its superior understanding, too limited in subject matter and intended audience).[84] In response he demanded greater freedom for creative experiment—and its particular capacity to elude rules and legislation—and an ostensibly new style of fiction that, rather than objectifying or representing its characters would manage to identify with them. By absorbing and transforming the people he depicted, the artist could surpass mere doctrinal political statement, so that his fiction would speak to the concerns not solely of workers, but of all people. Tellingly, however, the example Wright came up with to illuminate how such literary work should, and shouldn't, be done came in the figure of an imagined politician. Envisioning a novel that would follow an ambitious hack from local office all the way to the White House, Wright cast this character both as an object of literary sympathy and, by the same token, as a figure who demonstrated the achievement of fiction by counterexample. The writer must envision exchanging places with the politician, Wright explained. When the politician engages in campaign rhetoric, he should speak the words the writer once wished to hear from political leaders. His rhetoric should move the public and inspire the nation with the optimism and grand idealism that the writer dreamed of before he became disgusted with politics. Only by envisioning a figure who would act as he himself would wish to lead, Wright contended, could the artist create a politician who was not merely a thug.

There may have been in these words a subtle dig at the Communist Party with whose operatives Wright by this point was ever more frustrated. For, not only did Wright dismiss the protest fiction of the thirties—suggesting in particular that his audience shared with the American public deep national sentiments it preferred to disavow—he also implicitly cast the bad rhetorician as a figure whose promises were made false by his devotion to merely partisan purposes. Failing at what the good writer should do, the president becomes for Wright a negative to the writer to the same degree that he is the prisoner of a party machine. Like Whitman and Ginsberg, Wright effectively implied that the writer should aspire to the task envisioned by the theorists of presidential government, but traduced by actual politicians.

Wright himself suggested a possible reason for that similarity by referring to national characteristics that lay beneath even consciously held political differences. The symbols of conventional patriotism lay deep rooted in the psychology of all Americans, he contended. But to some degree, a more direct genealogy can be traced as well. The aesthetic theories Wright expressed in this lecture were influenced by his admiration for the unorthodox French Marxist Henri Barbusse, whose attitudes in turn were partly indebted to Whitman's 1872 jeremiad *Democratic Vistas*.[85] Whitman's essay, it is interesting to note, is itself an anguished vision of the way the failures of American democracy might be redeemed in a national "solidarity" expressed especially through executive power. Objecting to the corruption and divisiveness of the postbellum United States, and expressing outrage at "the alarming spectacle of parties usurping the government," Whitman imagined an alternative in the national "compaction" betokened by the fallen soldiers of the Civil War ("the People, of their own choice, fighting, dying for their own idea") and exemplified by the exercise of sovereign power: "Over those politicians . . . looms a power, too sluggish maybe, but ever holding decisions and decrees in hand, ready, with stern process, to execute them as soon as plainly needed—and at times, indeed, summarily crushing to atoms the mightiest parties." Though Whitman's essay envisions that power being expressed by "some great literatus" in particular, both in its definition of the problems bedeviling American democracy during the Gilded Age (crass materialism, urban squalor, "the depravity of the business classes," the insufficiency of an avowedly democratic political system controlled by "corrupt rings and electioneering") and in the solution it imagines (a "national literature" that would "permeat[e] the whole mass of American mentality, . . . giving it decision, affecting politics far more than the popular superficial suffrage"), Whitman's essay anticipates the visions of executive leadership then in the midst of germination.[86] When he invoked a "modern, image-making creation" as the solution to the crisis of democracy, Whitman in effect imagined just what his political successors would discover in the presidency.[87]

Wright may never have read *Democratic Vistas*, but, like Ginsberg he cited Whitman as a significant precursor, and it's striking to note how closely his concerns resembled his predecessor's. In particular, Wright's debt to Whitman highlights a rarely noted, yet central feature of his work—the frequency with which he, too, viewed national solidarity as the sine qua non of meaningful democracy and the degree to which he imagined that national identity being evoked by the exercise of executive power. Especially during the period of his most committed radicalism, Wright often made references to political struggles that cut across "racial *and* national lines of demarcation."[88] But frequently he indicated a nearly obsessive longing for the very kinds of national solidarity for which Whitman had yearned. Recalling his early attempts to become a writer in Chicago, Wright made this desire explicit in his memoir *Black Boy*: "I wanted a life in which there was a constant oneness of feeling with others, in which the basic emotions of life were shared, in which common memory formed a common past, in which collective hope reflected a national future."[89] But the theme runs all through his work, where, among other things, it provides the most consistent framework for his understanding of racism—typically cast most significantly as a failure of national sovereignty. "The oppression of the Negro" cast "a shadow athwart our national life."[90] Were it to be genuinely resolved, "we would all simply be Americans, and the nation would be the better for it. . . . But the contrary is true: The nation is split. White America dominates black America."[91]

With increasing directness Wright reacted to that injustice in much the fashion that Ginsberg later would. He didn't seek a flight from national identity so much as its redemption or full realization. "I criticize America," he told Gertrude Stein in

1946, "as an American."[92] Fittingly, then, his complaints against the racial division of the United States adopted a classic tenet of American racist discourse—that democracy cannot exist in a racially divided society—and, turning it against its traditional use, also accepted its fundamental concern, the emphasis on national cohesion. The problem with racism, in other words, was not merely that it was unjust, or cruel, or exploitative, but that, obviating the possibility of national community, it also rendered impossible the expression of the sovereign national will without which democracy appeared impossible. Perhaps not surprisingly in this context, Wright connected the problem of racism to the division between an ineffectual state and an ungoverned nation that exercised the proponents of presidential government. America and the United States were actually two separate nations, Wright complained. Though Congress theoretically represented the abstract localities of the United States, the owners of capital, who controlled the true sources of economic and political power, lived in the real world of America.[93] Much like the proponents of presidential government, in short, Wright traced the intractability of racism and injustice to the division of powers and the separation between formal democracy and genuine power it appeared to entail.

Not surprisingly, then, like many of his contemporaries, Wright consistently turned to executive power for a solution to the problem of national fragmentation. As Carla Capetti notes, throughout his career, Wright returned to a perception he had first formulated by way of Chicago sociology—a view of "modern social reality as the site of relentless conflicts between the individual and the group."[94] But just as significantly, he typically sought, as in "On Literature," for a resolution to this problem in the act of imaginative identification that could be achieved especially via executive power. Describing own goals, Wright made himself resemble both Whitman's "literatus" and Wilson's "constructive genius"—a personality able through his gifts of imagination and rhetorical power to bond with people in way that surpassed not just political institutions and personal conflict, but representation itself, thereby eliciting both identification and grandeur from his audience. In a lecture he gave after winning the Springarn medal, for example, Wright described himself as a leader of his people who alone might inspire them to put aside the caution of ordinary life and told his audience that he wished not merely to argue with or persuade them, but to literally enter their persons and through their sheer force of his rhetoric chemically transform their bodies.[95]

Similar comments run all through Wright's critical reflections, in each case emphasizing the pursuit of an imaginative identification that would evade conventional attitudes and forge a connection so profound as to approach corporeal identity. "My purpose," he wrote in *Black Boy*, "was to capture a physical state or movement that carried strong subjective impressions . . . [t]o fasten the mind of the reader upon words so firmly that he would forget words and be conscious only of his response" (280). It was fitting that Wright should find an analogue for that project in the, albeit falsely, inspiring rhetoric of presidential politicians. For, both in its tone and more seriously in its implicit theory of communication, Wright's call for imaginative identification resembled the visions of rhetorical leadership shared by the models of executive government prominent at the time. The artist "must be led by the sovereignty of his own impressions and perceptions; must be guided by the tyranny of what troubles and concerns him personally," Wright told his friend Antonio Frasconi.[96] But implicit in his theory of identification lay the suggestion that, if he were successful, the artist might articulate a sovereign power that spoke for his audience as well.

Wright's devotion to that possibility is most evident in his notorious lifelong attraction to tyrannical power. Defending *Native Son* from the tepid reaction of the Communist Party, for example, he asked whether left writers were "to be confined merely to the political and economic spheres of reality," leaving "the dark and hidden places of the human personality to the Hitlers and Goebbels."[97] Like his letter to Frasconi, that comment suggested that, in its need to break with "well-established lines of perception and feeling" (lines defended, Wright suggested, by party orthodoxy) and to plunge instead into the psychic terrain of demagogic power, the literary imagination was a close relative of tyrannical power. It also established an evident connection between the writer and his most famous creation. Like nearly all of Wright's protagonists, Bigger Thomas is depicted as not only drawn to dictatorial power, but as an incipient tyrant himself. Having killed Mary Dalton, Bigger comes to a sudden admiration for Hitler and Mussolini and begins to imagine himself as a black dictator: "Looking at the black people on the sidewalks, he felt that one way to end fear and shame was to make all those black people act together, rule them, tell them what to do, and make them do it. Dimly, he felt that there should be one direction in which he and all other black people could go wholeheartedly. . . . But he felt that such would never happen to him and his black people, and he hated them and wanted to wave his hand and blot them out" (130).

As Wright himself consistently stressed, what *Native Son* depicts in this context is not solely the evil of racism and the anger it produces, but a story that Wright suggested had still broader application. If Bigger Thomas is to be seen as a representative modern citizen—one of "a vast, muddied pool of human life in America"—what his suffering and anger reveal more generally is the attraction to dictatorial power that arises in the absence of genuine sovereignty—when one is faced by "a world which one did not make or own" (HBWB 514, 518). The first two books of *Native Son* confront Bigger Thomas with that disenfranchised condition in panoramic detail. Hounded by an oppressive legal system, solicited and abused by a manipulative media, badgered and ignored by a nonresponsive elite, and annoyed by the social customs of a minority culture, Bigger is confronted at every step by the unavoidable evidence of his powerlessness and, by the same token, with the absence of a "culture which could hold and claim his allegiance and faith"

(HBWB 520). His response is to dream of virtually totalitarian power. "He felt that some day there would be a black man who would whip the black people into a tight band and together they would act and end fear and shame" (130).

In this respect, Bigger represents not solely the black rage with which he is usually associated, but a more general longing for tyrannical power that Wright suggested was a constitutive feature of the modern world. But, while Wright returned to that longing often, the appeal of dictatorial power was always implicitly paralleled in his work by a less evident alternative. In a radio address he gave while working on *Native Son*, Wright argued that, in the chaos and desperation of the thirties, the U.S. devotion to "rugged individualism" threatened to culminate in what he suggested was its natural outcome, the "ruthless tide of fascism." But, anticipating the words spoken by Max in the concluding sections of his novel in progress, Wright also suggested that this dangerous individualism could be supplanted by an alternative model of civic identity—"rugged personality"—which would be less committed to inviolable liberty and more open to the collective guarantee of freedom and equality. Against the Nazi, the extreme face of the rugged individual, Wright therefore proposed as the ideal type of personality "a man in America"—Abraham Lincoln.[98]

References to Lincoln were, of course, commonplace in the culture of the Popular Front during the latter thirties. But the particular contrast between two forms of executive power that Wright draws here—between the compulsion exercised by the dictator and the solidarity evoked by legitimate democratic leadership—was also a central feature of the New Deal's effort to institutionalize presidential government. As Charles Merriam, one of the three leaders of the Brownlow commission, explained the year before *Native Son* was published, the conditions of industrial concentration had created a world in which either "a new despotism" or "a new democracy" appeared inevitable. In the development of "superior forms of public administration," Merriam perceived hopeful signs that the latter could be achieved. By drawing on the work of "scientists, educators, engineers, doctors, technical workers, [and] managers," executive leadership could "blend the elements of effective popular responsibility with those of unification of action, both in peace and in war." The result would be "a form of association where leaders no longer scream and curse and threaten, and where men no longer shuffle, cringe, and fear, but stand erect in dignity and liberty and speak with calm voices of what clear eyes may see."[99]

That contrast between two models of executive leadership and two forms of political association was a prominent feature of American culture in the thirties. It was central, for example, to Sinclair Lewis's sensational warning against the dangers of Fascism *It Can't Happen Here*, which managed to combine an attack on executive tyranny and the "Corporate State," with a simultaneous defense of the presidential leadership needed to create "a universal partnership, in which the State must own all resources so large that they affect all members of the State."[100] Despite his apparent political differences with Lewis and Merriam, Wright placed an analogous contrast between state tyranny and legitimate executive leadership at the core of his own political and aesthetic vision. If Merriam and Lewis each hoped that new administrative powers would enable a strengthened presidency to avoid the ordinary channels of representative government and forge a more democratic society, Wright suggested similarly that the gifted artist's ability to create sympathetic community—beyond parties, doctrines, and social conventions— might overcome the alienation and powerlessness he thought typical of the modern world. In both cases, the action of executive power would evoke a sovereign people who in turn would legitimate that power. Not coincidentally, therefore, the contrast between the tyrant and the leader—between, in Wright's terms, individualism and personality—provides the narrative framework for Wright's novel. For, in its most basic features, *Native Son* takes us from a world in which screaming, cursing, and threatening coexists with fear and cringing and replaces it with the vision of a world where dignity and liberty might prevail.

The crucial element in this transition—much as in the examples of Lincoln, Whitman, and Ginsberg—is martyrdom. In the first two books of *Native Son*, Bigger not only lives in a state of constant anger and fear, even before he murders Mary he resembles the tyrant envisioned by Wright as well as by Merriam. Killing the rat in the novel's legendary opening scene, ruthlessly bullying his friends (who "hate and fear" Bigger "as much as he hated and feared himself") dreaming of blotting out his antagonists with a wave of his hand, Bigger is at once the victim and the abuser of tyrannical power (31). He longs "to take life into his hands and dispose of it as he pleased" (170). But, importantly, he seeks more than to dominate his personal acquaintances, longing as well for a version of the rhetorical power that Wright envisioned novelists and politicians alike seeking. Having killed Mary, Bigger dreams of himself not solely as a commander, but as an unavoidable imaginative presence in the life of a mass public. "He wished he could be an idea in their minds; that his black face and the image of his smothering Mary and cutting off her head and burning here could hover before their eyes as a terrible picture of reality which they could see and feel and yet not destroy" (147).

Of course, neither Bigger's ability to dominate others, nor his fantasies of rhetorical power possess any substance or stability. Controlling others by fear, he is driven by fear himself. Establishing himself as a terrifying image in the collective imagination of white Chicago, he becomes for that very reason, vulnerable to its rage and superstition. The volatile exchangeability of tyrannical power and powerlessness is made especially apparent in the way that Bigger, who "all his life . . . had felt" that the newspapers should carry "*his* story," discovers that once they do, he becomes not the dictator, but the helpless scapegoat of an enraged people (256, emphasis in original). But the point is still more subtly indicated when, encountering the brutal private detective Britten, Bigger sees "in the very look of the man's eyes . . . his own personality reflected in narrow, restricted terms" (176). A cruel parody of "the response of recognition" that Bigger desperately seeks in the novel's final book, Britten's reflection points to a world characterized from top to bottom by cruelty and coercion—in which, Wright implies, the power to dominate, shadowed always by the knowledge of its own impermanence, can only sustain itself through the constant exercise of violence and fear (420).

But then, having established that panorama of domination, Wright seeks to reverse it in the novel's final book. Bigger, who has dreamed of himself as a dictatorial commander, now imagines himself not as the master of a subservient people, but as one member of a consensual public. "He was standing in the midst of a vast crowd of men, white men and black men and all men, and the sun's rays melted away the many differences, the colors, the clothes, and drew what was common and good upward toward the sun" (420). As in the era's visions of presidential government, and Wright's critical reflections on the work of fiction, this passage envisions a collective solidarity that transcends social difference, political conflict, and the various inadequate institutions of government and civil society. That the crowd includes no women is not a small detail, considering that throughout Wright's work it is women who most represent the constraints and confusions of civil society and who must be literally killed off so that the abstract public envisioned here can be imagined. But, the process is not complete, Wright implies, until Bigger's determination to create his freedom by force is displaced by his willingness to suffer and die to sustain it. Almost literally, the unified public Bigger envisions cannot be conceived without the catalyzing event of his own imminent execution. "He looked out upon the world and the people about him with a double vision: one vision pictured death, an image of him, alone, sitting strapped in the electric chair . . . ; and the other pictured life, an image of himself standing amid throngs of men, lost in the welter of their lives" (422). Without the former vision, it would appear, the latter is impossible.

We can understand Bigger's double vision in one way by noting how closely it accords with the analysis proposed by a theorist of the modern state like Giorgio Agamben. For Agamben, all avowedly democratic states are constrained to imagine their citizenry in a particular, bifurcated fashion. Despite their other differences in ideology or political culture, all may be best understood therefore in the terms proposed by a radically authoritarian philosopher like Carl Schmitt. To the extent any state claims sovereignty over the nation it claims to serve and represent, Agamben contends, it tends to imagine the people as a spiritual source of authority, transcendent and eternal. To the same extent, however, it tends also to con-

ceive the individual persons who make up that collective entity as the merely material bodies it cares for and manages and—in the limit case that proves its
authority—whose lives it may legitimately demand. Each tendency is exacerbated
as the power of the state is extended and as it vanquishes alternative sources of
authority, so that in extreme conditions the grandest aspirations of the state to
democratic legitimacy are matched by equally naked coercion (especially, in Agamben's view, through the definitive institution of the concentration camp). On Agamben's account, then, it is not too much to say that the dehumanizing technologies
of state control are not merely the complement, but the necessary condition for
the creation of the spiritual body of the people. More simply, in Agamben's view,
the deaths of individual people are needed to secure the life of the nation.[101]

Bigger's electric chair and his vision of the abstract crowd anticipate Agamben's
terms with striking exactitude. Though less evidently, so, too, do Merriam's tyrant
and leader or Lewis's "corporate state" and "Holy America." Each writer acknowledges the coercive power of government, only to ultimately dismiss its dangers
with an ideal image of the democratic people a new state might yet call into being.
But if this pattern suggests that at some level Merriam, Lewis, and Wright may all
have shared more in common with Carl Schmitt than they wished to acknowledge,
we might also note that each probably drew more directly on the native tradition
of political thought that had been implicitly used to justify the development of a
distinctly American form of the administrative government. If Wright anticipates
Agamben, in other words, he also more directly echoes the rhetoric of national
leadership and martyrdom that had descended by way of Whitman and the Progressive theorists of presidential government.

What we see in the last book of *Native Son*, in short, is a variation on the
symbolic drama that Wright tacitly invoked when he called on Lincoln as an emblem of personality. As in the rhetoric that Lincoln himself proposed, and that
was intensified on his death, the final passages of Wright's novel envision an
executive power characterized by conquest and command displaced, through
an act of martyrdom, by a mystically bound people. If, in postbellum popular
rhetoric, Lincoln and the fallen soldiers of the Civil War were to be the martyrs on
which a new nationality was founded, Wright recreates that story, seeking to replace the unified white nation that was in fact a prime legacy of the Civil War, with
a nonracial America. As with the Civil War, too, Wright suggests that such a new
nationality can only be established by a destructive act of power that wipes
away the prevailing institutions of a divided and unequal society—"a sudden and
violent rent in the veil" (456). But, just as the power of Lincoln and of his soldiers
to conquer and kill was seen to be redeemed by their willingness to die for the
cause they served, so, too, does Bigger become, in Whitman's words, an emblem
of "the People, of their own choice, fighting, dying for their own idea." In both

cases, martyrdom gives substance to the thought that the violent exercise of power is not merely arbitrary or abusive, but legitimized by a tacit popular will. In both cases, that is, the killer ceases to be a tyrant and becomes, in effect, a democratic executive when his death legitimizes the impression that he acts not solely for his own gratification but on behalf of a nation whose unknown wishes he articulates and serves.

Seeing *Native Son* in this context may help to clarify one of its more powerful and elusive features—the dramatic final scene in which Bigger famously rejects the pleas of his lawyer and declares, in the book's most memorable line, "what I killed for I am!" (501). Bigger's ultimate difference with his lawyer has long been something of a critical puzzle because there is little obvious reason for the two to disagree. Not only is it Max who has awakened Bigger's longing for recognition and "given him faith that at bottom all men lived as he lived and felt as he felt"; in his renowned closing statement to the jury, Max articulates a political vision, built on the importance of "personality and security," that closely matches ideas Wright himself expressed elsewhere (493, 472). Though some critics plausibly have read the ultimate rejection of the lawyer as a sign of Wright's growing alienation from the Communist Party, by giving Max ideas to voice that were themselves out of keeping with orthodox Marxism, Wright appears to go out of his way to ensure that the split does not appear ideological.[102] There is no obvious political or personal conflict between Max and Bigger, but nevertheless Wright concludes his novel with a confrontation in which they dramatically reverse place. Bigger, who throughout the last book of the novel has stammered futilely in his "impulsion to try to tell," suddenly speaks with an unprecedented clarity and force, while Max, who has up to this point been Bigger's eloquent spokesman, is reduced to inarticulate fear: "No; no; no . . . Bigger, not that . . . . Max's eyes were full of terror. Several times his body moved nervously, as though he were about to go to Bigger; but he stood still" (501).

Part of the justification for the apparent rebuke dealt out to Max here may be, as a number of readers have suggested, that despite his dedication to Bigger's cause and despite his theoretical explanation of Wright's own principles, Max rarely perceives Bigger as an individual personality, preferring to view him as a specimen of a larger social injustice. By his account, Bigger is a "test symbol" of "the complex forces of society" (444). But, if we see the novel as I have been suggesting—as a book that attempts to imagine social injustice redressed by an act of transcendent national sovereignty—this accurate observation might be extended still further. Counseling Bigger on the eve of his execution, Max seeks to comfort Bigger with a developmental model of political change that views social justice as the product of general processes of "grow[ing] and unfold[ing]" (498). "It's too late now for you," Max tells Bigger, but not too late for him to see his issue in the fate of "millions of men desiring and longing" and restrained only by the fact that "a few men are squeezing those buildings tightly in their hands" (499, 498). In keeping with that incremental view of social progress, Max is strikingly unreceptive to the two facts of Bigger's life that Bigger himself takes to be paramount—that he has killed and that he must die. As Bigger faces the execution chamber, Max must be forced by his client to speak the words, "You're going to die, Bigger" (497). And even in this ultimate conversation he reminds Bigger, "you killed. That was wrong" (499).

What Max seeks to deny, in other words, are the two central elements in the symbolic drama of executive leadership—coercive power and martyrdom. Acting as Bigger's advocate, Max has no trouble perceiving their importance to the historical establishment of American sovereignty. "Did we not build a nation," Max asks the court, "did we not wage war and conquer in the name of a dream to realize our personalities?" (465) But, as a party intellectual, Max would have little commitment to the lasting significance of national sovereignty. Confronted, then, with Bigger's effective desire to refound the nation, he hesitates and offers instead what Wright portrays as a feeble promise that Bigger's "balked longing for some kind of fulfillment and exultation" will someday be realized by others.[103] In effect, Max is not only unable to identify with Bigger, by the same token, as a Communist Party intellectual he remains confined to those "merely . . . political and economic spheres of reality" that Wright described as the limitations of the left. Bigger, by contrast, taps into and, through his death, redeems "the dark and hidden places of the human personality" that Wright suggested were the wellsprings of mass power.

In Wright's final scene, then, we witness the stupefaction of the party operative before the profound mystery of the national martyr. In Wright's telling, even the Marxist radical shares the limitations that the devotees of presidential leadership perceived in the ordinary workings of government. Devoted to the maintenance of laws, theories, institutions, processes, Max is reluctant to acknowledge the actual exercise of executive power and dumbfounded by the expression of a transformative popular will. Precisely in his readiness to both exert and suffer violence, by contrast, Bigger becomes a version of just that figure that Wright suggested mirrored the presidency—able to speak the words the writer once hoped to hear from national leaders. The connection is virtually explicit. Earlier in the novel, Bigger muses on his frustrating inarticulacy. "Many times, when alone after Max had left him, he wondered wistfully if there was not a set of words which he had in common with others, words which would evoke in others a sense of the same fire that smoldered in him." But "the moment he tried to put his feelings into words, his tongue would not move" (422). That frustration is at last resolved, in the same scene where Max's theoretical wisdom is rendered mute. Bigger is finally able to speak—and, by implication, thus able to speak for others—when he expresses a vision of violent self-creation. "What I killed for, I am!" In both roles, now finally come together, we might say, Bigger becomes the man to whom the imprisoned madman wished to speak—the leader who embodies his nation.

Wright's colleagues on the left, then, were perhaps not wrong to follow Max and hesitate before approving *Native Son*. As one of Wright's closest friends realized, the novel owed little to "the Theory of the Proletarian Revolution."[104] By contrast, it shared a good deal of ground with the idea of presidential government so important to the developing New Deal. As he worked on *Native Son*, Wright referred to that political context and, not unlike Charles Merriam or the other members of the Brownlow commission, demanded the expansion of the powers of "liberal government." "If the heritage of our culture is to be preserved, extended, and enriched," Wright declared, "new instrumentalities of social and political action must be found."[105] As things stood, Wright later added, "some may escape the general plights and grow up, but it is a matter of luck and I think it should be a matter of plan. It should be a matter of saving the citizens of our country for our country."[106] Though he did not specify just what instrumentalities he conceived, in the context of the day's most heated political battles, it would have been clear that like the proponents of executive reorganization he referred to the development of administrative capacities to be directed by executive power.

The fiction that Wright wrote during the same period is but one example of a literary endeavor whose most basic terms were shaped by the rising theory of presidential government—a literary mission that drew on, imitated, and adapted that political theory, even as it sought to articulate such ideas for a rival agenda. The elements of national mythology are in all of us, Wright claimed. So, too, did many twentieth-century writers share the underlying premise that drove the expansion of presidential government in the twentieth-century United States—the view that popular sovereignty, which was constantly frustrated by the restraints of law and the institutions of government, might come to redemptive expression through the power of charismatic leadership. The remaining chapters of this book will consider the way that variations on that assumption informed the work of a number of major writers whose careers track the course of the twentieth century and the rising and then falling expectations that many American thinkers expressed for the prospects of presidential power.

CHAPTER ONE

Masters of Their Constitution:

Gertrude Stein and the Promise

of Progressive Leadership

*Each generation has something different at which they are all
looking. . . . [T]heir influences are the same as that of all of their
contemporaries only it must always be remembered that the
analogy is not obvious until as I say the composition of a time
has become so pronounced that it is past and the artistic composition of it is a classic.*

—Gertrude Stein, "Composition as Explanation"

*Napoleon could not write a novel, not he. Washington could.
And did. Oh yes I say so. And did. . . .*

*I say that George Washington was the first president of the
United States.*

I also say that he knew what a novel is.

—Gertrude Stein, **Four in America**

W HEN SHE LANDED in the United States in 1935 on the triumphal tour following the publication of *The Autobiography of Alice B. Toklas*, Gertrude Stein
returned to a country that she had not seen for three decades.[1] She had left
America in 1903, in the depths of a personal and professional crisis—a medical

school dropout, a frustrated lover, a writer who longed for "la gloire" but who was plagued by doubts about her ability. She returned a different woman, to what one would have imagined was a different country. Now a respected arbiter of avant-garde taste and a literary celebrity at the height of her recognition, Stein looked around at the country she had not seen for decades and observed little difference from what she had left. When reporters, alluding to the revolution in industry and communication that had transformed the country, asked, "do you find Americans changed," Stein replied: "no neither America nor Americans after all when you say changed how could they change what after all could they change to?"[2]

It was a typical Stein retort, a philosophical joke designed to confound the expectations of her audience by confronting them with premises inconsistent with their own. Responding to journalists who were preoccupied by the historical evidence of the changing characteristics of life in the United States, Stein proposed instead a formal definition that implied the narrowness of the concerns of the press. Americans were Americans by citizenship; whatever they did they would still be American. Preoccupied with their need "to remember what they are hearing," however, reporters inevitably repeated the clichés of popular discourse. "They would say what it was the habit for newspapers to say" and ignore more significant matters, like "original writing." That was "the trouble with newspapers and teaching," Stein explained, adding that it was a problem they shared "with government and history."[3] As the eminent Stein critic Ulla Dydo points out, "remembering is the demon of the writing world" for Stein, "It leads to dead repetition."[4] With their common interest in thinking historically, the major institutions of popular democracy in the thirties—the press, the schools, the state—all appeared by Stein's characterization to be agents of torpor.

Although her tone in such exchanges was always comic, Stein's point was a serious one and touched on both her most consistent aesthetic concerns and the political attitudes that she would express with increasing emphasis during the later thirties. Beginning with her first major period of creative achievement, which culminated in the publication of *Three Lives* in 1909 and the completion of *The Making of Americans* in 1911, Stein had defined her work by an increasingly radical refusal of the historicism and conventional empiricism that characterized ordinary narrative. Now, as she reiterated and extended her philosophical commitment to that program during the thirties, her new public writing often elaborated its political implications.[5] Only recently Franklin Delano Roosevelt had justified the need for a New Deal by referring to just the kinds of socioeconomic change raised by Stein's journalistic audience. Taking up the mantle of his cousin Teddy Roosevelt and, still more earnestly, of Woodrow Wilson, FDR had pointed to the recent history of industrial concentration and demanded "a re-appraisal of values": "Equality of opportunity as we have known it no longer exists. Our industrial plant is built . . . . Our last frontier has long since been reached. . . . [W]e are steering a steady course toward economic oligarchy, if we are not there already." What was needed, Roosevelt concluded, was agreement on a set of "new terms" for "the old social contract."[6]

Stein, who saw little difference between the New Deal and either Stalinism or Fascism, and who accordingly would make her opposition to FDR increasingly direct, declined to accept that diagnosis.[7] As an alternative to Roosevelt's narrative of historical change, she proposed instead a model of cyclic popular confusion and gave it weight by using her own experience as an example. "I began" college in the 1890s, she remarked "when evolution was still . . . very exciting" (EA 249). "I was a natural believer in republics a natural believer in science a natural believer in progress . . . just as the present generation are natural believers in Soviets and proletarian literature and social laws" (251). Those analogous attitudes were both mistaken, Stein declared. Ideas about historical development were seductive to "the kind of people that believe in progress and understanding," but they did "not really make" anyone "be living" (77, 251). In fact, Stein declared, sounding like a harbinger of Ayn Rand, the premise of the New Deal—that industrial society demanded new political structures to protect the traditional liberal ideal of personal freedom—legitimized "a passion for being enslaved" (65).

Given those beliefs, Stein's joshing dismissal of the press naturally tended to take on a more serious tone. For, in this light, the implication of her question—what, after all, could Americans change to?—shifted meaning. Having first contrasted a formal definition of American identity to an empirical description of American life, Stein went on to suggest that in falling prey to historicist visions of social change, young Americans failed to live up to the demands of their citizenship—implying in effect that if that failure became serious enough the people of the United States might well become something else. They could cease in effect to be good Americans. "Once a nation has lived long enough anywhere to be that nation," Stein remarked, "the character of that nation can naturally never be changing."[8] "If it were not somehow the same," she added still more forcefully, "it would not remain our country" (EA 204).

Those remarks directly contradicted the point of Stein's initial comment to reporters, rendering incoherent her joke on the difference between formal definitions and empirical descriptions. Stein's view of the United States, it turned out, was no less historicist, and no less dependent on "remembering," than that of her listeners. Confusing thought it may have been, that conflation of the formal and the empirical nevertheless cut to the heart of attitudes that ran all through the major part of Stein's career. Beginning with the legendary period of creative ferment that culminated in *The Making of Americans*, Stein obsessively ruminated over and sometimes sought to undermine, the distinction between empirical and historical understanding, on the one hand, and a kind of abstract or theoretical knowledge that seemed impervious to time and context, on the other. What's more, Stein consistently associated that obsession with her idiosyncratic definitions of "the disembodied abstract quality of the American character," so that her own aesthetic ambitions and philosophical convictions could seem indistinguishable from an ideal vision of national identity.[9] Stein brought that connection to the fore especially during the Depression, where implicitly and sometimes quite explicitly she used it to assail the political developments she opposed. But as she suggested when she compared her own immature inclinations to the progressive youth of the thirties, it was a vision whose roots lay—as did those of the New Deal itself—in the turn-of-the-century movements for political reform with which Stein briefly flirted while a student.

In fact, Stein's investment in American identity would lead her, much as it did the defenders of the New Deal to a fascination with the power of the presidency. She began *The Geographical History of America*, the book in which she first elaborated on the way her aesthetic principles ran counter to the New Deal, by pointing out that "in the month of February were born Washington Lincoln and I." In *Four in America*, she returned again to a still more elaborate comparison between herself and Washington, who she reimagined as an experimental novelist like herself. And these two instances of what might be called presidential poetics were merely the culmination of Stein's career-long habit of looking anxiously at the development of politics in the United States and comparing her work as a writer with the work of executive leadership. Like her friend and admirer, Richard Wright, Stein was deeply concerned to imagine her writing as a form of political leadership that might restore an imperiled American sovereignty. Indeed we can clarify Stein's aesthetic and philosophical visions by recognizing that in one significant aspect they amounted to a rival vision of presidential power—one that accepted the priority that recent political developments had given to the chief executive, while also seeking to mobilize that prominence in pursuit of a contradictory agenda. To see the significance of that disagreement, however, we must first recognize the way Stein drew on and departed from the ideas of her reformist contemporaries.

A National Life: Stein and the Language of Progressive Reform

Though the connection has only rarely been considered by her critics, Stein drew attention to an important aspect of her intellectual formation when she pointed out her engagement during the 1890s with the emerging forces of the Progressive movement. Her encounter at Radcliffe with William James and her presumed debt to pragmatism have been examined at great length; her several years of postgraduate study in medicine and experimental biology at Woods Hole and Johns Hopkins, and their influence on Stein's professional and theoretical concerns, have been examined to a lesser, but still illuminating degree.[10] Much more rarely noticed, however, has been the extent to which all these experiences, along with her connections to her New York and Baltimore relations and her friendship with recent graduates of Smith and Bryn Mawr, put Stein in contact with newly forming networks of intellectual innovation and political reform.[11] Stein soon rejected the political and intellectual culture of Progressivism. "Everybody knows," she later declared, "there is no progress."[12] But that very comment points to the enduring significance of the ideas Stein encountered in her youth. As an early influence and later a prime antagonist, the ethos of Progressive reform shaped Stein's attitudes in fundamental ways. So much so that the literary ambitions she formulated during the first decade of the twentieth century—as the Progressive movement rose to the height of its influence and Stein herself turned decisively against it—can be understood as nearly a competing, but analogous agenda to the political movement that gave rise to the theory of presidential government.

Stein's intellectual biography overlapped at several points with the paths of the major ideologues of the Progressive movement, and in certain respects both her experience and her youthful attitudes resemble the nearly standard concerns of a whole cohort of reformist thinkers. As a Jew and a Californian, Stein differed from the defining figures of the Progressive movement, who were predominantly from the Northeast and Midwest and strongly influenced by the legacy of evangelical Protestantism. As a rentier whose income depended especially on investments in rail transport, she had reason to be wary of a movement that would place heavy emphasis on the regulation of monopolistic public transport.[13] But, in other ways, her experience was typical of the Progressive intellectuals. As a student in Cambridge and Baltimore, she experienced first hand the rapid rise of the research university and the enthusiasm for expert knowledge it produced. As a researcher in psychology and biology, she worked in the hottest fields of the newly professionalizing sciences. And as a member of several, overlapping groups of friends excited by the new opportunities and advantages that higher education provided, she knew well a number of young people who were involved in both the growing political movements to reshape American institutions and the closely related social-scientific theories that would often be called on to justify those changes. Her closest friends at the turn of the century were aspiring scientists, educators, advocates for women's suffrage, and antiparty activists in the movement for urban reform.[14] In the words of her teacher Hugo Munsterberg, who called Stein an "ideal student," she was one member of an incipient "class of national leaders" whose experience with "higher education" enabled it to rise "above the social life of the masses" and provide the leadership by which "democracy is to be . . . perfected."[15]

Indeed her later memories of both the problems that distracted her in her youth and the solutions she imagined for them referred to ideas widely shared among the new university-trained elite at the turn of the century. Stein placed her belief in progress, science, and republics in the context of an anxiety about political and social decline common at the time. "When I was young the most awful moment of my life," she recalled, "was when I really realized that there were civilizations that had completely disappeared from this earth," a discovery, she added, that confronted her with the thought that, if "civilizations always came be dead," then "one was just as good as another one" (EA 12, 250). That intuition of the insignificance of human effort was no doubt a distinctive personal crisis for Stein.[16] But the terms in which she cast it were commonplace among Gilded Age intellectuals, who frequently read in the social upheavals of the late nineteenth century portents of the decline of the American republic and signs of the loss of the nation's exceptional mission. Stein might have encountered an especially stringent version of the warning, for example, in the influential writing of Henry George, whose *Progress and Poverty*, as she later recalled, had been urged on her by a radical uncle. But at Radcliffe and Hopkins, Stein also would have encountered the topic as a fundamental concern of the era's flourishing social and political thought, where a wide range of academics found, just as Stein would do, a solution to the specter of civic decline in the new vantages encouraged by biological science.[17] "After all," she wrote, answering her own fear of decline, "there was evolution and James' *Will to Live*" (EA 250). As a "natural believer in republics," Stein suggested, she had grabbed on to the promise of scientific progress as an alternative to the threat of American decline, finding in the new bodies of scientific knowledge a restored sense of both metaphysical confidence and national mission. "Evolution . . . justified life and it also justified death." It "was as exciting as the discovery of America by Columbus" (WIHS 61).

That discovery would have been recognized by a wide range of Stein's contemporaries among turn-of-the-century reform intellectuals, who shared her enthusiasm for the progressive vistas that seemed promised by evolution. What they meant by the term, however, had very little in common with Darwinian theory as it eventually came to be conceived. While Stein was in college and medical school, the mechanism of genetic transmission was still poorly understood. Although the rediscovery of Mendel would occur just as Stein was about to drop medical school, it would be several years before the significance of Mendel's observations was widely appreciated and still longer before the "modern synthesis" of natural selection and Mendelian genetics became the prevailing model of evolutionary biology. The theories of evolution Stein encountered, therefore, were just at the beginning of a period of turbulent change, but still dominated by speculative visions of inheritance that were vague about the means of transmission and often actively resistant to the emphasis that *The Origin of Species* had placed on the random nature of natural selection. Indeed Stein's years in college and graduate study, which coincided with a remarkable flowering in the mélange of biology and social theory, also overlapped with a "heyday of the new Lamarckism" in the still inchoate field of professional biology.[18] Though they faced growing challenge, the dominant schools of American science at the turn of the century tended to deny "hard" heredity. Accepting the Lamarckian premise that acquired characteristics could be passed on genetically, they emphasized instead the capacity for habit and will to direct the processes of biological—and perforce cultural—development.

Among biologists, that view would be relatively short-lived, and even at the height of its influence it was embroiled in dispute and uncertainty, raised in particular by August Weissman's recent, devastating experimental challenges to Lamarckian transmission. In the burgeoning social sciences, however, Lamarckism took deep root and exercised long-term influence, especially for the way it seemed to grant a role for purpose and education in human history. In the developing fields of psychology and sociology, as well as in the professionalizing domains of history, political science, and economics, Lamarckian versions of evolutionary theory provided the prevalent models of historical change, serving at the same time to imply a reassuring order to the apparent chaos of recent social conflict. If Lamarckism was correct, and acquired characteristics could be passed on genetically, then present social groups were directly the inheritors of the accomplishments of their ancestors, and they might hope by conscious effort to pass on still higher levels of learning and achievement to their descendents. In the words of pioneering sociologist Lester Ward, the theory of evolution appeared to justify a view of history in which humanity was "a race that is to develop through its own exertions."[19]

But for reform intellectuals the appeal of Lamarckian theory extended beyond the vision of ever higher levels of human development it appeared to guarantee. Because it conflated culture and biology, turn-of-the-century evolutionary theory provided an especially strong model of social cohesion at a moment when reformers were looking for ideas that could overcome the intense individualism of America's traditionally dominant political and moral philosophy.[20] There was a variety of different viewpoints in the Lamarckian theories of human history that dominated turn-of-the-century social science, and, a range of political uses across the spectrum to which they could be put. But all examples shared the assumption that contemporary social groups were the products of deep histories that intertwined biological and cultural transmission, and all viewed contemporary practices and institutions as the legacy of generations of inheritance. While racialist to the core, Lamarckian theories thus provided a vision of social groups bound by forces surpassing political institutions and economic relations that was deeply appealing to reform intellectuals. As the sociologist William Thomas explained, "a group having a common origin and a common history must have to some degree a memory, a consciousness, and a personality in common."[21]

Evolution thus appeared to provide a scientific warrant for the national solidarity that Progressive intellectuals saw as the prime engine of democracy, and it seemed to promise that with ever more conscious education, the nation would grow less fragmented and competitive and still more cohesive. "The bonds of nationality," as Albion Small explained, stood "for something more vital than the external accidents which are reflected in mere group forms."[22] By the same token, evolution promised to resolve the central paradox of both the social theory and political attitude commonly shared among Progressives, their simultaneous advocacy of democracy and enthusiasm for expert leadership.[23] From the Lamarckian perspective, leaders were the advance guard of groups to which they were bound by shared inheritance and whose common mission they were specially gifted to elicit—"mouthpieces of a folk-mind."[24] Stein's teacher Hugo Munsterberg offered a standard version of the theory. Munsterbeg saw in the rise of the national class to which Stein belonged, and more particularly in the recent presidency of Theodore Roosevelt, the happy development of "a quiet, aristocratic complement to the inner workings of the constitution." (He welcomed imperialism, rising racism, and immigration restriction for the same reason.) Because "the human race in America has begun to differentiate into a species which is anthropologically distinct," it had also begun to forge a sense of national solidarity that overcame "the other great divisions of social life." "The feeling grows that honor toward the state, sacrifice for it, and confidence in it are even more important than the respect for the totality of individuals," Munsterberg claimed. "The nation has come to that maturity where the public is ready to let itself be led by the best men."[25]

If Stein did not discuss such ideas directly with Munsterberg, she would have encountered variations on them virtually everywhere she turned in her time at Radcliffe—in her studies with William James, who was among the first to adopt Darwinian premises to psychological research, and whose pragmatist epistemology would be foundational to Progressive social theory;[26] in her classes with Josiah Royce, who was in the midst of rereading the history of idealist philosophy through the lens of evolution; in her role as secretary of the Radcliffe philosophical club;[27] and in her interest in "constitutional history," which was dominated at Harvard in the 1890s by the influence of Alfred Bushnell Hart's evolutionary nationalism.[28] At Hopkins, where her brother Leo briefly studied history while she enrolled in medical school, Stein would have encountered similar views in Herbert Baxter Adams's predominant "Teutonic" school of historiography, which viewed democratic institutions as the product of the deep ethnic history of the Anglo-Saxon people. Her apparently brief interest in the feminist theory of Charlotte Perkins Gilman would have familiarized her with a more consciously reformist version of comparable ideas.[29] In her laboratory classes, too, she would have been surrounded by experimental work aimed at testing the various hereditarian theories that dominated the era's social theory.[30]

That experimental work would eventually refute much of the period's Lamarckian lingua franca.[31] But the various, reassuring evolutionary theories of the day were slow to crumble. Progressive reformers in particular were strongly committed to the political virtues of evolutionary theory and reluctant to acknowledge what the influential economist Simon Patten referred to in 1912 as "the downfall of Lamarckianism." As long as such theories reigned, Patten pointed out, the efforts of reformers "to help individuals" seemed also to have "social importance."[32] Not surprisingly, then, the rhetoric of evolution ran all through the language of Progressive reform in the decades surrounding the turn of the century, playing an especially valuable role in the developing political theory that would seek to justify a renovation in constitutional attitudes. Teddy Roosevelt, who did perhaps more than any other writer to popularize the era's new narratives of racial history, turned enthusiastically to evolutionary social science to justify his visions of national destiny and civic leadership.[33] Woodrow Wilson's own widely popular versions of national history, which were nurtured by Wilson's education and employment at Hopkins, echoed Roosevelt closely, and Wilson drew still more explicitly on evolutionary theory to envision a deepened national compact, led by newly empowered leaders. Like Hugo Munsterberg, Wilson described Americans as "a new race" whose "organic structure" created a "community of feeling" that overrode "mere printed law."[34] "Governments are living things and operate as organic wholes," Wilson contended in his argument for presidential power. "There can be no successful government without leadership or without the intimate, almost instinctive, coordination of the organs of life and action. . . . Living political constitutions must be Darwinian in structure and practice."[35]

Stein, who would refer to Roosevelt and Wilson regularly over the course of her career, surely knew those theories and referred to them in her remarks about the salvation that evolution promised the republic. But she encountered a particularly poignant response to those ideas in the work of an acquaintance, Alfred Hodder, whose novel *The New Americans* she read when near the depths of the crisis that would give rise to her decision to trade science and reform for literary ambition. Hodder's writing was well positioned to speak to Stein's concerns. He, too, had been a student of Royce and James—reportedly among their most brilliant protégés before a scandalous career destroyed his reputation. While still very young, he had received acclaim for philosophical writing that found in James's emerging pragmatism both a refutation of skepticism and an inspiration for a view of society as an "organism" whose "corporate body" justified a utilitarian defense of the collective good.[36] Like Stein, too, Hodder was aligned with the emerging reform movement, working as a journalist for Lincoln Steffens and joining Leo Stein and others among Stein's associates as a member of a group of young activists who sought to challenge Tammany Hall.[37] But Hodder, who like Stein was from the West, remained by virtue of a reckless temperament distant from the zeal and intellectual sobriety more typical of the Progressive elite and doubtful of its hopes. In his novel, he managed both to celebrate the reformist mission of "educated intelligence" and to illuminate some of the reasons it seemed bound to fail.[38]

The New Americans combines a treatment of the shifting attitudes toward sex and marriage characteristic among Hodder's friends in New York's bohemian circles with a tale of the growing movement for political reform. By Hodder's lights, as by those of many of his contemporaries, the two themes appear aspects of the same issue. The romantic dissatisfactions of his characters, like their political frustrations, are but symptoms of customs that remain cruelly irrational because of their deference to tradition and local authority. The immediate subject of The New Americans is thus the soaring dreams and harsh disappointments of a group of wealthy and well educated young people living on the border of Kentucky and Ohio. But the novel's explicit theme is the way the hopes of both men and women are thwarted by expectations and institutions that prevent their full articulation. The novel's female characters yearn for "access to a larger world" and find themselves trapped in "the diminutive farce of marital fidelity" (198, 243). The male characters wish to reform a political system where the "real governor . . . is not the choice of the people, but the 'boss' of the 'machine.' " All find themselves, however, crippled by the expectations of their fathers, who as intellectual "contemporar[ies] of Patrick Henry" are "incapable of an idea . . . of later date than 1776" (258, 57).

Like the era's most prominent feminist reformers, then, Hodder builds a complaint against the conventions of bourgeois marriage on an appeal to the higher duties of national or, interchangeably, ethnic citizenship. Marriage is "an affair of the race, in which the individual played the part of conscious public servant or of dupe" (328). Indeed back of all the dissatisfaction it portrays, The New Americans finds one central vice exemplified by the novel's setting. Caught up in their personal concerns and local customs, few of the country's citizens are "accustomed to think of the nation as a whole" (420). Our protagonist, Alan Windet, who virtually embodies the ideology of Progressive reform, struggles against that parochialism, aspiring along with his small band of allies after the grandeur of the "national life" last illustrated by "the war between the North and South" (323). Youthful, noble, and supremely confident, he is at once contemptuous of the existing corruption of democracy and inspired by a vision of an as yet frustrated national destiny. "The Great Republic was not a gaunt illimitable province dotted with ragged villages," Windet thinks, as, in the mode common among Progressive intellectuals, he proclaims his decision to throw off the hauteur of his college days and commit himself to public life: "It was one of the most significant things in the modern world: the

States, with all their lynchings and vigilance committees, their tricks of politicians and insolent vulgarities, federated in the sheer rude determination, wherever the men concerned do not themselves render the thing ridiculous, to make civil liberty, equality, and at all events humanity, without respect to formulas, prevail" (56).

Windet's distaste for provincialism, constitutionalism, and party politics were all central features of the era's reformist politics. As in the ideology of Progressive reform, too, Windet is justified in his conviction of public mission less by direct popular or electoral support—which he neither has nor seeks—than by his assumption of an ethnic and spiritual connection to a people misrepresented by their political and social institutions. "He belonged to these people and had an instinctive knowledge of them" (57). Indeed Windet's political theory all but directly echoes the visions of national leadership that had recently been expressed by Woodrow Wilson. For, like Wilson, Windet envisions the democratic leader as a figure whose power is legitimized by his ability to exceed representative institutions and embody the force of an otherwise inchoate popular opinion: "The man who could divine them could govern them; the man who could divine himself could govern them; for they were his people, they belonged to him, and he to them; they were accessible to the same ideas, to the same passions, they spoke and could be spoken to in the same language, . . . the power of which was still a mystery to the generation at the moment in possession" (339).

It is thus a failure of some pathos in Hodder's design that Windet, crushed by his father's expectations and by the recalcitrance of local institutions, is never able to make good on his hopes. In the novel's climax, he is murdered by a former friend and now rival, a corrupt senator who is seeking to protect his empty marriage and lucrative sinecure. The incipient force of national leadership is crushed by the resistance of the partisan and parochial—as if, having echoed the dithyrambs of Wilson and TR, Hodder decided to answer them with the satiric voice of Henry Adams.[39] In the acid closing lines of *The New Americans*, Alan Windet is dead, and his father—"the chief of his clan"—lives on, uselessly sheltering Windet's infantilized widow (460).[40]

Stein read *The New Americans* twice as she was about to begin her own literary career and she remained fascinated by its author's own flamboyantly unsuccessful career. In one of her first efforts at fiction, she took Hodder himself as a subject—and implicitly as a comparison figure for her own situation. In Stein's rendition, however, Hodder took on the characteristics of his own protagonist and became a personification of the inevitable failures of Progressive reform. By Stein's telling, moreover, the failure was not, as Hodder had suggested, a matter of historical contingency or of the accidents of social design, but, in keeping with her growing doubt about Progressive evolution, of the inextinguishable qualities of human nature.

MASTERS OF THEIR CONSTITUTION

Not So Sweet or Virtuous: Stein's Critique of Progressivism

In the years following her departure for Europe, Stein moved with increasing seriousness away from the attitudes common among her university peers. The shift, which appears to have begun just as she was abandoning medical school, deepened with the frustration Stein experienced during her entrapment in the love triangle that would give rise to her first unpublished writings and ultimately to the breakthrough work "Melanctha."[41] It would culminate in a philosophical and personal transformation so complete that some of the allies of Stein's college and medical school days would find their former friend almost unrecognizable.[42] Stein herself underlined the significance of the transformation in the unpublished notebooks she wrote while working on *The Making of Americans*, describing an awakening that had proceeded in "stages"—beginning with the "questioning" she had undergone in an unsuccessful romance and deepening into a general reorientation catalyzed by "an experience in Spain." Only recently, Spain had been defeated in the war that had delighted many Progressives with its portents of national unification and international power. What Stein discovered on her visit to the country, however, was not evidence of America's rising stature, but a reminder of "the awful depression of repetition in history." The experience led to a realization. "I did not believe in progress, . . . I was in that sense not an optimist" and "not a pragmatist." The "aesthetic has become the whole of me," Stein recorded. "Not so sweet as I was or virtuous."[43]

The passage is illuminating, not only because it describes the foundation of Stein's artistic self-understanding, but because it emphasizes the degree to which that self-conception involved a reversal of what she later described as her first intellectual convictions and because it points to the way Stein's process of reconsideration led toward her radical experiments with literary form. In her first writing, Stein showed little interest in the formal and epistemological questions that would soon preoccupy her. The voice and narrative style of her early unpublished work is a rough imitation of Henry James. But her first literary efforts already reveal a writer whose personal frustration led toward a disenchanted perspective on the ambitions of Progressive reform and a keen critique of its aspirations for democratic leadership. "Does a reform start hopeful and glorious with a people to remake and all sex to destroy only to end in the same old homes with the same men and women," Stein asked in the unpublished novella "Fernhurst." If so, she contended, that denouement was typical of all movements for political change, and especially appropriate for what she cast as the inevitably doomed hopes of feminism. "Had I been bred in the last generation full of hope and unattainable desires I too would have declared that men and women are born equal," Stein's narrator explained. "But being of this generation with the college and professions open to me and able to learn that the other man is really stronger I say I will have none of it."[44]

If that disenchanted perspective owed something to the confusion and to the sexism Stein confronted in medical school, by most accounts it stemmed still more from the erotic education she had received in her unhappy pursuit of May Bookstaver—a recent graduate of Bryn Mawr and, notably, an activist in the woman's suffrage movement. In that long and painful romance, Stein found herself embroiled in subtle, yet intractable conflict, first with Bookstaver's more privileged admirer, Mabel Haynes, then still more disturbingly, with Bookstaver herself. The experience dramatized what would become the key intuition informing her first successful literary experiments, a tragic sense of the irrevocability of character— or, as Stein eventually phrased it in "Melanctha," of the "struggle, sure to be going on always" between any two people whose "minds and hearts . . . have different ways of working."[45] More generally, it attuned her to the subject that, as Leon Katz explains, lay at the center of Stein's first literary efforts. In the writing she composed up through the sudden shift that followed *The Making of Americans*, unavoidable personal conflict appears not simply as an element of narrative development, but increasingly as itself the overriding subject of concern and as something near to a bottom truth of life. "Love, friendship, even conversation are viewed as fundamentally naked struggles for dominance and power."[46]

That view was not simply a grim moral philosophy. It was also, as "Fernhurst" revealed, a fully conscious repudiation of the most basic attitudes inspiring the emerging reform movement. For, if there was a philosophical weakness especially damaging to Progressive ideology, it lay in the movement's reluctance to consider the psychological and political realities of conflict and power. Viewing the various targets and enemies of their reform agendas (unregulated finance and corporate enterprise, party machines, corrupt politicians, smug patriarchs, squalid urban environments), Progressive intellectuals saw a host of moral vices, including selfishness, chaos, ignorance, and narrow-mindedness. But they very rarely conceived of their antagonists as opponents who had defensible interests or who sought to protect the exercise of their power. Viewing themselves as the natural leaders of a democratic movement, Progressive intellectuals and activists likewise rarely acknowledged the coercion they hoped to exercise over others—or the resistance and legitimate resentment it might evoke. Indeed it was a central assumption of the reform ideology that began to cohere around the turn of the century that the deep ties that bound social groups made conflict unnecessary and even unnatural. "The dependence of classes on each other," Jane Addams contended, "is reciprocal." So, too, Progressive thinkers argued, was the relation between political powers and their democratic subjects. The Progressive leader, in Simon Patten's view, "comes not as the ruler of men, but as their servant." With democratic reform,

Charlotte Perkins Gilman agreed, "government ceases to be compulsion and becomes co-ordination."[47] Stein turned that assumption on its head and illuminated the key weakness of the Progressive ethos. By her telling, everyone sought to enjoy the psychic gratification of exercising power over others—none more so than the reformist leaders who cast themselves as the disinterested tribunes of the democratic will.

"Fernhurst" took advantage of Alfred Hodder's recent scandalous career at Bryn Mawr to dramatize that conviction. As a star among Harvard's philosophy graduates, Hodder had been appointed to teach at the vanguard institution of women's higher education, but he soon came into conflict with the school's legendary leader, M. Carey Thomas and, in an event that became a source of fascination among America's educational elite, began a secretive affair with Thomas's long-time partner, the school's esteemed professor of literature Mary Gwinn. That scandal ultimately erupted into public view when Hodder and Gwinn went on to marry and Hodder was sued by his common-law wife for bigamy.[48] Among Hodder's friends and admirers, like William James, who was horrified by the public revelations, the story became an object lesson in the significance of character—a moral underlined when Hodder died soon after, only thirty-eight, of illnesses likely brought on by alcoholism. But Stein drew a different lesson. Recognizing in Bryn Mawr's love triangle a situation similar to her own unhappy romantic experience, Stein centered her tale on the struggle for power and used that theme to discredit the ambitions of feminism and political reform. To emphasize the point she envisioned her male character, Philip Redfern, as a combination of Hodder and Woodrow Wilson and predicted the inevitable failure of their shared ambitions: "He plunged deeply into the political life of his time and failed everywhere. In this life as in all his human relations his instincts gave the lie to his ideals and his ideals to his instincts."[49]

By Stein's telling, the explanation for that failure was not so much a weakness of character as an unwillingness to confront the reality of power. Reframing the Hodder-Gwinn affair to more closely resemble her own experience with May Bookstaver, Stein imagined Redfern as a man defeated by his romantic rival—Dean Helen Thornton, the figure modeled on Carey Thomas. In Thornton, Stein rendered her antagonist as both an idealistic reformer, fired by "a pure enthusiasm for the emancipation of women," and a power mad tyrant (5). The dean "combined a genuine belief in liberty and honor and a disinterested devotion for the uplifting of the race with an instinct for domination." She controls her institution through an insidious "system of espionage and influence" that makes a mockery of its ideology of "self government" (5–6, 17). In the novella's denouement, the dean's Machiavellian skills enable her to "regain all property rights" in the love object over whom she and Redfern have competed (49).

Stein's cruel portrait of Thomas appears to have reflected a fair amount of psychological insight. But her primary interest lies less in probing the qualities of either Carey Thomas or Alfred Hodder, or for that matter Woodrow Wilson, than in demonstrating the way their inevitable conflict undermines their avowed aspirations for political change. Like other Progressive Era feminists, Stein's Thornton justifies a pursuit of female emancipation by emphasizing her dedication to "the future of the race" (17). In response, Stein emphasizes what late twentieth-century critics of the Progressives would frequently note—that their program for education and influence easily turned into a paternalistic system of social control. Unable to contest that power, Redfern fails in love and will similarly fail in politics because of his inability to exercise or even engage with the ruthlessness of his opponents. "He did not know how to win, how to avoid battle or how to yield" (48). But the same perspective leads to a sweeping dismissal of turn-of-the-century feminism. The power Thornton wields on campus is absolute, but it will be ineffective in a public world where more serious enemies than Redfern will defend their privilege.[50] The visions of social evolution prominent at the time had promised that such antagonism was unnecessary and that deep forces bound all in a common mission. Stressing in Redfern and Thornton the warring incompatibility of "ideals" and "instincts," Stein suggested that both psychologically and politically the theory was misguided.

In the decade that followed, as Stein clarified the methods and concerns that would be important to her first major achievement in *Three Lives* and *The Making of Americans*, she also developed the intuitions at the core of "Fernhurst," expanding them into a full scale philosophical critique. In the notebooks she kept during this time, for instance, Stein sketched a thorough-going rejection of Jamesian pragmatism, which she criticized on two of its central tenets. Referring skeptically to the central role given to "attention" by James—for whom the capacity to choose to focus on some particular object seemed both a function of human biology and a warrant for free will—Stein cast doubt on James's central effort to stake out a "via media" between materialist determinism and metaphysical formalism. "Each of us," James had written, "literally chooses, by his way of attending to things, what sort of a universe he shall appear to himself to inhabit." Attention was thus "the very hinge on which our picture of the world shall swing from materialism, fatalism, monism, towards spiritualism, freedom, pluralism."[51] In the obsessive, circular jottings of her notebook entries, however, Stein suggested that this picture of human freedom was itself but a self-deluding recreation of the very idealist philosophy James had sought to escape—in effect, the "contradiction in terms" of a "pragmatic idealism." "They used to universalise consciousness now universalise attention."[52] That view raised questions about what Hodder and others had recognized as a central, therapeutic pay off of pragmatism: the promise that freedom was to be found in the action of purposeful agency and rational investigation, or, as Walter Lippman would later term it, "mastery."[53] Stein rejected that pay off and went on to dismiss the core assumption of pragmatist epistemology—that concepts were "teleological" instruments whose use for distinct purposes guaranteed that the information they shaped was partial and provisional.[54] Confronted with the claim that "all classification is teleological," Stein declared that she was "not a pragmatist" and articulated in response the principle that would be central to her early work. She "did not believe" the Jamesian premise that knowledge was purpose driven, she noted, and believed instead "in reality as Cezanne or Caliban believe in it. I believe in repetition."[55]

There was a subtle two-sided point in that expression of faith. On the one hand, Stein's belief in repetition against teleology implied a repudiation of the value that her Progressive contemporaries would find in pragmatism and aligned theories—that both intellectual formalism and psychological alienation could be overcome in the commitment to purposive social engagement. By Stein's lights, that kind of plunging deeply into the life of one's time was bound to end in failure. But if her discovery of repetition implied a pessimistic rejoinder to the Progressive faith in growth and evolution, Stein also suggested that for those capable of appreciating its significance, a belief in repetition promised a rare form of emancipation—one that marked the "significant difference" between "pedestrianism" and "creation." Merely routine and reductive thinkers worked as James recommended, by "concentrat[ing] . . . attention," Stein wrote. "I concentrate myself." And in that distinct and total type of concentration, she suggested, the creative "genius" attained a fullness of knowledge and freedom unavailable to more commonplace thinkers. "Most people who are noted for logic are those having the clarity of non-appeal to experience." But "real thinking is conceptions arriving and arriving again and again always getting fuller, that is the difference between creative thinking and theorizing." In short, the believers in progress, who failed to acknowledge the fundamental truth of repetition, remained trapped by their own dubious belief in freedom. The "genius," by contrast, discovered in repetition an emancipation the ordinary lacked.[56] "Repeating is the whole of living and by repeating comes understanding, and understanding is to some the most important part of living."[57]

The experimental fiction Stein began to write after 1905 substantiated that paradoxical understanding. The grimly fatalistic stories in *Three Lives* are renowned for the way that, opening the project that would culminate in *The Making of Americans*, they begin to flesh out Stein's understanding of character as a deeply rooted "rhythm" of repetition independent of time and context—and demanding, therefore, the cyclic narrative form and the abstract, reiterative prose that blossomed particularly in "Melanctha." For those same reasons, though, Stein's volume went far beyond "Fernhurst" in the implicit challenge it presented to the aims of the Progressive elite. For, in nearly every respect, the world painted by *Three Lives* is antagonistic to the deepest hopes of Stein's reformist contemporaries. Not only are the unchanging rhythms of each protagonist's personality clarified, as Katz notes, by their inevitable and recurrent conflict with other, incompatible personalities. In keeping with that view, the environment in which Stein sets her characters reads like a point-by-point rejoinder to the social theory of Progressive reform. Stein's characters are not only fatally confined to their own repeating personal rhythms; they live in a world of impermanent, individualistic relations that lacks any intimation of public institutions, social bonds, or common culture.

In *The Making of Americans*, her most ambitious undertaking, Stein went on to radicalize and formalize that picture, gradually extending her fascination with the effort to write "a history of every kind of men and women and of all the mixtures in them" until, in the obsessive effort to describe the recurrent structures of personality, the book moved entirely beyond both conventional narrative form and the field of social relations on which the novel traditionally focused (MOA 176). Because "it is hard to know the kind of being in any one from just a description of some thoughts, some feelings, some actions," the traditional methods of narration were bound to prove inadequate and to give way instead to a meditative effort to perceive the unknown determinants of personality (399). By the concluding sections of the gargantuan project, narrative and even character has thus almost entirely disappeared in favor of an increasingly abstract series of statements of the writer's perceptions of personal types.

But while Stein's epic pursuit of "a description of being" and her effort to track it through an exhaustive investigation of various systems of classification is well known, the significance of that ambition is clarified when we take into account the fact that it emerged specifically as an alternative to the agenda of Progressive reform (540). Even in the most general sense, it is obvious that Stein's ever intensifying tendency to view personal identity as an ahistorical constant, best known through a kind of inspired intuition, ran counter to the Progressive desire to understand national cultures as deep-rooted and historically developing corporate entities. Against the soft collectivism of Progressive evolution, Stein's fiction implicitly posed a radically antisocial individualism. The first several hundred pages of *The Making of Americans*, in fact, show that alternative in the process of development. For, in accounts of several minor characters, Stein's narrative repeatedly follows out the process begun in *Three Lives*, depicting moments of social conflict and miscommunication, highlighting occasions where characters' spoken words do not match their conscious or unwitting intentions and essentializing those instances of social interaction into expressions of varying "bottom natures" and "kinds of being." With Mary Maxworthing, for example—a dressmaker and daughter of farmers who comes to the city as a nursemaid, becomes an independent craftswoman, and conceives and loses an illegitimate child—we shift gradually from the social history of class and manners to a natural history of essential kinds. "All that happened to her was from the impatient being in her" (220). So, too, with

Maxworthing's employer, who is said to have "completely in her being the feeling of rich country house living" (273).

All but explicitly here, social relations are transformed by Stein's imagination into expressions of essential personal qualities. ("My ultimate business as an artist," she later explained, "was not with where the car goes but with the movement inside that is the essence of its going" [LIA, 195].) But it's only in looking more closely at what Stein later called the "gradual making" of her novel, that it becomes clear just how directly Stein herself conceived the antagonism between reformist ideology and her developing psychological essentialism. For in the initial, elaborate plan she developed for *The Making of Americans*, the novel was to be a sweeping family saga—"a history of a family's progress" that was to culminate, much as Hodder's *New Americans* had, in a panoramic depiction of the death and decline of the hopes of a generation of bourgeois reformers. Stein's explanation, however, was to be nearly the reverse of Hodder's. It was not that the rule of the fathers dwarfed the hopes of their children. Both in her initial plans and in the book's final realization, fathers and grandfathers are quickly killed off. Rather, in an industrial civilization cut off from tradition by development and migration, the young, who are thrown back on their own resources and immersed in a ruthlessly emulative society, lack the ability to make substantial lives for themselves. "We moderns must create a complete tradition and live into it, for we do not follow teaching. Hence our art and ourselves, and . . . the dreadful failures."[58]

Aspects of both this theme and of Stein's narrative armature survive in the final version of the novel. To the extent they remain tangible figures in the dense weave of abstract description that assumes the forefront of Stein's composition, for example, the depiction of the novel's major characters (David Hersland, Alfred Hersland, Julia Dehning) retains traces of Stein's original design. Likewise, the central and anomalous "Martha Hersland" chapter almost directly implants the surviving narrative of "Fernhurst." But in the unpublished notebooks for the novel, the outline of a far more traditional narrative can be discerned, and the story that book would tell is one of the crushing disappointments that meet the hopes of the American-born children of a pair of aspiring immigrant families. Not only is Redfern to fail in politics; Alfred Hersland is fated to lose his fortune in speculation and to go on to a demagogic career in "politics on the reform side"; his divorced wife, Julia Dehning, is due to take up bureaucratic employment in higher education, while his sister Martha, abandoned by her husband Redfern, is headed for a vocation in feminist organizing that Stein treats with withering disdain. (She is to end the novel covering Europe by bicycle, going country to country "to rouse up the women to [a] sense of what they should be.")[59] Most significantly, the novel's central personality, David Hersland is to see his hopes for a brilliant scientific career culminate in a useless appointment to a backwater college and ultimately in a suicidal embrace of illness and despair. The general picture, only emphasized by Stein's marginal invective, is of the ignominious defeat of the ambitions Stein and her friends had embraced in the 1890s.[60] If they had hoped to perfect democracy, as Munsterberg put it, by calling on national solidarity to overcome the limits of liberal individualism, they had not only failed; they had proven unable to rise to the challenge with which modernity confronted them.

Dead is Dead: The Ethics of Anti-Progressivism

The final version of *The Making of Americans* hints at a theoretical explanation for that general failure in keeping with Stein's philosophical convictions about the irreducibility of personal difference: "Disillusionment in living is the finding out nobody agrees with you not those that are and were fighting with you. Disillusionment in living is the finding out nobody agrees with you not those that are fighting for you. Complete disillusionment is when you realise that no one can for they can't change. The amount they agree is important to you until the amount they do not agree with you is completely realised by you. Then you say you will write for yourself and strangers" (485).

If Progressive social theory had hoped to amend the individualistic bias of liberal democracy by finding a basis for a deeper social contract in the laws of cultural history, Stein, rejecting that possibility, leaned drastically in the opposite direction, establishing her own literary mission on the premise that agreement of any kind was impossible. But in addition to this theoretical rejection of consent, *The Making of Americans* points to an allied and still more forceful reason for the intense antipathy Stein expressed to reform ideology. For, in the context of the vision Stein clarified as she worked out her aesthetic and epistemological theories, the agenda of the Progressive movement seemed increasingly not just doomed to failure, but miserably superficial and at odds with the grandeur Stein expected of genius. The most direct, although abstractly worded, critique of the reform agenda to appear in the final version of *The Making of Americans* implicitly views Progressivism, not wholly unreasonably, as a type of secular religion designed to ward off despair. The friends of her youth, Stein suggested, demonstrated a tendency—"now beginning to be true of men and women everywhere"—to "build up other people's convictions, other people's intuitions other people's loving and virtue and religion" (497). This agenda was not just a form of paternalist exhortation, however, but a program to deny the "awful depression" Stein had discovered in Spain—a crushing knowledge, she now suggested, not only of the fundamental truth of repetition, but of what she cast as an integrally related and ultimate fact—the inescapability of death.

"Dead is dead," Stein announces. "To be dead is to be really dead." And, yet, as the tautological and reiterative expression indicates, Stein worried that the truth of mortality was not a message that sunk in easily. "To be dead is to be really dead and yet perhaps that is not really the end of them, some men feel this in them. . . . [T]hey go on having their religion . . . and to their religion to be dead is not really to be dead" (498). Nothing in fact was more common—was, indeed, the essence of "general" as opposed to "concrete conviction"—than the wish to deny mortality (499). "They can have it in them as a generalization . . . that to be dead is not to be so very really dead, that things are not perhaps what they are." "This generalized conception is only sentimental," Stein declares, and "a very simple thing of being like everyone." For all people, she explains, are naturally drawn to the "conviction that dead is not really dead, that good is progressing" (499–500). Here, as in her later memoirs, Stein suggests that the allure of Progressivism came in the way that, in imposing false models of collective identity, it denied the mortality of both civilizations and individuals. "Everyone," she later recalled, "was refusing to be dead" (EA 250).

Stein's fiction, by contrast, is littered with corpses and dashed hopes. William James "always said there is the will to live without the will to live there is destruction," Stein later recalled. "But there is also the will to destroy, and the two like everything are in opposition" (WIHS 63–64). As her remarks about belief reveal, however, such comments reflect not just the obsessive awareness of mortality evident throughout the pages of *Three Lives* and *The Making of Americans*, but an intense ethical vision in a quasi-Nietzschean key. The greater part of human life was a conspiracy to deny the indistinguishable truths of death and repetition and opposition. Against that craven deception, however, Stein cast her own heroic effort to see the truth clearly and write it without obfuscation. "To some," Stein wrote, referring to herself and reiterating the antagonism she had scored against "pragmatic idealism" in her notebooks, "spirituality and idealism have no meaning excepting as meaning completest intensification of any experiencing, any conception of transcending experience has to some not any meaning" (779). The sentence neatly clarifies what it meant for Stein to "believe" in repetition, as opposed simply to perceive or understand it. Pragmatists and Progressives were like all religious believers, Stein suggested, in that they fashioned delusive promises of immortality by evading experience—necessarily "leaving out very much that should be being remembered" (780). But the genuine alternative to that self-deception was not so much a simple rejection of false belief as an alternative form of spirituality, and one that provided a more substantial version of the metaphysical confidence that religion ignobly supplied.

Indeed, by Stein's account, conventional religious convictions did not even attain the dignity of beliefs and amounted instead to an unthinking, natural credulity.[61] By contrast, in maintaining a stern commitment to full experience—to the effort "to live in the actual present"—from which everything conspired to distract one, the authentically creative thinker could attain a certain knowledge that transcended ordinary empirical awareness and that offered therefore a true alternative to the realization of mortality.[62] The intensification of experience, in short, was to be at once an acknowledgment of and an alternative to death: "I want to be completely certain . . . am wanting to be right in being completely certain and in this way only in me can it come to be in me that to be dead is not to be a dead one. Really to be just dead is to be to me a really dead one. To be completely right, completely certain is to be in me universal in my feeling, to be like the earth complete and fructifying" (574).

The echo in these lines of Stein's unpublished remark about real thinking as "conceptions arriving again and again" is illuminating. *Three Lives* emphasizes both the repeating structures of its protagonists' personalities and their mortality—setting their deaths, not incidentally, in a fictional landscape heavily shadowed by the omnipresent reality of childbirth. *The Making of Americans* goes on to intensify that depiction in a relentless catalog of death and decline. But Stein's most grandly ambitious novel also envisions an alternative to the fatal world of sex and death in the creative mind's full awareness of the truth of mortality. Conception and fructification for Stein thus would not involve the false immortality of growth and evolution, but a kind of intellectual emancipation—"a way to wisdom"—from the delusions of the commonplace (299).

Seeing Stein in this light helps to clarify the importance of one of the most often discussed, yet misunderstood features of her intellectual biography—the brief fascination, coinciding with the final stages of work on *The Making of Americans*, that she expressed for the notorious Viennese anti-Semite and misogynist Otto Weininger. Repellent as Weininger's crackpot ideas now seem, they had at the turn of the century an international caché that made his *Sex and Character* influential on a surprising range of anti-Victorian intellects, including Strindberg, Joyce, Musil, Krauss, and Wittgenstein. In Stein's case, Weininger's bizarre theorizing must have been especially appealing. For, Weininger drew on some of the same scientific training that shaped Stein. He was well educated in biology and psychology, for instance, and deeply admiring of James. And, like Stein, he developed his most intensely held beliefs in opposition to the prevailing social democratic tendencies, and Lamarckian theorizing, of his political environment.[63] Indeed Weininger's famous system of sexual and racial classification—like Stein's comparable efforts to develop an encyclopedic system of human character—were subordinate by his own account to a wildly neo-Kantian fantasy of individual autonomy as the willed transcendence of all social and biological constraint. "The birth of the Kantian ethics" was "the noblest event in the history of the world," Weininger enthused, "the moment when for the first time the dazzling awful conception came . . . , 'I am responsible only to myself; I must follow none other; I must not forget myself even in my work; I am alone; I am free; I am lord of myself.' "[64] Sincere though his anti-Semitism and misogyny were, for Weininger, the Jew and the Woman were merely the most concrete manifestations of the natural and conventional worlds he wished to escape.

Stein, who was no less anti-Semitic—and, at this stage in her life, no less misogynistic—than Weininger, embraced that vision by all reports wholeheartedly. She would have found in his *Sex and Character* both a confirmation of her political instincts and a clarification of the theoretical ambitions, and emotional uncertainties that had driven the development of her writing. The most prominent feature of Weininger's sensational book was his argument that recent discoveries in biology demanded a revision to conventional assumptions about sexuality. Groping toward something like the still unformulated distinction between genotype and phenotype, Weininger contended that each person's unique core sexual identity amounted to a particular spot on the continuum between masculinity and femininity and was therefore distinct from "the ready-made conventional shapes" that divided men and women (57). The payoff for this notion, however, came in the way that, in two respects, it undermined social categories and bolstered Weininger's extreme individualism. Most basically, by Weininger's account, the "innumerable" variety of individual types meant that it was senseless to conceive social groups in collective terms. A "psychology of individual differences" was required (59). More significantly, however, the distinction between the surface appearance and core identity of every individual provided for a self-confirming test of the hyperautonomy he wished to defend. At the far end of the spectrum of masculinity as Weininger conceived it stood the "genius"—the only full embodiment of "Kantian ethics" as Weininger imagined them. The mark of the genius, however, came not just in his struggle to transcend the constraints that imprisoned the less worthy (an effort that, in Weininger's intensely romantic view, meant that every genius must traverse a youth of struggle and obscurity) but in his ability to pierce the mysteries of human identity. Every genius was "a great discerner of men. The great man sees through the simpler man often at a glance and would be able to characterise him completely" (110).

It seems almost inevitable that, having read this account, Stein would declare herself a "masculine type" and say of her most esteemed contemporaries that "Pablo & Matisse have a maleness that belongs to genius. Moi aussi perhaps."[65] For Stein, who made her anxiety about recognition a recurring theme of her novel, Weininger's speculations must have come as a welcome reassurance. Since her youth, she had prided herself on her ability to diagnose the character of her friends. Beginning with *Three Lives* she had developed that talent into a strange program to identify and classify the essential personalities that lay back of every person's manifest appearance and that made themselves known, in characteristic inflections and rhythms, only to the most gifted and patient observer. Weininger's philosophy confirmed that all this was a mark of Stein's unique genius and simultaneously legitimized a rejection of the genteel femininity she had come to despise.

With the encouragement he offered, Stein went on to reemphasize what over the course of several years of experimental writing had in any case emerged as her main concern. Now fully jettisoning both the genealogical and the narrative interests with which she began, Stein made her novel into a drama of perception in which the social relations among fictional characters all but disappeared and were replaced by the author's struggle to perceive and describe her subjects correctly.

Among the results of Stein's commitment to that project was the toneless seriality of her prose. Throughout *The Making of Americans*, but especially, in its most radical late stages, Stein's novel increasingly displaces narration with a rhetorical method emphasizing the incremental variation among extended chains of sentences whose composition is limited to the most basic vocabulary and syntax. ("Certainly every one can have been one, can be one imagining something, some are imagining everything to be anything, some are very carefully imagining something to be anything, some are dreamily imagining something to be anything, some are daintily imagining anything to be something" [794].) Given Stein's theory, that combination of minimal diction and maximal qualification makes perfect sense. For, if on the one hand, the abstraction and limitation of her prose seemed necessary to avoid the shallow empiricism and symbolic resonance typical of literary characterization; the determination to record the most precise variations of perception required, on the other, continual restatement—with the result that Stein's descriptive project extends in countless pages of cascading reiteration.

But, importantly, this is only one side of Stein's ever more streamlined rhetorical structure. Running counter to that dominant strand of *The Making of Americans'* narration are recurrent interruptions that break the surface of Stein's text with exclamations of doubt and despair. Time and again, over the course of *Americans'* nine hundred pages, as she tries out various systems of classification and various ways of conceiving the morphology of character, Stein describes herself falling into a slough of despond. "Sometime and that will be a great thing there will be a history of each one, of the bottom nature of each," Stein announces as her quest gets seriously under way (182). But, she also points out that the effort to clarify it "is a complicated question" and requires continual efforts "to begin again," importantly revealing the project to be less the pseudoscientific enterprise it sometimes appears than a constantly beset spiritual trial (299). "There was a time when I was questioning, always asking," Stein reports. "Then I did not know repeating, I did not see or hear or feel repeating" (302). Later: "Sometimes I am almost despairing. Yes it is very hard, almost impossible I am feeling now in my despairing feeling to have completely a realising of the being of any one" (458). And again, "an unreal lonesome feeling" descends. "Perhaps not any really is a whole one inside them to themselves or to any one" (519). Finally Stein rises to her most anguished expression of doubt: "I cannot bear it this thing that I cannot be realising experiencing in each one being living, I say it again and again I cannot let myself be really resting in believing this thing, it is in me now as when I am realising being a dead one, a one being dying . . . and I am filled then with complete desolation" (729).

It is true, as critics have noted, that, joined to Stein's several shifts in terminology, these repeated expressions of despair impart a "revisionary quality" to *The Making of Americans*. But it does not follow that they show Stein engaging in a "continual undermining of her . . . Weininger-like project," or that they suggest her dissatisfaction with her own theoretical premises.[66] Rather the novel's occasional lamentations only emphasize the greatness that Stein perceived in her task. Indeed Weininger himself underscored the significance of the ambition he and Stein shared by stressing its profound difficulty. "The obstacles in the way of characterological investigation are very great, if only on account of the complexity of the material. Often and often it happens that when the path through the jungle appears to have been cleared, it is lost again in impenetrable thickets." But, as "behind the fleeting physiological changes there is a permanent morphological form, so in characterology we must seek the permanent, existing something through the fleeting changes" (80–81, 83). So, too, Stein, following each expression of despair, returns to the pursuit of certainty in an indubitable knowledge of personality. As in Weininger, too, the project culminates in a wisdom that surpasses the rough methods of social classification for an immediate awareness of individual personality. "Types of people I could put down," she later explained, "but a whole human being felt at one and the same time, in other words while in the act of feeling that person was very difficult to put into words" (LIA 145). Hence the climax of the novel: the celebrated lyric passage, extended for dozens of pages, in which Stein's narrator (now surpassing the personal expressions of despair indicated by the use of "I" and rising as before to the "disembodied" state of pure knowledge indicated by the pronoun "some") achieves a complete awareness of the life of David Hersland in the moment of his death. "He had come to be a dead one and he was then at the ending of beginning living. He had come to be a dead one and some then were knowing that thing knowing then that he was not any longer being living. Some were then knowing that he was a dead one" (902).

In later years, Stein would describe the conclusion of *The Making of Americans* as a significant transition in her artistic career. "When I began *The Making of Americans* I knew I really did know that a complete description was a possible thing," she wrote. But once that point had been proven, there was no need to pursue it further. "If it can be done why do it" (LIA 156, 157). Placing the moment in the context of Stein's intellectual and political development, however, we can see that it amounted not merely to the fulfillment of a methodology, but, also to a symbolic resolution to the long process by which Stein dispatched the theoretical paradigms of Progressive reform.[67] For, as her notebooks make clear, David Hersland amounts in the initial design of Stein's novel to the brightest hope of the novel's ambitious youth and the personification of Stein's early enthusiasm for science.

Synthesized from Stein's memories of her much admired friend and mentor in psychology Leon Solomons, and from Stein's view of her young self, David represents the aspiration of science "in its reform movements." His end both reflects Stein's reaction to Solomons's own early death by peritonitis and the personal conviction of mortality Stein experienced as she rejected her failing scientific career. Stein had told Hodder that her departure from medical school had been a kind of "mental suicide."[68] In the invention of David Hersland, she combined that experience with the story of Solomons's death and in the process dramatized both her own fear of insignificance and her own triumphant escape from the limits of Progressive ideology. "29 year old failure of influence, finds has not really affected people," reads the outline of the character in Stein's notebooks. "David constantly surrounded by thought of death—puts it away from him—then endeavors to embrace it . . . to conquer it, almost, never quite." "Fear of feminization" kills him.[69]

In these respects, David Hersland is clearly Stein's mirror image. Much as *Three Lives* showed Stein discovering her artistic prowess in the unbreachable gulf that divided the author from her hopelessly confined subjects, *The Making of Americans* enables Stein, by depicting David, to avoid the failure and sexual oppression that destroys him. By Stein's telling, that destruction could be laid to the same ultimate absence of the will-to-power she saw in Alfred Hodder and Woodrow Wilson. Ironically the very term she came up with to describe David's decline—"a dead one"—might well have been drawn from the phrase Hodder himself had used to refer to those who, in the race of life, "go to pieces all of a sudden."[70] In the final version of her novel, Stein attributes such a failure to David ("he was not one who had been one being fighting") and makes clear that his decline, and his ultimate decision to embrace the death that shadows him, can be explained by the fact that, like all reform-minded intellectuals of the turn of the century as Stein saw them, he lacked the will to commit to the full knowledge of conflict, repetition, and mortality that Stein's work itself represented (902). "He almost came to be certain that one could *not* be experiencing something more complete than any experiencing, he came to be almost certain that one *can* be experiencing something that is more than experiencing," Stein writes, thus marking David's difference from herself in his susceptibility to the "pragmatic idealism" she had critiqued in James (781, emphasis added). The fine distinction drawn there becomes the organizing principle of the final pages of her book. For, the pathos of David Hersland's death arises from the fact that he simultaneously glimpses the awareness Stein defined for herself, while lacking her own commitment to enduring it. Although he can die and rise to an admirable stature in the process, unlike Stein, he cannot "live in the actual present."

At the acme of his life as Stein depicts it, then, David resembles the genius envisioned by Stein and Weininger alike—beyond the confusions of ordinary society and the time-bound constraints of ordinary knowledge. "He was not needing to be remembering anything. He was not needing to be forgetting something. He was understanding that he was being living." He "was one who was completely a different one from any other one" (900, 901). In that moment, David nearly attains the stature Stein envisions for the writer—"he could have been one . . . clearly, completely clearly expressing that thing"—but, as the final peroration repeatedly emphasizes, he falls short for lack of effort (900). "Some are being ones being living and are in a way not ones interested in being living," Stein summarizes the case (880). The conclusion reinforces Stein's affinity for the hyper liberal fantasies found in Weininger's *Sex and Character*. Weininger argued that many people possessed, although failed to realize, the possibility of autonomy and that, in the right circumstances, that potential could be quickened so that the ordinary person might approach the intense consciousness and moral and intellectual liberation he thought characterized genius. "For most men," Weininger explained, "this moment is the point of death" (129). Giving David a glimpse of that awareness at the brink of his own mortality, Stein implicitly reserved a more durable and impressive form of accomplishment for herself—and in the process sealed her dismissal of Progressive evolution. "In the scientific sweep of their social theories," a late nineteenth-century observer noted, "the philosophers of the ultra-evolutionary school put out of sight . . . two commonplace facts—individuality and death."[71] Stein reasserted both, and, casting them as mutually dependent, made them definitive of her account of literary creation.

Clarity is of no importance: Anti-Progressive Leadership

In the work she published during thirties, Stein returned to the themes raised in *The Making of Americans* and made clear that the convictions she had arrived at in writing that book amounted to a complete philosophical vision—one that joined the aesthetic, epistemological, and ethical principles foregrounded in the epic novel to a political theory exemplified by her idealized vision of America. The series of artistic credos expounded in *Lectures in America*, and the analogous, though more abstruse works of the period like *The Geographical History of America* and *Four in America*, prescribe a radical form of neo-Kantianism similar to Weininger's—in which "writing" shucks off "associative habits" and, in its achievement of "disembodiment," surpasses the experience of time and the constraints of social "identity."[72] Art, which was the only means "to completely express" the "complete actual present," was also the only way to displace "human nature" by the "human mind" and thereby to achieve the superior form of self-realization that Stein described as "entity."[73]

But, while "master-pieces" as Stein envisioned them escaped association and "had nothing to do with time," they also paradoxically seemed particularly appropriate to the modern world and to the industrial United States that appeared to be its vanguard (WMP 155). "The strange thing about the realization of existence is that like a train moving there is no real realization of it moving if it does not move against something and so that is what a generation does it shows that moving is existing. . . . [But], this generation has conceived of an intensity of movement so great that it has not to be seen against something else to be known and therefore does not connect itself with anything, that is what makes this generation what it is, and that is why it is American" (LIA 166).

Stein's Progressive contemporaries had found in evolutionary cultural history a basis for democratic solidarity and a reason to feel confident about American progress. Having dispatched that vision, Stein replaced it with a reinvigorated version of the classic idea of the United States as a country whose unique "vitality of movement" enabled it to escape history. "The American way has been not to need that generations are existing" (LIA 173, 166). Against the historicism and culturalism of her contemporaries, then, she proposed a vision of the United States that resembled nothing so much as the new styles of academic social science that increasingly replaced Progressive social theory during the twenties. Like the rising schools of behavioral psychology, pluralist political science, and neoclassical economics, Stein cast the United States as a highly individualistic, mobile, and fluid society whose unique social order emerged from the undirected collective action of countless individual choices.[74] Though she is sometimes called a conservative, it would probably be more accurate to say that, like the neoclassical economists of the time, she responded to the reform movement by highlighting her long-standing libertarian beliefs.[75] The main value of the attention to syntax that became a focus of her work during the twenties, she thus claimed, was that, in the knowledge of grammar, "one is completely possessing something and incidentally one's self" (LIA 211). A significant benefit of art, likewise, was that it contested the hand of the state. "If there was no identity no one could be governed . . . . [G]overnments are occupying but not interesting because master-pieces are exactly what they are not" (WMP 156). Seen in this light, her famous vision of America as "a space . . . filled with moving" can be taken for what it surely was—a libertarian vision of the freedom promised by the market and civil society (LIA 161).

If in these ways, Stein implicitly rebuked the reformism prominent during her youth, she was still more direct when it came to the core feature of Progressive political theory—its assumption that, in the ability to articulate and mold popular opinion, elite leadership could forge a more democratic nation out of the fragmented individualism of American society. While her distaste for association and mimesis were themselves challenges to that assumption, Stein elsewhere revealed the antagonism to be no coincidence. Her first major creative achievements in

Three Lives and *The Making of Americans* had coincided, in fact, with her realization that the effort to instruct "public opinion" threatened a "destruction of individual power and liberty."[76] The result was a growing distaste for the idealization of civic virtue that ran through the writing of Progressive intellectuals and that had once been important to Stein herself. In college, she had rhapsodized about the example of William James. "He stands firmly, nobly for the dignity of man."[77] As she worked on *The Making of Americans*, however, James's example gave way to Stein's admiration for Picasso, whose combination of artistic integrity and juvenile bad manners she grew to admire. "The kind of originality that is genius," she came to decide, "has nothing to do with character."[78]

From this perspective, the type of civic leadership that Progressives had hoped for from the presidency seemed both impossible and counterproductive. And, indeed, during the twenties and especially the thirties, Stein spoke with increasing directness about her disdain for the several figures later described by historians as "the progressive presidents." Woodrow Wilson, who she had first mocked in "Fernhurst," returned as Stein's model for "patriarchal poetry" and as an exemplar of hapless, "seductive" demagoguery (FIA 174).[79] Teddy Roosevelt and his cousin Franklin appeared as imperial outlanders to a democratic country they failed to represent. Each resembled Napoleon, Stein claimed. "Even though they belonged to the country to which they belonged," because of their determination to force unwanted change on a public they deceived, they "were foreign to it" (GHA 127). The very emphasis that Progressives put on public rhetoric as a means of forming civic community seemed to Stein absurd. "It is not clarity that is desirable," she declared, "but force" (FIA 127).

And indeed, all through Stein's writing runs a subtle admiration of force, and an implicit contrast of it to seduction and demagoguery, that seems all but explicitly directed against the Progressive ideal of democratic community. When she thought back to the Civil War, for example, Stein recalled it not as the moment of national founding that appealed to her contemporaries, but as an example of the kind of erotic will to power lacked by David Hersland. "My attack on Alice is like Grant's on Lee," she recorded in her notebooks. When she considered analogs for artistic genius, she likewise turned to Caesar—whose "extraordinary versatility and plasticity of mind" corresponded with an "indifferen[ce] to all moral distinctions"—and to other renowned commanders.[80] It was not incidental that she spoke dismissively of Lincoln, selecting him as a counterexample to the aesthetic she preferred (FIA 195), or that in her frequent admiring references to Grant, she focused solely on his military career and left his later public life aside, or that when she imagined an alternative vocation for Henry James in *Four in America*, she envisioned him as a general. Describing the public reception of her own work, Stein imagined it not as an analog to the oratory she disdained, but as a kind of cultural assault on her audience. "A long complicated sentence," she advised her readers, "should force itself upon you, make you know yourself knowing it" (LIA 221). No other reception was possible she later curiously explained. "Nobody listens and nobody knows what you mean no matter what you mean, nor how clearly you mean what you mean. But if you have vitality enough," Stein wrote, surely thinking of her own surprising popular success, "somebody and sometime and sometimes a great many will have to realize that you know what you mean and so they will agree that you mean what you know, . . . which is as near as anybody can come to understanding any one" (FIA 127).

But for a writer who doubted both the possibility and value of public communication, Stein engaged in an awful lot of it during the thirties—publishing two accessible memoirs, a volume of widely attended lectures, a series of editorializing essays in the *Saturday Evening Post*, and multiple statements of artistic and political principle. What's more, the ends Stein hoped to achieve by the force of her own literary example appear to resemble quite closely the program of civic education she disdained in her political contemporaries. For, no less than Progressive reformers, Stein implicitly cast her own public expression as an inspiring and educational force that promised to issue in democratic renewal.

That curious symmetry might be taken as symptomatic of a larger pattern apparent throughout Stein's work. For, while it is evident, on the one hand, that Stein rejected the social and political theory of Progressive reform, in other respects, lingering signs of its influence can be seen all over her oeuvre. In her oft quoted claim, for example, that the United States was "the oldest country in the world because by the methods of the civil war and the commercial conceptions that followed it America created the twentieth century," Stein repeated a commonplace of Progressive social theory (ABT 78). So, too, with her description of the United States as a continental nation whose vast expanse created a culture at odds with the traditions of European nations. Even the aesthetic innovation introduced by *The Making of Americans* resembled to a degree a fundamental ambition of Progressive ideology. No conviction was more widely shared among turn-of-the-century reformers than the notion that the emerging elite must point the way to a realization of national identity that would supercede the restraining influence of region, custom, and the traditional family. The aim, Simon Patten explained, was to "take men out from under the domination of local, objective conditions" so as to "create a common subjective environment."[81] In its brisk rejection of both the family saga and ordinary characterization, and in its indifference to conventional sociability, Stein's writing similarly abstracted the people it depicted from mere local context, with the intimation that they might thereby conceive an emancipation related to their status as Americans. In both cases, moreover, the process required the unique gifts of an intellectual who stood apart from the ordinary life of the nation, but who possessed, by virtue of both that estrangement and her birth, a unique ability to discern the national will.

Each of these features, moreover, was but a mark of the deep investment in national mission Stein plainly shared with her Progressive contemporaries and that she touted in her titles' recurrent invocations of America. That patriotic sensibility is all the more striking in that, as Stein herself realized, in rejecting the cultural history of Progressive theory, she fashioned a psychological and ethical theory that cut against the significance of national identity. Summarizing a point made repeatedly in *The Making of Americans*, Stein noted in effect that her theory went Progressivism one better and revealed national affiliation to be but one more of the arbitrary conditions that obscured the bottom truth of psychological identity. "It is a very simple thing to be knowing that there are kinds in men and women. It is a simple thing to be knowing that being born in a religion, in a country, in a position is a thing that is not disturbing anything."[82] By the same token, the radical, antisocial individualism to which Stein gave the name "entity," should logically have been indifferent to nationalism as to any other form of association—a point Stein perhaps referred to when she noted that "the discovery of America" had been both "an opening up and a limiting" (WIHS 61).

Stein squared that circle in the classic fashion, celebrating America as a nation distinct only for its overriding commitment to individual freedom. The culture of the United States was anticultural. But, the upshot, of course, was the paradoxical implication Stein conveyed to the reporters who greeted her in 1935—that in fantasizing about collective history or national solidarity, Progressive Americans were in fact untrue to the ethical purposes enshrined in their national origins. "The eighteenth century began the passion for individual freedom," Stein wrote. Beginning with Lincoln and the rise of industrial "organization," however, there began an ominous "passion for being enslaved" that had culminated in the New Deal (EA 65, WL 336–37). The present moment, she suggested, was merely the culmination of a long-term flight away from the disembodied, abstract character that rightly belonged to the nation.

From this vantage, it is easy to see how, despite the universalizing aim of providing "a history of every kind of men and women," Stein might have justified using the title *The Making of Americans* for her epic novel and how that perspective might have led her to recreate the very models of executive leadership she appeared to distrust. For, what Stein's writing, with its insistent invocation of America, did in the thirties was to elaborate the implicit ethical lesson of her earlier work and, in so doing, expand on by democratizing the message of Weininger. In effect, she demanded that all Americans be geniuses and implicitly suggested that all people who similarly lived up to the demands of modernity could be in effect American. "Everyone when they are young has a little bit of genius," Stein told Thornton Wilder, explaining further that the receptiveness and courage she valued were merely lost with age and exhaustion. As Wilder himself perceptively observed, with "those gay and challenging eyes" Stein turned on the hundreds of American soldiers who visited her in Paris, she "asked nothing less of them than their genius" (FIA xxvii).

The point might be generalized to describe the whole range of work Stein published during the latter part of her career. It was implicitly cast as a challenge to the torpor of a complacent public and in that way demanded that Americans recall an origin at odds with the shallow remembering that dominated popular culture. The peril of freely chosen enslavement, and the virtue of self-possession, had been in fact a main theme of Stein's work from her first major phase. All through *The Making of Americans*, for example, Stein refers to the ethical agenda inspiring her book's more manifest theoretical ambitions. If in David Hersland's death we encounter both the possibility and failure of radical autonomy, Stein repeatedly sees similar problems elsewhere and casts her efforts to perceive personality as coextensive with the "anxious" effort that citizen of the modern world faces in the effort to "make an individual of her[self]"—to be "real in existing (83, 98). What's more, Stein tells us that her own writing surpasses the merely decorative pleasures of genteel culture because of the virtually pastoral role it thereby promises to fulfill. *The Making of Americans* was "not for anybody's reading," Stein commented, but "to give to everybody in their living the last end to being, it makes it so of them real being" (177). That few people live up to the burden of becoming who they are only underscores the significance of the heroic example set by Stein herself: "Many go on all their life copying their own kind of repeating, many go on all their life copying some one else . . . . Everyone mostly has in them their own repeating sometime in their living, this is real being in them . . . . [But] it is easier for such of them just to go on with an automatic copying of their own repeating rather than really live inside them their repeating" (192).

In *Lectures in America*, Stein takes up the topic again and emphasizes the way this ethics of heroic self-realization underlies her most familiar literary methods. Defending herself strenuously against the charge of redundancy, Stein contends that the incremental variation evident in her most monotonous writing marks not "repetition" but the conscious act of "insistence." "Insistence is always alive and if it is alive it is never saying anything in the same way. . . . [I]f anything is alive there is no such thing as repetition" (171, 174). "What one repeats," by contrast, "is the scene in which one is acting, the days in which one is living, the coming and going which one is doing, anything one is remembering is a repetition, but existence as a human being" involves other qualities—"listening and talking . . . action and not repetition" (179, 180) As a defense of intentionality, these comments might be taken as a capsule expression of Stein's aesthetic and social theory, both of which envision freedom as the accomplishment of a highly conscious individual striving against the constraints of habit and sociability. Such freedom was rightly the possession, and burden, of all Americans, Stein suggested, but with the rise of organization and the omnipresence of oratory it was constantly threatened by the dead hand of repetition.[83] In response, her public writing called in effect for a revival of America's revolutionary founding. "Organization is a failure and everywhere the world over everybody has to begin again," Stein announced in the *Saturday Evening Post* in 1936. "Perhaps they will begin looking for liberty again" (WL 337).

Strangely, though, that exhortation echoed almost precisely the point made by Stein's Progressive contemporaries and reaffirmed later during the New Deal. Teddy Roosevelt, Woodrow Wilson and their allies and supporters, too, had seen themselves contending with organization and struggling against what Walter Lippman condemned as "barren routine" (174). The whole premise of the reform movement was that the industrial transformation of society had created illegitimate powers and undermined the prospects of self-rule. And, against that civic corruption, Progressives, too, envisioned a rebirth of America in a renewal of the nation's revolutionary origins. Invocations of the founding fathers accordingly run all through the philosophical writings of Roosevelt and Wilson and of many of their supporters. But the most dramatic expression of the logic came in the platform created by the Progressive Party in the presidential election of 1912. In the legendary convention that gave birth to that party, and that occasioned TR's famed "Standing at Armageddon" speech, the Progressives laid out a policy agenda and, perhaps more importantly, a political vision that two decades later would become the core of the governing philosophy of the New Deal and the philosophical justification for the rise of presidential government.[84] In its advocacy of the initiative, the recall, and the referendum, but still more in its legendary popular fervor, the Progressive Party convention envisioned a political movement that would replace party competition with the direct expression of a reinvigorated popular will. The preamble to its platform cast the moment as a revolutionary refounding of American democracy:

> The conscience of the people, in a time of grave national problems, has called into being a new party, born of the nation's sense of justice. We of the Progressive party here dedicate ourselves to the fulfillment of the duty laid upon us by our fathers to maintain the government of the people, by the people and for the people whose foundations they laid.
>
> We hold with Thomas Jefferson and Abraham Lincoln that the people are the masters of their Constitution, to fulfill its purposes and to safeguard it from those who, by perversion of its intent, would convert it into an instrument of injustice. In accordance with the needs of each generation the people must use their sovereign powers to establish and maintain equal opportunity and industrial justice, to secure which this Government was founded and without which no republic can endure. . . . Unhampered by tradition, uncorrupted by power, undismayed by the magnitude of the task, the new party offers itself as the instrument of the people to sweep away old abuses, to build a new and nobler commonwealth.

There is no doubt that Stein would have opposed the policy initiatives suggested here and outlined more clearly in the remainder of the Progressive Party platform. But, it is worth noting the similarity in their diction and historical vision. For the rhetorical and theoretical framework in which Stein cast her disagreement with Progressivism and the New Deal all but replicated the grounding assumptions of her antagonists. For Stein as for the Progressives, the fundamental question—at the core of her aesthetics as of her cultural criticism—concerned the hope of popular sovereignty and of individual self-determination. For Stein, as for the Progressives as well, the fact that individual freedom and collective self-government seemed to be at odds was only the mark of the corruption of the political and economic order that needed to be overcome in the expression of popular sovereignty. Indeed, while the phrase would not have had precisely the same meaning in her case, Stein, too, shared the Progressive Party's concern that the American people become "the masters of their own constitution." That they so rarely rose to the task and remained imprisoned by routine and contented by demagoguery, explained the depth of the frustration she expressed during the thirties.

Here, too, though, Stein became almost a mirror image to those reformers who she had begun her career by criticizing. For the Progressive elite that emerged at the turn of the century, the prospect of a democratic renewal led by a national class of gifted leaders was both the most invigorating source of inspiration and a contradiction that would lead in later years to confusion and frustration. In this way, the Progressive movement gave rise to but the first example of the exaggerated hopes and bitter disappointments that would swirl around the belief that executive leadership could resolve the problems of a liberal polity. Stein had begun her career with a cruelly perceptive depiction of the dangers of such paternalism, but her very belief in democratic self-rule strangely led her to recreate it. Her Progressive contemporaries saw leadership as a kind of democratic revivalism that through exhortation and example could lead Americans to a fuller citizenship. Stein likewise suggested that a heroic struggle would be needed to overcome a society built on emulation and put herself in a still more paradoxical version of the stance taken up by the Progressive elite. Although she disdained public speaking—and advised her readers remarkably that "one discusses things with stupid people not with sensible ones"—she returned time and again during the thirties to public performance, with the implication that by forcing herself upon her audience, and thereby stimulating its self-awareness ("mak[ing] you know yourself knowing" her), she might inspire them, just as *The Making of Americans* had suggested, to live up to her example (EA 17).

It should hardly be surprising in this light that, even if antagonistically, Stein consistently compared her own ambitions to the goals of the era's most powerful presidents. For in imagining that avant-garde writing might somehow speak compellingly to a national public and recreate a forgotten democratic citizenship, she envisioned herself playing much the same role that Woodrow Wilson and Teddy Roosevelt, like Alan Windet, had each sought for himself. Indeed Stein imagined herself not only as a kind of president, but fittingly as the president imagined to found a new democratic nation. The George Washington depicted in *Four in America* is a novelist whose work strikingly resembles Stein's own and who in that role is viewed as the founder of a democratic society. Napoleon as he is imagined by Stein cannot write a novel, presumably for the reason that Lincoln cannot, or for the reason that each is associated with Teddy Roosevelt and FDR. All are joined in Stein's telling with both the demagogic manipulation and the narrative conventionality Stein condemned, and all thus stand in the way of the realization of "individual power and liberty." All, in short, become examples of the very debased conventional politics that the advocates of presidential government believed executive leadership could rise above.

But Washington, who "never began a novel with 'Once upon a time,' " writes as Stein does: "he wrote what he saw and he saw what he said. And this is what I do" (FIA 168). It was not enough, then, for Stein to view the writer as merely any president. Against the petty paternalism that she throughout the world during the 1930s, she envisioned the novelist as the father of her country.

Governable Beasts: Hurston, Roth,

and the New Deal

*Men and women—your fathers and mine—came here from
the far corners of the earth with beliefs that widely varied. And
yet, each, in his own way, laid his own special gifts upon our
national altar to enrich our national life. . . . I like to think of our
country . . . as one home in which the interests of each member are bound up with the happiness of all.*

—Franklin Delano Roosevelt

*Anyhow, who wants to be a peasant? What glory is in it, I
ask you?*

—Zora Neale Hurston

IN THE PASSAGE leading up to climactic scene of Henry Roth's 1934 novel *Call
It Sleep*, the protagonist's aunt Bertha arrives at the Schearl home to identity the
novel's central problem.[1] The moment is rife with tension. Young David Schearl,
an eight-year-old Jewish boy growing up on the Lower East Side, has been discovered fabricating a blasphemous tale to his Yeshiva instructor—that he is the bastard son of a Christian organist—a fantasy close enough to some family secrets to
be incendiary. Still worse things are to follow. His uncle is steeling himself to reveal
that David has sought to pimp the affections of his cousin Esther in an effort to win
the friendship of a Polish ruffian from the neighborhood. To add insult to these

injuries, a rosary will soon slip from David's pocket, as if to confirm both his apostasy and his illegitimacy. For his Aunt Bertha, though, none of David's sins are as awful as the reaction they are likely to encourage from his father. All through the novel we have seen Albert Schearl from his son's oedipal perspective—seething with rage and barely suppressed power. Now, as he seems on the verge of beating David to death, Bertha points out what we have suspected all along. Albert Schearl, she cries, is an "ungovernable beast."[2]

Except that the novel soon proves her wrong. In its climactic moment, David runs from his home and in a secularized reenactment of the Crucifixion plunges a milk scupper into an electrified trolley rail. The explosive short circuit that results transforms both David's family and his world. Only moments before, the Lower East Side had seemed a terrifying, multiethnic nighttown—a rancorous, disordered realm of vice, conflict, and sexual commerce.[3] David's near immolation changes everything. The Jewish, Italian, Irish, Armenian, and Anglo American city bonds over his innocent body and, in the person of a policeman—who takes the child from the crowd and carries it back to the Schearl's apartment—confronts his now broken father. Having attempted to kill his "false son" with his bare hands mere hours before, Albert, now "slack-mouthed" and "stooped," humbly acknowledges to the cop who has entered his home, and to the neighborhood crowd behind him, that, "Yes. Yes," David is "My sawn. Mine. Yes" (434, 437). The ungovernable beast turns out to be surprisingly governable.

Zora Neale Hurston's *Jonah's Gourd Vine*, published in the same year as Roth's novel, opens with a scenario much like the one that closes *Call It Sleep*. When the novel begins, its young protagonist John Buddy is threatened with a beating by his stepfather—a man like Albert Schearl terrifying for his brutality and for his rage at the "bastard" son he refuses to claim as his own.[4] Like David Schearl, John Buddy escapes that beating only by fleeing his father's realm for a larger world. But the problem of patriarchal violence haunts Hurston's novel much as it does Roth's. Indeed John Buddy, soon to be renamed John Pearson, will grow to be not only the victim but the unwitting purveyor of that force. The novel, which memorialized the father with whom Hurston had bitterly struggled, was originally titled with the name Hurston and her siblings had called John Hurston behind his back—"Big Nigger"—and it imagines its preacher protagonist as a figure of awesome virility and charismatic force, "God's Battle-Ax."[5] Like his stepfather and like Albert Schearl, John Pearson becomes a man who gains stature by threatening bodily harm to everyone he encounters. As in *Call It Sleep*, *Jonah's Gourd Vine* suggests that such violence can only be contained by a mass public that paradoxically is itself formed by the currents of violence that run through the likes of John and Albert. John's brief moment of happiness and redemption in the novel comes, surprisingly, after the community he has built has turned on him, viciously stripped him of his power, and left him humble and emasculated—like young David Schearl, "as shy as a girl" (JGV 160). Much as in *Call It Sleep*, in other words, Hurston's novel depicts both the terrifying power of tyrannical violence and its containment by popular community. Like Roth, it portrays that transition, in Hurston's phrase, as the "sacrifice of a God" (105).

That these two novels are similar—and that, in turn, their outline resembles that of other broadly political novels from the era like *Native Son* or *All the King's Men*—does not mean they are telling identical stories, of course, nor that the tale of the black rural South is interchangeable with that of the immigrant Lower East Side. In fact, the more closely one looks, the more evident are the profound differences, in political sensibility as well as literary aesthetics, that divide Hurston and Roth. But despite those differences, the points of comparison between the two writers are worth considering. For Hurston and Roth faced analogous problems as their literary careers developed during the early thirties; they imagined similar methods of conceiving and handling those difficulties; and the stories they crafted in the process spoke resonantly of a historical transformation addressed in similar, if less dramatic terms by their contemporaries. Like many among their generation of writers, both were centrally concerned with the tension between a traditional or vernacular culture and a modern, urbanized world that seemed hostile to the authority of custom. More importantly, both faced that problem from a distinctly belated position. Hurston and Roth wrote their major work during the Great Depression—in the wake of the literary movements of the twenties that had established powerful modes of conceiving the problematic relation between tradition and modernity. During the twenties, each had been marginal participants of those movements, but neither writer flourished in the vibrant coterie culture of the period. It was during the Depression, as both literary modernism and the cultural nationalism of the Harlem Renaissance fell on hard times, that Hurston and Roth each discovered their distinctive gifts and wrote the work for which they are remembered.

In fact, the narrative scenario we see in *Call It Sleep* and *Jonah's Gourd Vine* became a common one in the literature of the American thirties—which is full not only of sacrificial figures like David and John, or Bigger Thomas, but of tales like the one they are used to tell: stories of the effort to displace the claustrophobic realm of the patriarchal family and the ethnic community with the larger body of an implicitly national community. As Walter Benn Michaels has pointed out, a broad swath of American writing in the 1920s preoccupied itself with a nativist desire to make conventional social relations seem natural, so that citizenship would appear a matter of inheritance rather than legally enforced consent. That effort surfaced, among other ways, in the longing to render the family impermeable and to supplant, as Michaels points out, exogamy with endogamy.[6] Taking *Call It Sleep* as a paradigmatic example, we could say that a central fable of the thirties was a con-

GOVERNABLE BEASTS

trary tale: the story of a young person who attempts to flee family and parochial tradition to find his or her place among a larger body, bound not by religion or race, but by a combination of sentiment and law. That story—of the desire not to preserve but to displace the family—was told time and again during the Depression, where it expressed some of the central issues at the heart of the political transformation brought about by the New Deal.[7] It is also a story in which sacrificial violence plays a crucial role. As Jim Casy explains in the definitive New Deal novel, *The Grapes of Wrath*, democracy in the literature of the thirties seemed to demand the elevation and destruction of its leaders. "Look a Washington," Casy demands, "fit the revolution, an' after, them sons-a-bitches turned on him. An' Lincoln the same. Same folks yellin' to kill 'em. Natural as rain."[8]

In a novel that consistently casts political and economic developments as equivalent to natural forces, that line takes on a particular resonance.[9] And, indeed, Jim Casy's words predict the fate he is soon to meet. Steinbeck's own Christ figure, Jim Casy dies to dramatize the evils of social injustice, but, more importantly, to give rise, in the evangelical role assumed by his friend Tom Joad, and in the spontaneous charity of Rose of Sharon, to the intimation of a newly democratic people. Like Washington and Lincoln, Jim Casy becomes a sacrificial victim to a nation that can be unified only in the mutual sympathy that his martyrdom enables—so that his death both reveals the cruelty of an inadequate political order, and, in its intimation of a democratic rebirth, implicitly places the New Deal in a history of sovereign refoundings of American democracy.

That Steinbeck's own prime symbol for the limitations of a socioeconomic order built on private interest is the family nicely underscores the point. As a social "unit," the "family government" of Steinbeck's Joad family is likened to a "congress," and it shares many of the features traditionally associated with congressional government (189, 135). Less the natural organism depicted in the literature of the twenties than a system of negotiation and deliberation, the family as Steinbeck views it is a collection of rationally self-interested agents who struggle to consider any but the most immediate and personal concerns. As the prophetic figure who first breaches its walls and who points the way toward a sympathetic transcendence of the family's limitations, Jim Casy surpasses the deliberative democracy of the family to exemplify what the era's liberal reformers expected from presidential government. Washington and Lincoln each presided over a revolutionary recreation of an American compact, Steinbeck implies; so, too, might the current generation make use of executive leadership to surpass conventional institutions and call Americans back to their democratic purposes.

Though neither Roth nor Hurston drew the same direct analogy to the presidency that Steinbeck did, their fiction, too, was deeply informed by the political transformation Steinbeck allegorized, and in their concern to give that transition dramatic form, each explored the new ways of conceiving the relation between executive power and political community that the New Deal made prominent. Before contributing to the creation of that widely shared story, however, each first followed a path through the cultural politics of the twenties, when a markedly different set of values prevailed.

An Age of Islands

Ludwig Lewisohn's once celebrated narrative of Jewish cultural identity, *The Island Within* (1928) ends with its protagonist Dr. Arthur Levy leaving his Christian wife to "resurrect the Jew" from his "inner self"—a decision he makes in the effort to "save his son's heritage for him."[10] Though it requires him to reject the assimilation to which he was once committed, the effort has nothing to do, Arthur understands, with "ritual or dogma." It concerns, rather, "one's racial poetry, one's ancestral history" (342, 320). As his own father points out in the scene where the two men reconcile, then, Arthur must be concerned less with the religious beliefs and practices he has never been taught than with "remembering" the history of abuse that generations have Jews have suffered and a pride in the ancestors who endured that suffering (348). In Arthur's case, the effort is literal. He learns that, although his own parents had forgotten their heritage, he is the heir of a lineage of eminent rabbis, and the discovery leads him at the novel's close to accept his responsibility to join a commission that will travel to Romania to investigate pogroms.

The Island Within, in short, is a definitive expression of the cultural pluralism that flourished in American writing during the 1920s. It begins accordingly with a statement of the anti-Progressive assumptions on which that pluralism was typically premised. Claiming that Progressivism sacrificed the legacy of Whitman and Lincoln and tarnished the memory of "Fourth of Julys and Washington's birthdays," Lewisohn announces that America's "Golden Age" now lies far "in the past" (4). "The Spanish War came, and a weak man, shouting, like all weak and therefore cruel men, for blood and war and dominance and glitter, became the idol of the nation. The World War finished what Roosevelt had begun. The state is an image— brazen, remote, implacable, except by stealthy magnates." Thus neatly bookending the Progressive era with two images of war and tyranny, Lewisohn inverts the Progressives' own claims to the mantle of the founding fathers and their own language of civic revival. "The duped and stupid populace" created by two decades of reform, Lewisohn announces, is "no more a people" (5).[11]

Such attitudes were far from unusual in the decade following World War I, when virtually everyone agreed that the agenda of Progressive reform had been discredited. The Wilson administration, along with its supporters among Progressive intellectuals, had sold entry into the War in part as a means to finally achieve the egalitarian national community after which Progressives had long aspired. Mobilization would "jumble the boys of America together," Wilson's chief propagandist George Creel declared, "smashing all the petty class distinctions that now divide, and prompting a brand of real democracy."[12] But in the wake of the War, and of the sharp rightward swing that followed it, such ideas no longer found support in any quarter. Warren Harding swept into office in 1920 promising not only "normalcy" but an end to "executive autocracy" and a return to "party government."[13] His successors followed suit, making the twenties not merely a low point in the twentieth-century history of presidential power, but a period when the kind of pluralist alternative to state power espoused by Lewisohn seemed appealing across the political spectrum. In the context of Progressivism's demise, there were few who did not share the conviction that, as Barry Karl summarizes the view, "the Nation was an abstraction" that could exercise little legitimate emotional or political authority over its citizens.[14]

The most evident symptoms of that attitude came in the sensational "tribal" politics that dominated popular awareness in the twenties—the eruption of racism and nativism, the wave of lynching and race riots, the recrudescence of the Ku Klux Klan, and the obsession with cultural mores and religious difference. But what a novel like *The Island Within* makes clear is the degree to which the forces of cultural reaction in the twenties shaped the terms that were adopted even by the era's newly emerging cosmopolitan intelligentsia.[15] Among the avant-garde writers who would later be labeled modernists, for example, a suspicion of the coercive powers of the state, and a preference against it for the virtues of cultural inheritance, was a given. When William Carlos Williams constructed his imaginative cultural history *In the American Grain*, for example, he pointedly dismissed conventional political history precisely because, in following "government and never men," it appeared to legitimize a centralization of political power that Williams regretted. "Steadily the individual loses caste, then the local government loses its authority; the head is more and more removed. Finally, the center is reached—totally dehumanized, like Protestant heaven." Fittingly Williams underlined his point by ending his book with a dismissal of Lincoln. The Progressives' favored prophet of national citizenship and executive power became in Williams's satiric depiction "a woman in an old shawl—with a great bearded face." And the symbolism of presidential martyrdom was redescribed as a form of manipulative sentimentality that epitomized America's cultural failures. "The age-old torture reached a disastrous climax in Lincoln," Williams writes in the final passage of his book. "Failing of relief or expression, the place tormented itself into a convulsion of bewilderment and pain—with a woman, born somehow, aching over it, holding all fearfully together."[16]

Against that sentimental coercion, Williams offered in *In the American Grain* precisely what *The Island Within* gave Arthur Levy—a patriarchal history that would counter the psychic confusion and spiritual emptiness of industrial society by helping his readers to preserve rather than to abandon their "caste." "Americans have lost the sense . . . that what we are has its origin in what *the nation* in the past has been," Williams complained. "Their history is to them an enigma" (109, emphasis in original, 113). His interest in redressing that disinheritance by providing an idiosyncratic gallery of heroic ancestors resembled not only Lewisohn's discovery of cultural descent, but the tales of inheritance that were prominent throughout American literature at the time. As Arthur Levy's father points out, everyone in the twenties seemed to be discovering that "it's natural for people to be proud of their ancestors" (348).

But, like *The Island Within*, *In the American Grain* makes especially clear the political assumption on which such filial piety rested—that the "nation," as a "people" defined by genealogy, had to be rescued from the oppression of "the state," as an organization defined by government and law—along with the characteristic imaginative geography that accompanied the premise. The Progressives had envisioned the United States as a solidaristic political community that, through the organ of executive government, might transcend parochial custom, cultural difference, and the "old idea" of "the particularist individual." In effect, they imagined civil society subsumed by what Mary Parker Follett called "the New State," and they typically envisioned that new state in the form of a unified continental United States.[17] The writers of Williams and Lewisohn's generation turned that ambition on its head, replacing the vision of the United States as a nation unified by its collective political aspiration with an image of America as a confederation of ethnic groups and local communities marked by what Williams called "actual peculiarity" and "unique force" (v). In the words of Lewisohn's ally Horace Kallen, the United States at its best should be viewed as a "Federal Republic; its substance a democracy of nationalities . . . . [E]ach nationality expresses its emotional and voluntary life in its own language, in its own inevitable aesthetic and intellectual forms."[18] Kallen's sometime colleague, and the major theoretical influence on the Harlem Renaissance, Alain Locke made nearly the same point. "It is not the facts of the existence of race which are wrong," Locke emphasized, but the use of race as "a political instrument." Once ethnic identity had been disentangled from the organizational demands of the nation-state, though, Locke anticipated that "the cult of race" would be "free to blossom almost indefinitely to the enrichment and stimulation of human culture."[19]

For Kallen and Locke, as for the era's other leading theorists of cultural pluralism, the legitimacy of a centralized state was challenged primarily by the ethnic diversity of American society. But the stress on ethnic difference was further emphasized throughout the writing of the period by a complementary interest in geographic variety and local community. Hence, for example, Malcolm Cowley's declaration of 1929: "My country is tangible, small, immediate, . . . not an abstraction for politicians." The sentiment is one that rings not only with the familiar modernist yearning for the particular but with the characteristic political and geographical imagination of the period. Like Hemingway's Frederic Henry, who complains famously that the "abstract words" manipulated by statesmen are "obscene beside the concrete names of villages," Cowley and his peers turned to "our regionalistic forces" against both the distasteful "collectivism" of politics and the unpleasant effects of industrial capitalism. "Our nation," Cowley announced, "is much less standardized than its critics like to believe."[20]

Running alongside that localism, however, was the deep interest that Cowley and his contemporaries expressed in the era's international flow of people, goods, and money. Cowley's own paean to the small and immediate was written during the same period when he and his friends pursued the cosmopolitan sojourns that Cowley would later eulogize in *Exile's Return*. The implicit connection between those two interests in the global and the local—or in the world and the parish, as Willa Cather expressed a similar idea—lay in the fact that, as Cowley later explained, both were expressions of an "age of islands," when a booming publishing market and a strong dollar enabled artists to pursue "a flight from social uniformity" in various locales (Paris, Greenwich Village, the Connecticut river valley) apparently distant from the metropolitan center.[21] The same logic runs through the work of Lewisohn, who averred that "all sound creative art is rooted in a ghetto."[22] Though it was itself composed on the Left Bank, *The Island Within* echoes Cowley and Cather's concern with the local by focusing largely on the small world of New York's Jewish elite and by highlighting the hope that, despite differences in education, income, and taste, that elite might be led by ties of inheritance to devote paternal care to poor fellow Jews. Arthur Levy's pivotal discovery of his lost ancestry comes at a prominent institution of that world. Volunteering his services to "the Beth Yehuda Hospital," where he is "wholly surrounded by Jews," Arthur stumbles across Reb Hacohen, an Orthodox rabbi who immediately recognizes their familial connection (303).[23] Importantly the moment, which brings together the man of faith and the man of science in their literal kinship and their shared benevolence toward their poorer neighbors, also reveals an ancestry that ties Arthur to "Jewish communities in Persia, in the Caucuses, in North Africa" (310). The ghetto, like Cowley's archipelago, is at once a minute local world and a transnational community.

What joins the two sides of this diasporic geography—the dizzyingly international and the intensely local—is, of course, a hostility or indifference to the nation-state and an assumption against it that social groups should be defined not juridically, but genealogically. The United States as a national body plays little role in the literature of the twenties, and its government, if it appears at all, seems pathetically inadequate or corrupt. H. D.'s 1927 novel *HERmione* puts the predominant understanding of "this business of the United States" perfectly. Highlighting both the modernists' distrust of sentimentality and their complementary emphasis on the regional and ethnic autonomy they often conflated, Hermione complains, "You get no sort of cohesion out of a thing so immense. You can't expect every one of us equally to sympathize with southern Spanish California and New York Dutch and Middle Western and French from Louisiana. This thing that any one can say *united we stand* is all rot. We can't stand united. Divided we would probably stand."[24]

The major literary innovations of the 1920s, along with the era's prominent theories of cultural pluralism, can all be understood as, in effect, efforts to understand how Americans might "stand" in the absence of the political structures that, in the wake of the War and the end of Progressivism, found few supporters. All were concerned, in other words, with how Americans might negotiate the effects of an industrial economy without the national community and forceful state action once advocated by Progressives. Typically the leading thinkers of the 1920s took variations on the stance sketched by *The Island Within*. Viewing the state as dubious, per se, they invoked the promise of ethnic affiliation to create the kinds of local and paternalistic communities that might shield people from the worst hazards of the marketplace. Alain Locke summarized the prevailing view with an apt metaphor. Describing race consciousness as "a dam in the social stream," Locke praised the way it reminded African Americans of their "corporate destiny." Racial solidarity would prevent the "representative classes" of the black population "from being dissipated and lost" in the larger society, Locke claimed, and thus "harness" those privileged members of the community to their "submerged" brethren. Such "group self respect," Kallen agreed, was "the one thing that" stood "actually between . . . [ethnic communities] and brutalization through complete economic degradation."[25]

Much of the literature of the Harlem Renaissance dramatized Locke's vision almost directly, bringing together educated and wealthy African Americans with their less privileged neighbors in a world that seemed defined by intimacy and proximity. (In the memory of playwright Lofton Mitchell, Harlem in the twenties was not only an international "race capital," as Locke called the neighborhood. It seemed also "a distinct nation that was much like a small town.")[26] Indeed Nella Larsen's novel *Passing*, to choose one obvious example, turns largely on the question of whether a wealthy African American doctor can be reminded of the racial bonds that obligate him to "uplift the brother." Much like Dr. Arthur Levy, who learns that he has ethnic obligations to the poor Jews of New York and Romania, or, like Dr. William Carlos Williams, who is confronted in Elsie with his responsibility to "the pure products of America," Dr. Brian Redfield discovers that, however much he despises "smelly, dirty rooms" and "stupid, meddling families," his race obliges him to continue serving his Harlem community.[27] All, in short, look for the way that highly paternal, local communities, bound by ethnic and cultural bonds, might displace the political work that Progressive reformers once hoped could be done by the state.

Like a King Trying to Reduce the Barons

Put Arthur Levy's reconciliation with his father next to David Schearl's victory over his, however, and it becomes evident that matters changed profoundly between the twenties and the thirties—in a way that is not only reflected but thematized by the work of both Roth and Hurston. During the twenties, each had come in close contact with prominent exponents of the era's cultural pluralism. While still a student at City College, Roth became the lover of Eda Lou Walton, a poet and critic twelve years his senior who introduced him to a Greenwich Village circle of Boasian anthropologists (including Margaret Mead and Ruth Benedict) and modernist poets who were concerned, in Walton's words, to recreate the fading virtues of "self-contained communal existence."[28] During the same years, Hurston was studying with Boas himself and moving in the most prominent circles of the Harlem Renaissance. Neither began their most significant work, though, until the thirties, when, along with the era's avant gardism, the vision of ethnic autonomy and paternalistic self-help promoted by writers like Kallen, Locke, Larsen, and Lewisohn fell suddenly on hard times.

Though it was not apparent at the time, that vision had depended in large part on prosperity those writers and their contemporaries took for granted. During the teens and twenties, the black and immigrant neighborhoods of America's northern cities, though full of impoverished laborers, were often thriving enclaves presided over by local merchants, independent cultural institutions, and informal networks of neighborhood welfare. Even before the crash, however, their apparently robust independence had begun to falter. The severe antiimmigration laws of the twenties meant that there had been little in the way of new arrivals to remind the immigrant communities of their cultural roots. (Henry Roth was working on a term paper on the subject when he met Eda Lou Walton.)[29] Many second and third generation children attended public schools and Americanization programs, moreover, and had grown up speaking English and using the products of America's new mass industries. In short, local enclaves that often had been literally diasporic—characterized by the steady circulation of international migrants and remittances—gradually lost their ties to their overseas connections. The same was not true, of course, of the nation's northern black neighborhoods, which expanded rapidly throughout the twenties, but beneath the apparent prosperity of places like Harlem, low wages and the effects of segregation in overcrowding and exploitative rents had begun to stretch community resources to their limits. With the upheaval of the Depression, the once vital institutions of ethnic community in both immigrant and black neighborhoods suffered badly, as economic disaster wiped out countless businesses and taxed the networks of community welfare beyond their resources.[30]

This was a development that Hurston for one managed to praise—precisely for the way it undermined the authority of people like Alain Locke. During her apprentice years, Hurston, who had long distrusted the "mirage" of "Race Solidarity," often bridled at what she considered Locke's paternalism. He was "a malicious spiteful little snot," she later complained, "that thinks he ought to be the leading Negro because of his degrees."[31] Now she thrilled at the destruction of the authority that men like him had wielded. America has "produced a generation of Negroes who are impatient" of "Race Men," she crowed. "They want to hear more about jobs and houses and meat on the table."[32] Locke himself tentatively echoed the sentiment. Though he had only recently celebrated Harlem as "a realm of social and economic freedom," he now acknowledged that "we must become aware of the class structure of the Negro population," along with the challenge it presented to visions of racial community. Eventually he decided, though ambivalently, that African Americans "must do our share in the liquidation of segregation and all forms of separatism."[33] Horace Kallen still more enthusiastically dropped the cultural pluralism he had championed in the teens and twenties to embrace the New Deal. An industrial economy made ethnic difference less significant than class stratification, he now claimed. Where he had once defended economic laissez-faire, precisely because he believed ethnic affiliation more important than economic equality, he now cast cultural difference aside and demanded that governmental control be asserted over "the management of the financial-industrial establishment."[34]

The inhabitants of the nation's northern black and immigrant communities followed a parallel track, rushing in vast numbers to align themselves with the Democratic Party and the CIO. The "crash of 1929," Langston Hughes recalled, had sent the Harlem Renaissance "rolling down the hill toward the Works Progress Administration." Writing some decades later, Henry Roth was more lugubrious. As a child, he claimed, he had thought of the Yiddish neighborhoods of the Lower East Side as "a kind of ministate of our own," but that world had disappeared "like Atlantis."[35] "All were expected to continue," he lamented, "the folkways, the people, their pursuits. And they didn't. That's the whole point. . . . The cosmopolitan world displaced the parochial one."[36]

Looking back on that transition from the late eighties, Roth appeared to forget, or to repudiate, an aspect of it that was in fact crucial to his early work: the most widespread response to the crisis of the Depression was not cosmopolitan but nationalist in spirit. This was a transformation evident throughout American culture in the thirties. Malcolm Cowley, for example, who in 1929 praised "our regionalistic forces," offered a striking reversal by 1934. In remarks that managed to rebuke not just his own parochialism but the political and economic complacency of a whole generation of writers who had mistakenly believed they could withdraw from America's "business civilization," Cowley, like Kallen, now emphasized the awesome deracinating force of capitalism. The truth was, Cowley explained, his generation of writers had been "wrenched away . . . from their attachment to any locality or local tradition" and had "become merged with the lives of a whole class in American society" (ER 94, 206, 207).

The point was echoed by countless writers who, like Cowley, often saw the Depression as a nearly providential event that would reawaken Americans to the value of a "common life" (ER 214). This was the transformation that Roth's lover Eda Lou Walton endorsed when she noted the "growing tendency for people to join together in some sort of union for security" and that popular novelists like Steinbeck celebrated as the movement "from I to We."[37] Like Cowley's *Exile's Return*, *The Grapes of Wrath* characteristically envisioned that movement beginning only after economic catastrophe had wiped away regional economies and local cultures, laying the ground work for a newly national perspective. "This here's United States, not California," an anonymous character proclaims of the FSA camp that serves as the moral center of *The Grapes of Wrath* (456). A decade's worth of road books, travel guides, and documentaries—nearly all of which set aside the localism of the twenties in favor of efforts to bring the country's regions into a coherent national body—echoed the sentiment.[38]

No doubt many factors contributed to that shift, but to a large degree the political and material underpinnings for the change lay in the language and policies of the ascendant New Deal, both of which placed a heavy emphasis on what FDR called "our national life" against international relations and regional and ethnic distinctions. In FDR's description, the whole justification for the New Deal stemmed from the fact that industrial capitalism had made a once diffuse and open country into a self-contained, continental nation. "Our last frontier has long since been reached," Roosevelt explained in 1932. "There is no safety valve in the form of a Western prairie . . . . We are not able to invite . . . immigration from Europe." "We are compelled," he added in 1934, "to employ the active interest of the Nation as a whole through government in order to encourage a greater security for each individual who composes it."[39] The whole nation and the endangered individual—those were the primary terms of FDR's rhetoric. What had disappeared from his formulation were the key factors of the landscape of the twenties: on the one hand, the international movements of capital and migration; on the other, the presence of the once powerful mediating institutions of party, neighborhood, region, ethnic community, and local government. The "international" economy, Roosevelt explained in his first inaugural address had "in point of time and necessity [become] secondary to the establishment of a sound national economy."[40]

Apart from the more specific consequences of its policies, that language of social democratic nationalism was one of the prime political and cultural legacies of the New Deal. So common was that way of thinking that even enemies of the New Deal adopted the view that the United States was caught up in a battle between feudal provincialism and national sovereignty. Complaining about the way FDR had sought to use the federal government to break the back of local party machines and regional powerhouses, Senator Burton Wheeler worried that Roosevelt was "like a king trying to reduce the barons." Though he was not happy about it, Wheeler's assumption was much the same as Steinbeck's: that the power of local grandees could be contained only by submitting them to the authority of a centralized state. Roosevelt himself sometimes made the same point. The New Deal intended to be the "match" and then the "master" of "the forces of selfishness and lust for power." Its arrival meant that "the day of . . . the economic Titan . . . is over."[41]

Key to that transformation was the New Deal's resuscitation, yet also revision of the idea of presidential leadership. In the rhetoric advanced by Progressive champions of the presidency like Woodrow Wilson and Teddy Roosevelt, the chief executive was to be the medium and molder of the popular will. Especially in Teddy Roosevelt's militant rhetoric, the president was to make his people "a better race" by "training" them to rise above their individual desires and embrace a stern duty to the nation. "O my fellow citizens," TR declaimed, "each one of you caries on your shoulders . . . the burden of doing well for the sake of your country."[42]

The New Dealers who had seen the Wilson administration's repressive use of state power during the War, along with the disenchantment and political backlash that followed, disowned that civic hectoring. Teddy Roosevelt had called for the president to lead a crusade for "permanent moral awakening."[43] But recognizing the limits of exhortation and inspiration, FDR and his advisers would seek to expand governmental power by developing the administrative capacities of the executive branch, thereby enabling the New Deal to evade the instabilities of legislative brokering and theoretically lessening the need for political leaders to achieve legislative victories by whipping up popular enthusiasm. In keeping with that strategy, the New Deal would emphasize the state's role in guaranteeing its citizen's expanded rights rather than in demanding their duties—thereby remaking Progressivism into the political creed FDR renamed liberalism. Reversing the Progressives' demand that the American people prove themselves worthy of the national mission (an attitude that led them to restrict political participation even as they espoused a renewal of popular sovereignty), the New Deal stressed instead the state's obligations to ensure, via social welfare and economic regulation, the well being and autonomy of its citizens.[44]

In keeping with that transformation of Progressive ideology, FDR likewise crafted a new presidential persona that famously cast the president not as a stern authority or militant leader, but as a benevolent figure who brought together state and nation through sympathy rather than command or inspiration. In the disenchanted description later offered by Theodore Lowi, the new, "mass anti-party politics" created by the New Deal made the "personhood of the presidency" seem "a combination of Jesus Christ and the Statue of Liberty." Referring less critically to the same phenomenon, FDR himself remarked, "We seek not merely to make government a mechanical implement, but to give it the vibrant personal character that is the very embodiment of human charity."[45] The new voters who flocked to the New Deal coalition embraced that ambition, dropping their connections to local officials, party machines, and neighborhood associations in favor of a direct relation to the chief executive. As one New Dealer explained, FDR elicited "a newly aroused consciousness of United States citizens of their own part in the Government and of an actual, intimate bond between themselves and the man in the mansion on Pennsylvania Avenue."[46]

Though obliquely, it was the potential for just that kind of transformation that novels like *Call It Sleep* and *Jonah's Gourd Vine* took up. In fact, the crucial difference between Roth and Hurston's works could be said to come down to the different ways their critical scenes staged the assumptions at the core of Roosevelt's formulation. Both novels achieve their resolution in a scene of human collision with a "mechanical implement" that emblematizes the forces of industrial civilization—a train in Hurston's case, the electrified trolley rail in Roth's. Only in Roth's novel, though, can that event be given, almost literally, the kind of "vibrant personal character" that FDR called for, the type that promised to redeem personal suffering by making it the occasion for sentimental community. In Hurston's case, by contrast, the train remains a figure of crushing force, and nothing can be done to humanize it or to soften its blows.

The Violence of the Street

In the early seventies, several decades after he published *Call It Sleep*, Henry Roth explained to an interviewer that he had never had "any great attachment to Diaspora Judaism." Indeed, only ten years before, he had advised American Jews to assimilate as quickly as possible—to "orien[t] themselves," as he put it, "toward ceasing to be Jews." Now he found that the 1967 war had "changed . . . [his] whole way of thinking." But he took care to emphasize that he still felt little interest in what he called "Jewish history." What inspired him, he said, was "the Israeli state" and the way it appeared to represent "a people in the making."[47] The Jews of the "Diaspora," Roth later explained, "the mercantile, the professional, the urban, the business Diaspora," were "a people of the past." Israel was a "people of the future."[48] Even here, in other words, what was moving about conflict in the Middle East was the way it showed a people "ceasing to be Jews" so that they might become Israeli. "Only two courses remain open to the Jew in America," Roth explained to an interviewer in the late sixties: "he assimilates and disappears completely" or "he goes to Israel and does the same thing there."[49]

The sentiment was one that Zora Neale Hurston, who, like Roth, admired "the rule of the majority," might well have understood (TMH 340). Time and again her writing criticized traditional African American communities in order to celebrate a vanguardist appeal to the noble "experiment of self-government" (DTR 566). Visiting the Caribbean, for example, Hurston condemned Jamaica and Haiti for their custom-bound and minutely stratified societies. The problem, she concluded, was that an interest in popular self-rule had never been widely diffused in either country. Haiti, for example, had not yet been able to overcome the problem it confronted at its founding: "it had never been a country. It had always been a colony so that there had never been any real government there" (TMH 346). Viewing the recently concluded seventeen-year occupation by the U.S. military as an occasion for the "rebirth of a nation," Hurston hoped that Haiti's new president, Stenio Vincent, might take heed from "dynamic and forceful" Rafael Trujillo, the strongman of neighboring Dominican Republic, and force an as yet unrealized "national unity" (359, 356).

In her 1939 *Moses, Man of the Mountain*—a novel written while Hurston was employed by the WPA and a book evidently shaped by the rhetoric of New Deal state-building—Hurston called on the same assumptions in terms that closely anticipated Roth's critique of the diaspora. The novel is opened by a conversation between the Elders of Goshen and the Pharaoh that seems designed almost directly to dispense with the premises of the Harlem Renaissance. When the Pharaoh asks the Elders why he should respect their people, the Elders point to their "memories," arguing like Alain Locke that their commitment to cultural inheritance makes the Hebrews "good citizens" of Egypt. In Hurston's rendition, however, that belief signifies their willingness to accept a subservient role in a society that oppresses them. When Moses leads the Hebrews out of Egypt, by contrast, he replaces hidebound custom with a newly invented religion. Indeed in Hurston's version of the African American "concept of Moses"—an allegory of a black nationalist pursuit of self-determination—the crucial issue concerns Moses's effort to use every means at his disposal to remake the Egyptian "Hebrews" into the "great state" of "Israel," to replace "a horde of slaves" with a nation defined by "citizenship."[50]

By contrast to their predecessors, in other words, Hurston and Roth alike became unabashed statists, enamored not only of national identity but of the way it might be realized through the centralizing governmental structures their predecessors disavowed. And both reflexively assumed that such political ambitions depended on the repudiation of the customary relations symbolized by patriarchal authority. That assumption may be most striking in *Call It Sleep*. For Roth's novel is ruthless in its depiction of Jewish tradition. Young David's religious training, for example, first represented by his memorization of the Chad Godya, is an induction into a "long ladder of guilt and requital"—an ideological parallel, Roth implies, to an ancestral legacy of paternal abuse and vengeful patricide (233). As the novel progresses, we make the shocking discovery that Albert Schearl may be responsible for his abusive father's death—that he watched impassively as his father was gored by a bull—and that he is now haunted by the apparently reasonable fear that he faces similar retribution from his son. From the novel's first chapter, the six-year-old David dreams "of his father's footsteps booming on the stairs . . . and of himself clutching at knives he couldn't lift off the table" (22). What seems to make a Schearl a Schearl, in other words, is that the fathers torture their sons and that the sons come to manhood (and to the sexual virility symbolized by the motif of the bull's horn), by killing their fathers.[51]

But, Roth goes on to emphasize that this is not a problem of the Schearl clan alone. David overhears his mother and aunt discussing the comparable patriarchal abuse of his maternal grandfather, and cruelty, manipulation, and coercion characterizes almost every relation David has in the book except the intensely erotic connection with his mother. When, in the manuscript version of the novel, David's Aunt Bertha cries, "there's a curse on this tribe" it seems deliberately ambivalent as to whether she refers to the Schearl family in particular or to the whole Jewish people.[52] Certainly Roth emphasizes that the entirety of religious instruction is built on a hierarchical chain of coercion and abuse. David's Yeshiva instructor Yidel Pankower, whose first name means literally "little Jew," worries that the "Yiddish youth" of America are becoming a "sidewalk and gutter generation," lacking in "piety and observance . . . , veneration of parents, deference to the old" (374). But his nostalgia for the "discipline" of the past makes it clear why a boy like David might want to make himself, as he thinks, "somebody else" (371). Recalling his own training by the fierce Reb R'fuhl, Pankower remembers the "pleasure then in hearing another howl, in watching another beaten, seeing the naked flesh squirm and writhe and the crack of the buttocks tighten under the biting thongs" (374). What makes a Jew "truly a Jew" in Reb Pankower's eyes is the way "memory" serves to remind him of his place in an ancient hierarchy of erotic cruelty (376, 233). "Before God," he notes approvingly, "none may stand upright" (235). [53]

Cowed and repelled by that tradition, David inverts the career of Arthur Levy fleeing religious community and rushing off toward the secularized Christianity he finds at the trolley tracks. Hurston's novels tell a similar story. Though less dramatically, she, too, casts traditional community as a culture of abuse that her various protagonists must escape. *Jonah's Gourd Vine* begins with John Buddy escaping from his stepfather to symbolically cross the river that will separate him from the world of his parents, much as the significant action of Moses begins when Hurston's protagonist flees the oppressive world of the pharaonic court. Arvay Henson, the protagonist of Hurston's last novel, *Seraph on the Suwanee* only begins her quest for self-realization when she burns down her childhood home, a building that encapsulates all the "ambitions for littleness" that Hurston saw in the small-town South.[54] But *Their Eyes Were Watching God* makes the case most directly. In order for Janie to proceed in pursuit of "self-revelation," she must first kill off the several parental figures who speak for respectability, her grandmother and her first two husbands. Each of these characters is distinguished by a willingness to use cruelty in the service of bourgeois uplift, and, much like Albert Schearl, each must be vanquished by Hurston's protagonist. "All dis bowin' down, all dis obedience under yo' voice," Janie complains to Joe after she has stripped him of authority. "And now you got tuh die to find out dat you got tuh pacify somebody besides yo'self."[55]

What is striking about Hurston's fiction, though, is that the pacification of cruel authority does not result in the lessening of violence, but rather in its intensification. Here, too, she articulates an understanding present in a slightly different way in Roth's novel. In the moments after he flees his father's house and before he arrives at the trolley tracks, David Schearl encounters a terrifyingly brutal world. Throughout *Call It Sleep*, New York City has seemed an ominous place, but now David encounters it at night, and the urban geography erupts into a bewildering landscape of hostility, conflict, and rapacious desire. In a montage of disjointed voices, indebted to the Circe chapter of Joyce's *Ulysses* and reminiscent of other modernist depictions of urban fragmentation, Roth shows David wandering through the overlapping monologues of melancholic prostitutes, thuggish drunks, contentious gamblers, angry workers, and radical soapbox orators—their mutual isolation emphasized both by their conflicting voices and by their ethnic diversity. The result is a classic vision of the metropolis as corrosive free-for-all. "The violence of the street burst upon him like a tidal wave."[56] When David has merely run from patriarchal domination, in other words, and has yet to force his father to submit to the authority represented by the police, he enters a world that appears to lack authority altogether—where American liberties not only unleash dangerous appetites and resentments, but leave the weak vulnerable to the predations of the ruthless.

Something similar to Roth's nighttown characterizes the world inhabited by Hurston's protagonists. It is, above all, a harsh and combative place, characterized by what Hurston praised as "the strife of freedom" (MMM 591). As many readers have noted, Hurston's fiction celebrates and reinterprets the vernacular creativity of the black South, turning the oral song and story that Hurston loved into literary material and, in an example of the brash creativity she most admired, placing a black woman at the center of what was in many respects a masculinist culture.[57] Among the features emphasized by Hurston in her portrait of folk vitality, however, is its inseparability from conflict, insult, and humiliation.[58] It is when the townspeople of Eatonville are wallowing in "mass cruelty," strikingly enough, that Hurston gives their expression its most lyrical description: "They passed nations through their mouths. . . . Words walking without masters; walking altogether like harmony in song" (175).

This is, moreover, just the tip of the iceberg. The verbal cruelty of Eatonville is but our introduction to a series of fairly dramatic examples of physical violence: Tea Cake's knife fight; the beatings he and Janie deal out to each other; the mob violence and vigilante justice on the muck; the moment the rabid Tea Cake sinks his teeth in Janie's arm, just as she shoots him to death in self-defense. If, as many critics have pointed out, *Their Eyes* offers a variation on the quest romance or the initiation tale, one prominent feature of that narrative concerns the way Janie passes beyond the indirect, sometimes playful social cruelty of Eatonville's oral culture and comes into increasingly immediate contact with physical violence itself. Nor is it easy to dismiss this violence as incidental or as entirely a side effect of the encompassing environment of racial oppression. For, throughout her work, Hurston emphasizes how deeply attractive she finds aggression, struggle, and power. "Discord is more natural than accord," she notes, both more dramatic and, in some unexplained way, more vital to the "communal life" at the center of all her work. In grandiose public displays of aggression, "one does the community a service," Hurston claims. "There is nothing so exhilarating as watching well-matched opponents go into action."[59]

In the early short stories she wrote in the twenties, Hurston often emphasized one aspect of that violence by stressing the oppressiveness and the drama of life in the rural South—the ordinary cruelty, along with kindness and love, that characterized its day-to-day existence and the struggle it demanded from people who sought to confront or simply to evade it. "You got what your strengths would bring you" (DTR 599). But rather than attempt to deny or dismiss that violence, Hurston (like her contemporary Richard Wright, an enemy with whom she had far more in common than either writer realized) placed it at the core of her fiction, emphasizing its significance to the vernacular culture whose vitality she celebrated and, still more subversively, making it the center of a spiritual vision to which she returned repeatedly.[60] The second "law of nature," her Moses explains, is that "people talk about tenderness and mercy, but they love force" (MMM 411).

Variations on that observation are repeated often throughout Hurston's oeuvre. Indeed that violence and domination are not just sources of beauty, but of spiritual renewal seems to be the conviction behind the title of Hurton's most famous novel. In one brief excursus in *Their Eyes*, Hurston's narrator echoes a theme repeated often in her writing and editorializes about the connection between violence and divinity. "Fear is the most divine emotion. . . . Half gods are worshiped in wine and flowers. Real gods require blood" (293). But the understanding put theoretically here is still more emphatically demonstrated in the events of Hurston's narrative. The most dramatic moment in *Their Eyes* comes in the novel's rendition of an awesomely destructive hurricane (Hurston's dramatization of the legendary storm of 1928)—a force of sublime destruction that, like Roth's nighttown, all but literally apotheosizes the many currents of violence that run through Hurston's world.[61] It is at this moment significantly that Janie confirms the authenticity of her marriage to Tea Cake and that she is finally fully united with the rural folk she has sought throughout the novel. Not coincidentally, it is in this scene as well that Hurston brings her characters face-to-face with the awesome face of divine power. "Through the screaming wind they heard things crashing and things hurtling and dashing with unbelievable velocity. . . . They sat in company with others in other shanties, their eyes straining against crude walls and their souls asking if He meant to measure their puny might against His. They seemed to be staring at the dark, but their eyes were watching God" (151).

Higher Than Pity and Mercy

Despite their other similarities, it is here that Hurston and Roth most revealingly part ways. It is not that Roth fails to share Hurston's view of divinity as awe inspiring power. Like Janie and all Hurston's protagonists, David Schearl is on a spiritual quest, and what he seeks is precisely what Hurston's Moses or John Pearson desires—"power unekal to man" (JGV 124). David also imagines a divinity who speaks in thunder, who "has all the power" to "break . . . everything" (CIS 241). Both Hurston and Roth, in fact, might be said to share the modernist habit of joining an apocalyptic sensibility to a fascination with premodern sacrificial religions. "The Negro is not a Christian really," Hurston claimed, but in the "barbaric poetry" of syncretized religion, "calls his Congo gods by Christian names."[62] The web of symbols and talismans David Schearl desperately cobbles together likewise amounts to a kind of *pensée sauvage* that enables Roth's protagonist to seek in poetic correspondence and resonant images for a means to counter his otherwise overwhelming sense of powerlessness.

Where Roth differs from Hurston, however, is that he both demonstrates the appeal of such divination and ultimately puts it aside. Throughout *Call It Sleep*, David seeks to escape the sordid depths of basements and closets that he associates with death and sexuality ("everything belonged to the same dark") by aspiring after the blinding light and brilliant heights—the "durable purity"—he sees as the mark of divinity (70, 295). But, in the concluding passage that gives the book its title, David abandons this quest for eminence. "It was only toward sleep one knew himself still lying on the cobbles, felt the cobbles under him, and over him and scudding ever toward him like a firm black foam, the perpetual blur of shod and running feet, the broken shoes, new shoes, stubby, pointed, caked, polished, buniony, pavement beveled, lumpish, under skirts, under skirts, under trousers, shoes, over one and through one, and feel them all and feel, not pain, not terror, but strangest triumph, strangest acquiescence" (441).

With the novel's conclusion, in short, David surrenders a hope for sublime power and accepts his place in a democratic union of the abject and powerless. Leaving aside the quest for transcendence, moreover, he implicitly finds a path out of the tradition of filial violence stressed throughout the novel. As Roth notes at the pivotal moment in the novel, David's symbolic immolation has "stilled the whirling hammer" that symbolizes oedipal fury throughout the book (431). Unlike Albert, who had to effectively murder David's grandfather to become an adult, then, David does not have to slay his father to gain acknowledgment. Submitting himself to the "*Power! Incredible barbaric power!*" of the industrial city instead, David finds a way to escape the tyranny of his father and, indeed, to dispatch all the tensions of sexual commerce, ethnic conflict, and even radical politics that erupt in the final book of Roth's novel (419, emphasis in original).

That resolution is all the more striking in that Roth reminds us often that David seems destined to reproduce the life of his father. His mother teases early in the book that her little boy will become "a tyrant" when he's married, and, affectionate though her tone is, the remark underscores a pattern of association that runs all through the novel (65). In David's own fantasies, Albert Schearl is himself, not just violent, but an awe inspiring dictatorial figure—"standing on a high roof of darkness, and below him . . . faces uplifted, so many, they stretched like white cobbles to the end of the world" (28). David, who in his hatred for his father aspires after still greater eminence, likewise shares his father's wrathful temper, and, when David kicks and bloodies a friend in "blind, shattering fury" or knocks a schoolmate to the ground, Roth reminds us that his ressentiment is primed to blossom into feral rage (91). The implication is beautifully summarized when David free associates on the story of Puss in Boots, imagining that with magical gifts like Puss he, too, might "bound . . . high as the roof" and then considering what would happen "if the mouse changed back into an ogre inside the puss" (36). The image functions as a concise allegory of David's likely future. Should he destroy and swallow the terrible power embodied in his father, then David will surpass his father's authority, but he also will find the monstrous force of his father's rage exploding inside himself.[63]

The crucial intimation of Roth's novel, then, is the suggestion that David finds a way to escape the cycles of patriarchal violence. In the novel's critical scene, David's autoelectrocution transforms himself and his world. Summoned by the scene of a suffering child, the disordered city suddenly comes together in pity and the whole structure and tone of Roth's novel suddenly shifts dramatically. "Christ, it's a kid!" one character exclaims, and the remark highlights two crucial themes, underlined by carefully handled motifs, running throughout the novel: that, like Jim Casy, David becomes a secularized version of the Christian redeemer, and that his ability to fulfill this role depends on the sense that he is a sacrificed innocent able to unite a community in shared feeling (420). In the moments after his near immolation, the previously antagonistic and disjointed voices of the city begin to address each other in sympathetic dialogue, working together to remove David from the rail and exclaiming together over his suffering.[64] Even the fragmented, collage form of the novel's last section begins to cohere, moving toward the more conventional third-person narration that will soon replace it. As it does, the crowd of urban individuals—"swirled about" David "in a dense, tight eddy"—takes on the form of an organic collective. "Conch-like the mob surrounded, contracted, trailed him within the circle, umbiliform" (421, 429). Joined to the sexualized imagery of his sacrificial act ("the wavering point of the dipper's handle found the long, dark, grinning lips"), the description renders David the newly delivered child of a sentient, but inarticulate people (413). When an intern removes him from the rails to place him in the waiting arms of a policeman, David is shown almost literally to have been delivered from the body of the crowd and, placed in the care of the law, born again.

As the city is remade by its pity for David, and David is reborn in it, moreover, Roth's protagonist fittingly abandons his lust for power and vengeance. Taken by the cop back to his home, David briefly exults when he witnesses his father's terror. "For the briefest moment," he "felt a shrill, wild surge of triumph whip within him, triumph that his father stood slack-mouthed." But the scene ends with David collapsing weakly and is soon replaced by "a vague, remote pity" for his father (434, 440). What is unfamiliar about David's "strangest triumph," in short, is precisely that it amounts not to the sublime power he once sought, but to "acquiescence" in his own powerlessness and a willingness to see such victimization even in his most hated oppressor.

That resolution is one that Hurston would not countenance. Where Roth turns to a kind of sentimentalized, secular Christianity to rescue his protagonist, Hurston explicitly rejects that option. "If he weeps in compassion," the narrator of *Jonah's Gourd Vine* declares in a sentiment echoed throughout her writing, "let us lynch him" (138). In this particular instance, Hurston paraphrases the thoughts of John Pearson's treacherous people, who turn on him only when he begins to weaken. But the striking feature of this passage, as of the similar excursus in *Their Eyes* and others like it in Hurston's fiction, is that she makes it evident that, however much she regrets vindictive popular resentment, she accepts both its inevitability and, strangely, its justice. On those occasions when Hurston shows herself troubled by religious passion, it is not the violence of men like John Pearson or the patriarchal power of Moses that disturbs her, but the Christian rhetoric of love and mercy that strikes her as mealy mouthed and insincere. Religion in this guise is a reflex of the "feeling of weakness," and offers "a feeling of security" in response. "Strong, self-determining men," she adds, "are notorious for their lack of reverence" (DTR 222, 225).

What Hurston fears most, in other words, is less the domination that disturbs Roth, than servility. What she regrets in the scene of John Pearson's humiliation, as in similar examples throughout her fiction, is not cruelty so much as the weakness that allows cruelty to flourish. "There is another reason for the lower class of society besides the greed of the ruling class," Hurston wrote one of her patrons during the twenties, "and it is the lack of something in the ruled" (ZNH 62). Obsessed with the need for *amour propre*, Hurston returned time and again to denunciations of ressentiment and dismissive renditions of the emptiness of pity. There are no scenes of redemptive sympathy like the one that resolves *Call It Sleep* anywhere in Hurston's work. But still more revealing may be the fact that the most moving and celebrated picture of emotional connection in all of Hurston's fiction—the conversation between Janie and her friend Pheoby that frames the narrative of *Their Eyes Were Watching God*—is explicitly offered as an occasion not for empathy but pedagogy. Janie first waits for her friend to make a deferential approach (Pheoby comes bearing food and extravagant compliments) and then explains that she must "give" Pheoby "de understandin'" to assimilate her story (180).

As Carla Kaplan has noted, Hurston's narrative all but directly juxtaposes this moment to the parallel story of Annie Tyler—a pitiful woman so "broken" when she is left by a younger man that "she told those who asked what had happened" (271). The comparison reveals Janie not only to be one of Hurston's "strong, self-determining" figures, but a person who protects herself, in a community quick to turn on the weak, by refusing any offer of pity and by making effective use of a willing retainer to ensure her protection.[65] In a moment often praised for its portrait of intimacy and reciprocity, Pheoby has virtually nothing to say, and serves less as an interlocutor than an acolyte. ("Ah done growed ten feet higher from jus' listenin' tuh you," she tells Janie at the end of her narrative [332].) Indeed, perhaps the most celebrated line of the novel—Janie's claim that Pheoby can speak to their community on her behalf because "mah tongue is in mah friend's mouf"—is explicitly nonreciprocal (179). The line casts Pheoby not as Janie's equal but as her messenger. And their friendship is but one of the several master/student bonds that Hurston builds around her various protagonists, including John Pearson's friendship with Hambo (his Pheoby), Moses's tutelary relations with Aaron, and Janie's role as "pupil" to her third husband Tea Cake (316). Pheoby does not miss the implication herself, replying deferentially to Janie, "If you so desire Ah'll tell 'em what you tell me to tell 'em" (6).

It is true that, as a number of Hurston's critics have noted, Janie's alliance with Pheoby is strongly eroticized (they are "kissin'-friends") and that their friendship is the culmination of the narrative of sexual education that characterizes much of Janie's story (7). But that fact simply underscores how consistently Hurston, somewhat like Rabbi Pankower, assimilates erotic pleasure and domination, and how often she casts each in violent terms. Janie's first sexual feelings are sensations that "struck her outside observation and buried themselves in her flesh" (183). Tea Cake, who looks "like the love thoughts of women," seems "to be crushing scent out of the world with his footsteps" (261). Filled with love for his wife Lucy, John Pearson feels "another and stiffer bone down his back" and yearns "to feel himself taking and giving blows" (57, 56). Nor is there much sign that Hurston intended these comments to be seen as a critique of sexual domination. *Moses, Man of the Mountain* carefully dismisses the merely consensual relations of legal marriage (what Moses calls his "impersonal" arrangements with a "treaty wife") in favor of genuine erotic compulsion—the desire to "find a woman and crush from her body that essence that made men live" (393). And *Seraph on the Suwanee* goes on to emphasize the point by directly and approvingly equating the "violent ecstasy" of rape to marriage (877). By Hurston's account, one she only very rarely tempers, "love ain't nothing else *but* compellment" (759, original emphasis).

From such a perspective, it is easy to see why Hurston would not share Roth's vision of empathy as an instrument of social democracy. Indeed, she remained consistently suspicious of its power to undermine authority and level social relations. Hurston's Moses, for example, informs the weak and undependable Aaron that "the future of Israel is higher than pity and mercy" (583). It is an argument that reflects Hurston's attraction to the martial style of civic virtue espoused by Teddy Roosevelt. ("I never said I'd make [the Israelites] happy people," Moses points out. "I promised to make them great" [581].) It also indicates an assumption apparent throughout her writing, that collective feeling is not, as a New Deal sentimentalist like Roth would suggest, a solution to the problem of politics, but the heart of the problem itself. "What we have been trying to do," Moses explains, is "to channel the intentions of men" (587). But rather than imagining as Roth implies, that such a channeling could spring up out of common feeling, Hurston suggests, much as Teddy Roosevelt had, that it requires a high degree of authority and political coercion. "You can't have a state of individuals. Everybody just can't be allowed to do as they please." A nation that forgets that fact risks allowing "all the stupid but greedy and ambitious to sprout like toadstools"—exactly the urban discord Roth's sentiment is meant to control (586).

Like Roth, then, Hurston evinces a collectivist sensibility characteristic of her era, and like him, she envisions her collective being formed by a violence that overcomes the disparities in individual interests and intentions. What she can't imagine is that that violence can somehow by dismissed or transcended, and the strife that characterizes her communities thus comes to seem interminable. John Buddy, who is abused by his stepfather, will go on not only to be celebrated for his oratorical power over his congregation and his physical domination of other men, but to beat two of his three wives, to pull a knife on his own son, and to die a violent death. Janie of *Their Eyes*, mistreated by two husbands, will shoot the third, and by one reading (on which more below), she may slated for still more conflict and an ugly death of her own in the future. Just as there is no religion without blood, Hurston suggests, there is no real community without internecine violence.

A Broken Sword

Why should this be so? If we place *Call It Sleep* next to Hurston's fiction, an interesting possibility appears. In addition to its invocation of collective sentiment, Roth's novel makes reference to a means of ending violence that Hurston explicitly considers and then rejects. What's more, that rejection could be taken as Hurston's rejoinder to the New Deal, whose paternalism she often denounced, and in a larger sense to the implications of American racism in general. The method to which I am referring is law, and Hurston's complaint—which is inseparable from her celebration—is that it has a slim relation to the black community she depicts.

In order to grasp the weight of this complaint, it is necessary first to note how crucial legal authority is to young David Schearl. The importance of the law is most apparent in the novel's denouement, when Albert Schearl bends significantly not to David but to the police. All through the novel, David's father has doubted his son's legitimacy; in the scene's leading up to the novel's crisis, he announces to the world that, just as his "blood . . . warned," David is "no part of" of him. "I'm free," he exults, reaching at the same moment for a whip with which to slaughter his son (401). In the novel's closing scenes, however, Albert talks directly to the police and, speaking in English for the first time in the novel, acknowledges his son's legitimacy, so that David's paternity is established by the third party of legal authority rather than by blood, intuition, or sentiment.

Long before this moment, though, Roth prepares us for its implication. At the end of the novel's first book, David had already scored a partial victory over his father by running away from home—a moment significant for the way it brings David under the care of the police, temporarily removing both him and his mother from his father's control. Even earlier, though, Roth prepares us for such events. In the book's preface, we enter New York Harbor with David and his parents, passing Roth's striking version of the Statue of Liberty: "the rays of her halo were spikes of darkness roweling the air; shadow flattened the torch she bore to a black cross against flawless light—the blackened hilt of a broken sword. Liberty" (14). Establishing the first notes of a motif that will run throughout the novel, Roth casts the entry into America as a kind of symbolic castration; liberty follows from the broken sword. Like FDR, in other words, Roth suggests a national sovereignty that protects the weak by curbing the authority of titans and fathers. It is a message that Albert Schearl appears to understand. At this moment, he looks at his son and, noticing that the hat he wears resembles a "crown," tosses it overboard (14).

In *Call It Sleep*, in other words, the police and the legal authority they represent are on the side of the son, and it is fathers who embrace custom and flee from the law. That fact becomes especially salient when we consider that Albert's pivotal surrender—"Yes. Yes . . . My sawn. Mine. Yes"—all but directly echoes and re-writes the closing words of *Ulysses*, Molly Bloom's: "yes I said yes I will Yes."[66] From the first publication of *Call It Sleep*, critics have emphasized how deeply Roth was influenced by Joyce, a fact they have seized on to damn or praise his literary sophistication. Less noticed has been Roth's highly motivated revision of his model, a transformation encapsulated by the difference between the "yes" spoken by Albert Schearl and the more renowned "yes" of Molly Bloom. Spoken to Leo-pold Bloom in the heat of passion, Molly's assent signifies something like an eternal feminine bounty ("I gave him all the pleasure I could . . . and I thought well as well him as another") and a liberality that becomes invaluable for the way it undermines the restrictive boundaries of national identity. In this regard, it is an affirmation closely linked not only to Molly's sexual receptiveness, but to her delight in the pleasures of commerce and her appreciation for transnational exchange; it arises suitably in her memory as she muses about shopping for delicacies and remem-bers Gibraltar, where she encountered "the Greeks and the jews and the Arabs and the devil knows who else" (643). In short, Molly's "Yes" becomes the crucial term in Joyce's renowned cosmopolitanism—the vital openness that brings to-gether "Jewgreek" and "greekjew," that enables Leopold to become surrogate father to Stephan Dedalus, and that thereby allows Stephen to escape the nar-rowness of provincial Dublin and Bloom to overcome, however uncertainly, his ethnic exclusion from Dublin society (411). Like the commercial exchange with which it is closely associated, female sexuality becomes the force that loosens the vice of national identity—"the link," as Bloom puts it in words addressed to a prostitute, "between nations and generations" (488).

For Roth, however, cosmopolitanism offers not an escape from oppressive in-heritance but a confirmation of its power. *Call It Sleep* underlines that point by showing young David attempting with little success to negotiate something quite like Joyce's model of erotic exchange. Arranging an assignation between his cousin Esther and his Polish friend Leo, David bargains for Leo's rosary—an instru-ment, he believes, of magical power and more obviously a symbol of David's long-ing to overcome the authority of his father and religion (not to mention, in a parallel Roth underscores repeatedly, an object that seems analogous to coins). But if Joyce makes sexual and consumer appetite seem welcome routes out of the nightmare of history, Roth quickly renders them seamy and exploitative. Erotic free-dom becomes less than appealing when it means selling your cousin to an anti-Semitic thug from down the street, and in this respect David's disappointing expe-rience of sexual commerce points both backward, to his mother's memory of being seduced by a Christian musician in Europe, and forward, to the landscape of urban vice that will flower in the last section of the novel. What David needs—as Roth makes clear when his father assents not to a lover, but to the cops—is less the freedom of the market than the protection of the state.

It is the invocation of that protection that also distances Roth from Freud, another figure whose influence on him is sometimes overstated. *Call It Sleep* is heavily laden with oedipal symbolism, and it reflects strongly Freudian styles of thought that Roth probably encountered among Eda Lou Walton's circle.[67] As with Joyce, though, *Call It Sleep* suggests not just an absorption of Freud, but a critical reflection on the ways in which his psychoanalytic version of political theory must have seemed inadequate to Roth. At the core of this theory, as both Ernest Gellner and Carl Schorske have noted, lay a kind of nostalgic apotheosis of the classical liberalism that flourished briefly in mid-nineteenth-century Vienna.[68] Imagining "a sort of social contract" arising among the primeval band of brothers who had defeated their tyrannical father, Freud celebrated, while simultaneously lamenting, the "beginnings of morality and law" and their continued dependence on "dread of the father."[69] But, as Gellner points out, that vision of the social contract remained "virtually unrelated to the problem of the state," making no allowance for the coercive powers of government.[70] "The essence" of political society "lies in the fact that the members of the community *restrict themselves* in their possibilities of satisfaction."[71] In direct parallel to the Freudian account of familial socialization, Freudian civilization flourishes solely on the oedipal internalization of norms—indeed, it casts the family as the origin and the epitome of political relations—so that Freud's theory looked notably akin to Kallen's and Locke's. All fashioned a latter day, newly reinforced vision of a stateless society guided mainly by the interiorized legacy of patriarchal authority.

In Freud's case, too, much as in Kallen's and Locke's, that theoretical vision was inspired in good part by distrust of democratic passions—a fear of the mob and, more specifically, of the way in the early twentieth century the libidinal force of politics seemed to lead toward dangerous collectivist fantasies. That anti-Semitism often played a central role in those fantasies came to seem quite natural. By Freud's reasoning, Christianity had replaced the "Father religion" of Judaism with its own "Son religion," setting in motion a process of "cultural regression" that culminated at its extreme in "the German National Socialist revolution" (MM 111, 112, 117). In his ultimate statement in this vein, *Moses and Monotheism*, Freud cast the Jewish people, who "mostly live as a minority among other peoples," as holdouts against that regression (115). Captives of a "feeling of guiltiness" that Christianity had dismissed, the Jews became for Freud paragons of the "moral asceticism" that his own devotion to reason epitomized (172).[72] They were the last liberals in a world gone over to irrational, democratic passions.

For Roth, though, who was the son of working-class, eastern European immigrants, Judaism looked less like the tradition of learning and refinement celebrated by Freud or Lewisohn than a legacy of provincial superstition, and when he embraced the Christian symbolism that swirled about the New Deal he consciously sought to distance himself from it. (Explaining his success as "a matter of grace,"

Roth was delighted when the bemused Margaret Mead asked, "that isn't a Jewish concept is it?")[73] And, as if to mark exactly where he differed from Freud, *Call It Sleep* includes a remarkable scene that in a brief moment manages to invoke and deflate the oedipal paradigm at the core of Freud's political theory. When the crime of pandering his cousin is discovered to his family, David takes the situation into his own hands and, approaching his father with a whip—nominally a tool of Albert's job as a dairy cart driver, but more importantly a symbol of his terrifying power—offers himself for a beating. For David, this is a moment that realizes the lessons of tradition and religious training; his act feels "ordained, foreseen, inevitable . . . , a channel of expertness, imbued for ages, reiterated for ages" (400). Significantly, though, the whip David hands his father is a broken one, which Albert has recently discarded for a new model, and though Roth passes lightly over the fact, the implication of David's choice seems clear. Submitting himself to his father's authority for the first time in the novel, David declares himself ready to suffer punishment, so long—the broken whip implies—as Albert is willing to accept limitations on his ability to do harm; David will be a dutiful son, if Albert will be a responsible father. If that is the implication of the broken whip, however, the striking feature of David's bargain is that it fails entirely. Unrestrained either by David's submission or by the imperfect tool his son hands him, Albert gives way to lethal passion, promising to "rid the world of a sin" and leaving David no option but to flee into the street for the freedom and, later, the authority he will find there (402). The power of contract, like the freedom of the market and the authority of tradition, offers no protection to the weak. As Freud might predict, David's religion of the son must turn for an alternative to the nation represented by the crowd and the state symbolized by the police.

That Mighty Hand

Ironically, for all Roth's carefully manipulated oedipal motifs, Hurston's work was far more in tune with Freud's thinking. Not only did Hurston narrate her own version of the Mosaic legend, one that appeared in the same year as the English translation of *Moses and Monotheism*, her version of that story rang a striking echo with Freud's, imagining as did his that Moses was an Egyptian who aligned himself with a disheartened tribal people and remade them into a nation. More significantly, Hurston's political psychology matched Freud's closely. Like him, she envisioned irrational passions as the essence of politics, assuming, as he did, that "libidinal ties are what characterize a group."[74] And like him she was obsessed with "the creative glamour of leadership" and the abject submission it called forth from the mob.[75]

Where they differed sharply, however, was in their reactions to that assumption. For where Freud showed a frequent revulsion from the political passions he anatomized, Hurston embraced them for their dramatic qualities, a project that required a systematic debunking of the juridical authority *Call It Sleep* invoked. Like her fascination with power and her doubts about sympathy, Hurston's skepticism toward the law runs all through her writing. The pattern begins with Hurston's suggestion that the "highly developed languages" of "the white man" are a debased form of "legal tender," which the rich vernacular language of the black South avoids. It ends with her notorious opposition to *Brown v. Board of Education*, which she denounced as "Govt by administrative decree."[76] Its most strikingly direct expression appears in the preface to *Moses, Man of the Mountain*. Explaining "what Africa sees in Moses," and the way it differs from the more familiar view, Hurston notes that in black accounts of the "Mosaic legends," the authority of their protagonist "does not flow from the Ten Commandments," but from "his rod of power, the terror he showed before all Israel and to Pharaoh and THAT MIGHTY HAND." Law, like sympathy, is empty. Force is what counts (338).

A compelling reason for that antinomianism appears in two dramatic but patently ineffectual courtroom scenes. In the most well-known, Janie Woods is brought to trial for killing her husband Tea Cake. She is acquitted, but as many readers have noted, the moment provides little gratification. In a novel that emphasizes the crucial role of self-expression, this scene fails to show Janie speaking and stresses instead the empty formalism and manufactured sentiment of the law. The court speaks for Janie, dispenses with her case, casts her as the helpless victim she is not, and thoroughly ignores both her own voice and the outraged sentiments of her community. *Jonah's Gourd Vine* makes the point more directly when John Pearson is publicly humiliated in divorce court, yet refuses to defend himself. "Courtrooms were bad luck to colored people," he thinks, and, noting the combination of distraction and "smirking anticipation" that appears on the faces of the judge, "the lawyers, the Court attendants, [and] the white spectators," he determines not to unveil himself. The "white folks . . . knows too much about us as it is," John tells his friend Hambo. "Some things dey ain't tuh know (137, 139, 140). For Hurston, in short, the law is illegitimate because of its racist indifference to individual black citizens and its salacious curiosity about the details of their private lives.

If, then, we take Roth's embrace of the law as a tacit endorsement of U.S. sovereignty and of the New Deal project of asserting national authority over regional and ethnic traditions, Hurston's antinomianism looks like a rejection of that vision—or perhaps, to be more precise, of her marginal relation to it. In its climactic moments, *Call It Sleep* may envision something like a New Deal coalition: a multiethnic body whose combination of legal and sentimental bonds transcends the limitations of inheritance and the hazards of the market. If that is so, the striking thing about it in this context, is that Roth's sentimental public includes no black members. Hurston had not missed similar implications throughout American life at the time, and indeed they would have been difficult to avoid. Despite the fact that the rise of industrial unionism and the New Deal led massive numbers of northern blacks to align themselves with the Democratic Party, and despite the fact that that political realignment would lead eventually to a genuine transformation of the American racial order, the Roosevelt administration remained ambivalent about its black support throughout its tenure, often deferring to southern opposition to Civil Rights measures. Its most ambitious programs—the NRA (referred to by skeptical blacks as Negro Run Around or the Negro Removal Act), the AAA, the WPA, and the Social Security Act—targeted white farmers and workers who had been displaced by the upheaval of the Depression. They did nothing to address the poverty and peonage of the black South and relatively little to repair the massive unemployment of the black North, and in fact they often lent a kind of governmental imprimatur to the second-class status afforded black workers.[77]

No surprise, then, that Hurston, who despised all forms of paternalism, developed a hearty disdain for the New Deal and the Democratic Party. *Seraph on the Suwanee*, a love song to entrepreneurialism if there ever was one, includes a withering portrait of a southern New Dealer, a "monied aristocrat" who, in an effort to be "a man of the people" spends vast sums on ceremonial funerals for people who had "lived on scraps and crumbs," and it directly contrasts that empty symbolic politics to the beneficial transformation of the South brought about by private development (808, 809). *Moses, Man of the Mountain*, paints pharaonic Egypt as a country undergoing something very much like a New Deal. Establishing a "new order" under a "new government," Hurston's Pharaoh recreates the political ambitions of FDR (341, 343). He "work[s] to reorganize the country into a unit intensely loyal to the new regime" through an ambitious program of "public works" and "government projects" (372, 489, 449). By Hurston's account, however, that new solidarity comes at the expense of the country's racial minority. "Hebrews were . . . prevented from becoming citizens . . . , they found out that they were aliens, and from one decree to the next they sank lower and lower" (342).

In Hurston's rendering, the consequences of that marginalization were profound. On the one hand, as she suggested when she claimed that Negroes did not speak in "legal tender," the exclusion of African Americans from the American political compact made them seem vibrantly creative and alive. It also meant, of course, that at least in Hurston's depiction, they remained outside the "new order" created by the New Deal. Indeed where David Schearl becomes a member of a new community formed by shared pity, Hurston denies the very possibility of such sympathy. And thus, because she has already rejected the diasporic federalism of writers like Locke, all she can imagine at her most politically grandiose is an unlikely project of black separatism—a prospect she raises in *Moses, Man of the Mountain*, only to reject when she considers it again.[78]

The more serious consequence of Hurston's antilegalism, though, comes in her understanding that there can be no end to violence and force. "The world is to the strong," she claims, and thus resolutions of the type imagined by Roth will always seem unbelievable.[79] This is the implication of John Pearson's rise and fall in *Jonah's Gourd Vine*. Having mastered his community by the charisma of awesome force, John sees it turn on him when he weakens, "like a wolf pack about a tired old bull" (119). Stripped of his power, he then undergoes a rare experience of serenity, a brief moment when he does not have to struggle for dominance and can submit himself to the love of a good woman. A sentimental victim like David Schearl, he becomes "jes' lak uh li'l boy," and, in fact, he yearns to remain in that immature condition. Having abused and abandoned his first wife, John prays "fervently" and "abjectly" that he will not be tempted again, a submission that leads his new wife to "exul[t] in her power" (161). The pathos of Hurston's novel, however, hinges on the fact that this unusual peace cannot last; John's irrepressible prowess begins to return. When it does, and he finds that he remains charismatic and sexually potent, he takes David Schearl's self-sacrifice beyond its merely symbolic dimension and drives himself beneath the wheels of a train—tellingly, the "greatest accumulation of power that he had ever seen" (89). The message is clear. John can become a potent and dangerous figure like his stepfather, or he can allow himself to be extinguished beneath a greater power. What he can't do is imagine a solution like Roth's that will do away with the reality of force itself. There is no way for the man to stay a little boy except by dying.

Not only is violence inextinguishable, though. For Hurston, it becomes a mark of legitimacy and inclusion. When John Pearson goes to court he notes that the "waves of pang that palpitated in the room [among the black spectators] did not reach up to the judge's bench" (139). Unlike in *Call It Sleep*, where empathy makes law a means of binding strangers into a community, here law and people, white authority and black folk, are disconnected. What does bind Hurston's people, however, is precisely the pain and self-inflicted violence that the law ostensibly controls and transforms. A similar point is made in the courtroom scene of *Their Eyes Were Watching God*. There, the fact that the court pities Janie is a mark of its estrangement from her. That the people of the muck are prepared to "beat her to death," however, is a sign of their intense emotional investment in her affairs—just as earlier, the fact that Tea Cake and Janie beat each other served as a symbol of their profound love: they do "things with their bodies to express the inexpressible" (287).

In fact, the logic of Hurston's violence runs still deeper. When the rabid Tea Cake bites Janie, he does so because he is inflamed not just by disease, but by the suggestion that a member of the light-skinned bourgeoisie threatens to "class

[Janie] off" (and perhaps, its is more subtly hinted, because he fears that the woman who was once his pupil may be moving beyond his control) (289).[80] That he would rather kill her and die himself than be dispossessed thus tells us of the intense connection between Janie and Tea Cake, and more broadly between Janie and the folk community Tea Cake represents. That connection is deeper than skin color or class distinction, Hurston suggests, but the major evidence she offers for it is mutual violence. The way you know that you are a member of a community in her world is that it is always ready to hurt you or to be hurt by you. The counterpart to "mah tongue is in my friend's mouf" becomes, in this context, my lover's teeth are in my arm, and the rabies that deranges Tea Cake becomes the fitting correlative for the intense and highly contagious passions—of love, but also of jealousy, anger, and resentment—that course through every community Hurston depicts.

To look at Hurston in this way is to recognize in her work a profound awareness of the moral ambiguity of power. Indeed, placed next to each other, both Hurston's fiction and Roth's *Call It Sleep* take on a complexity otherwise difficult to see. The concluding moments of Roth's novel are often read as a scene of failure in which David aspires to a kind of transcendent power and discovers not divinity, but the mundane world of the ordinary city.[81] "Something went and something was gained" in that process, Roth later remarked.[82] What David loses, we might say by comparing him to John Pearson, is what he first aspires to: the force to crush his father—and, more generally, the "god-like" power to make the world do his will (305). What he gains by surrendering that prospect is a place in a civic order that allows him to abandon the tradition of patricidal struggle.

But if Roth associated religion with magical power and envisioned trading both for the more worldly force of public sympathy, Hurston refused to countenance that exchange. In her anthropological writings, she was careful not to discredit the folk belief in magic, often marveling at its power herself, and her fiction likewise stressed the wonderful and mysterious. Indeed the conclusion to *Moses, Man of the Mountain* directly repudiates the trade-off accepted by *Call It Sleep*. Understanding that his people follow him "only through fear and awe," Hurston's Moses realizes that they cannot see him "sickened and crumbled like ordinary men," and he determines, in a kind of reversal of the *Wizard of Oz*, to stage manage a divine disappearance for himself. "He would end in mystery as he had come." Only by fabricating that religious aura will he be able to escape vulnerability to the "conniving politicians, stupid, but stubborn pushers and suspicions and avarice" that threaten to undermine Israel's high purpose, and only in that way will he be sure that "his laws . . . [will] stand" (593). Like so many other aspects of her work, that passage reflects Hurston's obsession with charismatic power and her corollary assumption that law is not an alternative to force, but merely its outer garment. Hurston's Moses rules Israel, and will continue to rule it, not because of the impersonal code he transmits, but because of the fear and awe he inspires.

GOVERNABLE BEASTS

In that respect, Hurston's Moses, like John Pearson and Janie of *Their Eyes*, appears the very opposite of David Schearl, a person who does not surrender power but who rather seizes it in a triumph of self-assertion. In Hurston's world, however, there can be no victory without violence, no triumph that is not won at the cost of some one else's submission, and thus no power that is not always shadowed by resentment and destruction—which is why Moses must go to such lengths to avoid the problem of succession and why John Pearson finally kills himself. The most striking instance of this stark lesson may come in the otherwise triumphant conclusion to *Their Eyes Were Watching God*. In the final pages of Hurston's greatest novel, Janie is at the peak of a power that resembles Moses's in its near divine grandeur. As she mounts the stairs to her bedroom, in a progress that anticipates Moses's final journey up Mount Nebo, she takes on mythic dimensions: "The light in her hand was like a spark of sun-stuff washing her face in fire. Her shadow fell black and headlong down the stairs. . . . She pulled in her horizon like a great fish-net. Pulled it from around the waist of the world and draped it over her shoulder" (333). But like John Pearson's, Janie's victory may be fleeting, and the shadow she casts may be a significant one. For when *Their Eyes Were Watching God* ends, as Ann duCille points out, Janie may well be infected with the rabies that Tea Cake has passed on to her.[83] Leaving open the possibility that she carries the disease may be Hurston's way of suggesting that Janie cannot put on Tea Cake's knowledge without his power; that she cannot transmit the legacy of vernacular creativity and popular vitality he has taught her without preserving the violence that come along with it. "Of course . . . [Tea Cake] wasn't dead," the novel concludes. "He could never be dead until she herself had finished feeling and thinking" (333). If Janie is indeed infected with rabies, that line might take on a rather ominous tone. For, it would mean that, so long as the community Hurston depicts remained cut off from the legal order Roth celebrates, the "waves of pang" that palpitated through it would be bound to continue.

So, too, would the endless political struggle that formed an important subtext to Hurston's work. When Theodore Lowi identified the personhood of the modern president as a "a combination of Jesus Christ and the Statue of Liberty," he identified an important feature of the symbolism of the New Deal—capturing not just its invocation of sentimental power, but its aspiration to found a whole new political order. As Christ was said to replace the authority of law by the power of love, the Roosevelt administration envisioned the plebiscitary president as a figure who might be capable, through the administration he employed and the emotional commitment he forged, of overcoming an outmoded political system built on representative institutions and party competition.

In *Call It Sleep*, Henry Roth imagined much the same transformation, envisioning the creation of a new civil religion founded on sympathy and the benevolent attention of the state. Zora Neale Hurston's distaste for that vision and her conviction of the inescapability, and grandeur, of power politics never wavered. Toward the end of her career, she hoped to publish one final novel, a historical recreation of the rule of Herod the Great that would cast him as a misremembered hero of the Jewish people. The last of Hurston's strong leaders, the Herod she imagined rejected sentimental Christianity and served as a reminder of the unending need for the man on horseback—"a great soldier, a great statesman . . . a very handsome man astride an Arabian stallion" (ZNH 664–65).

The Myth of the Public Interest: Pluralism

and Presidentialism in the Fifties

Eisenhower isn't a bad man, I think, just formless, banal, effi-
cient—smiles without personal wit or passions. He's so appall-
ingly typical . . . [the] figure of a country looking at itself in the
mirror for instruction.

—Robert Lowell

I did not know my true relationship to America—what citizen of
the United States really does?

—Ralph Ellison

F ROM AT LEAST ONE ANGLE, J. D. Salinger's *The Catcher in the Rye* looks like a strong rebuke to the majoritarian visions displayed in the work of writers like Hurston, Roth, Steinbeck, and Wright.[1] This is so not only because Salinger's sensibility is so strongly individualistic and so suspicious of bureaucratic institutions like the military and the school, but because, quite explicitly, his novel appears to reject the pathos of martyrdom central to the social democratic writing that flourished during the thirties and early forties. Like much of the "new liberalism" that arose along with the Cold War, the advice offered to Holden Caulfield by his former teacher Mr. Antolini seems a repudiation of the affective power of sacrifice. "The mark of the immature man," Mr. Antolini says, "is that he wants to die nobly for a cause, while the mark of the mature man is that he wants to live humbly for one."

Given that Holden will come near to self-destruction himself ("I thought I'd just go down, down, down, and nobody'd ever see me again"), those words appear both prophetic and wise.[2]

And indeed such wisdom was common among the liberal writers of the fifties, who like Salinger discovered in the wake of World War II, and in the context of the growing global conflict between the United States and the Soviet Union, a deep suspicion of the state and an often intense revulsion against collectivism and mass democracy. "No ideology, however noble, can justify the sacrifice of an individual to the needs of the group," David Riesman declared in 1954, and his moral defense of individual autonomy was echoed widely at the time, when it was often invoked by writers who wished to distance themselves from what they now viewed as the dangerously sentimental politics of an earlier, more ideological age. Looking back on the literary politics of the thirties, for instance, Mary McCarthy mocked the era's fondness for tales of victimization, casting them as a seductive weakness of the left. "Perhaps it is always martyrdom, in one form or another, that one childishly feels one must ready one's soul for," McCarthy considered. In her campus satire *The Groves of Academe*, she accordingly gave the rhetoric of "the martyred President" to her most repellent character. The conniving demagogue and faux leftist Henry Mulcahy uses it to elicit the "feeling of sacrifice and blind obedience that we give to a leader of a cause."[3]

A similar distrust of demagogic sentimentality runs all through *The Catcher in the Rye*—most evidently in Holden's distaste for the movies or in his disgust at the "Abraham Lincoln, sincere voice" used as a technique of seduction by his roommate Stradlater (64). But a more subtly devastating depiction of the malevolence of sympathy appears in Holden's own, confused attempts to empathize with the various people he encounters. When he meets the mother of an obnoxious classmate, his initial attempt to shield her unknowing love for her child turns into an indulgence in rhetorical gifts that appear not unlike Stradlater's ("I had in her a trance, like") and then slides into a self-serving pursuit of pity (73). When he talks with two nuns whose cheap suitcases depress him, he first offers them a donation and ends by blowing smoke in their faces. When he encounters a mismatched pair of boys on a see-saw, he tries to even their balance and discovers his attention is unwanted. "One of them was sort of fat, and I put my hand on the skinny kid's end to sort of even up the weight, but you could tell they didn't want me around" (159). Salinger thus repeatedly echoes a point that had recently been put in a more philosophical vein by Lionel Trilling in his own complaint against the welfare state. "Some paradox of our natures leads us, when once we have made our fellow men the objects of our enlightened interest," Trilling worried, "to go on to make them the objects of our pity . . . [and] ultimately of our coercion."[4]

Learning not to be unduly interested thus appears to be a main goal of Salinger's novel, which, as Carol Ohmann and Richard Ohmann pointed out some time ago, manages to combine an aggrieved complaint against the injuries dealt out by a capitalist society with the implication that such dissatisfactions are a passing phase of adolescent rebellion.[5] If "kids want to grab for the gold ring," Holden discovers in the novel's climactic passage, "you have to let them do it"—a moral that appears to imply the mature acceptance of accident, inequality, cruelty, and all the sorrows of life, including sex and death (273). Most resonantly, of course, the whole direction of Salinger's novel suggests that, in order to mature beyond his own version of the theatrical pity that McCarthy likewise distrusted, Holden must surrender his fantasy of being a catcher in the rye. As that fantasy proceeds from a strong misreading of Burns's "If a Body meet a Body"—replacing the poem's references to poverty and sexual license with sentimental affection—Salinger's point seems clear. The adolescent Holden needs to grow up and come to grips with the inescapable pain, injustice, and pleasure of adult life.[6]

In this manner, *The Catcher in the Rye* could be said almost directly to reject the New Deal sentimentalism of a novel like *Call It Sleep* and to celebrate, in a manner typical of fifties liberalism, what Gary Wills would later, in summarizing its central principles, define as "the discipline of consent."[7] Speaking of the rigors of scholarly training, an education that he hopes will take Holden out of his solipsistic grief, Mr. Antolini says that the culture of letters amounts to "a beautiful reciprocal arrangement" (246). And, it's worth noting that this is but one of many images of consensual agreement Salinger casts in glowing terms. From the opening of novel, when Holden's repeated willingness to pick up the papers feebly dropped by Mr. Spencer is contrasted to his teacher's heartless lecture, Salinger establishes a running contrast between authoritarian coercion and the ordinary social practices of custom and manners, between abusive pity and the implicit respect and tacit consent built into conversations and ordinary sociability. Especially in the novel's fondness for games and play (Holden's checkers with Jane Gallagher, his chaste dance with Phoebe, his memory of playing catch at sundown), we see a subtle paean to social convention that Holden will implicitly defend when he says, speaking about the insincerity of ordinary manners, that "if you want to stay alive, you have to say that stuff" (114).[8]

At least from Mr. Antolini's perspective, that line might be taken to articulate the key wisdom of the novel. Having, in grief at his brother's death, pursued a near suicide of his own, Holden discovers that survival and happiness depend on the tacit consent involved in mundane insincerity. To put the point in more elevated terms, seen in this light, Salinger's novel takes the same view that Hannah Arendt would later call on in her defense of constitutionalism. "Every man is born into a community with pre-existing laws which he 'obeys' first of all because there is no other way for him to enter the great game of the world."[9]

But, if *The Catcher in the Rye* seems to be ultimately on the side of such civic minded maturity, it only makes that case after providing a far more memorable complaint against the insincerity and cruelty of ordinary social life. If Holden's path to adulthood is to be significant, his anger and despair must first seem convincing. Fittingly, then, Salinger gives us plenty of reason to doubt Mr. Antolini's sententious advice. After all, Antolini has himself carried the martyred body of the novel's Christ figure—the young suicide James Castle—and appears to have been culpably untouched by the experience. He drinks, he is unhappily married, he is a stuffy pedant who is complicit with Holden's father, and, most notoriously he betrays Holden's trust—accusing him of being "a very, very strange boy" when Holden suspects that Antolini has taken a sexual interest in him (250). Given Holden's resemblance to James Castle, Mr. Antolini begins to look like an inadequate apostle of the novel's true martyrs—a priest who has lost the spirit to dogma and convention. Ultimately, then, it is famously difficult to decide just where Holden, or Salinger, wants us to come down. Is the novel a defense of maturity or a celebration of the youthful sensitivity to injustice and cant? Is it a warning against the dangers of Holden's prudish distaste for a licentious and cruel world, or a complaint against venality and selfishness? Should we share Mr. Antolini's distrust of sacrifice, or wonder why the world seems unable, as Holden fears, to remember its martyrs?

The fiction of the fifties is full of novels like Salinger's that intensify such uncertainties and that like *The Catcher in the Rye* work formally as well as thematically to stress both the inescapability and the virtue of uncertainty and irresolution. Like much of the new literature of the period (Bellow, Kerouac, Nabokov, Ellison, Lowell, and his fellow confessionalists), *Catcher* is a first person narrative whose rhetorical hyperbole emphasizes the indeterminacy of its voice and narration, while also encouraging us as readers to take our own recognition of that uncertainty for itself a reassuring vantage on the truth. Holden explains in a celebrated passage that "it's more interesting" when "somebody digresses," and, as that remark would suggest, his own narrative is emphatically wandering and circular, full of contradiction and unconscious self-revelation, and marked by self-undermining attempts to establish its own sincerity and authority (238). Similarly in the countless conversations that make up the main body of Holden's recollection, manipulation, misunderstanding, conflict, and abuse prevail. "You could see there wasn't any sense trying to have an intelligent conversation" (173).

But, shored against that confusion, Salinger implicitly places the narrative address of the novel itself—which importantly is more in second than first-person and thus implicitly one half of an intelligent conversation with the reader. "If you really want to know about it"—the novel's memorable opening line—positions those readers who continue as people who, wanting to know, consent to Holden's narration in the way his worldly interlocutors rarely do. If the reality Holden describes is one of confusion and misapprehension, the frame his narrative creates is thus alternatively one of sympathy and understanding, so that the apparent disorder and uncertainty of Holden's rambling thoughts becomes in the reader's responsiveness to them itself a shape to Holden's tale.

To be more direct, we become the readers Holden lacks in his day-to-day life, and our attention enables the narrative that allows Holden to see his experience anew, now not with anger and revulsion, but with acceptance. Nowhere is the transformation that results more evident than in the novel's striking final lines. "All I know," Holden remarks, "is, I sort of *miss* everybody I told about. Even old Stradlater and Ackley for instance. I think I even miss that goddam Maurice. It's funny. Don't ever tell anybody anything. If you do you start missing everybody" (277, emphasis in original). At one level, those lines suggest a therapeutic breakthrough appropriate to the hospital setting from which Holden speaks. Now freed of the anger and grief that marred his life, Holden is presumably able to miss not merely the companions he earlier disliked but the brother whose death he could not accept and whose name he still avoids speaking.

By the same token, however, the passage recuperates the very catcher fantasy the novel has appeared to reject. Earlier, when Holden reports that he imagines himself the distant protector of a crowd of playing children, we are asked to recognize the desperate sentimentalism of that fancy and perhaps, in keeping with the example of the boys on the see-saw or of Holden's useless efforts to control his sister Phoebe, its implicit will-to-power. With the novel's conclusion, however, Salinger reverses polarity. Where earlier Holden was full of ethical proclamation and prescriptions, now he admits to knowing nothing but his own feeling. Where before we saw the self-deception that undermined Holden's pretenses to benevolence, now we know not to trust his own disavowal of sentiment. Where once the catcher fantasy implied an illegitimate form of paternal control, now Holden again watches over the figures of his world by placing them in a retrospective narrative. In the end, he still looks very much a catcher in the rye, but now his sympathetic care, no longer intrusive and combative, is evident only in his ability to perceive and represent the people of his life with generosity and affection. As Carol Ohmann and Richard Ohmann note, "Art forms the needed bridge between the desirable and the actual" (64).

The problem to which Salinger found a solution in that artful ending was widely shared in the fifties—when Salinger had many imitators among writers who, like himself, were inclined to believe there was an important political significance to questions of novelistic form. As Arthur Mizener remarked toward the decade's end, Salinger was "probably the most avidly read author of any serious pretensions of his generation," and among the rich cohort of young novelists who rose to prominence at the time, he was often admired especially for the way Holden Caulfield's freewheeling first person narration appeared to challenge the limits of both modernist formalism and the seemingly outworn conventions of realist fiction.[10] Salinger had created "new room for shapelessness," John Updike remarked gratefully, "for life as it is lived." His admirers and kindred spirits took up the picaresque style and the colloquial diction, often giving still greater emphasis to Salinger's suggestion that the informality amounted not just to an artistic accomplishment, but to a political challenge to the orthodoxies and institutions that appeared to dominate American life.[11]

But if many of the new writers of the fifties became fascinated with the appeal of shapelessness, almost inevitably many of them were therefore troubled to some degree by the question of what would give structure to their artistic, and implicitly political, flights. Saul Bellow, for instance, later remarked of the frenetic narratorial excursion that announced his breakthrough novel, *The Adventures of Augie March*, that, emboldened by "the excitement of discovery," he'd taken "off too many [restraints], went too far."[12] But in fact, in its first person rendition of Augie's own "larky and boisterous" excitement, and in its determination to "get outside of law and opinion," Bellow's novel itself repeatedly dramatizes that concern. Like Salinger and Trilling, Bellow positions the vigor of literary imagination against the bureaucratic impositions of social democracy—"the life of organization habits which is meant to supplant accidents with calm abiding." But like his contemporaries, as well, Bellow also imagines political domination as a kind of overextension of exactly that literary power, and he heroizes Augie for his stubborn resistance to its seduction. "This is what mere humanity always does," Augie reflects in the passage that underlines the assumption Bellow shared with his contemporaries:

> It's made up of these inventors or artists, millions and millions of them, each in his own way trying to recruit other people to play a supporting role and sustain him in his make-believe. The great chiefs and leaders recruit the greatest number, and that's what their power is. There's one image that gets out in front to lead the rest and can impose its claim to being genuine with more force than others. . . . Then a huge invention, which is the invention maybe of the world itself, and of nature, becomes the actual world. . . . That's the struggle of humanity, to recruit others to your version of what's real. . . . But the invented things never became real for me no matter how I urged myself to think they were.[13]

For Bellow, as for many of his contemporaries, in other words, novelists, dictators, and presidents all look pretty much alike, and this leads, of course, to the question of how Augie, and implicitly Bellow, will avoid becoming versions of the domineering, short-lived tyrannical personalities we repeatedly encounter. Much as in Salinger, then, Bellow's novel dramatizes a simultaneous indulgence in and suspicion of rhetorical power, where the ability to invent and entice seems at once a valuable means to resist the rule of law and custom and, at the same time, a dangerous form of imperial overreach. Just as in Salinger, moreover, Augie's main resource in the struggle to resist the enticements of that power is the delight in, and care for, the autonomy of others that Bellow defines as love—"the only answer" to "the conditioning forces" of the world (449). So, while Bellow is a far less prudish writer than Salinger, happy to show Augie in a series of passionate extramarital affairs, like Salinger, he too draws a bright-line distinction between power and love (403). The mad theoreticians of Bellow's novel seek acolytes. They are "big wheels and imposers-upon, absolutists" (524). Augie as lover, by contrast, is a serial admirer, briefly infatuated by women of whom he demands little. In Bellow's telling, in short, a tendency to erotic fascination serves as a counterforce to the worldly power of political coercion.

None of the Caesars and Macchiavellis who crowd Bellow's novel can withstand that force. Having sought to colonize the mind of their pupil Augie, they discover in him a resistance that repeatedly prefaces their own Ozymandian destruction. But, given that by Bellow's account there's no difference between recruitment and coercion, the only genuine affiliations must seem still more contingent and insubstantial. "Wives don't own husbands, nor husbands wives, nor parents children" (407). Thus Augie's erotic life amounts not only to a series of "temporary embraces," but to an ever deepened appreciation for the virtues of impermanence that looks remarkably like the lesson taught in *The Catcher in the Rye* (403). In each of the major movements of his serial tale, Bellow shows Augie rapt beneath the tutelage of one of the novel's recurrent chiefs and leaders; and in each Augie is led by that temporary subordination to an encounter with brutality and death that awakens in him the necessity of caring for, rather that coercing others. But, in each case as well, his very flight from domination also leads him to an increased tolerance for the fact that, in their own struggles to maintain their independence, other people are, like himself, "not the honestest type" (522). Fittingly he ends the novel in a condition of irresolution. He is a dealer in contraband lingerie and married to Stella, a compulsive fabricator whose resistance to fixity and recruitment mirrors his own. Traveling lightly over the battlefields of Western Europe, he feels a "laughing creature, forever rising up" beneath his breast to dispel the atmosphere of sorrow and gloom (536). That he is not a person weighted down, either by deep commitments or a tragic sensibility, is the novel's main point.

In this manner, Bellow more directly thematizes an issue that is implicit in Salinger's novel as well: the commitment to shapelessness could seem to require an investment in contingency and impermanence as evident in the serial construction of the novels as in their depiction of a social world of countless ephemeral connections. Salinger's accomplishment, echoed less markedly by Bellow, came not only in the way he rendered that vision with the brio that made it compelling, but in his ability to make the appreciation of fluidity seem itself like a reassuring stay against confusion. In both novels, that is, the emergent design of literary narration, which seems spontaneously created, serves as an almost explicit alternative to the bureaucratic structures created by political power. "It'd drive me crazy if I had to be in the Army and be with a bunch of guys like Ackley and Stradlater and old Maurice all the time," Holden reports (182). But in his narrative recollection, those obnoxious characters become not merely tolerable, but the objects of sentimental affection. So, too, with Bellow's novel. In his own rhetorical flights, Augie's narrative resembles the mad enthusiasm of the novel's countless tyrants and visionaries, the inventors and artists who turn others into supporting players. But in its own diffidence about political realization, Augie's story appears distinctive, inoculated from the incipiently tyrannical appetites that drive almost everyone he encounters. Significantly among the last of the lessons Augie learns is that his dream to found "a foster home and academy" where he might "educate children" was "one of those featherhead millenarian notions" that can never be brought to physical realization (514, 516). As in *Catcher*, his narrative itself serves as an implicit form of counter-education, thankfully free of the coercion represented once again by the military and the school.

In short: the spontaneous form of writing versus the brute hand of the state. The contrast runs all through the literary renaissance of the fifties. Some measure of its wide resonance and of the interests at stake can be seen in the fact that the resolution that Salinger and Bellow alike discovered can be found also in fiction that in other respects might seem quite different in attitude and provenance. Consider, for example, *Lolita*, yet another picaresque saga of the education and manipulation of the young. Nabokov himself later praised Salinger, along with Updike, as one of the living writers he most admired, and in several respects his most famous novel shows a surprisingly close resemblance to *The Catcher in the Rye*.[14] Like Salinger's novel, *Lolita* comes to us as the first-person narrative of a social outsider who speaks from within the confines of a therapeutic institution. As in Salinger's story, too, sexual predation and the mistreatment of the innocent occupy center stage in *Lolita*—where, in their association with manipulative sentimentality, they appear paradigmatic of every abuse of power. Like Salinger's, as well, Nabokov's novel associates its picaresque form with the expansiveness of postwar consumer culture and, less directly, with a vision of social competition characterized by deceit and emulation. Most strikingly of all, despite the distrust of sentimentality that Nabokov appears to share with Salinger, *Lolita* resembles *Catcher* by finding an alternative to abuse and competition in the pathos created by the death of the innocent and beautiful. Once more, as well, that pathos appears to offer a warrant for an obscure, but welcome intimation of social harmony.

In Nabokov's case, that intimation comes especially in the famed concluding passage that follows Humbert Humbert's murder of Clare Quilty. The preceding dozen chapters, detailing Humbert's pursuit of Quilty, and Quilty's "ingenious play" with Humbert, bring to a baroque climax Nabokov's fascination with aesthetic legerdemain. In the doubling of Humbert and Quilty, the atmosphere of guile and confusion that has characterized Humbert's narration throughout comes to a comic extreme. ("We rolled all over the floor in each other's arms," Humbert reports of the litterateurs' ultimate battle. "I rolled over him. We rolled over me. They rolled over him. We rolled over us.") With the death of Quilty, however, Humbert appears able to leave that bewildering emulation behind. In his immediately subsequent memory of overlooking a western town from a roadside, his literary gifts seem turned from trickery and manipulation to elegy, and we encounter a lyric vision remarkably similar to Salinger's closing recuperation of Holden's catcher fantasy. By Nabokov's own account, the scene—which alludes strongly to Humbert's depiction of the earlier western town of Elphinstone, where Lolita makes her escape—acts as one of "the subliminal coordinates by means of which the book is plotted." As readers sensitive to the intimations of its artistry and undistracted by prurience or censoriousness, we are implicitly asked, much as Holden's readers are, to join Humbert in recognition of its latent significance:[15]

> As I approached the friendly abyss, I grew aware of a melodious unity of sounds rising like vapor from a small mining town that lay at my feet, in a fold of the valley . . . . And soon I realized that all these sounds were of one nature . . . . Reader! What I heard was but the melody of children at play, nothing but that, and so limpid was the air that within this vapor of blended voices, majestic and minute, remote and magically near, frank and divinely enigmatic—one could hear now and then, as if released, an almost articulate spurt of vivid laughter, or the crack of a bat, or the clatter of a toy wagon, but it was all really too far for the eye to distinguish any movement in the lightly etched streets. I stood listening to that musical vibration from my lofty slope, to those flashes of separate cries with a kind of demure murmur for background, and then I knew that the hopelessly poignant thing was not *Lolita*'s absence from my side, but the absence of her voice from that concord.[16]

For Nabokov, as for Salinger, then, the agreement between writer and reader appears to offer an alternative to the narrative events of exploitation and competition. What that literary contract enables, Nabokov along with Salinger suggests, is an aesthetic perception of childhood play that turns it into the tacit model of a social compact—or "concord"—and one that can be placed in opposition to the novel's depiction of intrigue, abuse, and all the cunning, forced bargains into which Humbert and Quilty alike compel Lolita. In the aesthetic connection between speaker and reader, an agreement is forged that highlights the cruelty that otherwise runs rampant through Humbert's narrative. Alfred Appel refers to the moment as Humbert's "moral apotheosis."[17]

Of course, making his version of that resolution far more intensely lyrical, Nabokov also gives us much more reason to be aware of the doubtful service it may be providing. Humbert can hear the sound of children playing as concord, he himself reminds us, only because he perceives it from the requisite distance that turns rivalry and squabbling into harmony and, more importantly, because he has removed Dolores Haze from the world of play and led her toward her death. And not only Lolita, but Quilty, Charlotte Haze, Lolita's infant brother, Lolita's first seducer Charlie Holmes, Humbert's first wife Valeria, and of course Humbert himself are all dead by the time the reader encounters his narration—so that "the refuge of art" and the image of social harmony it descries all seem directly premised on the death of the actual individuals who might interfere with Humbert's grandiloquence. Indeed the pathos of the erasure of the individual person in the harmony of social concord is stressed by Humbert's paean itself, with the mournful pleasure it takes in the way the flashes of separate cries emerge only fleetingly from the demure background hum.

Even Humbert appears to recognize that there may be something false and self-regarding about this concluding lament. He recalls his vision of the town, in the same terms he uses to turn Dolores Haze into the nymphet Lolita, as "a last mirage of wonder and hopelessness" (307), and the suggestion of bad faith here becomes still more forceful in Humbert's following, final remarks—his ultimate, self-justifying explanation for his murder of Quilty. "One had to choose between him and H. H.," Humbert addresses Lolita, explaining his decision to kill the pederast Lolita is said to have loved, "and one wanted H. H. to exist at least a couple of months longer, so as to have him make you live in the minds of later generations" (309). Who is this "one," we might imagine Dolly Schiller wanting to ask? Why does he conceive the apparently false choice he presents here? (Both Humbert and Quilty might well have gone on living had Humbert not killed his rival.) And, more importantly, to whom does Humbert imagine he is speaking? Considering that Humbert requests that his memoir "be published only when Lolita is no longer alive," he knows a fact that we are reminded of in John Ray, Jr.'s preface, that his ideal reader, and the only person who can give him exculpation, will never hear his apology.[18]

What Nabokov does by planting those questions, of course, is to subtly undermine the satisfactions offered by Salinger and Bellow alike. If they suggest that literary eloquence might be freed of its association with power and manipulation, he hints that even this hope might amount to gratifying self-deception. If they imagine a literary contract alternative to a social world of competition and abuse, he points toward the imaginary investments on which that compact might be thought to depend. And, if they invoke the sufferings of the innocent, seeking to distinguish the pathos thereby produced from the demagoguery of mass culture and mass politics, he suggests that they too might be engaged in a self-deluding form of higher poshlust.

The Misty Figment of the State

The problems Nabokov thereby resuscitated cut to the heart of the attitudes prevalent in the new fiction of the 1950s, but for much the same reasons they also resemble the issues at the core of the era's prevailing political discourse. The search for a reliable image of social concord that appears in

Nabokov, as in Salinger and Bellow, for example, can be compared, in a very rough sense, to the main problem addressed in James M. Buchanan and Gordon Tullock's classic work in the theory of public choice, *The Calculus of Consent* (1962). In their influential effort to apply the tools of economic theory to constitutional government, Buchanan and Tullock sought to answer a question widely discussed in the pluralist theory that dominated academic political science in the fifties. Given the premises of methodological individualism that pluralism shared with neoclassical economics (that societies are made up of "separate individuals" who can be assumed "to have separate goals both in their private and in their social action" and that such individuals are "the only meaningful decision-making units"), Buchanan and Tullock sought to answer how reasonable structures of collective self-government might be conceived. Their answer, arrived at through the use of game theory, reiterated and expanded on a point they saw anticipated by Hume, and that in a somewhat different form would soon be echoed by Arendt: that rational individuals would agree to be bound by constitutional norms that might limit their own pursuit of satisfaction because it was in their self-interest to adhere to rules of the game that applied fairly to all. Even though such rules were the product of individual interests, Buchanan and Tullock stressed, they differed from the "operational" bargaining and competition of mundane politics because constitutional rules established collective procedures rather than distinctive policies and thus depended ideally on unanimous consent rather than minority interests. In "the good society" Buchanan and Tullock believed that free and rational individuals should agree to create, in other words, the constitution amounted to a bedrock social contract that restrained the omnivorous wheeling and dealing of the market.[19]

Salinger, Bellow, and Nabokov took a similar view. In the literary agreement they envision with their readers, each of those writers could be said to aspire after a kind of constitutional vantage on the operational bargaining and conflict their narratives otherwise describe (and one likewise premised on the narrators' willingness to give up certain satisfactions in favor of mutually beneficial collective norms). The aesthetic satisfaction they imply in that concord resembles, moreover, the philosophical satisfaction Buchanan and Tullock find in their model of collective choice. In effect, both enable "a theoretical determinacy" about political structures even in the face of a "purely individualistic postulate" that appears to make such foundations doubtful (5, 4). In the major fiction of the fifties, just as with Buchanan and Tullock's highly abstract theory, in other words, satisfaction comes from the way a reassuring collective agreement can seem to arise naturally from the apparent randomness created by individual choice.

The need for such satisfaction seemed pressing to many liberal intellectuals in the fifties precisely because nearly everyone agreed that, in the postwar atmosphere, the plebiscitary implications of presidential government had been discredited—and that, as Buchanan and Tullock noted, a "theoretical indeterminacy," or as Riesman more emphatically stated, a "chaos of democratic politics," seemed inevitably to follow.[20] During World War II, as during previous wars, the power of the federal government and of the executive branch in particular had expanded to previously unanticipated degrees. That expansion was spurred on, moreover, not just by the demands of wartime mobilization, but by overwhelming popular support for the role of presidential leadership. With FDR announcing that Dr. Win-the-War had replaced Dr. New Deal, the doubts about executive power that had flourished during the late thirties disappeared almost overnight. In the midst of a war effort that demanded massive national commitment, the reformist agenda of the Roosevelt administration took on new life, and liberal intellectuals in particular reinvigorated a "cult of leadership" that cast FDR, in the words of the *New Republic*, as the voice of the "whole people" and Congress as the craven home of "special interests."[21] By the later forties, however, that cult appeared to be buried. Roosevelt was dead, Truman excited little popular or intellectual devotion (and was successfully tarred by Republicans with a fondness for "executive dictatorship"), and in the context of the Cold War, state leadership seemed a dangerous fantasy.[22] Even admirers of FDR now worried about the excesses of executive power. "We've had our bellyful of great leaders," the former New Dealer John Franklin Carter announced in 1953: "Stalin, Hitler, Mussolini, Churchill and Roosevelt."[23]

Such attitudes were central to the tastes of postwar literary culture, which often generalized the political sentiments of the day into a sweeping vision of the evils done by charismatic leaders atop powerful state bureaucracies. Lionel Trilling, who warned against the dangers of liberal paternalism, likewise worried about "the great executive force" that appeared to link totalitarianism and the New Deal. Edmund Wilson sought repeatedly to disenchant the cult of Lincoln, depicting in his brilliant revisionist accounts, not the national martyr enshrined by memory, but an ambitious politician who left behind "a lasting trauma" and "a rather gross period of industrial and commercial development." Robert Lowell cast Eisenhower in similar terms, making him, in "Inauguration Day: January 1953," the object of a satiric love sonnet and suggesting that the American public's infatuation with military conquest signaled the decadence of the republic.[24] Most imaginatively of all perhaps, John Updike constructed in his first, widely admired novel *The Poorhouse Fair* a futurist allegory that worked almost directly to reverse the premises of presidential government. In the process, he created a near blueprint of the political thinking that ran through much of the literary excitement of the era.

For the young Updike, the "contemporary decadence" of the United States pointed toward a mildly dystopian future in which an extension of the New Deal (the "enforced reforms") would lead to a paternalist, one-party state exemplified by a public nursing home. The world that results from that progressive development is interracial and sexually permissive and also free of great suffering. "There was no cause for tears. Everybody had insurance." But, by the same token, the future lacks profound happiness as well. To fully reveal its limitations, Updike offers a drama built almost entirely on the conflict between two types of executive leadership. Literally overseeing the poorhouse is Connor, the officious administrator who "has vowed to bring order and beauty out of human substance." Opposed to his rule is the novel's protagonist Hook, a retired schoolteacher who is the unofficial "mayor of the place" and the reminder of "an older America." His memories significantly emphasize not merely a lost age of individual liberty and religious piety, but nostalgia for a forgotten era of intensely partisan politics. For, Hook is cleverly imagined as a Bryanite Democrat entirely out of place in the world of the welfare state. Like Edmund Wilson, he speaks of the Union victory in the Civil War as an imperial triumph for northern capital, and he scoffs at Lincoln as a modern Nero who toadied to corporate interests. His own heroes are the lost men of the late nineteenth-century presidency: Chester Arthur, Grover Cleveland, James Garfield, Benjamin Harrison. Thus, although Hook himself conceives his life directly in the context of national politics—his past is "a long smooth gallery hung with portraits of presidents of the United States"—the chief executive he idealizes is not the plebiscitary leader of the whole people, but the party servant central to nineteenth-century democracy.[25] For him, much as for the antebellum Whitman, the ideal president does not look all that different from a mayor.

If it were not clear enough that his novel acts in this way to reject the visions of presidential government that had been central to the New Deal, Updike adds an acute rejoinder to the rhetoric of presidential martyrdom. In a scene that initially appears slated to become a climactic moment in the novel, the residents of the poorhouse, who have been impressed by Connor into repairing a damaged wall, turn on the administrator and begin spontaneously to stone him. For Connor, who imagines himself a Christ figure and "their leader," the moment comes as "a revelation" (111, 109). But Updike neatly undermines Connor's self-importance, and the whole drama of presidential leadership, by making the scene embarrassingly anticlimactic. The stones are a "harmless pepper of tiny black objects," and the event serves to resolve none of the novel's tensions (110). It is as though Updike aimed to invert the vision of novels like *Native Son*, or *Call It Sleep*, or *The Grapes of Wrath*. In Updike's story, collective violence makes nothing happen. There is no powerful emotional bond between the people and their leaders. (Even Hook is estranged from the poorhouse residents.) And the inhabitants of his institution are explicitly not citizens of a nation-state, but merely the vectors of aimless imperial dissemination. "They were just people, members of the race of white animals that had cast its herds over the lands of six continents. . . . [T]he conception 'America' had died in their skulls" (131–32).

For Updike, as for Wilson and Trilling, in short, the basic premise of presidential government—the affiliation of executive leadership and national sovereignty—

seemed politically a sham and spiritually a dead letter. Ironically, while all those writers believed themselves to be offering a pointed criticism of their society, the message they proffered was one that their contemporaries seemed eager to hear. Updike's novel includes some digs at the Eisenhower administration—the one party of the novel's future state is significantly Republican—but the animus that he, like Trilling and Wilson directs against presidential power was shared by Eisenhower himself. As his speechwriter Emmett Hughes later recalled, Eisenhower "brought to the White House of the 1950s a view of the presidency so definite and so durable as to seem almost a studied retort and rebuke to a Roosevelt. . . . Where Roosevelt had avidly grasped and adroitly manipulated the abundant authorities of the office, Eisenhower fingered them almost hesitantly."[26] Nor was this diffident persona solely a matter of style. As Hughes suggested, it stemmed also from an underlying political philosophy that, much as in the memory of Updike's Hook, emphasized a view of liberal society as a fluid negotiation among diverse interest groups. Both in its economic relations and in its political processes, Eisenhower suggested, the United States should be seen as an affiliation of bargaining parties whose shifting, informal associations (rather than "regimented statism") would act to restrain the dangers of demagogic power and destructive selfishness.[27] "Without allies and associates," he remarked, fittingly in private, "the leader is just an adventurer, like Genghis Khan."[28]

Variations on that attitude were as prominent in the political discourse of the fifties as they were among literary writers. In the years following the war, popular journalists, public intellectuals, and academic specialists all seemed to fear the dangers of executive force and to rediscover the virtues of the separation of powers. The era's prevailing theoretical account of the presidency, for example, was Edward Corwin's bestselling constitutional analysis, which warned that a presidency that slipped the traditional and legal restraints on executive power was "a potential matrix of dictatorship."[29] Echoing that view, Corwin's contemporaries among popular novelists and journalists began restoring the reputation of the legislative branch. In numerous admiring works (*The Citadel*, *Profiles in Courage*, *Advise and Consent*, *The Manchurian Candidate*, *The Best Man*), popular culture now venerated not the presidency, but the Senate, which for the first time in decades appeared not just a center of national power, but the model of a courtly, civic culture whose insular routines created a welcome resistance to democratic passions.

Academic writers were only slightly less enthusiastic in their praise for a "pluralist" democratic culture whose "endless bargaining" was epitomized by the legislative process.[30] Indeed the very assumption that had been central to the idea of presidential government—that there was a sovereign will, or simply a national interest, articulated by the chief executive—now appeared doubtful. There was no "mystical general will" to be discovered, Buchanan and Tullock argued, stressing a point made often by political scientists during the fifties; nor was there any "'public interest' apart from, and independent of, the separate interests of the individual participants" of any social group (12). The state itself was but one more organization in a society of jockeying interest groups, and "not different from other associations." And the chief executive was merely one negotiator in the endless process of social give and take. [31]

From at least one vantage, in fact, the central appeal of this pluralist view was the way it made sovereignty in general and the power of government in particular appear virtually unnecessary. Pluralism, in the words of Charles Lindblom, demonstrated how "people can coordinate with each other without anyone's coordinating them, without a dominant common purpose."[32] For Riesman similarly, the distinctiveness of American democracy lay precisely in the fact that it did not demand any "agreement on fundamentals." Because of "a party system that serves as broker among special interest groups," and because of "our expanding economy," the United States seemed able to tolerate a collocation of divergent interests that made its political order resemble "that of Switzerland."[33] So strong was this consensus view, that even to appeal to "the misty figment of the state" could seem an admission of craven superstition. The political scientist Earl Latham thus counseled his readers to accept a "view of the political process [that] may seem formless, inchoate, ambiguous, and disordered." Such a view lacked "the *mystique* of the law," Latham acknowledged, "with its authoritarian constructs, its assumption that there *must* be a supreme power, like father in the household or the Absolute, some authority which arranges disorder and judges our transgressions and supplies us in an infinite universe with a finite demesne of which we can see the walls, and feel secure." But mature citizens had little choice other than to do without such reassurance. "We deceive ourselves to clothe men in gowns and call them supreme, or sovereign, or all-powerful."[34]

As if to emphasize the point, the new American fiction of the late forties and fifties was full not only of repellent demagogues, but of protagonists like Holden Caulfield and Augie March—young men who (in an especially striking contrast with David Schearl or John Pearson or Tom Joad) find themselves in distinctly post-oedipal situations, without fathers and in search of a route beyond their own temptation by authority. Jack Burden of *All the King's Men*, Sal Paradise and Dean Moriarty of *On the Road*, Neil Klugman of *Goodbye, Columbus*, Harry Angstrom of *Rabbit, Run*, Frank Wheeler of *Revolutionary Road*, Ellison's *Invisible Man*—all are figuratively or literally orphans who have no immediate father against whom to contend. Even an apparent exception to the rule like John Grimes of Baldwin's *Go Tell It on the Mountain* turns out to fit the pattern. For, if John's father Gabriel resembles Willie Stark or, say, Ras the Exhorter in figuring the perils of the tyrannous personality, we eventually learn that he is neither the biological father, nor any kind of paternal figure to his young son. Almost everyone turns out to be poignantly fatherless in the literature of the fifties.

In the very attraction to commanding authorities that many of those protagonists demonstrate, however, the new fiction of the fifties dramatized a nagging issue at the core of the pluralist vision. Having shrugged off the mystique of the law and the dangers of executive force, what should American citizens look to in their place? How reassuring should they find the idea of a pluralistic process itself?

Our Beautiful History

Some years later, in the midst of a late twentieth-century revival of contractualist political theory, the philosopher Norberto Bobbio offered a more formal statement of the problem. "A basic feature of an agreement based on a bargaining relationship between two parties who consider themselves mutually independent is that it is by its very nature unstable," Bobbio noted. "Contracts based on private law prosper, and promote social development, under the protection of the coercive force of the state." No sovereignty, in other words; no meaningful pluralism to shield against its excesses.[35]

Though the predominant political thought in the United States during the fifties was reflexively antistatist, a nagging awareness of the problem articulated by Bobbio ran through the mainstream political writing of the day, just as it did through the era's new literary expression. Even at the height of the pluralist heyday in the early to mid-fifties, there were signs that its stoutest defenders shared the realization that some underlying framework was necessary to ground the diversity of interests that made up a bargaining society. Though Eisenhower himself was an instinctive pluralist, for instance, and distrusted the demagoguery and statism he associated with prewar leadership, he also tended to share the assumption that it was the responsibility of the national government to defend an underlying constitutional order that private actors were naturally inclined to neglect. "All of us," he claimed, must be bound by "commonly agreed-upon rules and regulations in order that the accidents of mass production . . . not defeat or destroy the right of the individual to political and economic freedom." In his increasing dissatisfaction with the demands of defense contractors and corporate enterprise, and in his distaste for the extreme right wing of his own party, Eisenhower began to mention doubts about the capacity of cooperation and bargaining alone to compel such civic responsibility.[36]

Similar views were especially common, of course, whenever the Cold War was emphasized. When the concern was global competition with the Soviet Union, U.S. policymakers and opinion leaders often spoke of the need for national commitment and frequently invoked what John Foster Dulles called "our spiritual heri-

THE MYTH OF THE PUBLIC INTEREST

tage." George Kennan had similarly conceived the Cold War as an international struggle that defined the nation's sovereign identity—"a test of the overall worth of the United States as a nation among nations." The Cold War was valuable by Kennan's lights, in other words, precisely because it demanded that the American citizenry commit to the exercise of their collective will and to their national destiny. He wished to see Americans "pulling themselves together and accepting the responsibilities of moral and political leadership that history plainly intended them to bear." Over the course of the fifties he and a host of similarly minded social critics would complain that in pursuing barbecues and tailfins the American citizenry was failing to rise to that collective mission.[37] In *The Poorhouse Fair*, for instance, Updike summarized the decadence of the imperial future, not by envisioning a swaggering warfare state, but by complaining at an enervating sense of stalemate that sapped public commitment. "There was to be no war; we were to be allowed to decay of ourselves" (131). It was not surprising in the context of such views that the Republican Party went beyond Eisenhower's preferred reticence about executive power to claim that the president was "not only the political leader, but the spiritual leader of our times" or that liberal Democrats would follow by investing similar prophetic expectations in JFK.[38]

The academic voices of pluralist theory disliked that prophetic stance and disdained "our nationalistic and politically illiterate glorifiers."[39] They preferred to champion democracy with an air of scientific detachment that fit well with their doubtfulness about collective identity and democratic passions. But they, too, felt compelled to acknowledge, if only in the last instance, a fundamental role for national sovereignty. Even if the state was but a misty figment, it was still the case, Earl Latham argued, that the ceaseless action of social bargaining depended on a "body of agreed principles that forms the consensus upon which the political community rests." From one vantage, then, the government appeared to Latham but one organized interest amid a sea of competing groups, and therefore a political actor whose own agenda was qualitatively no different from any other. But from another perspective, the federal government possessed great symbolic importance because, it "represent[ed] the consensus by which the various groups exist in mutual relations." The influential pluralist E. Pendelton Herring had asserted a similar view when he claimed that democratic politics depended on at least "the myth of the public interest." By "its very vagueness," Herring asserted, a sheerly mythic sense of the common good, enabled "the freest interplay of group interests."[40]

Though such references to national sovereignty were themselves vague and unenthusiastic, the pluralist defenders of American democracy shared with the rhetoricians of the Cold War a basic way of conceiving the underlying authority they felt compelled to acknowledge. In nearly all cases, pluralist thinkers alluded reflexively to a distinctly cultural and implicitly historical source of authority—a foundational set of "extraconstitutional" assumptions passed down by history that could seem at once necessary to, and outside of the mundane wheeling and dealing that was their properly political subject of interest. They made reference, that is, not just to the market or to civil society, but in the final analysis, to the nation. Robert Dahl, the era's preeminent voice of pluralist theory, put the issue most clearly:

> In a sense, what we ordinarily describe as democratic "politics" is merely the chaff. It is the surface manifestation, representing superficial conflicts. Prior to politics, beneath it, enveloping it, restricting it, conditioning it, is the underlying consensus on policy that usually exists in the society among a predominant portion of the politically active members. Without such a consensus no democratic system would long survive the endless irritations and frustrations of elections and party competition. With such a consensus, the disputes over policy alternatives are nearly always disputes over a set of alternatives that have already been winnowed down to those within a basic area of disagreement.
>
> Lest anyone conclude that these basic agreements are trivial: a century ago in the United States it was a subject of political debate whether the enslavement of human beings was or was not desirable. Today the question is not subject to political debate.[41]

Like many of his contemporaries, Dahl assumed that a prepolitical agreement must underlie the narrow range of the nation's legitimate disputes about public policy. But the specific example of consensus he provides here—almost, it seems, as an afterthought—is equally representative. While his diction is restrained, Dahl resembles the earlier defenders of presidential government in that he, too, appeals to a foundational moment in national history as the source of an ultimate, sovereign authority. Indeed the very moderation of Dahl's tone is illuminating. For, the effort to wall off mundane politics from occasions of profound conflict, and the habit of handling the latter with kid gloves, bespeaks a paradoxical attitude that runs through much of the liberal thought of the era: a combination of reverence for and wariness of the great crises that define national sovereignty. On the one hand, Dahl needs the events of "a century ago" as an example of the nontrivial origins of an American consensus. On the other, he shunts them aside as a nearly unnameable example of the incendiary matters properly ruled off from political debate. The Civil War in this treatment looks virtually taboo.

Such a sacred source of common identity, we might say, is what's absent from Nabokov's writing and whose disappearance Updike explicitly warns against. Among the aspects of Lolita's world to which Humbert is indifferent is "some great national celebration" marked with "firecrackers and veritable bombs" (245). Independence Day comes fittingly just as Lolita flees Humbert with Quilty, the coincidence highlighting both Humbert's complete estrangement from the shared context of national culture and, more subtly, the illusory promise of freedom it offers

Lolita. If, as Nabokov later claimed, "the writer's art is his real passport," he would suitably have expected little good from the promise of national sovereignty.[42]

But Nabokov's contemporaries were less skeptical about the grounds of national consensus, and quite frequently their writing demonstrates the same kind of hesitant allusion to profound national origins evident in Dahl. In the final lines of *Augie March*, for example, Bellow's protagonist announces to us that he is: "a sort of Columbus of those near-at-hand and believe you can come to them in this immediate terra incognita that spreads out in every gaze. I may well be a flop at this line of endeavor. Columbus too thought he was a flop, probably, when they sent him back in chains. Which didn't prove there was no America" (536).

Without that stirring peroration, Bellow's novel would end on a note as anticlimactic as Nabokov's. With it, Augie's aimless wanderings take their place in a history of national striving whose significance almost literally depends on the thought that there is an America that lends them meaning. Following, too, as it does Augie's journey over the battlefields of Normandy, the passage implicitly casts the origins of America in the simultaneous acknowledgment of and effort to overcome an ancient history of European violence—so that the final passage functions as a kind of crowning reiteration of Augie's repeated attraction to and escape from tyrannical power. Likening himself to a Columbus in chains, Augie becomes by his own analogy a prophet who suffers at the hands of the powerful in the name of an as yet unrealized, democratic nation.

Though the examples differ, similar references give structure and symbolic resonance to much of the new fiction of the fifties, functioning in Nabokov's useful phrase, as the "subliminal coordinates" that shape their otherwise disorderly tales. *The Catcher in the Rye*, for example, reminds us of the importance of underlying consensus in Holden's fascination with the Museum of Natural History, an institution contrasted to the bureaucratic impositions of the school. Holden famously celebrates the museum as an institution where "everything always stayed right where it was," but equally important to its status as a marker of stability is the particular history the museum records. Holden's memory latches on to "some movie . . . always showing Columbus discovering America" and to diorama displays of Native Americans that refer to a past both thrillingly dangerous ("this long, long Indian war canoe") and now pleasantly resolved. Like Augie's Europe, the museum almost literally houses a reminder of violent national origins that provides both ballast for and a contrast to the consumer society of the present. The Indian war canoe, Holden notes, is "about as long as three goddam Cadillacs in a row" (156).

For Holden, then, the national culture established by the museum provides what Mr. Antolini believes, more or less like Humbert, he should find in the cosmopolitan culture of higher learning. "It isn't education. It's history" (246). That such a source of collective identity is important to the underlying structure of Salinger's novel is suggested by the novel's opening scene in which Holden recalls "standing way the hell up on top of Thomsen Hill, right next to this crazy cannon that was in the Revolutionary war. You could see the whole field from there, and you could see the two [football] teams bashing each other all over the place" (5). Formally Holden's position here is similar both to the stance he envisions in his catcher fantasy and to the imaginative status he demonstrates in the novel's closing passage. In all cases, he assumes a superior vantage that enables him to look with detachment on the competitive striving of ordinary social life. Here, though, Salinger adds a suggestion that the perspective is historical and cultural as well as imaginative or theoretical. Considering that Holden has just told us of the false advertising of Pencey Prep—"since 1888 we have been molding boys"—the hilltop almost directly contrasts the deep origins of the revolutionary past to the more recent history of snobbery and fraudulent manipulation (4).

Subtle though that intimation may be, it was echoed often in contemporaneous writing and bolstered by contemporaneous enthusiasm in the academic and popular press for America's revolutionary origins.[43] Although literary writers were less direct, they similarly reached for allusions to the revolutionary generation, especially when they wished to indict the failings of the present. Trilling pauses, for example, in his novel *The Middle of the Journey* to note of a wealthy patron of a liberal magazine that "he would never put his ideas or his life or his fortune or his sacred honor to the test of establishing them at Yorktown" (243). Richard Yates similarly titled his novel *Revolutionary Road* to contrast the nation's heroic origins to the suburban decadence of the present. (When the last remnant of that spirit, Yates's heroine April Wheeler, is most disgusted, she repairs like Holden to a hilltop that enables her to look down on the petty striving of her world.)[44] In a particularly eloquent version of the fashion, Frank O'Hara responded to Larry Rivers's parodic revision of Leutze's "Washington Crossing the Delaware" with a lyric invocation of Washington that cast him as a genealogical forebear and the predecessor to O'Hara's own preferred social and aesthetic sensibilities—the founder of "a nation of persons":

> Dear father of our country, so alive
> you must have lied incessantly to be
> immediate, here are your bones crossed
> on my breast like a rusty flintlock,
> a pirate's flag, bravely specific.

Rivers claimed of his painting that he wanted both to assault the piety of abstract expressionism and to rescue Washington from "national cliché."[45] Responding to his irreverent veneration, O'Hara exults that "our hero has come back to us" and finds in the painting's unorthodox Washington something much like what Augie sees in Columbus—an aesthetic and historical warrant for a preferable America: "secular and intimate" and alternative to the most crass features of social competition.

> Anxieties
> and animosities, flaming and feeding
> on theoretical considerations and
> the jealous spiritualities of the abstract
> the robot? they're smoke, billows above
> the physical event. They have burned up.
> See how free we are!

Just as in Salinger and Bellow, then, "our beautiful history" becomes the ultimate means to surpass the failings of an emulative society, and one that appears necessary even to a literary project that wishes to celebrate the individual pursuit of ephemeral pleasures. Like his contemporaries among fiction writers and pluralist theorists, O'Hara distinguishes the genuine personal freedom he wishes to defend from the craven privacy and imitation of mass society by associating it with a forgotten history of national aspiration. "Don't shoot," O'Hara apostrophizes Washington, "until, the white of freedom glinting / on your gun barrel, you see the general fear."[46]

Sacred Principles

Perhaps the most elaborate invocation of revolutionary origins came in the era's most celebrated novel, Ellison's *Invisible Man*. Like his contemporaries, Ellison used an appeal to the founding of the nation as a means to resolve the tensions inherent to a pluralist theory of democracy. But from Ellison's perspective, those tensions rightly seemed far more critical than many of his peers allowed, with the result that *Invisible Man*, and later Ellison's essays and his incomplete second novel, offer a more profound exploration of the issues at the heart of the era's emerging political and literary consensus. Indeed, in some respects, the full significance of Ellison's work cannot be appreciated without recognizing how thoroughly it explores and rearticulates the ideological and aesthetic predispositions that circulate through the writing of his contemporaries.

To look at Ellison in this manner is to see a writer perched ambivalently on the edge of a developing critical orthodoxy. As the National Book Award committee recognized when it commended *Invisible Man* in 1953, Ellison's novel shared the antiformalism of the era's new trends in fiction. "With a positive exuberance of narrative gifts," the committee declared, Ellison had "broken away from the conventions and patterns of the tight well-made novel." But, while Ellison himself would come later to stress his appreciation for the "fluid, pluralistic turbulence" of democratic society and the "random assemblies" of styles and tastes it encouraged, *Invisible Man* itself leans less far in the direction of "shapelessness" than did many of Ellison's contemporaries, tending instead toward a structure that the author himself described as "near allegory."[47] In its didactic epilogue, and still more in the elaborate patterns of motif and allusion over which Ellison labored for years, *Invisible Man* showed itself eager to revise and combine, rather than to reject, both the committed political writing and the modernist techniques of formal construction that had been the prevalent methods of "well-made" fiction before the fifties.[48] "To be unaware of one's form is to live a death," the prologue remarks in words that are difficult to imagine elsewhere in contemporaneous fiction.[49]

So, too, with the democratic institutions to which Ellison often connected his aesthetic practices. In the homiletic epilogue to *Invisible Man* and many times thereafter, Ellison underscored the significance of his narrative exuberance by offering a defense of pluralism more direct than almost anything in the work of his contemporaries. "Whence all this passion toward conformity anyway?" Ellison's epilogue famously asks. "Let man keep his many parts and you'll have no tyrant states," an imperative directly aligning his novel with the Madisonian premises then common in political discourse. But here as well, Ellison carefully hedged his bets. "Our fate is to become one, and yet many," *Invisible Man* immediately follows, marking a defense of national cohesion that in coming years Ellison would consistently and emphatically balance against his celebration of diversity (577).

Ellison had good cause for mixed feelings on such issues. His experience of American racism and his anger at the Communist Party made him acutely sensitive to the ways that dominant majorities are always prepared to sacrifice the interests of minorities in the name of the collective good. At the same time, he was aware that the argument from cultural diversity could be used to prop up segregation and, by the same token, to serve the interests of a Negro elite whose failure to provide adequate leadership in the struggle against racism was the main inspiration for his novel.[50] Yet, if Ellison was more intensely ambivalent than many of his peers, his means of resolving such uncertainties look at first glance virtually standard in the mainstream discourse of the era. Invoking a paradoxical understanding widely shared among the defenders of pluralism, Ellison suggested that the commitment to diversity served the public interest so long as cultural identity aspired not to exclusivity but to a place in a larger national dialogue. The view, which amounted to a latter day cultural translation of the Madisonian defense of faction, resuscitated the arguments of Kallen and Locke.[51] Like those predecessors, and like his contemporaries, moreover, Ellison found a reason to be confident of that paradoxical relation by appealing to an underlying constitutional order that he suggested would ideally serve to channel various private interests toward the public good. The view was put most clearly in the essay "The Little Man at the Chehaw Station":

> In relationship to the cultural whole, we are, all of us . . . members of minority groups. . . . Holding desperately to our familiar turf, we engage in that ceaseless contention whose uneasily accepted but unrejectable purpose is the projection of an ever more encompassing and acceptable definition of our corporate identity as Americans. . . . The rock, the terrain upon which we struggle, is itself abstract, a terrain of ideas . . . that draw their power from the Declaration of Independence, the Constitution, and the Bill of Rights. We stand . . . united in the name of these sacred principles. But indeed it is in the name of these same principles that we ceaseless contend, affirming our ideals, even as we do them violence" (CE 500–1).

Invisible Man builds its narrative structure in large part on the assumptions summarized in this passage, negotiating between the "ceaseless contention" of mundane life and the "corporate identity," which ideally provides a ground of collective agreement. We begin, of course, with the narrator's near lethal collision with a white stranger on the street, an encounter that—like the comparably murderous accidental entanglements in *Lolita*, *The Adventures of Augie March*, and *The Catcher in the Rye*—serves to dramatize the hazard of urbanized society, the absence of a collective agreement and, more generally, the social violence that appears necessarily to ensue. "Responsibility rests upon recognition, and recognition is a form of agreement," Ellison's narrator remarks, thus reminding us of the need for an underlying consensus to ground the interaction of civil society (14). Nearly the whole of the remainder of his story goes on to depict the consequences of its absence, showing the many diverse, but always comparable forms of abuse and manipulation that result from the fact that such a mutual commitment is missing from his world. Only in the novel's final lines do we approach the suggestion of an alternative. When, in the famous concluding sentence, the narrator asks, "who knows but that, on the lower frequencies, I speak for you," he gestures toward a suitably profound, but inarticulable collective understanding (581). Much as in Salinger, Bellow, or Nabokov, the narrator's address to the reader stands in for a larger, social compact that, because it is not an event, but a framework, cannot be narrated by the means the novel reserves for its account of social confusion.

Characteristically Ellison's allusion to that framework is both unusually emphatic in expression and tentative in its hopes of realization. As a consequence, *Invisible Man* highlights a strategy that Ellison shares with writers like Bellow and Salinger. Placed in comparison, all can be seen to stage a variation on what may be the central myth of liberal political theory—the transition from the state of nature (or "chaos" in Ellison's usage) to the social contract. To the extent *Invisible Man* is, as

Ellison suggested, an allegory, that transition might be said to provide the rudiments of the novel's organizing framework. Throughout its episodic narrative, we witness various forms of illegitimate and coercive power. Then, in the novel's climactic moment—the extended riot scene—we see both political authority and individual distinction briefly crumble. "I was one with the mass . . . my personality blasted," the narrator reports. As Harlem descends toward a state of open civil war ("the crash of men against men"), we observe the ultimate extension of the series of violent encounters that began in the novel's opening pages (550, 553). The looming prospect of race war is confirmed when the narrator finds himself set on by a mob of white vigilantes and literally chased into the novel's lower depths.

But, then, in the epilogue that follows, the novel shifts suddenly in tone and address as the narrator summarizes his experience. "So there you have all of it that's important," he begins, replacing his earlier most prominent characteristics—blindness, foolishness, ambition—with a determination, underscored by his address to the reader, "to study the lesson of my own life" (572). That transition, however, is fittingly far from a merely personal development. Alluding now to the terms that he may share with his readers, white and black, *Invisible Man* meditates on "the principle" that the founding fathers "dreamed into being out of the chaos and darkness of the feudal past" (574). Almost literally, then, the form of Ellison's narrative—the transition from the street-level riot to eloquence on the lower frequencies, the narrator's progress from political oratory to literary craftsmanship ("from ranter to writer"), and the novel's shift from picaresque narrative to philosophical meditation—echoes the founding creation of the nation's political order (CE 111).[52] In all dimensions, we are asked to sense the aesthetic, emotional, and political satisfaction that might arise as form and agreement displace coercion and confusion. Fittingly the narrator first hears the riot as "a distant celebration of the Fourth of July" (535).

Here and throughout his writing Ellison hit much harder an implication that many of his contemporaries were content to leave as a subtle intimation. Time and again in the essays he wrote after *Invisible Man*, Ellison invoked the constitutional principles and sacral founding of the American nation—"our national beginnings"— stressing how fundamental they were to democratic society and how desperately the United States was in need of their redemption (CE 107). He spoke so emphatically, however, precisely because, unlike his contemporaries, he could not be confident of the underlying consensus to which he referred. His contemporary Robert Dahl referred glancingly to the Civil War as the foundation of an indubitable national consensus. Ellison, by contrast, repeatedly stressed that little had been resolved by the conflict and that, indeed, the United States continued in the state of undeclared civil war that blossomed in Harlem's riots. *Invisible Man* alludes to that understanding in its opening chapter, when the narrator's grandfather instructs him that "our life is a war and I have been a traitor all my born days, a spy in the enemy's country ever since I give up my gun back in the Reconstruction" (16). A similar implication appears when the narrator conflates the Emancipation Proclamation with the accomodationist rhetoric of Booker T. Washington: "About eighty-five years ago [slaves] . . . were told that they were free, united with others in our country in everything pertaining to the common good, and, in everything social, separate like the fingers of the hand" (15). The premise of *Invisible Man*'s story is thus a condition that Ellison would often describe more explicitly in subsequent essays: that emancipation created no genuine freedom or citizenship for African Americans, that Reconstruction had been betrayed by a corrupt agreement among white Americans, and that the regime inaugurated with Jim Crow had amounted to chronic race war ever since.[53]

The most obvious features of that war are the nightmarish conditions depicted in the bulk of *Invisible Man* and anatomized often by Ellison in his more critical comments on American society. In the absence of a substantial corporate identity, life in the United States is "a social nightmare, a state of *civil* war, an impersonal and dreamlike chaos." Notably, in his darker moods, Ellison emphasizes the anarchic features of that condition by pointing out precisely the absence of the collective agreement whose significance on other occasions he stressed. "Even the word 'democracy'—the ground-term of our concept of justice, the basis of our scheme of social rationality, the rock upon which our society was built—changes into its opposite, depending on who is using it" (CE 31, emphasis in original).

But, if, on one level, *Invisible Man* stresses the pain and confusion the narrator suffers in coming to grips with his world, we miss the full significance of his story if we fail to recognize that Ellison also sees much that is ennobling in that struggle. After all, the naiveté and superficiality of the narrator are most evident when he is slow to realize what admirable figures like his grandfather, or the unnamed veteran of the Golden Day, or Tod Clifton, Brother Tarp, and Dupre—all not just subversives, but warriors—intuitively understand: the life of black Americans is an unending battle for justice. Likewise when the riot finally breaks out, it not only threatens the narrator with death, just as in the classic invocations of war, it coincides with his "fierce sense of exaltation" and his profound awareness of his connection with his people (548). Ellison emphasizes the point by making his narrator witness the death of a stranger shot by the police. "I looked at the dead man. He lay face forward, the crowd working around him. I realized suddenly that it might have been me huddled there, feeling too that I had seen him there before, in the bright light of noon long ago" (537). Until this moment, the narrator's relation to the people of Harlem has been a source of anxiety. But shot down, the anonymous man becomes—like Tod Clifton, to whom he bears a structural resemblance—not just a victim, but a martyr, and he therefore becomes in his very anonymity resonant of a collective history. His death thus serves finally to underscore the narrator's identity and to bring home the significance of his grandfather's words: "*our* life is a war." As in the classic treatment, war is the alembic of collective identity.

Ellison's attraction to that stirring vision of conflict makes for an interesting comparison to his contemporaries. Trilling, Updike, and many others among the Cold War liberals suggested often during the postwar years that there was a high price to pay in the apparent placidity of consumer society. In the absence of declared war, the American people avoided the evils of demagoguery but lost also a sense of public good and collective mission. "We were to be allowed to decay of ourselves," Updike predicted. Ellison answered that lament by pointing out that Americans were in fact already engaged in an on-going race war they seemed determined to ignore. To the extent they acknowledged the conflict, however, they might discover precisely the revivification of citizenship whose disappearance liberal thinkers regretted. Thus, Ellison's excoriating comments about American racial injustice and his uplifting invocations of America's democratic mission turn out to be entirely consistent—just as the two major tonal registers of Ellison's novel, the satiric and the homiletic, are meant to be as complementary as the comparable voices appear to be in Salinger and Nabokov. In both voices, Ellison casts himself as a prophetic figure who calls his fellow citizens to the demands of a common struggle they too easily neglect. "Consciousness and conscience are the burdens imposed on us by the American experiment. They are the American's agony, but when he tries to live up to their stern demands they become his justification" (CE 59).

The duple structure of *Invisible Man*, then, rests on an analogously two-sided model of America's racial order. On the one hand, there is the false peace initially trusted by the naïve narrator, a structure of racial subordination that is exemplified by the various repressive institutions depicted in the novel—the college, Liberty Paints, the Brotherhood. All impose a manufactured reality that obscures the chronic, low-intensity race war on which it rests. On the other hand, though, there are the outbreaks of open warfare, at the Golden Day and in the ultimate riot scene, whose full conflict reveals the hidden truth of America's racial order and in so doing enables Ellison's male characters to achieve briefly a civic dignity they are otherwise denied. That contrast between false peace and open war, it is helpful to realize, resembles the distinction that Ellison's pluralist contemporaries frequently drew between the grubbily "operational" and grandly "constitutional" levels of political action, and it corresponds fittingly with a similarly stark distinction between two types of social agreement that runs all through Ellison's work.

The more evident of those two agreements comes in the model of the relation between racism and democracy that Ellison developed during the late forties, when, dissatisfied with the traditional theories of inequality proposed by the left, he drew on a combination of Hegel, Freud, and Kenneth Burke to fashion a symbolic as well as material account of the subordination of African Americans. "It was . . . when white men drew up a plan for a democratic way of life, that the

Negro began slowly to exert an influence upon America's moral consciousness," Ellison writes in the breakthrough essay, "Twentieth-Century Fiction and the Black Mask of Humanity." "Gradually he was recognized as the human factor placed outside the democratic master plan, a human 'natural' resource who, so that white men could become more human, was elected to undergo a process of institutionalized dehumanization" (CE 85). At the root of racism in the United States, in short, lies an illegitimate agreement among white Americans to exploit African Americans—both for their labor and, still more importantly, for their ability to symbolize the various forms of enslavement that white Americans only thereby rose above. But that illegitimate compact will always be haunted by the ineradicable presence of black Americans, Ellison points out. As the nation's scapegoats, they are the ever present reminder of white America's bad conscience and of its material and symbolic dependence on the very people it wishes to disavow. As claimants who increasingly seek their rights as citizens and as victims of injustice, they constantly threaten the stability of the racial order. The result, Ellison suggests, is an unending project of psychic and material repression that deforms white and black Americans alike.

This is the situation that Ellison's narrator summarizes in *Invisible Man*'s epilogue, decrying the effects of a social bargain that, as his own history symbolizes, black Americans nearly as much as whites are compelled to misrecognize. "One of the greatest jokes in the world is the spectacle of the whites busy escaping blackness and becoming blacker every day," he complains, "and the blacks striving toward whiteness, becoming quite dull and gray" (577). But, a richer and more concrete rendition of that deformation is dramatized in the narrator's countless, failed attempts to negotiate his world, nearly all of which feature his effort to engage in systematically unjust contracts and exchanges. "By pretending to agree I had indeed agreed," the narrator laments in remarks that, although directed at his manipulation by the Brotherhood, could be applied to nearly every one of his encounters (553). Much like Dolores Haze, in other words, the narrator is forced, by the terms of an illegitimate social compact, to engage in an endless, demeaning series of contracts to which he has no effective power to consent or demur. The injustice of his world, in other words, is characterized by the omnipresence and systematic illegitimacy of the very bargaining his pluralist contemporaries praised, so that his picture of American life looks like a sharp variation on theirs. Like the pluralists, Ellison views civil society as a complex and unending system of fluid exchanges. Unlike them, he sees that social fabric systematically malformed by the presence of an underlying, inegalitarian social contract.

But if this operational picture of American racism assumes the foreground of Ellison's fiction, it is often implicitly compared to a superior constitutional alternative gestured to in the final lines of *Invisible Man*—an invocation of a foundational covenant that holds out the promise of a more democratic agreement among all of

America's citizens. Ellison returns to that promise often in his essays, but the most striking version may appear in his tribute to an Oklahoma newspaperman and Negro leader who influenced him in his youth. "Roscoe Dunjee understood what it has taken me many years to understand," Ellison writes in that essay, perhaps implicitly comparing himself to his slow learning protagonist: "He understood that not only were the American people a revolutionary people, but that in the shedding of blood, sacrifice, agony, and anguish of establishing this nation, all Americans became bound in a covenant. Roscoe Dunjee understood, at a time when hardly anyone else did, that there was an irrational element in the American Constitution, a mysterious binding force which was the secret to moving people" (CE 452).

If his contemporaries distinguished between "operational" and "constitutional" levels of agreement, then, Ellison called on a similar contrast—between "plan" and "covenant"—to explain the relation between racism and democracy. But Ellison heightened both sides of this contrast still further by emphasizing the cost in violence and suffering essential to both. For, in Ellison's telling, both these forms of social agreement depend for their survival on sacrifice, although in ways that are markedly different and mutually exclusive. In the quotidian world of American race relations, white Americans, and the powerful more generally, maintain their status, and their sense of psychic balance by excluding African Americans and abusing their interests—or, as Ellison more melodramatically puts it, through "rites of symbolic sacrifice in which cabalistic code words are used to designate victims consumed with an Aztec voracity for scapegoats" (CE 501).

Hence the various abuses of power *Invisible Man* portrays. Both Bledsoe's notorious promise to "have every Negro in the country hanging on tree limbs" to preserve his power and Brother Jack's explanation, in defense of his own, that "discipline is . . . sacrifice, sacrifice, SACRIFICE," demonstrate the ugly logic of organized coercion (143, 475). The illusion of democracy depends in both cases, Ellison implies, on symbolic and material repression. But while this abusive kind of sacrifice assumes the foreground of Ellison's fiction, a less apparent, consensual form of sacrifice hovers in the background as the crucial vantage point from which the existing order can be criticized. "Morality still claims us," Ellison editorializes, "because these words in whose name we act [, the words, that is, of the founding fathers,] were made luminous by human sacrifice, with the shedding of blood" (CE 412).[54]

Unrecognized Compulsions of Being

As Ellison himself acknowledged, the language he makes use of in such moments descends straight from the vision of patriotic martyrdom that developed in the wake of the Civil War.[55] His terms are those that were advanced by Lincoln's inaugural addresses and by the Gettysburg Address, and that have been echoed countless times since—in which the willing death of America's citizens establishes the bedrock of collective solidarity and sacralizes the nation's distinctive mission. By the same token, the contrast to which Ellison repeatedly returns—between plan and covenant, racial domination and willing sacrifice, the squalor of civil society and the grandeur of sacred principle—corresponds not only to the contrast between ranting and writing that he shared with contemporaries like Salinger, Bellow, and Nabokov. It likewise echoes the central dynamic constantly replayed in the symbolism of presidential government inaugurated by Lincoln: between coercive state power and the democratic expression of the nation's sovereign will. As in so much postbellum American writing, martyrdom, in its testimony to the life of the nation, becomes the foundational political act, the crucial, symbolic means of transforming the abusive exercise of power into a spiritually ennobling, collective agreement.

The point is worth making because it highlights an element of Ellison's political sensibility that is often overlooked, but that he himself stresses in his comments on Roscoe Dunjee, its "irrational element." Ellison is often praised, not only as a great novelist or brilliant essayist, but as a philosopher of democracy whose perceptions of the demands of political life offer a universally applicable model of the just society.[56] But, both in his fiction and in the prophetic mode of his essays, Ellison himself referred less to abstract principles than to spiritual legacies that were powerful precisely to the degree that they exercised a compelling, exclusive, and irrational hold over people. *Invisible Man* stresses the ever present significance of that irrationality when the narrator remarks that "in going underground, I whipped it all except the mind." He warns us, that is, against the unending temptation to be seduced by falsely comforting abstractions that exclude "the chaos against which that pattern was conceived" (580).

His phrasing at such moments is highly abstract. But Ellison's address on Dunjee may suggest more concretely just what it was Ellison feared might be excluded by the reductive and doctrinaire theories he came to perceive in orthodox Marxism. In a word, the central mystery, or original chaos, exerting spiritual power here and throughout Ellison's essays is national history, and the event that testifies to its binding force is the blood sacrifice that inevitably gives national identity its grandeur. The point is often passed over by critics who praise Ellison for his universality or his commitment to the principles of constitutional law.[57] But Ellison's comments on Dunjee make emphatic a point touched on often throughout his writing. The value invoked there comes less from any particular idea or scheme laid out in the U.S. Constitution than from the "revolutionary people" who authored it and from their willingness to fight and die to give it meaning. Much as in the theories of Ellison's pluralist contemporaries, in other words, it is not philosophical principles that matter so much as the national will that stands behind them.

Ellison's deep investment in a distinctly American nationalism runs all through *Invisible Man*, and not only, or most importantly in the vulgar images of patriotism that appear, say, in the flag tattooed on the stripper's belly or in the Washington facades painted in "optic white." Just as democratic "covenant" always shadows the "plan" of racial domination, behind those satiric references to a debased version of American patriotism runs a more approving appeal to national identity. Many critics have noted the innovative use that *Invisible Man* makes of African American folklore and of its central place in the novel's aesthetic and ideological design. In a complement to those readers who celebrate Ellison for his putative universalism, some even take the novel to gesture in this way toward the black cultural nationalism that would flourish during the latter sixties and seventies. But Ellison himself spoke otherwise. "For better or worse," he declared, "whatever there is of value in Negro life is an American heritage" (CE 80). And consistently over the course of his career after *Invisible Man*, his writing would defend African American vernacular creativity precisely for the way it exemplified a democratic culture that he cast as an interracial, but also distinctly American inheritance.[58]

The importance of that inheritance to *Invisible Man* can be glimpsed among other places, in Ellison's process of composition. In his initial outline for the novel, Ellison envisioned the narrator being presented by an admirer with "a primitive African fertility god, an ugly little figure which he imagines argues with him concerning the aesthetics of democracy."[59] In the completed novel, however, the resonant icons of heritage—Bledsoe's leg shackle, the scattered possessions of the evicted couple, the Sambo bank the narrator finds at Mary Rambo's boarding house, above all Brother Tarp's length of chain—all testify to the distinct history of black slaves and their descendents in the United States. It is not Africana, in short, but as the narrator emphasizes, "Americana" that provides his crucial legacy and that engages him in implicit argument (319).

That fact, while worth considering, is more or less obvious. What is more rarely noticed is the key role that national identity plays in giving normative weight to Ellison's narrative design. As is often pointed out, *Invisible Man* is a novel preoccupied by the problem of leadership. It offers both a critique of the prevailing Negro elite, and a narrative of the protagonist's path beyond the seductions of illegitimate power toward a position of genuine, democratic authority. In his journey toward that stature, the narrator contends against a series of antagonists and false models culminating in his conflict with the paired enemies of the leftwing politico Brother Jack and the black nationalist Ras the Exhorter. Complementary representatives of illegitimate power, each of those men shows himself ultimately willing to slaughter black Americans in the misguided effort to advance his followers' interests. But, Ellison goes beyond that complaint and makes the bad leadership the two share inextricable from a more fundamental fact. Brother Jack and Ras alike are strangers who speak notably in alien tongues. At exactly the moment he reveals his indifference to the people of Harlem ("our job is not to ask them what they think but to tell them"), Brother Jack slips, "spluttering and lapsing into a foreign language" (473).[60] Likewise with Ras. In the midst of the riot, as he shifts from Exhorter to Destroyer and demands the narrator's execution—"to teach the black people a lesson"—he is said to be "yelling something in African or West Indian" (563). A "madman in a foreign costume," his words have become incomprehensible to the rioting southerners who appear as the true heroic actors of Ellison's narrative (558).

In one sense, there is an important perception summarized in the complementary depictions of Jack and Ras, beyond even the recognition that in their most radical forms Communism and black nationalism aspire to be mass political movements that take power through revolutionary means. Each, too, as Ellison's caricatures suggest, are avowedly internationalist movements opposed to the claims of the nation-state. But to put things this way is to see, by contrast, just how significant is Ellison's own devotion to the American nation and how much political and moral force he expected it to exert. His comments on the illegitimate sacrifice demanded of African Americans hint at the logic in the references to "cabalistic code words" and "Aztec voracity." Not unlike his friend Bellow, in other words, Ellison suggests that political injustice is somehow finally a foreign or primitive precursor to America's revolutionary people. His treatment of leftism and black nationalism in *Invisible Man* depends on the same assumption. Both movements appear to mislead African Americans necessarily, not solely because of their ideological convictions or undemocratic means, but because they represent the incubus of alien seduction. Ellison's narrator himself underscores the point when, arguing to the people of Harlem against Ras, he exhorts, "We are Americans, all of us, whether black or white, regardless of what the man on the ladder there tells you" (481). No surprise then that, directly in response to his confrontation with Ras and his disgust with the Brotherhood, the narrator finally realizes "who I was and where I was" and comes to an appreciation of "the beautiful absurdity" of his "American identity" (559). As the white cops remind the narrator that he is a Negro, Ras and Jack show him he is American.

Seen from this vantage, the desiderata *Invisible Man* implies is not merely an end to racism or injustice; nor a greater dedication to the substance of democracy; nor an abandonment of demagogic political ideologies and an appreciation for freedom and the wealth of cultural diversity; nor an emancipation from a shallow, mechanized society and the rediscovery of a greater spiritual and civic purpose. All these are central themes of *Invisible Man* and all are taken up repeatedly in Ellison's subsequent essays. But in every case as well Ellison makes each of these ambitions appear inextricable from the achievement that he suggests guarantees them all, a rebirth of the American nation. Little in Ellison's novel can be fully understood without appreciating how central that vision is to the book's design. Thus, for example, when the narrator reminds us that "recognition is a form of agreement," what he refers to evidently is the due recognition of common national identity, not mere humanity, that racism denies. Much the same implication appears in the prologue's densely Freudian and Danteasque fantasy—in which the narrator imagines, at "a still lower level," a "beautiful girl the color of ivory pleading in a voice like my mother's as she stood before a group of slaveowners who bid for her naked body" and then goes on to talk with a "singer of spirituals" who loved the master that fathered her murderously angry sons (9, 10). Here the narrator discovers the "unrecognized compulsions of his being," not primarily in the current unjust features of American society, nor even in their historical sources, but in the fact that he is the genealogical descendent of slaves and slaveowners, whose interracial ancestry is denied in the present (13).

It is the refusal to recognize that genealogical origin Ellison implies here and throughout *Invisible Man* that drives the literally patricidal fury of African American men. Against both that destructive force and the injustice that inspires it, he will ultimately invoke a complex and emotionally intense filial piety toward the founders of American democracy. The transition can only be effected, though, through the kinds of martyrdom Ellison celebrated in his paean to Roscoe Dunjee. The determining role of that sacrificial nationalism appears most directly in *Invisible Man* in the novel's concluding passage between the riot and epilogue—a transition which all but literally marks a shift not just between picaresque and meditative form, or between chaos and order, but, by the same token, between Ellison's two alternative models of sacrifice. In the riot, we see not just race war and the disorder of an implicitly preconsensual (or "feudal") society, we likewise witness the ultimate extension of the illegitimate sacrifice that a racist society imposes on African Americans. That abusive order is epitomized in the tacit conspiracy between Ras and the Brotherhood to provoke the slaughter of Harlem's residents, an apotheosis of the earlier alliance between Bledsoe and Norton. "Can't you see it?" the narrator pleads, warning Harlemites of the alliance of corrupt white and black elites, "They want you guilty of your own murder, your own sacrifice!" (558). But the white coercion of African Americans takes on a more directly allegorical form in the narrator's ultimate, hallucinatory vision of himself as a lynching and castration victim of Brother Jack. Cast over a bridge, and now useless for biological reproduction ("my generations wasting upon the water"), the narrator's testicles become the symbolic center of America's illegitimate racial hierarchy ("your sun . . . and your moon"). They are, in short, the mythic center of a primitive society built on "Aztec voracity."[61]

But, that vision of coercive sacrifice is answered in the novel's concluding epilogue, where the narrator counters his hallucination of being lynched with an alternative and equally imaginative vision of something closer to a freely chosen martyrdom. The relevant passage, which comes with the narrator's recollection of his grandfather's "deathbed advice," is often noted and often taken to summarize the central and most admirable wisdom of Ellison's novel (574). But it is almost always truncated. To see its full significance, we need to quote the passage at length. "Perhaps he hid his meaning deeper than I thought," the narrator considers:

> Could he have meant—hell, he must have meant the principle, that we were to affirm the principle on which the country was built and not the men, or at least not the men who did the violence. Did he mean say "yes" because he knew that the principle was greater than the men, greater than the numbers and the vicious power and all the methods used to corrupt its name? . . . Or did he mean that we had to take the responsibility for all of it, for the men as well as the principle, because we were the heirs, who must use the principle because no other fitted our needs? Not for the power or for vindication, but because we, with the given circumstances of our origin, could only thus find transcendence? Was it that we of all, we, most of all, had to affirm the principle, the plan in whose name we had been brutalized and sacrificed—not because we would always be weak nor because we were afraid or opportunistic, but because . . . they had exhausted in us, some—not much, but some—of the human greed and smallness, yes, and the fear and superstition that had kept them running. . . . Or was it, did he mean that we should affirm the principle because we, through no fault of our own, were linked to all the others in the loud, clamoring semi-visible world, that world seen only as a fertile field for exploitation by Jack and his kind, and with condescension by Norton and his, who were tired of being the mere pawns in the futile game of "making history"? Had he seen that for these too we had to say "yes" to the principle, lest they turn upon us to destroy both it and us? (574–75)

For many of Ellison's readers, the first two sentences of this passage summarize his novel's central meaning: the principles of liberal democracy transcend their abuse by American racists. But if, as seems likely, we are intended to read the passage as a series of rhetorical questions that build progressively toward an ultimate inference, that reading is not fully adequate, and Ellison's meaning can be seen to be both far more specific and more complex than most responses allow. For the implication of Ellison's questions pointedly extends beyond the thought that the vaguely described "principle" is good in itself, or good for all people, and suggests rather that it suits African Americans because of their special genealogical relation to American history—because, that is, of "the given circumstances of our origin."

What Ellison means more specifically in this passage is difficult to grasp until we recall his contemporaneous use of the word "plan" to describe the historical relation between American democracy and racism. Seen in that context, the passage reminds us that the "principle" of democracy cannot be separated either from the men who "dreamed it into being" or from the victims on whose subjugation it has necessarily depended. For American democracy in this depiction is not a set of universal ideas or abstract truths, but an ethnically distinctive history binding white and black Americans in an inescapable embrace. "Weren't we *part of them*?" Ellison's narrator asks (575, emphasis in original). African Americans, by this account, have a distinctive national mission precisely because they are "the heirs" of a history of abuse, which makes them both the victims and the potential redeemers of the nation. Much as in the Lincolnian rhetoric from which it descends, the passage suggests, then, a secularized and nationalized version of the myth of the Christian redeemer. Having suffered the brutalities of racial oppression, and thus in some respect having purged themselves, and potentially their oppressors, of "greed and smallness," African Americans by this account possess the capacity to show all Americans the means to rise above their failings and thus to live up to the full potential of their origins.

But even this does not capture the full significance of Ellison's millennial rhetoric. In its final sentences, the passage shows just how fully Ellison embraced a fervent American nationalism and, not coincidentally, how closely that vision suited the novel's Cold War context. For, when his narrator speaks of being "linked to all the others in the loud, clamoring semi-visible world" seen "as a fertile field for exploitation by Jack and his kind," he can only be referring to the colonial subjects of European empire. Ellison had long been concerned with the oppression of those people, and as a fellow traveling leftist, he had been eager to indict the imperial incursions of the capitalist states. Here, having abandoned Leninist theory for the creed of American nationalism, and now apparently troubled by the success of Marxism in the decolonizing world, he suggests an alternative stance. (Notably, for the Ellison of the fifties, it is the left who exploits victims of imperialism, while white industrialists—Norton and his kind—merely condescend to them.)

Racism creates a natural affiliation between African Americans and subject people around the globe, his narrator thus admits, but Ellison then goes still further to suggest that, for just that reason, black Americans have a special leadership role in relation to the people of the colonized world. Earlier in his narrative, the narrator famously discovers the obligations of the black elite to the working-class residents of Harlem "who shoot up from the South into the busy city like wild jacks-in-the-box." He implies there that the failure of Negro leadership accounts in part for the hipsterism and juvenile crime Ellison had seen developing in Harlem during the forties (439). The young black men of Harlem are "the stewards of something uncomfortable, burdensome, which they hated because, living outside the realm of history, there was no one to applaud their value and they themselves failed to understand it" (441). If his suggestion there is that the narrator himself bears the responsibility of appreciating and speaking for his inarticulate people, in the epilogue Ellison globalizes that paternalist vision.[62] Black Americans, he suggests, must rise to the defense of American democracy or risk seeing themselves overrun by an angry horde of colonial subjects who in their resentment threaten, like Ras or like the Brotherhood, to destroy both the preeminence of American power and the distinctiveness of African Americans themselves. "We had to say 'yes' to the principle, lest they turn upon us to destroy both it and us?" Strikingly the epilogue puts the "we" defended by the narrator in something much like the place occupied by the white man he assaulted on the street in the novel's opening scene—threatened by the violent dissatisfaction of people who emerge quite suddenly from the "semi-visible world." Extraordinary though it seems, the people of the decolonizing world, play for him the role that Ellison saw the Negro serving for white Americans. The objects of the narrator's defensive paternalism, they are the marginalized and dangerous people who remind him of his special status.

Ellison's epilogue, in short, is a classic variation on the vision of America as redeemer nation—one that must bring democracy to the world or see it destroyed by the legacy of feudal resentments. The "principle" to which the narrator refers is fittingly vague in this context because it cannot be limited to any particular concept, which might appeal equally to all people, but is instead an expression of national identity. At college when he aspired to be an orator, the narrator found his best and most discomforting audience in the former slave Miss Susie Gresham, the "bearer of something warm and vital and all-enduring." As an "old connoisseur of voice sounds, of voices without messages," she challenges the narrator because she listens not to "the mere content of words," but only to the "echoed noise of the promise" that the speaker himself represents (113, 114). Similarly, during his funeral oration for Tod Clifton, when the narrator affirms in the common history of his people something that "wasn't political," something "deeper than protest, or religion," he suitably communicates not ideas, but the incommunicable identity of which he is a vehicle. His audience listens intently, but, "as though looking not at me, but at the pattern of my voice upon the air" (457, 453, 455).

In the epilogue, as the narrator speaks on the lower frequencies implicitly for all Americans, he continues the motif, articulating not ideas so much as a common destiny authorized by a shared history and tracing patterns that, in their mythic and "irrational" resonance, are more powerful than any particular set of ideas. The undefined "principle," in other words, is less, say, the value of democracy itself, than the conviction that the American people are themselves an essentially democratic nation, burdened and blessed therefore with a special mission and fated to pass through episodes of great strife and self-sacrifice in the effort to realize it. Like many a previous voice of that mission, Ellison excoriates his fellow citizens' failure to live up to their destiny. Caught up in defending illegitimate power and pursuing petty satisfactions, they fall prey to the greed and smallness that characterizes the quotidian life of democratic society. But, when they are mindful of their revolutionary origins, and of their historical failure to be worthy of it, they may accept their unique stature, rise to their better selves, and become a light unto the world. Indeed, in asking his readers to maintain both a "plan of living" and an awareness of the "chaos against which that pattern was conceived," Ellison's narrator not only reminds his readers to be wary of intellectual rigidity, he likewise effectively recalls the Jeffersonian demand for the periodic renewal of the tree of liberty with the blood of patriots. He asks Americans, that is, to remain a revolutionary people by keeping always in the forefront of their minds the grandeur of their self-constitution as a nation.

Ellison adds a critical variation to that nationalist rhetoric by suggesting that slavery and the subsequent history of racial domination are the keynotes of U.S. history. His means of doing so, however, so closely aligns the solution to racism and the mission of America that the two are made to seem inextricable. Indeed, when the narrator suggests that African Americans "affirm the principle" and "the plan in whose name we had been brutalized and sacrificed," he revealingly transforms his grandfather's martial rhetoric. For, if men like his grandfather and Tod Clifton and the anonymous riot victim are the novel's warriors and martyrs, the narrator himself occupies the position memorably staked out by Lincoln. He is their eulogist and the interpreter of their meaning to a waiting nation. (Among the last things we learn of Clifton, interestingly, is that he is located in the place from which the narrator ultimately speaks: "Tod Clifton was underground" [460]).

Like the narrator's earlier experience with Tarp's chain and Mary's Sambo doll, the narrator's recommendation to "affirm the principle" and "the plan" thus suggests that African Americans must not only acknowledge, but in some fashion accept and approve the history of racial subjugation. In the context of the complete passage and of Ellison's aspirational nationalism more generally, it becomes clear why. For what Ellison requests is that black Americans trade their own legitimate resentment at being forced to occupy a subordinate position in American life for a willing embrace of the suffering that has been imposed upon them—to in effect, replace bad sacrifice with good. As in the secularized protestant theology from which the vision ultimately descends, the victims of injustice are asked to exchange mere endurance or even justified anger at their subordination into the conscious approval of the place of their suffering in a vision of redemptive destiny. In so doing, Ellison implies, they swap an awareness of the demeaning bargains of civil society for a profound appreciation of the deep contract of the nation's providential history. Black Americans come in this way to resemble the soldiers of the Civil War, who were ultimately celebrated not for their conquests or their immediate political convictions, but, in Whitman's phrase, for their readiness to die "of their own choice, . . . for their own idea." In willingly giving their lives so that the nation might live, they implicitly sanctify America and elevate themselves.

Become President

Several decades later, in a preface to *Invisible Man*, Ellison proposed a fitting analogy to explain his artistic and political inspiration. "If the ideal of achieving a true political equality eludes us in reality," Ellison explained:

There is still the fictional *vision* of an ideal democracy in which the actual combines with the idea and gives us representations of a state of things in which the highly placed and the lowly, the black and the white, the northerner and the southerner, the native-born and the immigrant are combined to tell us of transcendent truths and possibilities . . . . There are, of course, other goals for fiction. Yet, I recalled that during the early, more optimistic days of this republic it was assumed that each individual citizen could become (and should be prepared to become) President. For democracy was considered not only a collectivity of individuals . . . but a collectivity of politically astute citizens who, by virtue of our vaunted system of universal education and our freedom of opportunity, would be prepared to govern (CE 482–83, original emphasis).

Invisible Man by this account looks much like what Ellison's pluralist contemporaries referred to as the myth of the public interest. As counterfactual representations of ideals rooted in shared inheritance, both the pluralist myth and Ellison's novel were meant to guide American citizens and thus to act to elicit a civic behavior that the conditions of liberal democracy might not otherwise encourage. Without demanding a revolutionary change in institutions, or in the distribution of wealth or power, both were expected to lead Americans gradually in the direction of a more democratic world. Both, in short, were supposed to inspire without coercion, and, in encouraging Americans to become their better selves, to help create a more just society. "Unless we continually explored the network of complex relationships which bind us together," Ellison explained in another essay, "we would continue being the victims of various inadequate conceptions of ourselves, both as individuals and as citizens of a nation of diverse peoples" (CE 523). The obvious counterimplication was that, if Americans did appreciate their common history, they would emancipate themselves from their most disabling restraints and rise to a better citizenship.

It is not obvious why, by Ellison's reasoning, the appropriate analogy for this kind of fiction is the presidency, until we recall just how closely Ellison's aims resembles those of the advocates of presidential government. What he demands here and throughout his major writing is what they sought as well: a reassertion of popular sovereignty. Like them, he laments the institutional disenfranchisement of a divided people, demanding that American citizens not only pursue their individual desires but collectively govern themselves. Like them, too, he operates under the nearly mystical assumption that the realization of popular sovereignty—the rebirth of the nation—would be indistinguishable from the defeat of injustice. Though the analogy is only implicit, it seems clear that *Invisible Man* is itself Ellison's model of presidential leadership and that in its claim to speak for all Americans, and, more particularly in its capacity to speak on behalf of the nation's martyrs, the novel gestures to the possibility of an otherwise frustrated national self-rule.

Ellison's presidential analogy thus illuminates the theoretical assumptions that helped inspire his major writing, but, for the same reason, it also highlights the common ground that the tradition of pluralist political theory always shared with the visions of presidential government. Their political implications differed sharply, but the Madisonian tradition of valuing divided power and the Wilsonian tradition of calling for the chief executive to embody the national purpose often shared a common philosophical inspiration. Both were frequently invoked as solutions to the problems of liberal society and more particularly to the grievances created by the fact that the democratic ideology of the United States is continually traduced by an undemocratic state apparatus. If many Progressive defenders of executive leadership had believed that the president could burst the trammels of law and representation to voice the national will, many among the pluralists believed that American citizens could take immediate part in the democratic governance of their world through their membership in voluntary associations. At their most extreme, both made the problem of government and the irritation of politics disappear.

By the latter part of the fifties, the pluralist version of that faith looked ever more doubtful. The consensus among academic political scientists came under increasing assault by critics who pointed out that the ideology of pluralism often concealed the reality of oligarchy or of an ineffectual and bureaucratic government, and those critics sometimes called for the assertion of more active and democratic state power. From the perspective of a growing number of observers during the latter fifties and sixties, Americans appeared in E. E. Schattschneider's resonant phrase at best a "semi-sovereign people."[63] More significantly, perhaps, liberal supporters of the Democratic Party took advantage of a brief recession and of the uncertainties of the Cold War to demand that, as the Kennedy campaign declared, America get moving again. The result was an intense, if brief enthusiasm for executive leadership that erupted across the political spectrum in the early sixties.

During the same years, Ellison was working on the second novel, whose completion would be permanently delayed. His hesitation may have reflected Ellison's unexpressed doubts about the viability of his own most prophetic hopes. For all Ellison's tendency to the homiletic, his increasingly rapturous defense of the possibilities of democracy during the sixties and seventies only rarely concealed his doubt about the chances of its realization. At one point in the midst of the Johnson administration, he explained some of his difficulties in writing by pointing to the massive resistance to desegregation that followed in the wake of *Brown v. Board of Education* and the striking absence of a collective national will it betokened. Explaining that he had been stymied in the effort to imaginatively conceive the national condition that he had so strikingly demonstrated in *Invisible Man*, Ellison concluded his remarks by admitting defeat, saying, "I returned to my novel [in progress]—which, by the way, has as its central incident the assassination of a Senator" (CE 46).

THE MYTH OF THE PUBLIC INTEREST

Summed up in the remark was a pivotal moment in the history of presidential symbolism. In its reference to the regional and legislative power that he, like the advocates of presidential government wished to transcend, Ellison's comment, and the story to which it referred—the part of his incomplete novel published posthumously as *Juneteenth*—conveyed the cruel trivialization of Ellison's hopes. After the grandeur of national martyrdom, there seemed only the confusion of a corrupt Senate. The transition said much about the lowered expectations that accompanied even Ellison's increasingly fervent rhetoric and could speak as well for the profound disappointment in executive leadership many American writers discovered during the sixties.

CHAPTER FOUR

Come Home, America: Vietnam and the

End of the Progressive Presidency

*America, the unterrible country, not susceptible to the Russian
treatment, comprehensible only in bits and pieces.*
                    —Ward Just, A Soldier of the Revolution *(1970)*

*In the old days, when I was doing nothing but trying to stop
the war, we assumed that, whenever the time finally came that
someone who had been through at least some of what we
were enduring sat in Lyndon Johnson's chair, things would
be different.*

                                        —David Harris, Our War *(1996)*

NORMAN MAILER'S 1967 novel *Why Are We in Vietnam?* offers an unorthodox
answer to what may have been the defining question of culture and politics
in the late sixties.[1] Despite its boldly interrogative title, Mailer's book has nothing
to say about foreign policy or the Cold War, and it does not even mention Indochina
until its final lines—in which the reader is informed that the novel's protagonist, a
testosterone-charged Texas teenager named D.J., is due to ship out to Vietnam
the following morning. Avoiding the banal concern with the details of public policy
that he elsewhere dismissed as "housing projects of fact and issue," Mailer instead
traces America's military adventures not to its interests or to its ideology, but to its

barely conscious psychic impulses. "He had come to decide," as *The Armies of the Night* noted a year later, "that the center of America might be insane."[2]

Such thoughts were increasingly prominent, of course, among opponents of the war during the late sixties, perhaps especially so among literary intellectuals whose talents inclined them to emphasize the importance of cultural forces and, with growing frequency, the relative insignificance of more traditionally conceived political factors. "The problem" evident in the war, Allen Ginsberg thus argued, was not in Vietnam, but "here in America"—in a crass and violent society that seemed fated to export its pathologies around the globe—and the overwhelming question the war raised was: "how do we get out of ourselves, our own minds?" So deeply did the evils run, Ginsberg contended, that we might need "to bomb out the entire public consciousness of the USA with LSD or some therapeutic equivalent."[3]

Yet, characteristically, Mailer himself did not exactly indict U.S. aggression per se. Like all his writing, *Why Are We in Vietnam?* relishes the antinomian glamour of violence, and it complains most forcefully about the way the "psychic glug" of a commercial society obscures the elemental truths of combat and struggle. "The country had always been wild," Mailer observes in *The Armies of the Night*. But now, "the existential sanction of the frontier" had given way to "the abstract ubiquitous sanction of the dollar bill" (AN 152, 158), and "the fever had left the blood" (152). By Mailer's account, in other words, it was not that war or aggression themselves were blameworthy. What was wrong with U.S. military action in Vietnam, rather, was that, bureaucratically managed and badly fought, it epitomized the soul of a decadent empire. "America needed the war," Mailer worried. "It would need a war so long as technology expanded on every road of communication, and the cities and corporations spread like cancer" (AN 189).

That point is made most revealingly in the final chapters of *Why Are We in Vietnam?*, which follow D.J. and his best friend Tex on a quest into the wilderness of Alaska's Brooks Range. In the preceding chapters, we have already seen D.J.'s disgusted experience of a deluxe "safari" arranged for corporate bigwigs like his father. Now, in contrast to the callow brutality of that expedition, we see D.J. and Tex venture off into the wilderness without weapons or equipment of any kind, leaving behind the "mixed shit" of civilization to experience the genuine violence of America's last true frontier (200). There the two pause briefly on the threshold of homoerotic combat, only, in the novel's critical moment, to turn anxiously away. "They hung there each of them on the knife of the divide in all conflict of lust to own the other yet in fear of being killed by the other and as the hour went by . . . something in the radiance of the North went into them, and owned their fear, . . . and they were twins, never to be near as lovers again, but killer brothers, owned by something" (219). When the boys return from this experience to camp, they discover themselves under the dominion of their fathers' corrupt world and bound for war. D.J. will be going to Vietnam, in other words, not because he is brutally violent, but because he was not man enough to make himself his friend's lover. That Tex is described as part Native American—of "fearless Eenyen blood"—and a descendant "in the direct line of the heroes of the Alamo" emphasizes the point (219, 177). He stands the fading remnant of a heroic native land, now corrupted by commercialism and abandoned for adventures in foreign parts. The "Indian haunts from Maine to the shore of California," Mailer's novel laments in conclusion, have been "all gutted, shit on, used and blasted" by "the United Greedies of America" (221, 222).

Bleak though that picture looks, however, Mailer revised it sharply in his immediately subsequent book, 1968's renowned work of new journalism *The Armies of the Night*. A comic-heroic celebration of the 1967 march on the Pentagon, *The Armies of the Night* reverses the implications of *Why Are We in Vietnam?* on an almost point-by-point basis. At the center of this latter book is the experience of our first-person narrator and protagonist—"Mailer," the buffoonish antihero, who in his readiness to risk civil disobedience, ultimately rises above his self-absorption and joins the rebellious children of "a dead de-animalized middle class" in a courageous "rite of passage" (280, 279). In their willingness to endure violence and particularly imprisonment, Mailer imagines that he and those young men and women revitalize themselves and reinvigorate a distinctively American history of founding struggles: "Valley Forge, New Orleans in 1812, . . . Sutter's Mill, Gettysburg, the Alamo" (280). Where earlier Mailer had portrayed young machismo falling prey to timidity, then, here he shows middle-aged foolishness rising to admirable courage. Where before he portrayed the dissipation of national character, here he envisions the country reborn in the moral challenge posed·by direct action. "Brood on that country who expresses our will," he ends in peroration. "She is America" (288).

In keeping with this reversal in tone and implication, Mailer also intriguingly turned the current, literary preoccupation with metanarrative experiment in a direction that fit his book's redemptive purpose. *Why Are We in Vietnam?* underlines its depiction of national confusion by raising what, in the theory of postmodern fiction, might be called an ontological question about the narrative's authorship.[4] We are encouraged to wonder whether the book's narrator D.J. may not be, rather than the white teenager he seems, an African American evil genius. "Is this D.J. addressing you a Texas youth for sure," the novel challenges us, "or is he a genius of a crippled Spade up in Harlem making all this shit up?" The question foregrounds Mailer's central and apparently irresolvable concern about the character of his nation and its affinity for either the virtuous frontier ("Indian haunts") or the enslavement of corrupt society (Harlem). In *The Armies of the Night*, however, that question no longer exists. And the particular metanarrative experiment Mailer takes up now—the way his book plays with its definition of "history as a novel" and "the novel as history"—is used instead in the service of the writer's identification with his country. In book 1, "history as a novel" Mailer as character is "a clown of an arriviste baron," bumblingly preoccupied with his personal reputation, exhilarated and abused by the mass media in a way that makes his individual story an apt representation—"a document"—of a confused and privatized county (41, 255). In book 2, "the novel as history," Mailer the writer transforms that embarrassing document into what he calls "a collective novel" by abandoning public reputation for a redemptive encounter with "the interior." Despite the fact that the voice is third person and the subject matter an historic event, we now "enter that world of strange lights and intuitive speculation which is the novel" (255). Though deliberately paradoxical, the point is clear. History and the housing projects of fact are appropriate for an incoherent, media-besotted society, as is the self-preoccupation of the egocentric author. The novel as personal exploration and act of courage, on the other hand, delivers the genuinely collective nation. "For the novel . . . is, when it is good," Mailer declares, "the personification of a vision which will enable one to comprehend other visions better" (219).

In the transition between the two books of *The Armies of the Night*, in short, Mailer dramatizes a transformation that is also evident in the difference between that work as a whole and the immediately preceding *Why Are We in Vietnam?* Although the genius of Mailer's writing comes in his ability to make the drama vivid, the transition itself can be easily summarized. We move from the denunciation of an atomistic, liberal empire to the vision of a virtuous republic characterized by the heroic action of its citizens and by their mutual commitment to their shared national purpose. What Mailer discovers in the march on the Pentagon, and what he suggests must be shared by his readers if the Vietnam War and the evils it epitomizes are to be ended, is a "sharp searing love for his country" that echoes the patriotism sanctified by the Civil War—"as if the ghosts of the Union Dead accompanied them now" (113).

Not surprisingly, then, Mailer echoes, while making far more self-conscious, the ambivalent attitude toward the chief executive that so many of his contemporaries placed at the center of their work. Since the publication of *Advertisements for Myself* in 1959, which he began with the declaration that, "like many another vain, empty, and bullying body of our time," he had imagined himself "running for President these last ten years," Mailer had positioned his distinctive vision of the writer as self-created public combatant in counterpoint to the modern presidency.[5] Before the 1960 presidential election, he had blazed his own path into the undeveloped country of new journalism with a paean to JFK, who he envisioned as the existential hero of a "national psyche which was . . . at last, again, adventurous." Over the course of the first years of the sixties, as he lamented the fact that Kennedy had "lost the way," Mailer cast himself as an alternative figure—a national prophet who spoke directly to the chief executive and reminded the president of his duty "to enrich the real life of his people."[6] Now, in the last years of the decade, he viewed himself as both a rival and an analog to LBJ. At his most bathetic, Mailer announced, he was "Lyndon Johnson's little old *dwarf* alter ego" (49, emphasis in original).

For Mailer, in sum, president and novelist were more explicitly analogous and contending figures than any previous writer had had the temerity to suggest. Both the writer and the chief executive possessed "the responsibility to educate a nation," and each discovered that, "as the power of communication grew larger," his capacity to speak to a common people paradoxically declined. Both were victimized by the mass media, which "wrenched and garbled and twisted and broke one's words," and both struggled desperately to contend with the waves of public opinion (157, 65). "LBJ was the legendary surfboarder of them all" (286).

Yet, if Mailer looks most like LBJ in the first part of *The Armies of the Night*, where he presents himself as at once a brilliant political diagnostician and an insecure publicity hound, it is in the second part of his narrative, as he contrasts his own courage to the cowardice of LBJ and to the failures of the liberal state in general, that paradoxically Mailer most earnestly embraces the presidential imagination. For, the key distinction between the two halves of Mailer's text, and the feature that underlies the earnestness of the second book by contrast to the confusion of the first, is that in the second Mailer revivifies the language of national martyrdom that, since the Civil War, had been central to the elevated visions of executive leadership. In the second book of *The Armies of the Night*, "the novel as history," Mailer suggests that, by pursuing his personal vision of the march on the Pentagon, he is able to pass beyond merely journalistic accounts of political conflict to depict a truth about the protest—its "real climax"—invisible to the mass media (268). That truth is crucially one of a martyrdom suffered beneath the coercive hand of the state and endured, in Mailer's rendition, on behalf of the nation.

Thus, in the final pages of his account of the march, Mailer narrates the fate of a group of Quaker protesters who, up until this moment, have been entirely neglected. After Mailer and the other celebrities and politicos of the march have been released from their own brief encounter with the law, those protestors, who refuse to cooperate with the machinery of the criminal justice system, are placed in solitary confinement and begin a hunger strike. Mailer finds in their suffering—"these naked Quakers on the cold floor of a dark isolation cell in D.C. jail, wandering down the hours in the fever of dehydration"—the "last of the rite of passage" defined by the march as a whole. In their willingness to suffer, those martyrs redeem the circus atmosphere of the protest itself, rising above the clashing ignorant armies referred to by Mailer's title, and more grandly the waywardness of the American nation. "Who was to say they were not saints? And who to say that the sins of American were not by their witness a tithe remitted?" (287). By the same token, Mailer's ability not merely to bring those people to public recognition, but to engage in imaginative empathy with their suffering, redeems his own foolishness, securing his claim that as a writer of fiction he conveys deep truths invisible to the more conventionally minded. He goes "places no history can reach" (287).

In effect, then, Mailer gives us in *The Armies of the Night* a recreation of the visions of national renewal evident in writers as diverse as Whitman, Wright, Ginsberg, and Ellison. Here, much as in *Native Son*, for instance, the prison is the dramatic representation of coercive state power, and its most obscure depths, hidden from the conventions of public discourse, provide the setting for the ultimate mystery of national identity. Here again, too, the freely chosen suffering of martyrs beneath that power betokens a new birth of freedom. Once more, that is, self-chosen sacrifice becomes the means by which an abusive government is to be redeemed from its corruption and reunited with the people who authorize it. What the trial of the Quakers brings home to Mailer is thus the core lesson he delivers on his final page: "the country belonged to the people" (288). In his ability to convey their suffering and its significance, meanwhile, the writer—like the president envisioned by the most ardent defenders of executive power—overcomes his own embarrassments and rises to the prophetic stature by which he presides over the union of state and nation. In effect, Mailer trades his imitation of LBJ for an imitation of the mythic founder of the modern presidency. He becomes, as he suggests, an example of "Lincoln in hippieland" (46).

Yet, if Mailer offers a version of the by now familiar story of the linkage between presidential eloquence and national rebirth, *The Armies of the Night* also represents an important transition, both in Mailer's own career and in the larger history of popular conceptions of executive power. Since the turn of the century, the advocates of presidential leadership had seen it as the prime face of activist government. Invoking the capacity of a powerful administration, guided by enlightened and responsive leaders, to surpass the constraints of representative government and local culture, they had envisioned the presidency as a means to form a national community that would overcome the injustice, along with the parochialism, that seemed endemic to a society governed by commercial freedom and individual liberty. That vision had reached its high water mark in the bold vistas invoked in the rhetoric of the New Frontier and then the Great Society, where the capacity of the federal government both to transform the United States and to convey the blessings of democratic liberty around the globe were advanced with frankly imperial zeal. Coming to office with a determination to reinvigorate the presidential leadership he remembered in FDR, John F. Kennedy declared that the nation needed "a Chief Executive who is the vital center of action in our whole scheme of government," who could "summon his national constituency to its finest hour."[7]

Mailer himself had long been drawn to similar views. For all his cherished renegade status among liberal intellectuals, his first enthusiastic paeans to JFK hit virtually the same notes played by the rhetoricians of the New Frontier who, admiring

Kennedy's ability to "project a mystique," imagined that the new chief executive could use it to reinvigorate a sense of national mission.[8] Although Mailer claimed he was far to the left of such establishment liberals, his own attitudes toward JFK differed little from the rhetoric of New Frontier liberals like Richard Neustadt or Arthur Schlesinger, Jr., who celebrated JFK for his seeming ability to return "heroic leadership" to government.[9] He first celebrated JFK for a presidential campaign and a personal style that appeared to signal a break with conventional party politics and thus to reinvigorate the methods of FDR. (Roosevelt was a "hero," Mailer wrote; Eisenhower "the anti-hero, the regulator.") And like the New Frontier intellectuals, he imagined that Kennedy's readiness to emphasize the risk of Cold War conflict signaled a new hope of national regeneration. "The country and its people must become more extraordinary and more adventurous, or else perish." Indeed, like his more conventionally liberal contemporaries, Mailer invoked executive power for precisely the reasons that progressives had long placed their hope in presidential leadership—the conviction that by articulating the nation's "common danger," the president might overcome the fragmentation built into the political system and reestablish popular sovereignty. Americans had been "leading a double life," divided between "the history of politics which is concrete, factual practical and unbelievably dull" and "a subterranean river of untrapped, ferocious, lonely and romantic desires." Only a heroic president, who could soar above the trivialities of "social legislating" and encourage the "nation to discover the deepest colors of its character," could overcome that divide.[10]

Mailer soon lost his enthusiasm for Kennedy, indicting JFK for his failure to live up to the existential mission that Woodrow Wilson had first described as the president's core responsibility. ("He embodies nothing," Mailer complained, "he personifies nothing."[11]) Along with that enthusiasm departed, too, much of Mailer's excitement about the thrilling dangers of world politics. In this respect, *Why are We in Vietnam?* and *The Armies of the Night* mark a change in the tone of Mailer's writing that was echoed widely among his contemporaries. The fundamental concern with sovereignty and the distaste for conventional representative politics remained. But the orientation of the complaint had changed. Mailer was no longer the bold internationalist, obsessed like his contemporaries in the Kennedy administration with the significance of the Cold War for America's global mission, and had become instead what he described, in an apt phrase, as a "left conservative"—a writer forced to "think in the style of Karl Marx in order to attain certain values suggested by Edmund Burke" (AON 185).

That new Burkean slant to Mailer's social criticism can be seen in almost every aspect of his work—in the fact, for example, that Mailer now showed no interest in the international canvas and the visions of global communion that continued to inspire writers like Thomas Pynchon; or in the way his new veneration of victimized Native Americans took up a theme that had not been prominent among American writers since the twenties (AON 185). But the shift may be most striking in Mailer's newly discovered uxoriousness. Mailer had long cast himself as an antidomestic hipster, of course. His most recent novel before *Why Are We in Vietnam?*, *An American Dream* began with its protagonist (a former congressman who once double dated with JFK), murdering the "Great Bitch" of his wife.[12] But in *The Armies of the Night* Mailer portrays himself as surprised by the awareness that his rediscovered love of country includes a sudden enthusiasm for marital fidelity. Indeed, if it is Mailer's empathy with the Quaker martyrs that enables him to view the march on the Pentagon as a "quintessentially American event," by his own telling, it is his marriage itself that permits and encourages his "love affair with America" and that enables him, through nearly genetic transmission, to perceive the crucial significance of Christianity to American national identity (216, 171). "Some old pagan spirit of her part Swedish blood must have carried Christ through all the Southern exposures of her mixed part Indian blood, crazy American lass" (213). Mailer's love for country and his commitment to his wife turn out to be "damnably parallel" (171).

Similar parallels cropped up through much of the cultural expression that responded to the Vietnam War, where marriage often serves as the prime metaphor for the obligations of citizenship and the bonds of nationality—demands that American writers in similarly Burkean fashion would increasingly view as inseparable, if not indistinguishable forces).[13] Suggesting that "nations were like people, lovable and wonderful in their simple existence," for example, Mailer's sometime antagonist John Updike used the same analogy invoked by his rival. "He was pro-American," Updike remarked of himself, "in the sense that he was married to America and did not wish a divorce."[14] The force of that analogy, in Updike's usage as in Mailer's, was to counter the abuses of liberal government and the confusions of political conflict with an appeal to personal loyalties that appeared more profound than matters of ideology. If nations could be understood as people (rather presumably than as states), they could elicit obligations that seemed more profound than "the unaccountable influence," as Updike put it in his relatively late turn against the Vietnam War, "of our party politics upon decisions vindicated in human blood."[15]

For Updike, as for Mailer, in short, opposing the war meant not merely objecting to a particular set of policies; it involved as well an alteration in what seemed the appropriate terms by which to evaluate political decisions. For much of the twentieth century, American liberals had criticized the inadequacies of "party politics" by appealing to the grandeur of transcendent principles and a suprapersonal state. During the latter sixties Mailer and Updike spoke for many who now viewed that tendency as a terrible mistake. Against the evils of an unresponsive government and the obscurities of party competition, they would now defend the demands of an avowedly provincial nationality. Casting the nation as a body alternative and antagonistic to the state, they would with growing frequency seek to elevate the connections of family and blood above the errors of ideology and the coercion of political institutions.

To the extent writers like Mailer and Updike invoked presidential leadership, then—or called, as Mailer did in *The Armies of the Night*, on the rhetorical structures that had been used to legitimize executive power—they would do so in ways that managed both to preserve and to fundamentally alter the manner in which such leadership was understood. As before, presidential power would seem valuable for its apparent capacity to assert popular sovereignty against an unresponsive government and over the vulgarities of party competition. But its main antagonist would increasingly seem the federal government itself, and the role of executive leadership would often be to reassert against state abuses the distinctive and exclusive demands of American identity.

The Soul of America

Attitudes like Mailer's and Updike's were in fact an increasingly prominent feature of American discourse on the Vietnam War, much of which began from the assumption that, as one opponent of the war put it, "the problem of Vietnam is the problem of the soul of America."[16] Over the course of the sixties and early seventies, many commentators echoed Ginsberg to suggest that U.S. foreign policy and, still more, the country's military strategy revealed a profound ugliness at the heart of American civilization. A few novelists, like Gore Vidal and Robert Coover, extended the point to suggest that the executive tyranny evident especially in the Nixon administration was the inevitable consequence of the illusions of an increasingly imperialistic nationalism.[17] But such views always represented a minority perspective, and they would increasingly be answered with the contention that in aim and method the war represented not merely an expression, but also a betrayal of America—and not so much of the country's stated principles or ideals, as of its bedrock national identity. As the protagonist of Robert Stone's *A Flag for Sunrise* put it, in the wake of Vietnam, "our secret culture, the non-exportable one" appeared to be "dying."[18]

Though in less melodramatic terms, a similar anxiety ran through much of the public commentary on the evident disaster of the war. In the era's paradigmatic attack on the foreign policy elite, for example, David Halberstam reinvigorated the complaint of the old isolationist right and traced the origins of America's misguided involvement in Vietnam to the fact that "the best and brightest" had believed themselves "linked to one another rather than to the country." Paul Goodman raised a similar implication. Taking the war to be representative of the evils of a corrupt order, Goodman suggested that the nation had culpably permitted itself to be captured by an imperial bureaucracy. "I would almost say that my country is like a conquered province with foreign rulers, except that they are not foreigners and we are responsible for what they do."[19] Despite their other substantial differences, both Goodman and Halberstam suggested, in short, that the political evils of the Vietnam War could be best understood less as the creation of a misguided foreign policy or even as the consequence of political or economic interests than as a kind of cultural sin—an elite betrayal of national obligations in favor of the spurious universalism of imperial power. The United States, each implied, was being governed by outlanders.

With the growing signs of the inability of the United States to maintain its commitment to a global struggle against Communism, similar, once marginal, views gained traction among influential political advocates and policymakers. During the latter sixties, Democratic and some Republican politicians, along with mainstream opinion leaders, showed new appreciation for foreign policy realists like George Kennan and Hans Morgenthau, who sought to limit the irresponsible extension of U.S. power by reference to robust national interests that cut against the demands of ideological causes or moral campaigns. The shifting ground of mainstream opinion was nowhere more evident that in the famed appearance Kennan made in 1966 before the Senate Foreign Relations Committee, when Senator J. William Fulbright recruited him as part of a public relations effort to resist the snowballing war effort. Given a national pulpit by Fulbright, Kennan used the opportunity to puncture the grandiosity of Cold War imperialism. LBJ had defended U.S. engagement in Vietnam by appealing to a universal demand for freedom and democracy. "We fight for values and we fight for principles, rather than territory or colonies."[20] Kennan responded by suggesting that a foreign policy not rooted in the defense of the nation was bound to expand toward chaos, and he invoked the wisdom of John Quincy Adams in support of a knowingly exclusive nationalism. America "goes not abroad . . . in search of monsters to destroy," Kennan quoted Adams. "She is the champion and vindicator only of her own."[21]

A defense of our own would increasingly become the prevailing theory of U.S. foreign policy in the last years of America's engagement in Vietnam—most prominently in the realpolitik advanced during the Nixon years by Henry Kissinger. During the height of the Cold War (and, still more, during its recent twenty-first-century reassertion of global hegemony), the United States echoed earlier imperial powers in aspiring after a peaceful authority that would transcend the concern with borders and territory in the name of universal values—in Charles S. Maier's phrase, a "utopia" of "free worldwide transactions." But, with the United States, as with earlier empires, Maier points out, "when the utopia is punctured, the logic of territory reasserts itself."[22] During the latter sixties and seventies, as U.S. policymakers rediscovered that logic, their contemporaries among critical intellectuals simultaneously rediscovered the complementary logic of cultural difference and began to emphasize its power to override political ideology or economic interests.

Frances FitzGerald expressed the widely shared view in her influential study *Fire in the Lake*, which in its reference to the long history of Indochina argued that the ideological and material causes of the Cold War were but an epiphenomenal distraction to the more salient force of Vietnamese nationalism. The Vietnamese had "a different moral imagination than we have," FitzGerald contended. It was neither possible nor desirable to make a "direct translation" between "the basic intellectual grammar" of the two, profoundly different countries. Fulbright spoke more directly to LBJ, advising him to abandon the war. The Vietnamese, he claimed, were "not our kind of people."[23]

Kennan, FitzGerald, and Fulbright all sought to counter the crusading arrogance that had assumed a predominant place in U.S. foreign policy since the Kennedy inauguration. But their views, which were echoed frequently during and long after the war—and which would be reemphasized by the Nixon administration, even as it intensified the conflict—could also be used, of course, to vindicate American failure and to encourage a renewed appreciation for the allegedly nonexportable qualities of American culture. Defending the inevitable course of Vietnamese anti-colonialism and of the need for the "narrow flame of revolution to cleanse the lake of Vietnamese society," FitzGerald viewed the war less as a political conflict than as a cultural struggle that would culminate in a restoration of Vietnamese national integrity. The victory of the NVA, and the establishment of "revolutionary community" was "the only way the Vietnamese of the south . . . [could] restore their country and their history to themselves" (442). Many among her contemporaries began to view the U.S. side of the war in parallel terms, casting it less as a disastrous foreign policy error, or as a brutal, but failed exercise of imperial power, than as a grievous self-alienation that would be overcome only when Americans repudiated their universalist aspirations and rediscovered their special inheritance. Even an avowed radical like Susan Sontag—who in 1966 had declared, "choking with shame and anger," that the United States was "a criminal, sinister country"—returned from her journey to Hanoi two years later wondering whether it might still be possible to "revalidate the tarnished ideal of patriotism."[24] After withdrawal and the fall of Saigon, such inclinations grew only stronger. As Loren Baritz contended in his oft cited history, the United States had failed in Vietnam because, at bottom, the war had been "foreign to America's genius." "What we must learn" from the experience, he argued, was "not tactics or strategy, not technique, but who we are, what our culture requires."[25]

Sentiments like Baritz's help explain why so many people spoke in the late sixties and early seventies of "bringing the war home" and why the exhortation became such a compelling way of referring to the conflict.[26] For the Weatherman faction of SDS, which coined the phrase in 1969 and made it sensational during its "Days of Rage" protests in Chicago that year, "bringing home the war" was conceived as part of a "worldwide struggle" against "U.S. imperialism."[27] But for many of their contemporaries, the phrase was appealing for its ability to articulate a different, but more widely shared intuition—that U.S. forces were not just imperial, but by the same token, troublingly distant and illegitimately separated from the awareness and intentions of a fragmented citizenry. "The nation was living . . . in the dissociated state of a foreign and incomprehensible war," Stanley Cavell later explained, neatly capturing a diagnosis repeated on countless occasions at the time, and one commonly assumed to point to a fundamental crisis in American political culture.[28] "The underlying problems of our society" had been pushed "farther and farther from daily experience and daily consciousness," Philip E. Slater concurred, so that "the mass of the population" had lost "the knowledge, skill, resources, and motivation necessary to deal with them."[29] This was the sense in which George McGovern called on the rhetoric when he famously urged his fellow citizens to "Come Home, America," recalling his countrymen not just from the tragic distractions of Indochina but urging them to return to a national mission and an invigorated citizenship he feared lost beneath imperial decline.[30]

In retrospect, much about the complaint against dissociation appears doubtful. It seems unlikely that Americans in the 1960s were less aware, as Slater suggested, of the underlying problems of their society than predecessors or successors. Compared to when one might reasonably ask? Nor is it clear that a more engaged citizenry would make for a more just or judicious foreign policy (the Spanish American War, for example, was provoked at a time of record voter participation) or, as many appeared to assume, that the mere fact of greater civic engagement would itself resolve the intense, domestic conflicts over the war. The underlying premise of the argument from dissociation was that the United States had slipped into the Vietnam War in a fit of distraction or of unconsidered moral reformism. But neither assumption fits the historical evidence, which suggests rather that several administrations managed to convince themselves and the American public that support for the South Vietnamese regime was morally admirable, key to the vital national interests of the United States, and politically and militarily feasible. If anything, the Vietnam War was enormously popular in the United States precisely because of the strong national consensus that had emerged out of World War II and that had been solidified by nearly universal commitment to the cause of anti-Communism. Indeed the war coincided not with the fragmentation of the American public, but with a peak in civic participation and political agreement. As Robert Putnam has shown, on any number of measures, "engagement in community affairs and the sense of shared identity and reciprocity had never been greater in modern America" than they were during the mid-sixties.[31]

In retrospect, then, it seems clear that U.S. engagement in Indochina owed more to association than dissociation and that, as is usually the case with wars, until it became clear that the United States was losing, Vietnam acted only to deepen national consensus and to intensify the power and prestige of political leadership.

But the notion that the Vietnam War could be traced to the dissociated state of the American public was deeply appealing nevertheless, at least in part because it plugged the conflict into a well established political and moral narrative and because it therefore explained the disaster of the war in familiar terms. For, the complaint against dissociation was a version of the long-standing suspicion that liberal freedoms were inimical to good citizenship, and the conviction that it explained the debacle of the Vietnam War was a version of the corollary assumption that the most pressing problems facing the United States could be best understood as crises of sovereignty. "We pride ourselves on being a 'democracy,' " Slater wrote, "but we are in fact slaves. We submit to an absolute ruler"—"technology"—"whose edicts and whims we never question."[32] "We aren't fit to rule ourselves," a character similarly worries in *Couples*, Updike's contemporaneous effort to trace the crisis epitomized by Vietnam to the errors of New Frontier liberalism. "So bring on emperors, demigods, giant robots, what have you" (138).

Comments like Slater's and Updike's, along with the comparable remarks of Halberstam and Goodman, point toward a significant premise that informed many critical responses to Vietnam. All implied that the war flourished not on the assertion, but on the absence of the nation's collective will—or worse, on its distracted, undirected exercise. "Intent," Slater lamented, seemed "to have nothing to do with" U.S. military strategy in Vietnam, or with any of the public policies that pretended to address the country's most intractable problems. "Power is deployed," Andrew Hacker agreed, but "purpose is absent." Like their predecessors in the genre, the critics of dissociation usually found the source of that absence of sovereign will in the prevalence of a divided and individualistic citizenry distracted by the toils and pleasures of commerce from their national obligations. "War is not regarded as a dread emergency in which each does his bit," Goodman thus complained, "but as part of the ongoing business of society in which fighting and dying are usual categories of the division of labor."[33] In response, they frequently implied, as Mailer did, that the reassertion or rediscovery of collective will would itself be enough to resolve the nation's fundamental problems.

That was in any case the avowed position of unabashed elitists like Kennan who celebrated America's heroic national mission without having much fondness for either representative democracy or individual liberties. According to Kennan, the *national interest*—the interest, that is, of the country as a whole"—should take precedence over the "egocentricity of the participants in the American domestic-political struggle," just as, ideally, "hierarchy and authority" would take precedence over the "compromise and manipulation" that characterized civil society.[34] But analogous views existed among thinkers who, unlike Kennan, characterized themselves as liberals or leftists and who were less prepared than he was to advocate aristocratic rule. Sontag, for instance, explained U.S. policy by referring to a "superficial consensus made possible by the strongly apolitical character of a decentralized electorate" and implied the need for the deeper consensus that presumably would be created by a less decentralized citizenry. Morgenthau spoke similarly. While he denounced LBJ as "the Julius Caesar of the American Republic" and complained that Johnson had betrayed "the national ethos," Morgenthau also suggested that such imperial abuses had only been possible because of a general condition of civic decline—evident in "the disengagement of the citizens from the purposes of the government" and "the decomposition of those ties of trust and loyalty that link citizen to citizen and the citizens to government." Seen in this light, the war was but a symptom of a deeper evil. "The very identity of America" was in crisis.[35]

The lament was recapitulated almost obsessively during the late sixties and early seventies. The United States had become "an ungovernable nation," Andrew Hacker argued, for instance, because it demanded "no sense of national loyalty" and therefore no longer possessed "that spirit which transforms a people into citizenry and turns territory into a nation." Michael Walzer concurred, tracing the core problems of American life to the fact that its politics had become spectatorial. The liberal state had "simply outgrown the human reach and understanding of its citizens," and government had become "something to watch" a piece of theater characterized by an "aura of magic and mystification." Ordinary people were left feeling "compromised, anxious, guilty, impotent" and "the life of the citizen" grew ever more "flat, two-dimensional, marked by private and social concerns, but never heightened . . . by political aspiration." Baritz later summarized the common wisdom: the United States had become "a nation without citizens."[36]

Such indictments resembled the complaints that had long been made against liberal democracy, of course. Echoing Mailer, however, the new generation of communitarian and civic republican thinkers exemplified by Walzer gave the charge an important new turn by finding the cause of American decadence not merely in the complacency of a self-interested people, but in their very susceptibility to the ideological and institutional reform proposed by earlier generations of liberal and Progressive leaders. That "we went to war in Vietnam in the name of ideas, of principles, of abstractions," Baritz thus argued was precisely the problem because it encouraged a "sentimental imperialism" and, then, a ruthless frustration when the world resisted American will.[37] Walzer had already made a similar point. Suggesting that it was the specious claim to be acting on principle or in the name of impersonal obligations, that had created America's imperial crisis, Walzer proposed to do away with such mystifications and to emphasize instead what he claimed was the true core of citizenship—allegiance not to ideals or states, but to people. The idea of the sovereignty of the state was "no more than a venerable superstition," Walzer argued. Genuine "commitments" were not to such "vague and inclusive entities," nor to moral abstractions, but first and foremost "to other men" from whom principles were learned and by whom they were enforced.[38]

In essence, the claim formalized an intuition that Mailer had come up with during his experience in the 1967 march on Washington, when he had reveled in the realization that politics "existed in the nerves and cells of the people . . . rather than in the sanctity of the original idea." So it is fitting that the ultimate desiderata for Walzer turns out to be, much as for Mailer, Sontag, or Baritz, the creation of what Walzer called "an authentic patriotism." For all, the idea of collective membership promised to solve the problems of conflict and alienation and to hold the key to otherwise seemingly intractable policy dilemmas. Each would find an answer to political crisis in the determination to put loyalty first.[39]

The irony of such arguments, of course—apart from the fact that, as Mailer recognized, they contested liberal imperialism with a traditionally conservative appeal to national allegiance—was that, even so, they shared an important set of terms with the rhetoric that had been used to justify the creation of an imperial presidency. Critics like Mailer, Sontag, and Walzer all hoped that a revived citizenship and an authentic patriotism might be turned against the abuses of executive power. Yet the decadent conditions they saw in the American public—alienation, isolation, powerlessness, passivity—were nearly identical to the failings indicted by the reformers of the Progressive Era or that had been excoriated by the rhetoricians of the New Frontier and that led each to call for an extension of presidential power. Fittingly, then, like Mailer or, in a different fashion, like Mailer's contemporaries in the New Left, the critics of dissociation sometimes showed themselves drawn to the appeal of executive leadership. In his critical history of the imperial presidency, for example, Arthur Schlesinger, Jr., repeated the widely shared complaint against civic decline. Having ostensibly renounced his own earlier enthusiasm for a heroic vision of presidential leadership, Schlesinger now claimed to realize the way the modern presidency had culminated in an imperial office, and he worried that the "spirit of the American people" might no longer be equal to the demands of self-government. "A large praetorian bureaucracy," Schlesinger complained, "cuts off the nation from the President and the President from the nation."[40] And yet, precisely because, on this view, the ultimate problem with executive tyranny was that it lacked the backing of a clearly articulated popular will, Schlesinger did not so much reject as reiterate his call for the predominance of presidential power. Although he now claimed to realize that executive power could be used for evil as well as good purposes, "a strong presidency" remained in Schlesinger's view all the more "necessary to hold a spinning and distracted society together."[41]

A similar ambivalence was evident in much of the American commentary on the war. Morgenthau, for instance, first denounced LBJ as an emperor, and recommended (much as had the young Woodrow Wilson, before his discovery of the possibilities of the presidency) that the United States abandon its constitutional design in favor of parliamentary government. But he immediately followed that recommendation with an alternative invocation of presidential leadership that

COME HOME, AMERICA

echoed almost precisely the vision of the mature Woodrow Wilson, and, not inci- dentally, that of Schlesinger as well. It was up to the chief executive, Morgenthau claimed in this guise, to be the "molder of the national will, the educator of the people, the guardian of its interests, and the protagonist of its ideals, . . . the incar- nation of the nation-in action." In "that noble and vital mission," Morgenthau charged, LBJ had "completely failed," making him sadly "ineffective even in his dealings with Congress."[42] It was now as if Johnson had not been too much a Caesar, but not imperial enough.

A similar reversal can be glimpsed in the trajectory that led George McGovern to urge the nation home. McGovern had first spoken prominently against the Viet- nam War as a senator, when, in a celebrated speech he charged his colleagues with abandoning their public responsibilities before an arrogant executive. The "cruelest, the most barbaric, and the most stupid war in our national history," McGovern contended to his fellow senators, continued because Congress had allowed its constitutional authority "to slip out of our hands until it now resides behind closed doors . . . [in] the basement of the White House."[43] McGovern based his argument on a whiggish appeal to the deliberative and law-making responsibili- ties of the legislature and on the constitutional principle of the separation of powers. When he became a presidential candidate, however, McGovern put aside that constitutional emphasis and, speaking above the heads of his colleagues, ad- dressed the American people directly. By implication, the source of, and answer to, the country's problems now lay less in the behavior of their public servants than in the character of the nation itself. "Together," McGovern exhorted, "we will call America home to the ideals that nourished us in the beginning."[44] Envisioning a renewed compact between the president and the people, McGovern suggested in effect that he would be a leader who would use the power and mission of the chief executive to repair the injuries created by presidential government.

Stuck inside His Own Skin

The question that motivated thinkers like Walzer—of what might count as authentic patriotism and of how it might counteract the weakness of liberal citizenship and the arrogance of the liberal state—were at the heart of a wide range of American writing during the latter sixties and seventies. The concern was evident not only in the autobiographical dramas of public personalities like Schlesinger, Mailer, and Sontag, but in a host of novels and films that frequently responded to the anguish of the Vietnam War with various subtle and not so subtle allegorical fictions. Ward Just, for example, writing his first novel *A Soldier of the Revolution* after his stint as one of the legendary journalists of the war, transferred the issues raised by Vietnam to the South American altiplano where he recast the

conflict as a battle between U.S. economic missionaries and indigenous revolu-
tionaries. The protagonist of his novel, an American aid worker named Reardon,
must learn not only that the modernization theory of U.S. liberalism is an imperial
creed (akin to St. Paul), but that, to the extent he seeks to bring aid or development
of any kind, even radio, to the region's impoverished people, he is complicit in its
evils. What is most terrible about the United States, Reardon discovers in the passage quoted in the epigraph above, is precisely that it is unterrible and unsuscepti-
ble to the Russian treatment. Lacking a homeland and a national soul, it destroys
itself and imposes its shallow materialism on its resentful subjects around the
world. Salvation can only come for the indigenous victims of U.S. power, then,
with the reestablishment of territorial and cultural boundaries—when the Indian
civilization of the altiplano is free of "commerce, living a life of its own, unconnected
with anything except the land it occupied" (40).

Similar ways of thinking could be applied, of course, not just to native peoples
who opposed the incursion of the metropolis, but to Americans themselves, who
might now appear in the mode suggested by Paul Goodman—as the indigenous
victims of their own imperial power. That prospect was only briefly hinted at in
novels like *A Soldier of the Revolution*, which left merely implicit the suggestion that
the United States would be a better country if it were somehow comprehensible as
a unified whole. But it assumed the foreground in the sudden vogue beginning
during the late seventies for stories about the trials of U.S. soldiers and returning
veterans. If those stories responded most immediately to a new public sympathy
for the pain of American servicemen (and, to some degree, to a conservative public
relations offensive against opponents of the war), they were also plainly intended
to make retrospective sense of what was widely acknowledged to be a senseless
war—to articulate the sources of U.S. policy and its failures and, more significantly,
to resolve the domestic conflicts and ideological crisis occasioned by American
defeat. With striking regularity, they did so with tales of the suffering of soldiers
who were coerced and abused by an imperial bureaucracy and abandoned in a
foreign land. In stories of the mistreatment of the soldier by the state, American
writers and filmmakers thus offered what one of their number, Philip Caputo, aptly
described as "therapy . . . for a wounded nation."[45]

Caputo's widely admired memoir, *A Rumor of War* can be taken for a paradigmatic version of that story. A recollection of his service as a lieutenant in the 3rd
Marine Division during 1965 and 1966, when he was a platoon commander among
the first U.S. ground troops in the war, Caputo's narrative works by emphasizing
the gulf between the awful events the memoir describes and their later, therapeutic
translation into a coherent "story about the war"—a transition in short between
Caputo the soldier and Caputo the writer that is not unlike the comparable transition, between Mailer the politician and Mailer the writer, that organizes *The Armies
of the Night* (xiii). In its account of the young lieutenant's combat experience, the

memoir foregrounds Caputo's gradual disenchantment as his encounter with the miseries of war progressively undermines his belief in martial heroism and his conviction in the rightness of America's cause. "We had believed we were there for a high moral purpose. But somehow our idealism was lost, our morals corrupted, and the purpose forgotten" (345).

In its composition itself, however, and in Caputo's frequently drawn parallels to the Bible, Shakespeare, and the poets of World War I, the memoir emphasizes a counterprocess of what might be called resacralization, as the genuine value of literary expression is substituted for the false appeal of political ideology. In the painful effort of writing his story (a process that he notes "took as long . . . as it did for the United States to fight the Vietnam War"), Caputo views himself as "shaping enduring art out of the shapeless muck of experience" (347, 355).

In this fashion, *A Rumor of War* dramatizes the writer's emancipation—his triumph as an artist over his dehumanization as a soldier. But also and by the same token, it depicts his liberation from the ideology of the New Frontier and more broadly from the claims of the state in general. "I was finished with governments and their abstract causes," Caputo recounts at the memoir's climax. "I would never again allow myself to fall under the charms and spells of political witch doctors like John F. Kennedy" (332). The transition requires, however, not merely a preference for art over public rhetoric; it also hinges on a narrative design by which Caputo's identification with his fellow soldiers replaces his deference to political authority and his mystification by ideological visions. Like nearly every other text in the literature of Vietnam, *A Rumor of War* foregrounds the suffering of combat soldiers and contrasts it to the bureaucratic insensibility of the higher command and the cravenness of the nation's civilian leadership. Like nearly every other such text as well (at least among those published after the revelation of My Lai), it emphasizes the gulf that separates the veterans of combat from everyone else by depicting both the soldiers' suffering and the brutality they display when, maddened with anger and fear, they terrorize helpless civilians. In Caputo's memoir, however, those elements are arranged in a design of unusual dramatic clarity and that clarity is useful for our purposes for the way it reveals the common ground Caputo's story shares with other, less avowedly skeptical narratives of national destiny.

The pivotal passage in that narrative structure occurs when the young Lieutenant Caputo is subjected to court martial, and ultimately acquitted, for actions that he acknowledges amount legally to war crimes. In a moment of rage, after a long period of inconclusive and terrifying combat, Lieutenant Caputo has exceeded his authority and knowingly sent subordinates to kill two young men who, on slight evidence, he suspects of being Viet Cong. When he is charged with murder (and with subsequently concealing the crime), Caputo admits the formal accuracy of the charges and acknowledges the fact that they testify to the demoralizing effects of fighting a war against irregular forces shielded by a civilian population. But, while he affirms his moral responsibility, Caputo also denies his legal accountability and expresses his outraged contempt for the "precious law" of the military bureaucracy (327). He cannot justly be tried because, while his actions were indeed illegal, they merely epitomized the criminal nature of U.S. policy itself: "the war in general and U.S. military policies in particular were ultimately to blame" (330). In effect, Caputo appeals to the doctrine of sovereign immunity. In Vietnam, he was acting on the commands of the state and as a "reflection" of the will of the people (xxi). He is not therefore individually guilty, but the representative of a collective guilt ("we had killed the wrong man") (321). And that crucial fact is only emphasized by the moral and epistemological ambiguity ("neither a lie nor the truth") of the charges at the center of his trial (330). His court martial emphasizes, in other words, the impossibility of measuring the will of the nation by the narrow terms and methods of statutory law—a legal code that, from this implicit perspective, the people itself has ultimately authored and whose fetters now constrain its self-recognition.

In short, the legal drama that provides a climax for *A Rumor of War* serves virtually the same function that analogous scenes play in *The Armies of the Night* or *Native Son*. In each case, a bold transgression of the law both testifies to the illegitimacy of the existing political order and, in shattering the restraints of a corrupt legal structure, prepares the way for a revivified expression of sovereignty. As the victim of an abusive state, then, Caputo, along with his fellow soldiers plays much the same part as Bigger Thomas or Mailer's Quakers. All are martyrs whose suffering dramatizes the perverse distortion in law and policy of the nation's sovereign will and whose suffering thereby gestures toward its redemption. This is the implication of Caputo's title, as the epigraph that provides its context from the book of Matthew makes clear: "ye shall hear of wars and rumors of wars . . . . Then shall they deliver you up to be afflicted and shall put you to death. . . . But he that shall endure unto the end shall be saved." As Caputo subsequently explained, it was also the central premise of his memoir's self-consciously artful design:

> I tried to give meaning by turning myself into a kind of Everyman, my experiences into a microcosm of the whole. My own journey, from the false light of youthful illusions, through a descent into evil, and then into a slow, uncertain ascent toward a new and truer light of self-knowledge, I hope, reflects our collective journey. Our heroes were men like Walt Levy [Caputo's admirable fellow officer, slain in combat seeking to rescue another marine], who, in his act of shining self-sacrifice, showed that we can rise to the better angels in our nature even in conditions where it is all too easy to succumb to our demons. (355)

The collective journey invoked here is, of course, the path of the American nation. (As in all the major literature and film of the Vietnam War produced in the

United States, the Vietnamese themselves, and certainly the forces of the NLF and the NVA are almost entirely absent.) Its collective journey involves not only a return from the "moral no-man's-land" of battle, but, as in the classic literature of executive power, a transition from the exercise of coercive force to the national self-dedication symbolized by martyrdom—a shift in emphasis, that is, from the demonic face of the warrior exemplified by the young Caputo himself to the angelic self-sacrifice represented by Walt Levy and his fellow fallen soldiers.

In Caputo's telling, that journey likewise coincides with a return from imperial errors to a renewed sense of national identity and, by the same token, a movement beyond the ideological conviction and political disagreement that Caputo views as the underlying cause of the war and that he sees as continuing, in the years after U.S. withdrawal, to poison domestic life. In both the advocates of U.S. policy and strikingly in its opponents alike, Caputo sees only "smug righteousness" and an undemocratic willingness to abuse the nation's victimized soldiers. "The war was fought by the children of the slums, of farmers, mechanics, and construction workers. The debate was waged by elites" (349). When Caputo speaks of being done with governments and their abstract causes, then, he implicitly makes his own story anticipate a vision of the nation freed from the parasite of an imperial state and healed of the fruitless, internal dissension that its power has created. In discovering the forgotten martyrdom of the veteran, he suggests, Americans will overcome their falsely political divisions and abandon abstract ideologies for the concrete loyalties of national identity.

As the passage above clarifies, Caputo's own part in this therapeutic drama is directly analogous to Mailer's in *The Armies of the Night*. Like Mailer's, Caputo's stance depends on the premise that literature (because it is not "debate") surpasses merely political sources of disagreement, going beyond the disputing armies of ideological conflict. And like Mailer, Caputo legitimizes that stance by ultimately positioning himself less as the story's central martyr than as the prime witness to those victims typified by Walt Levy, whose ultimate sacrifice transcends and redeems the writer's own less noble service. While Caputo's authority is necessarily legitimized by his experience of war, then, his primary role is to be the prophetic voice (the "battle singer") of the story's true martyrs and therefore the crucial intermediary who conveys their meaning to a divided nation (355). It is fitting then that Caputo, though less directly than Mailer, also positions himself as a latter-day Lincoln and that he caps his analysis with an invocation of the first inaugural address ("better angels of our nature") in which Lincoln established the sanctity of the Union by appealing to "the mystic chords of memory, stretching from every battlefield and patriot grave to every living heart and hearthstone all over this broad land." *A Rumor of War* recounts Caputo's emancipation from presidential witch doctors, but in replacing the black magic of the state with the white magic of a national literature, it enables Caputo to play the role established by Lincoln himself. Like Mailer and like McGovern, in short, he becomes a presidential figure who contends against the evils of presidential government.

Most of the American writers who responded to the Vietnam War avoided the narrative coherence and stark moral definition apparent in *A Rumor of War*. But the attitudes that assume dramatic form in Caputo's memoir are so widely evident in the prominent literature of the era that they suggest an emerging consensus among America's intellectual elite about the proper attitudes toward both the war and the larger problems of state power the conflict raised. That ideology and political argument were to be scorned, for example, and that they were trivial beside the enormity of military disaster and the deep cultural forces that disaster revealed was, for example, a virtually stock attitude among the era's most celebrated writers. Policy debates and political disagreement struck Michael Herr, for example, as "political, square, innocent" beside the "blood consciousness" shared by those who experienced Vietnam at first hand. "We all had roughly the same position on the war," Herr explained. "We were in it."[46] That, by the same token, the war was not a political conflict so much as a spiritual trial for the American people was an equally prominent assumption—as, too, was the, often faint, hope that a divided nation might ultimately throw off an abusive state bureaucracy to discover a renewed national consensus built on the martyrdom of its soldiers.

Though with less drama or certainty, most of these assumptions appear, for example, in the major novels that John Updike wrote during the late sixties and early seventies, as he turned away from a war that, like Caputo, he had once supported. In *Couples* and, with still greater urgency, in *Rabbit Redux*, Updike built intensely complex narratives around the simple metaphor he proposed to explain his loyalty to America. Each novel took marriage as the emblem of national bonds that extended deeper than mere political conviction or legal obligation, and each used sexual freedom and divorce to epitomize the civic decadence that arose alongside the relentless expansion of the liberal state—as with "the Roman subjects all over the world in the period of the Roman empire."[47] In the latter book in particular, Updike arrived at a resolution that would come to seem common wisdom in much of the subsequent writing of the seventies. For, like *A Rumor of War*, *Rabbit Redux* can be concisely described as a tale of the humiliation and redemption of the liberal, its title almost explicitly casting that transformation as a return from sickness to health. When the novel begins, its protagonist—the erstwhile pseudobeatnik Harry Angstrom—is a flag-waving defender of U.S. involvement in Vietnam, an intensely committed ideological partisan, and a sexual adventurer, recently separated from his wife Janice (whose significance is underscored by the fact that she is described as an "Indian" and a "squaw"). By the novel's conclusion, he will have gratefully surrendered both his erotic and his political passions in favor of a gratifyingly asexual rapprochement with his spouse. Though his resolution is nowhere near so clean or so certain, Updike's narrative is, then, quite similar to Caputo's. Like *A Rumor of War*, *Rabbit Redux* describes a longing to return from foreign entanglements to what Harry nostalgically thinks of as "the old world of heraldic local loyalties."[48]

In *Couples*, Updike had already sketched the imperial conditions that would make such a narrative compelling. Tracing the growth of its small town New England setting to "the ubiquity of the federal government" and to the state's subsidization of suburban expansion, *Couples* mourns the way "federal grants" and personal license have combined to kill off the tradition of New England direct democracy. "There was . . . talk now of representative town meeting" (387). A still more revealing complement to this lament comes when Piet, who as a carpenter-cum-general contractor has fallen into the very suburban development he despises, worries over the way his "dreams without his volition began to transpose themselves into reality" (50). The danger of that phenomenon becomes especially apparent when Piet visits a job site to discover a black construction worker bulldozing an Indian burial ground. "By no extension of his imagination could Piet believe that he had helped cause this man and machine to be . . . churning and chuffing and throttling here. . . . He felt between himself and the colored man a continental gulf, the chasm between a jungle asking no pity and a pampered rectilinear land coaxed from the sea" (83). The corollary of representative government and federal power becomes here, in other words, not merely the vertiginous extension and dissemination of agency, but the simultaneous displacement of what the novel elsewhere invokes as "native land"—by both unwitting racial integration and a literally global network of commercial association.

What Piet discovers in *Couples*, in other words, closely resembles what Harry will eventually learn in *Rabbit Redux*—that Cold War liberalism's determination to export capitalism and democracy around the globe appears incompatible with a devotion to native loyalties and civic virtue. In *Couples*, there is no solution to that looming prospect of imperial decadence. In the novel's closing pages, Piet, who is made quite literally to represent the fading promise of American citizenship, has been assumed into both the U.S. military bureaucracy and the sexual and spiritual disenchantment that Updike paints as its corollary. "Your virtues are obsolete," he is told by the lover who conspires to ensure his cooptation (449). But, if in this way his tale of cultural failure resembles Mailer's pessimistic vision in *Why Are We in Vietnam?*, *Rabbit Redux*, by contrast, looks like Updike's version of *The Armies of the Night*.[49] For, in that subsequent novel, Updike hints at the prospect of a fundamental cultural reorientation. When his suburban home is literally invaded by a Vietnam veteran and angry black nationalist named Skeeter, Harry is forced to confront the dark underside of American liberalism—both in the history of racial oppression at home and in the imposition of military domination abroad. Updike figures this confrontation as an encounter with the coercive force of U.S. power— its "buried tortures" (284). And, much as in *The Armies of the Night* and *A Rumor of War*, he describes Harry's discovery of that concealed history as a descent into a nether region from which return brings the promise of rebirth. It is "like scouring the plumbing . . . down in the cellar."[50] As in Mailer and Caputo, in short, when Harry finally acknowledges the victims of American democracy, he learns to perceive both the shallowness of his once cherished political convictions and, by contrast, the depth of his ascriptive identity. "Everybody stuck inside his own skin," Skeeter ultimately teaches Harry. "Might as well make himself at home there" (335).

Given the patterns we have been tracing throughout this book, it should come as little surprise that Updike also echoes Mailer and Caputo in conceiving the protagonists of both these novels as presidential figures. Piet, who is compared to John F. Kennedy, resembles his historical analog in the fact that his unconsidered desires lead him to succumb to an imperial bureaucracy that extends his interests beyond his capacity to understand or control. He is the president, in sum, in the failed mode also represented by Mailer's version of LBJ or Caputo's witch doctors—a prisoner of the military-industrial complex and the craven symbol of a ruthlessly sentimental people.[51]

Harry becomes, by comparison, a counterfigure who resembles the Lincoln invoked by both Caputo and Mailer. That the pivotal event in his story comes with his painful acknowledgment of a black man, and that their exchange forces him to confront the legacy of America's ugly postbellum history is in this light no coincidence. For, it not only enables Harry to feel Skeeter's pain and, through that identification, to conceive himself an honorary black man and a victim of history. ("You want to be a nigger, right," Skeeter demands in the pivotal scene of humiliation in which Harry trades places with his antagonist [296].) It also suggests that, in that act of empathy, Harry begins to make good on the unredeemed promise of emancipation in order to move toward the full recognition of all U.S. citizens. "What I want to say to you . . . what I want to make ever so clear," Skeeter informs Harry, speaking of the history of racial domination that followed the Civil War, "is you had that chance. You could have gone some better road" (233). When, by the novel's conclusion, the two are no longer antagonists, but sympathetically united common sufferers, the suggestion is clear that Harry, and the nation he represents, may have begun down that better path. Much as in *The Armies of the Night* and *A Rumor of War*, then, Harry becomes a figure who rises to the grandeur associated with Lincoln because of his willingness to confront and endure the "violent tensions" of America's "political contract." "It's a kind of agony," Updike aptly says, summarizing Harry's admirable suffering.[52] In his willingness to acknowledge and empathize with Skeeter's pain, and to accept his responsibility for the abuses as well as the glories of American power, Harry becomes, like the self-created personas of Caputo and Mailer, the implicit voice of a potentially redeemed nation.

In a number of ways Updike's version of that story is more complicated and less certain in its resolution than the encouraging visions proposed by Mailer and Caputo. But the work of all three writers suggests a desire shared with many of their contemporaries—to find in the rediscovery of national identity a hope of moving beyond the ideological violence of recent years. Both the military conflicts of international relations and the bitter disputes of domestic politics, all three implied, could be overcome when Americans learned, like Harry, to be restrained by their ascriptive loyalties and natural interests—to be comfortably stuck inside their own skins. The same wisdom is summarized by Frank Holliwell, the protagonist of Robert Stone's *A Flag for Sunrise*, when he looks back on the Vietnam War and marvels at the unnecessary blood shed in the name of putatively universal ideological causes. "The most specious lunacy had been conceived, written and enacted on both sides of the Pacific," Holliwell muses. "Most of the survivors," he adds with apparent relief, "were themselves again" (28).

As it happens, Holliwell is mistaken in this last supposition. The premise of Stone's novel appears in Holliwell's discovery that the lunacy that was U.S. policy in Vietnam, along with the anticolonial lunacy that it produced in response, is being replicated in the squalor of the Central American proxy wars of the 1980s. But the conviction enshrined in that line—that Americans might finally restrain the ruthless imperial forces that acted in their name when they learned to abandon the distractions of ideology for the deep truths of cultural difference—became a principle assumption of the literary response to Vietnam. Indeed it was the core principle of Stone's most immediate reaction to the war, his novel *Dog Soldiers*, which, though again with much ambiguity, presents a narrative strikingly parallel to the stories told by Updike, Caputo, and Mailer. Once again, the Vietnam veteran—here a countercultural hipster named Ray Hicks—appears at first glance the embodiment of both America's coercive force and its moral decline, a "scented death's-head harlequin" (96). Once again, though, the veteran is rescued from that mistaken impression and made the center of a hesitant story of national rebirth. In a narrative that literally brings Hicks back from Vietnam and toward the geographic and (Stone implies) historical interior of his country, Hicks moves away from the confusion of war and the cynicism of a decadent counterculture. Placed in conflict with abusive agents of America's imperial bureaucracy, Hicks becomes no longer the aggressive arm, but the defiant victim of state power—"the little man in the boonies, . . . [on] the right side for a change" (296). And once more his ultimate martyrdom becomes the occasion for an estranged couple to overcome their cynicism and passivity and rediscover their deeper loyalties. What Hicks teaches those disenchanted liberals,

Marge and John Converse, is almost precisely what Harry learns from Skeeter and what Caputo learns from Walt Levy. In the absence of all other hope, and of the delusions of imperial ideology, there remain the bonds of shared history. "In the worst of times, there's something . . . . There's us" (337).[53]

To envision a world where there was just "us"—where the American people had freed themselves from the political apparatus, the ideological zeal, and the foreign entanglements that had led them into a disastrous war—was the implicit desire shared by Stone with literary contemporaries like Updike, Caputo, and Mailer. ("In Vietnam I found a mistake ten thousand miles long," Stone later remarked. "The logic of the thing required that everybody make their way back home to . . . America."[54]) Against what Baritz called the "sentimental imperialism" of U.S. foreign policy, such writers, that is, invoked a sentimental nationalism.

That effort is apparent in the numerous stories of return and reunion that flooded American literature and film in the 1970s, as it was in the many occasions those stories were joined to an angry rejection of an imperial state. But it was also evident in the way that many writers took such stories to resolve the problem of dissocia-tion at a stroke, in effect, transforming a complex and divided society into a coher-ent and unified entity through a narrative of moral reinterpretation. If the Vietnam War appeared to flourish on the absence of American will—of, in Andrew Hacker's terms, the exercise of "power" without "purpose"—stories like *A Rumor of War*, *Rabbit Redux*, and *Dog Soldiers* suggested that, when Americans ultimately con-fronted the actions of their government, they would come to the realization that ultimately such dissociation was a philosophic impossibility and thus a kind of col-lective self-deception that proper experience would necessarily correct. In *Rabbit Redux*, Harry is educated by a flower child in a theory of expression that turns out to be significant not only for Updike's novel, but for much of the literature of the era. "Matter is the mirror of spirit," she explains. Whatever a person "feels when he makes the mark—if he's tired or bored or happy and proud—will be there. . . . [W]e'll feel it. Like fingerprints. Like handwriting"(158). The virtue of such a theory of communication, of course, is that, in displacing representation with expression, it makes dissociation and thus disagreement and dissembling appear ultimately impossible. Quite literally, on this view, everyone is stuck inside his or her own skin and, like Harry, must only be brought to realize the fact.

No surprise, then, that variations on this expressive theory would appear widely in the writing of Updike's contemporaries and almost inevitably as a key feature of an understanding of collective action cast as alternative and superior to the prevail-ing confusion of contemporary politics. The culminating scenes of Stone's *Dog Soldiers*, for example, are set at a former Jesuit mission, El Incarnacion del Verbo, whose later countercultural occupants, "Those Who Are," believe "There Are No Metaphors" (229, 293). Fittingly Hicks, for whom at his best there is "no difference between thought and action," wears the Greek phrase "those who are" tattooed into his skin. That device is consistent with Stone's later suggestion that what differentiates the "secret culture" of a nation from communicable "information" is that the former is "beaten . . . into" its citizens (FFS 180). It is also, and by the same token, consistent with the fact that Hicks ultimately seeks to fulfill the role that Norman Mailer, like Woodrow Wilson, thought the chief executive must pursue: he personifies the collective desires of his people. "He's a serious man, like your President," a minor character thus observes, "a total American" (270).

The pathos of Stone's novel comes from the fact that the features of a modern commercial society appear to doom that ambition to almost complete failure. The insulation and identity that men like Hicks crave—and, Stone implies, that we all desperately need—cannot be maintained in a world of communication and appetite. There are no longer any total Americans. But the yearning to replace the confusion of politics with the certainty of embodiment, and the desire to make it alternative to the ugliness of international conflict and the nastiness of ideological dispute, is central not only to his fiction but to the similar views of many of his contemporaries. The attitude finds possibly its strongest articulation in the remarks of Michael Herr. Herr's *Dispatches*, perhaps the most highly praised of any of the literary responses to the Vietnam War, took the methods of new journalism to their most extreme realization. Putting aside official U.S. pronouncements of aims and methods, but also abandoning any effort to situate the war in terms of the objectives or interests of the parties involved, Herr focused instead on what he cast as the indubitable sensations of "real life," making the writer's experience of combat and his intensely ambivalent and erotic connection to American soldiers the exclusive subject of his reporting. Given his guiding assumptions, no other approach seemed plausible. "Politics is language," Herr claimed in a remarkable avowal, "and as such I find it completely worthless."[55]

Like Caputo, Mailer, Stone, and many others among his contemporaries, Herr suggested that such worthless verbiage flourished because Americans were insufficiently dedicated to their collective past and preoccupied with trivial ideological distinctions. "We're very ignorant of our history. We're great perverters of our tradition." And he went on to indicate the force of that assumption in a claim that not only repudiated dissociation in the strongest possible terms, but that emphasized the corollary understanding that to be a member of a group was in the final analysis necessarily to intend or rather to embody all of its actions. Seconding the point made by Caputo, and by Paul Goodman and Norman Mailer, Herr denied that American opponents of the Vietnam War could evade their own collective responsibility for state policy. Whatever they may have wanted to believe, Herr claimed, "in their dreams and in their wishes and in their hearts they were in Vietnam too. The Vietnam war was . . . an American manifestation."[56]

The charge—which was widely echoed at the time and which aptly summarized the premises Herr shared with writers like Caputo, Mailer, Updike, and Stone—

cast itself as a stern moral challenge to American complacence and to the alleged civic dissociation that preserved it. But precisely because it was so vague and sweeping, thinking like Herr's could exercise little critical force. Making all Americans metaphysically accountable for the war, it effectively indemnified any particular policy or policymakers from responsibility. Viewing the conflict as a distinctly "American manifestation," it likewise obscured the aims, interests, and experiences of the various Vietnamese factions involved in the war—as if, as Oliver Stone's *Platoon* would notoriously put it, "we did not fight the enemy, we fought ourselves and the enemy was in us." Casting Americans as a lost tribe who stumbled arrogantly into hostile territory, it shifted easily from viewing them as a people united in misguided imperial conquest into a nation joined by its shared victimization.

Here perhaps was the ultimate appeal of such thinking. The Vietnam War presented a serious challenge to the premises of democratic government and to the mythology of American destiny. Confronting Americans with the actions of an enormously powerful and secretive, but ineffective, executive branch, it raised fundamental question about democratic control over state power—both about whether there was any meaningful such control to speak of and alternatively whether the institutions of democratic accountability actually produced wise and just state policies. More fundamentally, of course, the war threw into doubt the deep rooted belief that Americans were the bearers of a redemptive democratic message to the world.

Jeremiads like Herr's highlighted, but also effectively assuaged such concerns. By his terms, there was little cause to doubt the institutions of government because all Americans had acted in Vietnam. Precisely because it was a spiritual trial for an arrogant and divided people, moreover, the war only affirmed the special burdens of the nation and its collective identity. That point, which was implicit in all the narratives discussed in this chapter, was ultimately put most clearly in an essay, composed several decades after the war, by the draft resistance leader David Harris. Looking back on Vietnam from a distance of three decades, Harris remained outraged by the ugliness of U.S. actions and the heedlessness of government officials. But, casting the conflict as a struggle to which the Vietnamese were virtually incidental—Vietnam was "our war"—he also viewed all Americans as victims of the disaster. And he suggested that, once they viewed the war in the ways recommended by the likes of Michael Herr (seeing it not as a product of "ideology," but as a matter of "behavior" and "experience"), the American people would discover in the conflict an ultimately uplifting understanding of themselves as members of "a single moral organism." "When a nation acts," Harris wrote, "all its citizens are joined insolubly in responsibility for the consequence of their national behavior, bound to that mutuality for as long as they remember their history, bound generation after generation, carrying its weight as part of their ancestral inheritance . . . . And in that communion, we eventually redeem ourselves."

COME HOME, AMERICA

For Harris, in short, the basic problem ultimately revealed by the Vietnam War was that, in its imperial stumbling, the United States had failed to act as a nation, and the ultimate solution to the evils the war caused was therefore to reassert the foundational significance of national identity. As the remark quoted as an epigraph above makes clear, moreover, Harris assumed, like his predecessors, that this redemptive communion could only be fully realized when it was articulated by an appropriately presidential leader—one who would not act on behalf of an imperial state, but who would feel and speak for a chastened nation. U.S. imperialism would be controlled, not, say, through the constitutional division and restraint of state power, nor by the obligations of international law, but only when the president had suffered the pain and thus perforce shared the assumed views of his fellow citizens.[57]

He Has Made Us Part of His Dying

The United States' ideological retreat from imperial mission was, of course, a brief one. With the election of Ronald Reagan, U.S. foreign policy turned away from realism and toward a renewed conception of the Cold War as a moral struggle between inherently conflicting, universal ideologies. But, as David Harris's words suggest, the literary conventions and aesthetic attitudes forged during the late sixties and seventies proved remarkably durable. They remained a prominent feature of the way American writers and filmmakers would conceive the projection of U.S. power and the excesses of presidential government for years to come. Indeed, over the course of the 1980s, as the Reagan administration renewed the United States' aggressive stance in the Cold War, and as neoconservative intellectuals, journalists, and pop culture producers began to press for a reassessment of the war in Vietnam, more self-consciously literary artists sometimes marked their dissent from the Reagan revolution by affirming their commitment to the chastened, sentimental nationalism that flourished in the literature and film of the seventies. Thus in *A Flag for Sunrise*, for example, Stone reiterated and expanded on the narrative he'd developed in *Dog Soldiers*, casting it explicitly as an effort to restore a damaged national dignity against the foolishness and ugliness of Reagan administration arrogance. Joan Didion told a remarkably similar story in the nonfiction essay *Salvador* and still more directly in the novel *Democracy*. And Tim O' Brien became the most widely recognized literary authority on the legacy of Vietnam with a story cycle, *The Things They Carried*, that merged the most current techniques of the short story with a nearly exact recreation of the themes established by Caputo. The most ambitious and elaborate example of the trend came, however, in Don DeLillo's *Libra*—the epic narrative of the Cold War that DeLillo built around the assassination of John F. Kennedy and that, like his predecessors, he made into a kind of antiimperial romance built around the repudiation of executive power.

In many ways, in fact, *Libra* is a defining work in the history of the literary representation of the presidency, both a culmination of trends that reach back to the nineteenth century and a pointed rejection of their traditional ideological associations. That DeLillo views the Cold War through the lens of executive power, and vice versa, is only the most evident feature of this engagement. In this most prominent aspect, *Libra* offers a discerning counterhistory to the Camelot legend, replacing the sentimental piety of pop culture with a critical reconstruction of two central elements of executive power that came to a critical stage in the Kennedy era—the use of covert force to conduct secret military operations beyond congressional legislation or public scrutiny; and the rise of the politics of personality that exploited the mass media to expand presidential prestige at the expense of the parties and representative democracy. These are notably the only features of modern politics to appear in DeLillo's novel. Together, he implies, they make up the core instruments of an arrogant, imperial power fated to be brought low at Dealey Plaza where, in DeLillo's telling, not only JFK is killed, but so also dies the grandeur of U.S. hegemony. The assassination, as perhaps the novel's most remembered line puts it, amounts to "the seven seconds that broke the back of the American century."[58]

DeLillo has been widely praised, and more rarely denounced, for aspects of this critical vision. But just as in the work of his predecessors and contemporaries, ideology critique accounts for only a minor part of his ambitions, and the narrative of disenchantment he provides by revealing a history of clandestine power is answered by a counternarrative of reenchantment apparent especially in the portions of the novel given over to the labors of the writer Nicholas Branch. In DeLillo's own metanarrative design, Branch is the novelist within the novel. A retired CIA analyst "hired on contract to write the secret history of the assassination of President Kennedy," Branch is charged with the impossible task of bringing order and meaning to the enormous mass of data that surrounds the oracular event (15). His constantly failing efforts are narrated alongside two parallel plotlines: the conspiratorial narrative of a group of rogue CIA agents and Cuban émigrés who plot to stage a failed and yet ultimately successful attempt on Kennedy's life; and the wandering story of the young Lee Harvey Oswald, whose desperate efforts to find a place in the world culminate when he falls into the plotters' design.

These latter two, dominant narrative strands—one of highly structured, but nevertheless finally uncontrolled planning, the other of undirected, but ultimately highly consequential wandering—come together in the novel's gripping climactic moments, as JFK is assassinated and Oswald is subsequently murdered by Jack Ruby. But their significance to the larger meaning of DeLillo's novel is dwarfed by the less extensive and less gripping, but more resonant plotline devoted to Branch.

COME HOME, AMERICA

Both DeLillo's conspirators and his version of Oswald are committed to placing themselves in an encompassing design that will discover meaning in the course of history. Both are, like Branch, thus analogs of the artist, composers and draftsmen who seek "to extend their fiction into the world" (50). Branch differs from them, however, in the fact that his invention will never take on that worldly significance—not only because it is generically a secret document that cannot be made public, but more fundamentally because his narrative can never be completed and thus communicated in conventional ways. The data through which he unceasingly combs is "an incredible haul of human utterance . . . , lost to syntax and other arrangement." What it repeatedly forces upon Branch's realization is that no amount of reconstructive analysis will ultimately discern a plausible relation between intention and consequence that will adequately explain the event of the assassination and the lives that surround it (181). The meaning of his unfinishable report is that there is no meaning susceptible of clarification there.

Placed in juxtaposition to the projective efforts of Oswald and his conspirators, then, Branch's reconstructive labor dramatizes the fatuity of their hopes. All three plotlines act in this way as accounts of the failure of artistry. But against what might be called the negative failure of the plotters and Oswald (negative in the sense that the events described by the novel reveal the shallow fabrication of their illusions), Branch's failure proves to be a redemptive experience of the limits of human reason and therefore implicitly an opening to spiritual wisdom. The assassination, he thereby discovers, is not a political event, but a higher mystery. "There is much here that is holy, an aberration in the heartland of the real" (15).[59]

A good deal of discussion has been devoted to the significance of *Libra*'s distinctive historical vision and the way it suggests a particular understanding of both U.S. politics and the special role of literature in understanding, or failing to understand, it.[60] But because it mainly treats DeLillo in isolation, most of that discussion misses the way his concerns can be clarified when they're seen in the context of the literary attitudes toward U.S. power that developed over the course of the seventies, especially in response to the Vietnam War. The story of DeLillo's invented plotters, for example, is a latter day version of the stories American writers told about the Kennedy and Johnson administration zealots who embroiled the United States in a fruitless war in Vietnam, and like those tales it emphasizes the inevitable, unanticipated consequences of allegedly expert designs and the perilous seductions of ideological fantasy. The portrait of Oswald, similarly, is an intensified version of the depiction of the American citizenry that flourished in the critical writing elicited by the war—disenfranchised, alienated, quietly and then loudly desperate for a source of civic purpose. The counternarrative that appears meanwhile in the story of Nicholas Branch can be understood as a version of the redemptive tale that appears in the likes of Mailer, Caputo, Updike, Stone, and Herr. As with those writers, Branch's story dramatizes two linked transitions: the displacement of the assertive use of force by an implicitly restraining political sentiment, and the parallel displacement of political argument by a superior, spiritual understanding such that ideological dispute and rational analysis come to seem insignificant before an awed appreciation of the sacred. Once again, moreover, that higher mystery hinges on the way the death of martyrs reveals a common national identity.

Seeing DeLillo in this context, we can also see that he is concerned with the underlying issue that often drove the literary responses to the Vietnam War and that, as we have seen throughout this book, has long been associated with the imagery of the presidency and in particular with the symbolism of presidential martyrdom. The central problem of *Libra* in this light is a version of the problem that also haunts *The Armies of the Night* and *A Rumor of War*, as it does *The Grapes of Wrath* and *Native Son*. The novel's subject, that is, is the breach between state and nation—understood to be now widened to a gulf which leaves government presumptively illegitimate and the people powerless and unrepresented—and the underlying question is whether that breach can be in any way healed. Once more, in short, the underlying issue is the crisis of popular sovereignty.

DeLillo presents that problem in several ways. It is most evident, for instance, in the depiction of Oswald, who in DeLillo's rendition is painfully sensitive, though suitably not quite articulate, about his family's poverty and social marginalization and who yearns for a compensatory place in a larger historical movement. "He knew what Trotsky had written, that revolution leads us out of the dark night of the isolated self" (101). Because Oswald's political ideas are juvenile and his various efforts to join the revolution are miserable failures, and because the various glimpses of the socialist state we see are all repugnant, we know that from DeLillo's perspective that view is mistaken. But, while Oswald's unfocused political aims are themselves shown to be absurd, the longing that drives them, by contrast, is made to seem not foolish but a profound and widely shared spiritual impulse. Oswald is thus but one of the various "men in small rooms . . . , struggling with secret and feverish ideas," who constitute the central figures in DeLillo's canvas (41). The conspirators and Nicholas Branch are the most prominent others, and their compulsions and methods are shown to be directly analogous to the desperation driving the would be assassin. All these men are troubled by a spiritual need to find a route beyond the prison of the private self emphasized by liberal society, a need that DeLillo suggests has reached a kind of critical impasse because of the way the forces of rationalization have stripped life of spiritual immanence and thereby destroyed the hope of finding a higher reality capable of anchoring the sense of religious transcendence. "If the world is where we hide from ourselves, " DeLillo asks in a question repeated in various ways throughout his work, "what do we do when the world is no longer accessible?" (148).

In this respect, despite the madness of their obsessions and the violence of their actions, *Libra*'s men in small rooms are clearly not meant to be seen as dismissible crackpots. Rather, as the phrase might suggest, they are spiritual athletes who bring to a pitch of refinement the needs that implicitly trouble all men. (Women, by contrast, appear almost without exception in *Libra* as the voices of the alternative and implicitly shallow model of domestic happiness: the "standard ways to stop being lonely" [371].) The novel thus begins with an epigraph taken from a letter the historical Oswald wrote to his brother Robert. "Happiness is not based on oneself," Oswald writes, "it does not consist of a small home, of taking and getting." Placed in the context of the novel's larger design, his observation appears to summarize DeLillo's guiding premise, which could be summarized as the spiritual inadequacy of the freedoms and pleasures promised by liberal society—a society whose orthodoxy and conformism in turn drives its most needful members into extremism, rabidity, and violence. "There was something about a long and low and open-space house with a lawn and a carport that made her feel spiritually afraid," one minor character appropriately thinks (123).

But, if the ultimate source of the Kennedy assassination lies in the spiritual poverty of liberal society, DeLillo—much like Mailer, Updike, and Stone—makes that diagnosis politically resonant by casting it as the complement of governmental institutions that ensure the disenfranchisement and the emotional hunger of the liberal citizen. This is the evident significance of DeLillo's emphasis on the covert power and the media image of the modern presidency. Both, in DeLillo's telling, are instruments that elevate the presidency to unprecedented levels of power. Acting effectively together to rob the American people of sovereignty, they serve to intensify the popular resentment and spiritual desperation of an alienated people—an emotional stew that in DeLillo's vision of history will ultimately culminate in the assassination itself.

This latter point deserves emphasis since it is not the most obvious explanation DeLillo proposes for the death of John F. Kennedy. Indeed the most striking feature of *Libra* is that, as Nicholas Branch's story appears to emphasize, it refuses an obvious explanation at all. Though like previous challenges to the Warren report, DeLillo imagines a conspiracy to kill the president and, though, conventionally enough, he views that conspiracy as arising from a combination of rogue CIA agents, anti-Castro zealots, and Mafia kingpins, DeLillo ultimately suggests that, enticing though such stories are, they are less important than the astrological angle emphasized by his title. "Oswald's attempt on Kennedy," DeLillo imagines, "was based on elements outside politics and . . . outside history," in "coincidences and even the . . . configuration of the stars."[61] Time and again, *Libra* underscores that point by reminding us that the conscious intentions of individual human agents count for little and that mysterious forces act to arrange the events of destiny— "dreams, visions, intuitions, prayers," a "force of connection" that "cuts across causality, cuts across time" (339).

But while *Libra* puts great stress on this noncausal, spiritual force, it nevertheless repeatedly implies a still vaguer, yet still ultimately causal explanation for why the intuitions and prayers it imagines assume the specific form they do—why, that is, the force of "dreams and coincidences" results in the assassination of a president and the murder of his alleged killer. If the Kennedy assassination takes on a kind of fatal inevitability, *Libra* consistently suggests, it does so because of the way it surpasses the intentions of individual agents to emerge instead out of the free floating longings of a whole inarticulate population, for whose desires Oswald and DeLillo's conspirators alike turn out to be merely vehicles. The deep root of those desires, we are shown in countless ways, lies in the spiritual hunger endured by all the citizens of a liberal society and suffered most acutely by men in small rooms. But their proximate cause comes in the resentment stirred by the imperial presidency. Wherever Kennedy goes, one conspirator thus acutely observes, "somebody wants a piece of him. Deep sweats of desire and rage. . . . Maybe he's just too pretty to live" (365). Another notes "how strangely and completely a hatred for this President reached into certain parts of the culture, into daily lives" (298).

DeLillo's astrological framework, then, serves much the same purpose evident in the comparably antiintentional remarks of David Harris or Michael Herr. Putting aside the conscious political aims of individual agents as ultimately trivial, it enables the discovery of what seems by contrast the deeper, more spiritual force of the unacknowledged wishes of a collective people. As in the long tradition of the presidential imagination, moreover, those wishes are both provoked by the embarrassment of the coercive force of executive power and elicited by the alluring promise that, by articulating the popular will, the president might rise above that embarrassment to reassert the sovereignty of the people.

DeLillo's conspirators are appropriately the most articulate voices of the complaint against the coercive power of the state. Themselves agents of clandestine executive power, they grow outraged when that power fails to serve their wishes—and, equally significantly, when they feel excluded from its concealed operations—and they therefore become both the creators and the spokesmen of a kind of metaphysical blowback theory that envisions the abuses of executive power being turned against the president. Thus Win Everett, the principle author of DeLillo's invented conspiracy, considers his plotting a means to exploit and vengefully uncover the operations of concealed state power and, if only ironically, to begin a restoration of democratic self-governance. "It was his personal contribution to an informed public" (53). His fellow conspirator T-Jay Mackey takes the thought to more extreme lengths. "When Jack sent out word to get Castro, he put himself in a world of blood and pain. Nobody told him he had to live there. He made the choice with his brother Bobby. So it's Jack's own idea we're guided by" (302).

From this eloquent perspective, JFK is fated to die for the reason that martyrdom always seems appealing in the literature of the presidency. As the chief executive, he exemplifies the U.S. government's willingness to pursue actions inconsistent with its stated democratic ideals and its avowedly constitutional system of government. More basically, he highlights the tension between the consent prized by democracy and the coercion fundamental to government—the world, one might say, of blood and pain. In this respect, Kennedy is only the most concrete representative of the state imposition that DeLillo casts as a virtually universal condition of government—as evident in the Cuba of Castro (whom Kennedy, in his "stain of greatness," is said to closely resemble) as it is in the police state of the Soviet Union or in the Marine brig experienced by Lee Harvey Oswald (187). Everywhere DeLillo's characters go, they are confronted both by the allure and the indignity of an unresponsive and abusive government. "There's something they aren't telling us," a third conspirator thus thinks of the secret dialogue he imagines taking place between Kennedy and Castro. "This is what history consists of. It's the sum total of things they aren't telling us" (321).

The Kennedy assassination is thus made to seem the inevitable consequence of the underside of the Cold War state. It emerges naturally out of the desires and resentments stirred up in a society whose leaders foster the impression that "it's always wartime" (64). But, if in this way, the vast power of the chief executive seem itself to elicit a suppressed popular desire to kill the president, a still more important factor in DeLillo's telling is the emotional fever evoked by the rise, alongside the mass media, of the politics of persona and style. Nothing does more in fact to feed the rage of DeLillo's conspirators than their frustration with the "Kennedy magic, Kennedy charisma," and they become, as a result, vividly accurate critics of the stylistic pretensions of the New Frontier (62). Win Everett first begins to plot against the state, for instance, when he is disappointed at the merely symbolic amends JFK makes for the embarrassment of the Bay of Pigs. "He respected the President for going to Miami . . . . But the ceremony had not renewed the cause . . . . He saw it now as pure public relations, the kind of gleaming imagery that marked every move the administration made." "The repressed material" of popular desire is "sent in reconverted waves into Televisionland" (61).

Everett's fellow conspirators are, like him, outraged by the public relations of the Kennedy White House and infuriated by JFK's ability, to, as the defenders of the New Frontier proclaimed, "project a mystique." "Did you ever see a man in such a hurry to be great," the conspirator Guy Bannister demands. "He thinks he can make us a different kind of society" (68). What irks them in the most abstract sense is the gulf between the rhetorical pretensions of the U.S. government and the reality of a concealed and concentrated power from which they feel unfairly excluded. But the larger significance of their dissatisfaction comes in the fact that it is only representative of a far more intense desire that DeLillo suggests courses through the unconscious mind of televisionland. That everyone wants a piece of the president is, in this sense, the obverse side of a popular obsession whose recognition DeLillo places in Marina Oswald's musings about JFK: "What must it be like to know you are the object of a thousand longings? It's as though he floats over the landscape at night, entering dreams and fantasies, entering the act of love between husbands and wives. He floats through television screens into bedrooms at night" (324).

Touting JFK as the face of a new existential politics, Norman Mailer had urged the aspiring presidential candidate to glory in that symbolic power and then reacted with disappointment when JFK failed to live up to his potential. Several decades later, DeLillo takes up the phenomenon of political charisma celebrated by Mailer and his contemporaries and views it in a sharply different light. If it was true, as Mailer claimed, that Kennedy had discovered in his exploitation of the mass media a means to evade the pettiness of orthodox politics and tap into "the real subterranean life of America," the consequence, DeLillo suggests, was not the national grandeur Mailer envisioned, but a surge of emotional hunger that inevitably overwhelmed the inadequate vehicle of the politician (PP 33). The theme reaches its culminating expression suitably in the climactic moments leading up to the assassination, in an extended passage of rising intensity that casts the shooting, not as a crime or a political murder, but as the completion of an orgiastic expression of popular need.

> There was a mood rising through the packed bodies, an eager spirit of assent. . . . A sound, an awe worked through the crowd, a recognition, ringing in the air. People called out together, faces caught in some stage of surprise resembling dazzled pain. . . . The sound was a small roar now, a wonder. They shook the fence, they came running from the terminal building, handbags and cameras bouncing. . . . (391)
>
> . . .
>
> Here he was among them in a time of deep division, the country pulled two ways, each army raging and Jack having hold of both. . . . it was important for the car to move very slowly, give the crowds a chance to see him. . . . The message jumped the open space from one press of bodies to the next. A contagion had brought them here, *some mystery of common impulse, hundreds of thousands come from so many histories and systems of being . . . a convergence of dreams . . .* They were here to be an event, a consciousness, to astonish the old creedbound fears, the stark and wary faith of the city of get-rich-quick. . . They were here to surround the brittle body of one man and claim his smile, receive some token of the bounty of his soul. . . . Here was a new city, an idea that traveled at the speed of sound, pounding over the old hushed heart, a city of voices roaring. Loud and hot and throbbing. . . . Did Jack think this fervor was close to violence? They were so damn close, nearly upon them. He looked at them and whispered, "Thank you." (393–94, emphasis added)

The passage can be read as a cruelly accurate parody of the exaggerated expectations of presidential government and a devastating critique of their unintended consequences. Beginning in the late nineteenth century, the advocates of executive power had defended the presidency especially as a rhetorical office— one that, by enabling political leaders to reach above the ordinary institutions of representative government to speak directly to the nation would permit them to lead the American people beyond their narrow concerns and ambitions and thus to evoke a more complete and meaningful citizenship. JFK had spoken the rhetoric more enthusiastically than any one. Casting himself as an heir to Lincoln (whose words he closely echoed), along with Wilson and FDR, Kennedy had, for instance, defended the idea of the New Frontier to "the American people" by bragging that it "appealed to their pride, not their pocketbook," and by demanding that they commit themselves to "national greatness" rather than "private comfort."[62] De-Lillo's rapturous account of popular hysteria echoes that rhetoric, but also revealingly distorts it. The people of Dallas have come together around the person of the president to make themselves a new city, superior to the vulgar acquisitiveness of their ordinary world. In doing so, however, they become not a prophetic nation, but a howling mob whose unconscious desires drive the killing of their leader.

That depiction suggests several telling observations about the rhetoric of presidential leadership and the political culture that enabled it. Viewing the reaction to JFK as a form of collective hysteria, DeLillo highlights an implication running through his novel's emphasis on magic and dread. If the modern presidency had, through the agencies of the mass media and the instruments of covert power, assumed a nearly monarchical stature, the public attitudes it called forth, DeLillo implied, were the ritualistic and theocratic forms suitable for a premodern court society. Dreams, visions, fate, and the supernatural agency of the stars are they keynotes of DeLillo's story, in other words, because they are the appropriate ways of conceiving the subrational appeal of a charismatic office. In a presidential system, as Mailer had intuited, all politics becomes ultimately magical.

But where Mailer, not unlike Woodrow Wilson, had imagined that magic uniting people and leader to resolve the problem of sovereignty, DeLillo suggests more nearly the reverse. The yearning set off by JFK taps into a subterranean river of popular need. But rather than making that desire part of an articulate national will, his frail presence only illuminates the disenfranchisement and spiritual emptiness that makes such hunger inevitable and, as a consequence, highlights the utter inadequacy of the politician to address them. Even more than the assassination itself, in short, the passage leading up to JFK's shooting marks DeLillo's shattering destruction of the myth of presidential leadership.

Yet, if *Libra* reveals the irrationality and the inadequacy of presidential government, and the way in which it thus exacerbates the political and spiritual complaints it was meant to repair, like so many of its predecessors, it also draws heavily on the very symbolic structures it rejects. For, while as a living president, JFK proves too small and conventional a politician to actually form a new city around himself, in his death—and more specifically in the ruminations on it of Nicholas Branch—he nevertheless serves to articulate an alternative collective story that would go otherwise unreported. The theme runs all through Branch's reflections. Musing upon the pattern of seemingly mysterious deaths that surround the assassination, for example, Branch discovers "the neon epic of Saturday night": "shot in back of head. Died of cut throat. Shot in police station. Shot in motel. Shot by husband after one month marriage. Found hanging by toreador pants in jail cell. Killed by karate chop." That, misleading appearances to the contrary there is "nothing statistically abnormal" in this pattern and thus no evidence of a conspiracy only underscores the significant point (57). "The assassination sheds a powerful and lasting light, exposing patterns and links" not because it points toward the work of conspiratorial power, but because it illuminates the ordinary violence and desperation of American society otherwise concealed by the falsity of political rhetoric and popular ideology.

Branch himself later draws this moral almost explicitly, generalizing from the lives in some way touched directly by the assassination to a conviction that the Warren report amounts to the material for an encyclopedic vision of American civilization.

> Everything is here. Baptismal records, report cards, postcards, divorce petitions, canceled checks, daily timesheets, tax returns, property lists, postoperative x-rays, photos of knotted string, thousands of pages of testimony, of voices droning in hearing rooms in old courthouse buildings, an incredible haul of human utterance . . . . [I]t resembles a kind of mind-spatter, a poetry of lives muddied and dripping in language.
>
> . . .
>
> Everything belongs, everything adheres, the mutter of obscure witnesses, the photos of illegible documents and odd sad personal debris, things gathered up at a dying—old shoes, pajama tops, letters from Russia. It is all one thing, a ruined city of trivia where people feel real pain. This is the Joycean book of America, remember—the novel in which nothing is left out. (181–82)

Branch is in these passages a figure strikingly reminiscent of the persona created by Philip Caputo or Norman Mailer or David Harris—the anti-JFK who finds in the rejection of presidential charisma an obscured story of national destiny that can be, if never quite completely, best articulated by himself. Against the false image of a new city fostered by Kennedy's political rhetoric, Branch's literary rumination discovers the true, "ruined city" of America. Against Kennedy's pretensions to raise the eyes of the nation above its citizens' pocketbooks, Branch finds a common identity, as it were, below them—in the failure, hunger, and poverty of his people. Against the New Frontier's call that Americans rise to the demands of their beliefs and principles, Branch reminds us of their obscured "real pain" and thereby becomes the memorialist of their inheritance. "He feels the dead in his room" (183).

COME HOME, AMERICA

The pattern of oppositions establishes an impressive symmetry between JFK's public speaking and Branch's private soliloquies. Both offer a rhetorical alternative to liberal society's emphasis on personal freedom and the pursuit of happiness—Kennedy, by demanding national aspiration, Branch by trumpeting the spiritual depths of humiliation and failure. Indeed JFK plays in this scheme much the same role that he, along with LBJ and Nixon, played in the works of DeLillo's predecessors. He is not just obnoxious for being a pseudomonarchical figure, but by the same token a false king who in fostering the illusions of national destiny, and the disastrous policies that went along with it, exploited without actually redressing the genuine hunger fostered by liberal society. Nicholas Branch's meditations suggest, by contrast, that there is an alternative story of America and imply that, because that story is a true collective expression rather than a false ideological vision, its acknowledgment, if possible, would restrain the abuse of power. He, rather than the politician, becomes the "agent of redemption."[63]

Just as in Caputo, Mailer, and their peers, that redemption requires a martyr whose willing death unites an otherwise divided people. The true martyr, however, is not JFK, whose life and death alike testify only to the embarrassment of the state's coercive power and the emptiness of a mass-mediated public life, but Lee Harvey Oswald, who exemplifies his people's otherwise obscured common suffering. That significance is perceived by the minor character Beryl Parmenter (another analog, as it happens, to Nicholas Branch and the artist) who, watching and re-watching the television footage of Oswald's death realizes, in the novel's epiphanic, penultimate passage, that Oswald has assumed the role that his wife imagined for Kennedy. It is in his death, rather than in his dream of wielding power, that Oswald finally achieves the place in a collective mission he long sought.

> [Beryl] began to cry again. She wanted to crawl out of the room. But something held her there. It was probably Oswald. There was something in Oswald's face, a glance at the camera before he was shot, that put him here in the audience, among the rest of us, sleepless in our homes—a glance, a way of telling us that he knows who we are and how we feel, that he has brought our perceptions and interpretations into his sense of the crime. Something in the look, some sly intelligence, exceedingly brief but far-reaching, a connection all but bleached away by glare, tells us he is outside the moment, watching with the rest of us. . . . [H]e has made us part of his dying. (447)

DeLillo published these words shortly after the United States had experienced a revival, not only of the rhetoric of the Cold War, but of the assertion of executive power—and, more specifically, after the revelation that the White House had once again, in the name of national security and in the pursuit of ideological zealousness, made use of secret forces to skirt congressional legislation and public scrutiny. No doubt DeLillo had those abuses in mind as he wrote and meant his novel at least in part to illuminate the political history that prefigured them. Like the predecessors who wrote about the Vietnam War, his novel suggested a strong desire to repudiate the ideological use of state coercion and to hinder it by an alternative consideration of the inevitable limitations of power and by the restraints of national identity.

But, if only to a limited degree, *Libra* may also say something about why, despite many significant complaints, Americans and their elected officials have done so little to limit the expansion of presidential power and at critical moments have rather welcomed it. There are surely many explanations for that fact, including the structural conditions of national power, the demands of international relations and international law, and the vagaries of domestic politics. But another relevant factor may be that Americans continue to be drawn to the idea that their nation inherits a special destiny and that it remains in need of leaders who can rise above factionalism and self-interest to personify that mission.

DeLillo no less than the celebrants of Ronald Reagan or George W. Bush is indebted to those assumptions. Like the predecessors who responded to Vietnam, DeLillo suggests that, in the ideological pursuit of the Cold War, the leaders of the United States had sacrificed its distinctive identity, risked what Stone called its "secret culture," and undermined its stature, and though he responded by suggesting that the United States had been cursed rather than blessed by its legacy, *Libra* can be understood to seek to restore the spiritual uniqueness and historical grandeur of its people. Indeed, the fact that Nicholas Branch's report must itself remain functionally secret and, because it is "lost to syntax," can never be put into the publicly communicable form of ideology, suggests, much as Stone's writing does, a desire to reassert the special status of the national identity it articulates. Against the secrecy of executive power, DeLillo's novel in effect casts a secret force of literary perception. Against the failures of the Cold War, it likewise envisions, in the irrational and unexplainable features of failure and loss, a resacralization of the United States. In the death of Lee Harvey Oswald, it imagines a better president for America.

EPILOGUE ▌███████████████████████

Philip Roth and the Waning and Waxing

of Political Time

I've never heard a president use words like "destiny" or "sacrifice" and it wasn't bullshit.

—Anonymous (Joe Klein), Primary Colors

The central paradox . . . was that in order to reduce federal power, it was first necessary to increase presidential power.

—Leonard Garment, White House counsel to Richard Nixon

I just want you to know that, when we talk about war, we're really talking about peace.

—George W. Bush

I N BUT THE FIRST FEW episodes of its premier season (1999–2000), the popular television program *The West Wing*, managed to present its viewers with vivid renditions of two different images of the late twentieth-century presidency.[1] Portraying the mundane politicking of a liberal administration beset by fierce opponents and unreliable allies, the program dramatized the view of the federal government that had come to prevail among mainstream opinion leaders over the two terms of the Clinton presidency. Like Bill Clinton, *The West Wing*'s Josiah Bartlett is a centrist Democrat from a small state who has come to office without the support of a strong majority and who must try to govern by negotiating a divided and fractious government. Like the Clinton administration after 1994, the fictional Bartlett administration concentrates on trying to assemble unstable majorities to support small bore domestic legislation, while worrying ceaselessly about public relations and the president's popular image. As in the last years of the Clinton presidency, the predominant image of politics we get is one of major squabbling and maximal posturing over what everyone agrees amount largely to minor stakes.

In this fashion, *The West Wing* not only captured the tone of the last years of the Clinton era, it also dramatized an understanding of the condition of the federal government that had gained increasing prominence among political scientists and public intellectuals over the previous two decades. If at one time, the visions of activist government and presidential leadership advanced by the likes of James McGregor Burns and Richard Neustadt earned widespread assent, by the mid-1990s their ideas had come into severe disrepute. Building on the critical diagnoses articulated by Arthur Schlesinger, Jr., and Theodore Lowi, a cohort of dissatisfied intellectuals had taken apart the once credulous celebrations of the modern presidency to show the diverse ways that the ideal of plebiscitary leadership had helped bring the United States toward a condition of political ennui. The modern presidency had not given rise to the vigorous leadership that its supporters predicted, such thinkers pointed out, but to a dispiriting mixture of rhetorical grandstanding and governmental stasis. Rather than national consensus, it had produced venal partisanship and a public life preoccupied by scandal. Rather than an enriched political discourse, it had undermined civic deliberation and replaced it with media spectacle and a slavish dedication to opinion polling. During the 1980s, Ronald Reagan had briefly made the idea of presidential leadership newly credible to his conservative supporters, convincing some observers that, in the hands of an effective politician, the rhetorical powers of the chief executive could be used to redirect public policy.[2] By the end of the century, however, the seeming irrevocability of harshly divided government had swamped that impression with a conviction that the presidency was the most ineffective branch of a lamely functioning government. In the view of a growing number of commentators, presidential leadership seemed less an imperial than an imperiled or even illusory force.[3]

The West Wing created a similar impression in several ways. Its large cast of characters focused especially on communications officers, whose work demanded an obsessive concern with media fashion and the fluctuations of public opinion. Its dramatic form—featuring multiple, overlapping plot lines—emphasized the piecemeal nature of contemporary politicking, and the ordinary confusion of triviality and substance. Perhaps most impressively, the program's visual style used a warren-like set and its signature steadicam tracking shots (which follow characters as they "walk-and-talk") to create an image of frenetic, but not especially productive activity. The combined impression was a vision of the "presidential branch" that gave dramatic representation to the prevailing academic view of the fin-desiecle presidency. The executive office the program showed was a well intentioned, but flailing institution profoundly limited in its power to achieve any goal apart from the desperate effort to track public opinion polls.

Perhaps because such a view might easily prove dispiriting, *The West Wing* complemented it with an alternative image of the dignity and stature of the presidency itself—so that the seemingly veristic portrait of mundane politics was always countered to some degree by an idealized vision of leadership and public service. As the program developed, audience demand encouraged its writers and its producer, Aaron Sorkin, to make this latter image increasingly prominent, with the result that a series initially designed to focus on the White House deputy communications director (Sam Seaborn, played by Rob Lowe) came to center around the president himself. In its first season that alternative image was only briefly evident, but it appears with particular clarity in moments when the program turns to what might be called boundary events—renditions, that is, of political crises that place the stature of the American nation and the common belonging of its citizens at risk. In those occasions, where the program reaches below political squabbles to touch the fundamental ground of national identity, the president speaks almost directly in the voice of god.[4]

That voice speaks most clearly in two episodes of *The West Wing*'s opening season. In the show's third episode, "A Proportional Response," the fictional President Bartlett orders a limited, tactical bombing strike on Syria in response to the terrorist downing of an American plane, reluctantly putting aside his desire to bring down devastation on the rogue state with "God's own thunder."[5] That this moment surpasses the ordinary confusion of representative politics for the deeper drama of national identity is highlighted not only by the shift from domestic policy to international relations, but by the program's skillful suggestion that the president's quasidivine rage is legitimized by his personal connection to the American citizenry. President Bartlett's urge to wield "the clenched fist of the most mighty military force in the history of mankind" is inspired, he asserts, by his responsibility to protect all Americans and, at the same time, by his personal friendship with the one named victim who represents those citizens—Morris Tolliver, an African American naval officer who was also the president's personal physician.

Summed up in this deft storytelling are several of the key components of the presidential imagination. Most obvious is *The West Wing*'s suggestion that the chief executive speaks with full presidential grandeur especially in his role as commander-in-chief—in which capacity the program implies, in keeping with the twentieth-century redefinition of constitutional law, he operates alone. But in addition to this implication, the program makes several further important suggestions: that the president's authority comes from the care he owes the lives of all Americans, especially in their conflict with foreign antagonists who threaten the nation's sovereign authority; and that his legitimacy is particularly underpinned by his obligations to the martyred military personnel who carried "the flag of the United States" and who surrendered their lives in the nation's service.

Finally, much as in *Native Son*—or *Invivisble Man* or *Rabbit Redux*—*The West Wing* gives particular emphasis to the sacral limits of American national identity by emphasizing the symbolic role of African American citizens, whose historically marginal status is particularly useful in highlighting the significance of national membership. That Morris Tolliver is loved by the president, but killed by the terrorists who represent a lawless challenge ("unwarranted, unprovoked, and cold-blooded") to the president's authority, foregrounds his crucial status as the representative of a nation finally democratic enough to fully include its African American members. To underscore this symbolism, and implicitly the continuing life of the nation, the episode ends by replacing Tolliver with President Bartlett's new, African American personal aide Charlie Young (a man who comes to his position, the program importantly stresses, without any experience of the institutional routes of ordinary politics) and by making him, in the final scenes of the episode, the awed witness to the charisma of presidential power. As the president prepares to address the nation to announce the military action he has commanded—a step that enables him both to surpass ordinary representative politics and *The West Wing*'s usual visual style—he also speaks especially forcefully to Charlie, who thus stands in for the public otherwise unrepresented by the program. "I've never felt like this before," Charlie remarks. What he feels, we may take the program to be implying, is something near to what Bigger Thomas wishes to feel—the emotions one might experience on moving from the periphery of one's society (where life is characterized by the indignity, impermanence, and isolation of liberal society at its cruelest) to the very center of the nation's power, where uncertainty is replaced by the dignity of command.[6]

In "A Proportional Response," then, Jed Bartlett rises to presidential stature in his willingness to use the awesome power of the state in defense of the nation (and, the program implies more subtly, in the psychic suffering he undergoes when he takes up that sacred power). In the final episode of its first season, "What Kind of Day Has it Been," however, *The West Wing* gives us the canonical response to that image of presidential grandeur. Once again, the president's stature is emphasized by his concern for endangered American citizens whose vulnerability marks the outer limits of national power—in this case, a pilot downed in Iraq and the crew of a space shuttle experiencing technical difficulties. Now, however, those threatened citizens do not die, but return to America unscathed, and the president rather than wielding righteous power on their behalf instead demonstrates his own personal vulnerability. In the program's cliffhanger season-ending, President Bartlett takes the occasion of a town hall meeting to once again address the American citizenry directly. Now, however, rather than speak of the state's coercive power, the president emphasizes his own accountability by invoking the Founding Fathers, who, he remarks had declared that "we were no longer subjects of King George III, but rather a self-governing people." In the immediately following moment, *The West Wing* calls on the time-honored symbolic association of that premise. The president, having wielded the coercive power of the state, must now prove his democratic legitimacy by demonstrating his willingness to lay down his own life for the nation. Leaving the lecture hall to meet the public, he becomes the victim of an assassination attempt.[7]

What we can see in these two episodes of *The West Wing*, in short, is the classic drama of presidential grandeur just barely peeking through an alternative far less grand image of the presidential staff. Taken together the various images presented by the program provide us with a remarkable distillation of the popular drama of the presidency. In its two fundamental renditions of the presidential office—one focusing on the seriocomic tribulations of the White House staff, the other featuring the dignity of the president himself—*The West Wing* recreated the ambivalent vision of government that has long characterized American political discourse. Though the emphasis has shifted from the conflict between Congress and the president to the tension between the president and his own advisers, once again we see the ambivalent conviction that the federal government is, at one and the same time, both a poorly functioning bureaucracy and ideally the eminent agent of the American people. More impressively still, however, in the two, anomalous episodes of its first season, the program neatly summarizes the mythology of the president's sovereign power. In "A Proportional Response," we see the president as the nearly monarchical figure who, confronted with the mortality of America's individual citizens, exercises the power of the state to affirm the enduring stature of the nation. In "What Kind of Day Has it Been," by contrast, the living people demand that the president demonstrate, in his own mortality, that his power comes not from his own monarchical command but from his subservience to its sovereign authority. The true president at once commands the helm of the state and martyrs himself to the nation.

In retrospect, of course, *The West Wing*'s brief image of presidential grandeur, and its suggestion that such grandeur might be elicited by a confrontation with terrorism and the allegedly lawless states of the Middle East looks virtually prophetic. In the months after 9/11, the Bush administration reinvigorated the ideal of presidential leadership, using the time honored argument that the nation had been thrown into a war that threatened its very existence in order to concentrate unprecedented powers in the hands of a virtually unchecked commander-in-chief. In the process, it both followed the lead of earlier Democratic administrations and, at the same time, sought to use the powers of the president to undermine the political order, governmental structures, and institutions of social welfare that the modern presidency had been used to create. In effect, the latter Bush administration followed out a strategy that, as Leonard Garment indicated, had first been conceived by conservatives during the Nixon years. It would reassert the legitimacy and stature of presidential leadership with the hope not solely of defending executive power itself, but of using that power to finally achieve a conservative counterrevolution that would break the back of the liberal state. "With Congress encircled by interest groups," the conservative intellectual Terry Eastland announced, "*only* the president stands much of a chance of changing the status quo." In the same era when liberal thinkers and political scientists had lost faith in the value of presidential power, the new right sought energetically to renew and expand it.[8]

One measure of the radical nature of those ambitions can be seen in just how unlikely they seemed throughout the last decade of the twentieth century. In its first year, *The West Wing* only briefly invoked the president's stature as commander-in-chief in order to counter its own predominant image of quotidian, mass mediated politics. The greater part of the program's time and energies were dedicated to the mundane dramas of political competition in a divided government. So, too, did many political thinkers throughout the 1990s stress the seemingly inevitable features of a nearly stagnant political system whose fundamental condition seemed unlikely to change anytime in the near future. In the words of the prominent political scientist Stephen Skowronek, the United States appeared in the nineties to have entered a state of "perpetual preemption"—of interminable "interest cleavages and factional discontent"—in which rival agendas could be expected to conflict endlessly without any one coalition being able to marshal the kind of partisan coherence and popular support that would enable it to seize commanding authority. It was a condition Skowronek welcomed for the emphasis it seemed likely to place on renewed "pragmatism" and "deliberation." Because of the deeply divided political order that had emerged in the last decades of the twentieth century, executive power would be, thankfully, perpetually constrained. From this point forward, Skowronek hopefully predicted in 1993, "no president will be able to tramp roughshod over the authority and independence of everyone else."[9] His prediction of the death of the charismatic presidency turned out to be greatly exaggerated, of course. But such views were not unusual throughout the last decade of the twentieth-century, and it is worth considering them briefly, both for the history of intellectual attitudes toward the presidency they help to reveal and for the way, more fundamentally, they may illuminate the persistent American ambivalence toward executive power.[10]

Skowronek himself was a leading figure in the late twentieth-century reconsideration of the idea of presidential leadership, his work presenting perhaps the most original and widely celebrated academic challenge to the long-standing hegemony of the theory of the "modern presidency." Reconsidering that theory, Skowronek questioned whether such an institution could even be said to exist. He did not doubt the reality of executive power itself. In fact, he accepted and intensified the view first articulated by Progressive advocates of the presidency, who had celebrated the capacity of a democratic executive to override the limitations of law and Constitution. "The presidency is an *order-shattering* institution," Skowronek affirmed, a "battering ram" particularly suited to "dislodging established elites, destroying the institutional arrangements that support them, and clearing the way for something entirely new."[11] But he questioned both whether such charismatic power was valuable and whether it was a distinctly modern force that had represented an advance in the political development of the United States.

In Skowronek's view it was a mere "modern conceit" to believe that a new ideal of presidential leadership had arisen in the twentieth century alongside the expansion of the federal government and the rise of national power. In place of that developmental narrative, he articulated instead a cyclic history in which the charismatic force of executive power was repeatedly yoked to large scale shifts in political alignment and major changes in the structure and mission of governing institutions. The history of national politics could be reduced in this way to a recurring pattern of the relation between aspiring political leaders and the larger political regimes that shaped the environment in which they came to power. Time and again, Skowronek thus argued, presidents either assumed office to grandly delegitimize and replace a tottering regime (as say, Thomas Jefferson, or Franklin Roosevelt, or Ronald Reagan had done), or to seek to extend and institutionalize the political commitments of an existing order (as James K. Polk and LBJ had done), or to seek to hold together a political consensus that was in the midst of falling apart (John Adams, Herbert Hoover, Jimmy Carter). Rather than seeing a vast rise in presidential power and prestige during the twentieth century, in other words, Skowronek saw the history of the United States replaying a series of political dynamics whose possible permutations were deeply rooted in the institutional design and cultural expectations of American government.

Like a number of his contemporaries, Skowronek thus issued a strong challenge to the once prominent view that the modern presidency was a radically new institution whose most energetic occupants had significantly expanded and democratized American politics. His emphasis on cyclic historical patterns and on the constraints imposed by the long-term fortunes of vast political regimes sharply undercut the grandeur of personal leadership. Presidents were able to exercise power, in Skowronek's view, less because of their distinctive qualities or because of their ability to articulate the popular will, than because of their chance relation to the highly contingent assembly of historical forces. Nor was it clear by his terms that presidential ambition and grand leadership were as benevolent as the defenders of executive power once thought. Presidents exercise great authority only when the stars align properly, Skowronek asserted—when a prevailing regime is shaking and the democratic legitimacy of the political system has come to such a crisis that a wide part of the citizenship welcomes a seemingly fundamental reorientation of the political agenda. Even, then, however, the "inherently disruptive" power of charismatic leadership does little to guarantee more just or more effective government. "It is worth noting," Skowronek pointed out, that "the commanding authority Presidents wield at these moments does not automatically translate into . . . effective solutions to the substantive problems that gave rise to the nationwide crisis of legitimacy in the first place."[12]

Thus it was that Skowronek welcomed a future where presidents seemed unlikely to wield such extraordinary power again. With each stage in the history of charismatic leadership, Skowronek maintained, the institutions of government and political participation had expanded and thickened to the point where it had become impossible for any single administration to initiate truly sweeping change, so that the battering force of presidential leadership was ever more likely to be deflected by opposition, resistance, and sheer inertia. Such continual "preemption," he argued, was likely to play the role once believed to be served by the separation of powers, restraining the capacity for profound change and checking the prerogative of executive power. "The traditional leadership postures" have "deteriorated into mere roles to be performed," Skowronek asserted—a point he emphasized by calling on a nearly elegiac description of their senescence. The great moments of reconstruction associated with charismatic leaders had taken place in an elevated order of history that Skowronek summarized as "political time." (He contrasted this highly charged form of temporality to the mere "secular time" of ordinary history.) In the 1990s, Skowronek seemed both disappointed and relieved to note, such foundational moments appeared a thing of the past. "We are witness," he proclaimed, "to the waning of political time."[13]

It is not difficult to see how closely in some ways a drama like *The West Wing* resembles the theories of a scholar like Skowronek. In its initial season, the television program also marked the difference between the grandeur of "political time" and the ordinariness of "secular time," and it, too, suggested that in the context of the battles of the late twentieth century, truly profound moments of political transformation seemed forever consigned to history. Jed Bartlett dramatizes the understanding in his frustrated realization that, rather than wield "God's own thunder" without restraint, he must remain bound by the norms of international and domestic politics to a mere "proportional response." Such assumptions about the limitations of presidential power in fact were common elements of public discourse in the nineties, and they echoed not only through academic political science and popular culture, but through some of the moment's most impressive literary writing as well—where not only Skowronek's historical diagnosis, but something like his deep ambivalence about charismatic leadership was evident as well.

Indeed it is striking to see the manner in which contemporary writers once again reconsidered the heroic examples of the historical presidency. In 1995, David Herbert Donald published his long awaited, antihagiographic biography of Lincoln, a work that reversed the traditional image of Lincoln as great leader and national martyr by stressing what Donald saw as Lincoln's more fundamental qualities—his alleged, essential passivity and his complete engagement in the mundane politics of party competition.[14] A number of imaginative writers drew on a comparable understanding. When Toni Morrison referred to the Gettysburg Address in her 1993 Nobel Prize lecture, for example, she invoked an image of Lincoln that almost directly inverted the terms for which his eloquence had long been celebrated. Against what she denounced as "statist language"—a rhetoric of "exclusivity and dominance" that served only to excite "reverence in schoolchildren" and provide "shelter for despots"—Morrison praised Lincoln as a writer whose work emphasized its own powerlessness. Her version of the Gettysburg Address was admirable for "refusing to monumentalize" the fallen soldiers of the Civil War. "His words signal deference to the uncapturability of the life it mourns."

Like many of her predecessors, then, Morrison redeemed the virtue of a presidential leadership (to which she, too, compared the work of the writer) by distinguishing it from a counterimage of purely coercive state power. But she seemed able to maintain that contrast only by imagining presidential rhetoric as a kind of poetry that made nothing happen. Unlike earlier artists and thinkers who had celebrated Lincoln and other examples of presidential greatness for uniting state and people in a renewed national compact, Morrison imagined the writer and president as a figure most admirable for the quality of "deference"—for "the recognition that language can never live up to life once and for all." At their best, she suggested, writers and presidents did not spin words of binding eloquence, but dramatized their own limitations and thereby freed their audiences to accept their own personal responsibilities.[15]

A similar doubtfulness of the mythology of presidential leadership appeared in some of the era's more extended fictional portraits. In his brilliant imagining of Abe Lincoln's formative years, for example, Richard Slotkin resembled Morrison in rearticulating the mythology of presidential leadership with remarkable fidelity. Slotkin's young Lincoln is an aspiring national leader who will stake a "claim to the whole American republic," particularly by virtue of an eloquence that is shown to surpass the restrictions of illegitimate law and the coercion of brute power. As in the classic visions of presidential leadership, moreover, Slotkin imagines a Lincoln who not only aspires to refound a more just and equal nation—one particularly freed of slavery and racism—but a presidential figure whose eloquence depends on his encounter with a martyr who sanctifies that cause. But, having established a compelling vision of presidential heroism, Slotkin closes his novel with a telling gesture toward the less grand arrangements that such visions often obscure. His Lincoln will begin the path to greatness by making opportunistic use of the Black Hawk war to establish a public reputation, thus reminding us that the president is first of all a politician and that his claim to national power depends above all on the collective solidarity produced by the very conquest and war his words claim to rise above.[16]

Similarly qualified visions of democratic leadership were prominent throughout the literary writing and public discourse of the turn of the century. In the terms proposed by Russell Banks's novel *Cloudsplitter*, "an Age of Heroism had acceded to an Age of Cowardice."[17] But the most elaborate and inventive of the antimythic renditions of presidential power may have come in the remarkable series of novels Philip Roth wrote during the later nineties, in a creative efflorescence that appears to have been stimulated at least in part by the sense, common in the years following the end of the Cold War, that the era of U.S. power that gave rise to the visions of presidential grandeur had drawn to a close. In *I Married a Communist*, for example, Roth all but literally echoed Skowronek's point that in such a world "traditional leadership postures" would be revealed as "mere roles to be performed" and that such postures both depended on and disguised their order-shattering disruption. For, the central figure of Roth's novel, Ira Ringold, is a radio actor and popular celebrity whose renditions of Lincoln make him the representative, in the dawning anti-Communist hysteria of novel's late forties setting, of the dying culture of the Popular Front and of New Deal populism more generally.[18] The more significant fact, however—revealed by Roth only in the closing pages of his novel—is that Ira Ringold's presidential impersonation only conceals the violent rage that underlies his populist bravado and that it belies his inevitably failed effort at "heroic reinvention." "The root at the root of everything was about to be exposed anyway. America was going to see the cold-blooded killer . . . underneath Abraham Lincoln's hat."[19]

I Married a Communist is the middle novel in the series of books often called Roth's American trilogy, and like its two companions, *American Pastoral* and *The Human Stain*, it offers an intensely disenchanted view of the course of postwar liberalism—a history that Roth views, as his frequent references to Shakespeare and Sophocles emphasize, as a tragic tale of great aspiration leading to terrible self-destruction. In *I Married a Communist* that tragic mode is directly contrasted to the epic celebrations of popular democracy that had been crucial to the Popular Front and more generally to the New Deal and to the creation of the modern presidency. The story of Ira Ringold's desperate rise and inevitable fall is cast against the populist sentimentality of Howard Fast and Norman Corwin and the sentimental affiliation that had held together the now splintering legacy of the Roosevelt coalition. But throughout his trilogy, Roth uses the grievous self-destruction of his protagonists to throw doubt on the great days of U.S. power and prosperity and to reveal a fatal cultural shallowness at the heart of the liberal ambition to expand the freedom and opportunity of all Americans. In Ira Ringold, he creates a hero of left populism who is brought down by the tawdry vindictiveness of red baiters and still more by his own unchainable rage. In *American Pastoral*, he gives us Swede Levov, whose great ambition—"vaulting his father" in pursuit of the nonsectarian promises of democracy—results in the destruction of himself and his family.[20] In *The Human Stain* we likewise see Coleman Silk, the African American man whose decision to pass as a Jew in the pursuit of "the passionate struggle for singularity" leads to humiliation and the bereavement of his family.[21] All three men are committed to what *American Pastoral* calls a "particular form of utopian thinking"—"the desire to go the limit in America with your rights" (86, 85). Each in his ideological zeal will betray the only world that looks remotely attractive in the late Roth's depiction, the little, localized milieus of ethnic community, the lost urban villages of the mid-century industrial city.[22]

Like many another intellectual who rediscovered the virtues of social capital in the last decade of the twentieth century, Roth often views those worlds through the gauze of nostalgia. The lower-middle-class neighborhoods of Newark are repeatedly limned in Roth's late novels with virtually ecstatic celebrations of humble dignity. Their patriarchal stewards, who Roth had long cast as the victims of the American liberalism they mistakenly supported, are viewed glowingly as the dignified tutors of the very women and children who undermine them. Their decline amid the urban crisis that accompanied the wave of postwar suburbanization is repeatedly depicted as a spectacle of civilizational collapse—with the African American residents of the inner city cast nearly explicitly in the role of coming barbarians. Roth's mythology of urban decline is often richer and more complex than that of many of his contemporaries; he consistently imagines, for example, the lost urban villages as willfully narrow communities that, in nurturing the virtues of hunger and ambition, could not help but ensure their own destruction. But the thought that nostalgia for the warmly parochial worlds of the industrial city might itself be a particular form of utopian theory seems only rarely to cross the late Roth's mind.

All but directly, Roth ties that parochial fancy to a repudiation of the myth of presidential leadership. In the climactic moments of *American Pastoral*, Swede Levov's faithless wife Dawn brags to a dinner party about the crowning moment of the family's past glory—the time some two decades earlier when the Levovs and their then young daughter sailed to Europe on the *U.S. Line*, honored guests in "the presidential suite." The memory exemplifies "the American pastoral par excellence," Roth's narrator Nathan Zuckerman suggests, as he unkindly juxtaposes the glib satisfaction of Dawn's public recollection to the unspoken depths of Swede's more painful and privately considered memories. The false glamour of the presidency, in other words, typifies the shallowness of mid-century American ambition and its false confidence that by sheer ambition Americans might triumph over the sorrows of family and the superstitious constraints of the old world (402).

By the time he published *American Pastoral* in 1998, Roth had been making similar observations about the charade of the presidency for nearly four decades. In "Writing American Fiction," the legendary essay in which he lamented the oppressive weightlessness of a mass-mediated culture ("It stupefies, it sickens, it infuriates, and finally it is even a kind of embarrassment to one's own meager imagination"), Roth found such banality epitomized by the newly televisual spectacle of presidential politics, whose prominence occasioned in him a sense of "professional envy." "I found myself beginning to wish I had invented," the theater of the presidential debates, Roth complained. "But then, of course, one need not have been a fiction writer to wish that *someone* had invented it, and that it was not real and with us." As the high style of the Camelot era declined toward the squalor of the Nixon years, Roth only intensified the complaint. Presidential politics produced only "frustration, the sickening disappointment of finding in the seat of power neither reason, nor common sense, nor horse sense—and certainly not charity or courage—but moral ignorance, blundering authority, and witless, arbitrary judgment."[23]

Such comments offered a summary judgment on the history of presidential government. If it had once seemed to Roth's predecessors and many of his contemporaries that executive leadership might restore the promise of democratic government and accomplish the redemptive achievement of popular self-rule, Roth saw a nightmarish inversion of that hope. What presidential politics dramatized, rather, was the utter absence of genuine popular sovereignty. The mass culture typified by the media presidency only intensified the awareness "that events and individuals are unreal, and that power to alter the course of the age, of my life and your life, is actually vested nowhere." It brought home to the writer the realization that "he does not live in this country."[24] Indeed, amid the snowballing revelations of governmental abuse and political corruption during the latter sixties and early seventies, Roth's anger at "dispossession and powerlessness" grew, until he felt oppressed by "a daily awareness of government *as a coercive force*, [of] its continuous presence in one's thoughts as far more than just an institutionalized, imperfect system of necessary controls."[25] Popular sovereignty was not only absent, in short, it was systematically denied by an abusive state that took illegitimate possession of its citizens.

The upshot of such a view was a guiding assumption that the craft of the novelist stood in direct antagonism to the coercion of the state, that the work of writing amounted to an endless, unresolvable effort to resist the manipulation of government and the signature seduction of politics—"the narcissistic illusion that" one "has been sprung from the realities of pain and loss, that . . . life is *not* futility" (IMAC 60, emphasis in original). Earlier writers, like Whitman or Stein or Wright or Ellison, who were more enticed by the image of presidential leadership, had found precisely such a solution to the problems of pain and loss in an idealized image of the nation-state.[26] Though in importantly different ways, all invoked the image of executive power to figure the grandeur and immortality of an American nation that was imagined to surpass what appeared in its light the merely temporary accidents of failure and injustice. Roth rejected the allure of that salvation, returning often to the reminder of the absence of a genuine national community. Thus the inverse collectivity portrayed in *Our Gang*, where Americans are united solely in hostility to a crude and abusive state, or the more poignant suggestion in *Portnoy's Complaint*, that the elder Portnoy's slavish devotion to upward mobility and assimilation (as to "Roosevelt in the White House in Washington") is of a piece with his social marginalization and his absence of a true homeland.[27]

It was not until the final years of the century, however, in his American trilogy, that Roth expanded that impression into a full scale tragic vision, deepening the contrast between the suffering of his protagonists and the shallowness of national politics and returning consistently to a determinedly postheroic image of the presidency. The major action of *I Married a Communist* takes place during the presidential campaign of 1948, when the legacy of FDR (the "great man," Nathan Zuckerman's father says, who "saved this country's capitalism from the capitalists") has been displaced by the undignified factionalism between the supporters of Truman and Wallace and the vicious, small-minded red-baiting of congressional conservatives—including the rising Richard Nixon (103). *American Pastoral* envisions Swede Levov as "our Kennedy," casting his destruction not as a martyrdom that will forever enshrine the hero's glamour, but as a grinding disenchantment that reveals the emptiness of hope and the dominance of "circumstantial absurdity" (83, 80). *The Human Stain* unfolds in the summer of the Clinton impeachment "when some kind of demon had been unleashed in the nation" and "the smallness of people was simply crushing" (3). In each case, Roth aligns his protagonist with a presidential figure to reveal not only the shallowness of that hero's hopes and the implicit repression concealed in his longing for national community, but the inevitable upending of the "narcissistic illusion" that the presidency consistently represents in Roth's depiction. "The jumble, the mayhem, the mess proved itself more subtle than this one's ideology and that one's morality. . . . Life, in all its shameless impurity, once again confounded America" (3).

Significantly, however, Roth consistently suggests that the obverse side of the false promise of postwar liberalism is not merely shameless impurity, but the far more disturbing fact that he refers to when he invokes "the cold-blooded killer . . . underneath Abraham Lincoln's hat." In *I Married a Communist* that phrase refers specifically to the late revelation that the ostensibly political passion of Ira Ringold's life has been a mere effort to conceal and control a more basic, "murderous rage" that defines Ira's character—a "scaffolding of politics" built up around the primal force of "the unreasonable" (299, 291, 304). But like *American Pastoral*'s allusion to "the presidential suite," the line is also meant to gesture toward a more fundamental point—which is that in Roth's depiction, the crucial bargain of the presidential vision, as it has descended from the memory of Lincoln, will no longer be honored. No invocation of the solemn dignity of the nation or of the sovereign will of the people can be called on to justify and thus dispatch the bottom truth of coercion and violence. This is the point Roth makes in the final lines of *The Human Stain* as well, where, encountering the murderously angry Vietnam veteran Les Farley and seeing the lethal drill Farley holds in his hand, Zuckerman considers "the terror of the auger"—"like the X of an illiterate's signature on a sheet of paper" (360, 361). So, too, is it the implication of the bombing carried out by the teenage Merry in *American Pastoral*. All are reminders of what Roth describes memorably in that novel as "the fury, the violence, and the desperation of the counterpastoral . . . the indigenous American berserk" (86). If the great stories of the presidential imagination had imagined violence and coercion redeemed by the achievement of a renewed national compact, Roth's late fiction denies the promise of that resolution. Indeed it suggests that the very pursuit of the pastoral dream of democratic community demands the coercion and repression, and produces the resentment, that will ultimately destroy it.

In Roth's world, in short, there will be nothing like that striking transition portrayed by *The West Wing*, where the confusion of ordinary politics is overcome by the valor of war and the exercise of state power is redeemed by the suggestion of the president's suffering. Or, at least there would not be until Roth answered the tragic narrative of his American trilogy with the surprising departure of his later novel *The Plot Against America*. In that counterhistorical novel, Roth again returns to the allure and deception of presidential politics, imagining that Charles Lindbergh defeated FDR in the 1940 race for the presidency and that his election gave brief rise to a Fascist state in America. But, despite the apparently paranoid imaginings that inform this narrative, *The Plot Against America* suggests a significant departure from the darkly pessimistic novels Roth wrote in the late nineties, giving us in almost every respect a far simpler and more reassuring story. Against the manifold, metafictional complexities of the trilogy—in which Roth's invented narrator, the reclusive Zuckerman, considers and reconsiders the deeply entangled tales that are recounted to him by other speakers—*The Plot Against America* gives us the compelling and seemingly straightforward (although invented) childhood recollections of "Philip Roth." Against the tragic mood of the trilogy, this latter novel provides us with an elegiac celebration of Roth's parents. (The novel "gave me an opportunity to bring my parents back from the grave," Roth reports, to "restore them to what they were at the height of their powers."[28]) Most significantly for our purposes, against the political pessimism of Roth's earlier fiction, *The Plot Against America* strangely imagines a redemption of American government—which, compared to the brief, nightmarish alternative of fascist tyranny, looks suddenly appealing. "There was something very patriotic in the endeavor," of writing the novel, Roth appropriately remarked. It reminds us that "instead of fascism we got FDR."[29]

What happened between 2000 and 2004 to shift Roth's attitude and to make him reconsider the accomplishments of the liberal presidency, of course, were the events of 9/11 and, more importantly, the disastrous administration of George W. Bush—a man, Roth declared, "unfit to run a hardware store let alone a nation like this one." Roth went on to suggest that the sheer enormity of Bush's tenure had "merely reaffirmed the maxim" that informed the novelist's complete oeuvre. It was a maxim, he added, that "makes our lives as Americans as precarious as anyone else's: all the assurances are provisional."[30] Yet, curiously, despite his evident disgust for Bush—and despite the fact that, half-hearted demurrers aside, his counterhistory seemed plainly intended as an allegory of recent history—Roth did not seem to recognize how similar his maxim was to the message the Bush administration itself sought to impress on the American public. For, in several respects, the Bush presidency, too, has emphasized the conviction that all assurances should be regarded as provisional. In its continually reiterated claim that the United States remains engaged in an existentially definitive war, the Bush administration has sought to convince Americans that they live in a perpetual state of peril and crisis, using that assertion much as earlier administrations had done to concentrate power in the hands of the president. Equally significantly, however, the Bush presidency has tried to use that power in service to the agenda predicted by Leonard Garment: to undermine the regulatory, administrative, legal, and diplomatic institutions that are in fact the main legacy of the modern presidency.[31]

In this manner, the Bush presidency has aimed to make use of the disruptive powers of charismatic leadership in the manner that commentators during the nineties thought a thing of the past, seeking to use executive power to dismantle the accomplishments, institutions, and political structures of liberal government. Like the predecessors who built the modern presidency, the Bush administration has sought to view the presidency as an expression of a national plebiscite and thus as a warrant for sweeping regime change. ("I've got the will of the people at my back," Bush remarked after the presidential election that took place in the year Roth's *The Plot Against America* was published. "When you win, there is a feeling that the people have spoken and embraced your point of view, and that's what I intend to tell the Congress."[32]) In pursuing that agenda, however, Bush aimed not just to use and expand executive power, but to alter its relation to existing political and governmental structures. Beginning with its prophets during the Progressive Era, and especially during the pivotal years of the New Deal, the creators of the modern presidency had sought to link presidential power to administrative government and had aimed in this way to free the executive branch from the decentralized systems of party competition and congressional representation. In so doing, the advocates of presidential leadership made consistent ideological appeals to the grandeur of a national community that transcended the limitations of party, region, state, and personal interest. In practice, they created an interrelated system of political elites centered on Washington (and located in administrative agencies, congressional subcommittees, foundations, interest groups, and universities) whose interests and sources of power were independent of party organizations and local communities.[33]

The Republican revolution that culminated in the second Bush presidency aimed to reverse every aspect of these developments. Against a liberal regime that had elevated presidential leadership over partisan organization, Republican activists rebuilt an elaborate party structure that acted to enforce ideological coherence and political coordination over the three branches of the federal government. Against the liberal emphasis on administrative and regulatory independence, the new Republican activists reinforced party unity and undermined established public institutions, by resurrecting the use of patronage appointments that stressed ideology and partisan loyalty over expertise. Targeting the legitimacy and power of the national elites that had grown along with the federal government, moreover, the leaders of the Republican revolution established widely flung networks of political activists rooted in local communities and organizations, acting frequently to remind the party base of its ideological mission and its moral superiority to Washington insiders.[34]

In keeping with this newly intensified partisanship, finally, the Republican revolution dispatched the liberal rhetoric of egalitarian national community. Arguing for a renewal of presidential power years before the second Bush came to office, the conservative intellectual Terry Eastland made a point of contrasting the new, Republican executive he envisioned to a liberal "concept of the presidency" that he claimed had "long ago hit its limits." "Liberalism from the first years of this century has argued against localism and for an ever more inclusive, more equal national community," Eastland accurately noted. "Toward this end it has posited the need for a powerful federal government brought about by a visionary President who would mount the 'bully pulpit' and lead the American people toward its special future."[35] A conservative presidency, Eastland went on to argue, would not merely avoid that concept, but actively contend against it. Rooting his electoral power in an energized base and an activist party, Bush followed Eastland's advice to the letter, emphasizing and intensifying the cultural and political differences that divided the United States and implicitly casting his supporters as a saving remnant who, in refusing to defer to formerly respected institutions of public culture, spoke for the true nation of America.

The curious feature of *The Plot Against America* seen in this light is how closely the story it tells resembles in a number of respects the vision of presidential leadership that conservative intellectuals brought to the fore during the Bush administration. For decades, Roth had been indicating his suspicion of the pretenses of postwar liberalism and the stultifying institutions of the welfare state. *The Plot Against America* takes those suspicions to a melodramatic extreme. FDR, as the novel's protagonist, the seven-year-old Philip Roth, recalls him, looks just as Eastland's liberal president does. "The inherent decorum" of his radio addresses "bestowed on our family a historical significance, authoritatively merging our lives with his as well as with that of the entire nation."[36] But Roth's point, much like Eastland's, is to emphasize the fragility and insubstantiality of the reassurance provided by Roosevelt, who in Roth's telling is able to do little to protect the beleaguered supporters who have been targeting by a sudden explosion of state-led anti-Semitism. Meanwhile, the administrative structures of the federal government that the Roosevelt presidency had built over the first eight years of the New Deal become in Roth's reimagining the apparatus of an abusive new racial policy. Their powers meet meaningful resistance only from the two figures whom Roth pointedly imagines as outsiders to the existing political system: the gossip columnist Walter Winchell who, in his decision to run for president against the anti-Semite Lindbergh, and in his ultimate assassination during the campaign, gives rise to a popular movement against state tyranny; and Roth's father Herman, who in his epic journey to rescue an orphaned Jewish boy abandoned by an abusive government in the midst of anti-Semitic Kentucky, provides the climactic events of the novel.

Together, those two characters resuscitate in a new key the language of presidential grandeur. Winchell is significantly cast as "the martyred candidate" whose casket, traveling from Louisville to New York, implicitly reverses the path of Lincoln's funeral bier, while acting similarly to gesture toward the reformation of the national community (305). Herman Roth, meanwhile, appears as the citizen soldier, who in his willing service to his people, justifies the politician's leadership and redeems his nation. The heroic journey he takes, we are told, amounts to Herman Roth's "Guadalcanal, . . . his Battle of the Bulge" (355). Though here importantly neither figure quite fits the standard definition, once again the presidential leader (the orator Winchell) and the soldier (Herman Roth) are joined in service to a nation whose stature is legitimized by their commitment and by their willingness to endure violence and to face death to prove it. Indeed, the implication of their shared role deepens with the ensuing disappearance of Lindbergh (who is revealed to have been blackmailed by the Nazis), the rapid dismantling of America's brief Fascist regime, and the subsequent restoration of the *status quo ante*—such that U.S. history as Roth imagines it returns without alteration or interruption to the actual course of events now familiar. In Roth's telling, that is, Herman Roth and Walter Winchell become the representative face of America's saving remnant. Their heroic commitment acts to purge their society of a foreign and oppressive parasite and restores their nation to its destiny.

In effect, Herman Roth is a more heroic version of *The West Wing*'s Morris Tolliver, with the young "Philip Roth" assuming the role of the television program's Charlie Young. Though for Roth it is the Jews who now represent America's symbolically crucial marginal citizens, Roth, too, envisions U.S. sovereignty redeemed in an ultimate confrontation with a foreign oppressor—here not the hostile states of the Arab Middle East, but the internal subversives of America's own, homegrown Fascism.

To see *The Plot Against America* in this light, however, is to recognize that Roth's novel mirrors to a remarkable degree the political movement Roth himself appears to despise. Though the values they prefer and the local communities and minority cultures they defend differ radically, the Bush administration and Roth's novel tell comparable stories. Both suggest that a marginalized people must throw off the false reassurance and actual oppression of an administrative state to revitalize the energies of partisanship and restore their country to its rightful stature. Against the Republican revolution, in other words, *The Plot Against America* might be seen as an attempt at an epic justification for the rebirth of Blue America and for the recreation of the political leadership necessary to revitalize it.[37] Though it would certainly be a mistake to read Roth's story as overtly allegorical, it may be significant that the leader of Roth's imagined political opposition, Winchell, shares some of the qualities that establishment Democrats saw in the development of the grassroots, Web-based insurgency that developed around Howard Dean during the 2004 presidential campaign. He is "too loud, talks too fast, . . . says too much," is vulgar, shrill, and lacking in the "decorum" shared by Lindbergh and Roosevelt, yet creates a political opposition where more reputable figures are slow to act (304). If, the United States was fortunate to get FDR rather than Fascism, in other words, Roth's celebration of his father and of the companion figure Winchell proposes an explanation for that history that is in keeping with the way a rising cohort of activists had begun to think of political competition in the first decade of the twenty-first century. The success of the New Deal from this retrospective angle looks to owe less to the leadership of FDR (who in Roth's depiction seems a largely passive figure), or to the innovations of administrative government, than to the intense commitment of the populist media and committed partisans who supported the Roosevelt revolution.

In this fashion, Roth's novel can be seen to take its place—alongside, say, the writing of Terry Eastland—in the historical series of efforts to reimagine the role of executive power. Along with the Bush administration, Roth's novel contributes to a reformulation of the concept of presidential leadership for the twenty-first century—one that has turned against the liberal presidency's earlier dependence on the administrative state and that looks forward to the further growth of intense mobilization and party competition. How precisely Roth wishes us to understand this story remains intriguingly unclear. It may be that in telling such a tale Roth really is true to a maxim that he claims runs consistently through all his fiction, and that, in giving us a child's view of the heroism of this narrative, that he wishes us to recognize, as Toni Morrison does, the dangerous appeal of such reassuring political epics. Or it may be that, as with a number of his contemporaries, Roth's literary talents were most suited to the institutions of American liberalism that he mocked and lamented for several decades and that in a new context dominated by the Bush administration and the Republican revolution, he finds less that is penetrating and subversive to say. Or, it may simply be that Roth, like many of his contemporaries among liberals has found himself so outraged by the Republican revolution that he is eager to imagine a redefined Democratic Party that will emulate the intense partisan organization and the pursuit of political dominance that has served to bolster the power of the radical right. However the case may be, *The Plot Against America* resembles *The West Wing* in that it demonstrates the continuing power of the presidential imagination to compel assent. One way or another, Roth reminds us of the lasting appeal of heroic leadership and its alleged indispensability to democratic government.

On this point alone, Stephen Skowronek proved to be badly wrong. The assumption that, in Roth's words, "a nation such as this one" demands a distinctive and charismatic leader who can reestablish popular rule and redeem the national mission remains a central and alluring element of American political ideology. Indeed the fervor greeting Barack Obama's campaign for the presidency demonstrates its resilience. In his eloquent appeals to the nation, and in his forceful advocacy of the importance of public eloquence itself, Obama has defined his candidacy as a revitalization of presidential leadership, reasserting the theory of the presidency that descends from Whitman and Wilson and FDR. Invoking especially Lincoln and JFK as his predecessors, he has cast his campaign as a vehicle for the collective American people to reassert control over their government and their destiny. And, like his predecessors, he has placed that ambition as the latest in a series of founding moments—the Revolution, the Civil War, the Civil Rights movement—in which the American nation overcame the illegitimate powers and unjust exclusions that frustrated its sovereignty. Not surprisingly, Obama's first electoral success led immediately to a wave of rumor predicting his assassination.[38] Not only does the image of the redeemer president survive; the mythology surrounding the figure remains deeply embedded in our political culture.

NOTES

Preface

1. Whitman, "Hero Presidents," *The Uncollected Poetry and Prose of Walt Whitman*, ed. Emory Holloway (Garden City, NY: Doubleday, Page, 1921), 196–98. In his earliest political writing, Whitman cast himself as an admirer not of heroic leaders, but of party organization. "True liberty could not long exist in this country without our party," he asserted in 1847, rallying Brooklyn Democrats to party loyalty. Whitman, *The Gathering of Forces*, eds. Cleveland Rodgers and John Black (New York: G. P. Putnam's Sons, 1920), II: 40. When he did praise a Democratic president like Polk as "a truly noble Magistrate," he viewed the politician mainly as a party leader and he emphasized the degree to which the politics of "president-making" surrounded even such impressive figures with "chicanery" and "small ambition." "President Making," *Brooklyn Daily Eagle* (June 12, 1846), 2. At least until the mid-1850s, then, Whitman placed his political hopes in the prospect that an effective presidential candidate could revitalize "a real live Democratic party." Whitman, *The Correspondence*, ed. Edwin Haviland Miller (New York: New York University Press, 1969), I: 39.

2. Whitman, "New Light and Old," *Uncollected Poetry and Prose*, 167.

3. Whitman, notebook entry, circa 1856, qtd. at Betsy Erkkila, *Whitman the Political Poet* (New York: Oxford University Press, 1989), 146.

4. Whitman, "To a President," *Collected Poetry and Collected Prose*, ed. Justin Kaplan (New York: Library of America, 1982), 410; *subsequent citations to this volume given as CPP*.

5. "impregnable," Whitman, "The Eighteenth Presidency!" *CPP*, 1321; "conquering march," Whitman, "Race of Veterans," *CPP*, 452.

6. Whitman, preface, 1872, to *As a Strong Bird on Pinions Free*, *CPP*, 4, 5, emphasis in original. On Whitman's experience of the War and its effects on his poetics and his political thinking, see, Daniel Aaron, *The Unwritten War: American Writers and the Civil War* (New York: Knopf, 1973), 56–74; Betsy Erkkila, *Whitman the Political Poet*, 190–292; George Frederickson, *The Inner Civil War: Northern Intellectuals and the Crisis of the Union*, 2nd

ed. (Champaign: University of Illinois Press, 1993), 19–22, 66–72, 90–97; Kerry C. Larson, *Whitman's Drama of Consensus* (Chicago: University of Chicago Press, 1988), 207–44; Mark Maslan, *Whitman Possessed: Poetry, Sexuality, and Popular Authority* (Baltimore: Johns Hopkins University Press, 2001), 93–141; Deak Nabers, *Victory of Law: The 14th Amendment, the Civil War, and American Literature, 1852–1867* (Baltimore, MD: Johns Hopkins University Press, 2006), 173–98; David S. Reynolds, "Politics and Poetry: *Leaves of Grass* and the Social Crisis of the 1850s, *The Cambridge Companion to Walt Whitman*, ed. Ezra Greenspan (New York: Cambridge University Press, 1995), 92–109.

7. Whitman, "The Eighteenth Presidency!" *CPP*, 1321.

8. Whitman qtd. at Erkkila, *Whitman the Political Poet*, 192.

9. Whitman qtd. at Justin Kaplan, *Walt Whitman: A Life* (New York: Simon & Schuster, 1980), 272.

10. Whitman, "The Eighteenth Presidency!" *CPP*, 1317, 1310.

11. Peri E. Arnold and L. John Roos, "Toward A Theory of Congressional-Executive Relations," *The Review of Politics* 36, 3 (1974), 412.

12. Whitman qtd. at Kaplan, *Walt Whitman: A Life*, 260.

13. Whitman, "This Dust Was Once a Man," *CPP*, 468.

14. Whitman, "Notes Left Over," *CPP*, 1071.

15. Whitman, "Spirit Whose Work is Done" and "When Lilacs Last in the Dooryard Bloom'd," *CPP*, 456, 467.

16. "Absolute triumph," Whitman, "A Backward Glance O'er Travel'd Roads," *CPP*, 661; "indomitable firmness," Whitman, "November Boughs," *CCP*, 1198; "Over the Carnage Rose a Prophetic Voice," *CPP*, 453.

17. Whitman, "Specimen Days," *CPP*, 764. As Erkkila points out, without noting the logic implicit in the point, Whitman's elegy for Lincoln, "When Lilacs Last in the Dooryard Bloom'd," offers "a politicopoetic myth to counter Booth's cry on the night of the assassination—*Sic Semper Tyrannis*—and the increasingly popular image of Lincoln as a dictatorial leader bent on abrogating rather than preserving basic American liberties." *Whitman the Political Poet*, 228.

18. Lincoln qtd. at Francis Fisher Browne, *The Every-Day Life of Abraham Lincoln* (Chicago: Browne & Howell, 1913), 310.

19. Whitman, "Specimen Days," *CPP*, 764.

20. Erkilla, *Whitman the Political Poet*, 203.

21. Whitman, "Death of President Lincoln," *CPP*, 1046, 1047.

Introduction

1. Alexis de Tocqueville, *Democracy in America*, vol. 1, trans. Henry Reeve, revised by Francis Bowen, corrected Phillips Bradley (New York: Vintage, 1990), 123; Ginsberg, "America," *Howl and Other Poems* (San Francisco: City Lights Books, 1959), 41; Richard Wright, *Native Son* and *How "Bigger" was Born* (1940. New York: HarperPerennial, 1993), 403, 356.

2. The definitive account of Wright's ambivalent relations with the New Deal can be found in Michael Szalay, *New Deal Modernism: American Literature and the Invention of the Welfare State* (Durham, NC: Duke University Press, 2000), 207–55.

3. See Craig Werner, "Bigger's Blues: *Native Son* and the Articulation of Afro-American Modernism," *New Essays on Native Son*, ed. Kenneth Kinnamon (New York: Cambridge University Press, 1990), 141.

4. Compare, e.g., Wright's impression of southern black sharecroppers' attitudes toward the New Deal: "We hear talk vaguely of a government in far away Washington, a government that *stands above the people and desires the welfare of all*. We do not know this government; but the men it hires to execute its laws are the Lords of the Land whom we have known all our lives. We hear that the government wants to help us, but . . . there are too many men . . . with their shoulders pressing tightly together in racial solidarity, forming a wall between us and the government." Wright, *Twelve Million Black Voices* (1941) reprint in *Richard Wright Reader*, ed. Ellen Wright and Michel Fabre (New York: Harper & Row, 1978), 176, emphasis added. Like *Native Son*, *Black Voices* was itself a work whose production was in part underwritten by the New Deal.

5. See, e.g., Houston A. Baker, Jr., "Richard Wright and the Dynamics of Place in Afro-American Literature," *New Essays on Native Son*, ed. Kinnamon, 85–88.

6. Wright, journal entry, 1945, quoted at Hazel Rowley, *Richard Wright: The Life and Times* (New York: Henry Holt, 2001), 313.

7. Ibid.

8. Theodore J. Lowi, *The Personal President: Power Invested, Promise Unfulfilled* (Ithaca, N.Y.: Cornell University Press, 1985), xi. Lowi's polemical book is a particularly strong version of an argument echoed in less dramatic terms by other historians and political scientists. See, e. g., Barry Karl, "Constitution and Central Planning: The Third New Deal Revisited," *Supreme Court Review* 1988 (1988), 163–201; and Sidney M. Milkis, *The President and the Parties: The Transformation of the American Party System Since the New Deal* (New York: Oxford University Press, 1993).

9. Harold Laski, *The American Presidency: An Interpretation* (New York: Harper & Bros., 1940), 278; like *Native Son*, Laski's paean to FDR's leadership was a Book-of-the-Month-Club selection.

10. On rising public concern about continental dictatorship in the U.S. during the late thirties, see Benjamin Alpers, *Dictators, Democracy, and American Public Culture: Envisioning the Totalitarian Enemy, 1920s-1950s* (Chapel Hill: University of North Carolina Press, 2003), 77–158.

11. James A. Morone, *The Democratic Wish: Popular Participation and the Limits of American Government*, rev. ed. (New Haven, CT: Yale University Press, 1998), 137; the main elements of the plan involved giving the president more power over a more professional civil service, bringing independent regulatory commissions under presidential control, moving the Office of the Budget out of the Treasury Department and into the White House, and, most significantly, giving the president command of a powerful planning apparatus.

12. Roosevelt, quoted at Alan Brinkley, *The End of Reform: New Deal Liberalism in Recession and War* (New York: Vintage, 1995), 22; by contrast to the writers cited in note 8 above,

Brinkley suggests that FDR may not have shared the ambitions for an administrative presidency expressed by his advisers.

13. As reported by Luther Gulick, quoted in Sidney N. Milkis, "Franklin D. Roosevelt, Progressivism, and the Limits of Popular Leadership," *Speaking to the People: The Rhetorical Presidency in Historical Perspective*, ed. Richard J. Ellis (Amherst: University of Massachusetts Press, 1998), 258n55.

14. Charles E. Merriam, *The New Democracy and the New Despotism* (New York: McGraw-Hill, 1939), 256; Luther Gulick, quoted at Sidney M. Milkis and Michael Nelson, *The American Presidency: Origins and Development, 1776–1998*, 3rd ed. (Washington, DC: CQ Press, 1999), 271. Gulick and Merriam along with Louis Brownlow were the leaders of the commission of academics and reformers whose report formed the basis of the reorganization bill.

15. "Report of the Brownlow Committee," quoted at Sidney M. Milkis and Michael Nelson, *The American Presidency*, 270.

16. Ernest Cuneo, quoted at Milkis, "Franklin D. Roosevelt, Progressivism," 202.

17. Richard Polenberg, *Reorganizing Roosevelt's Government: The Controversy over Executive Reorganization* (Cambridge, MA: Harvard University Press, 1966), 154; see also, Ellis Hawley, "The Constitution of the Hoover and F. Roosevelt Presidency during the Depression Era, 1930–39," *The Constitution and the American Presidency*, ed. Martin L. Fausold and Alan Shank (Albany: State University of New York Press, 1991), 102–4.

18. FDR, *Public Papers and Addresses* (New York: Random House, 1938–1950), 7, 179, *subsequent citations given as PPA*.

19. Brinkley, *End of Reform*, 23.

20. See, e.g, William M. Lunch, *The Nationalization of American Politics* (Berkeley: University of California Press, 1987); Richard L. McCormick, *The Party Period and Public Policy: American Politics from the Age of Jackson to the Progressive Era* (New York: Oxford University Press, 1986), 143–96. Historians and political scientists disagree about how fundamentally the "modern" system of presidential government (so dubbed by Fred Greenstein) differs from the "traditional" patterns of U.S. government. Elements of the strong view include the contention that modern presidents bear greater responsibility and exercise vastly greater power with respect to the other branches of the federal government, especially Congress, and to state governments and civil institutions than was the case for most of the nineteenth century; that since World War II, presidential power has depended not solely on charismatic leadership or the context of national crisis, but has been institutionally based in the vast expansion of the national security apparatus and of the administrative powers of the executive branch; that the expansion of presidential power has coincided with a transformation of political participation, deemphasizing party affiliation and elevating personal charisma and ideology; and that public expectations of the prerogative and style of presidential leadership (now emphasizing the president's need to be a symbolic presence in the popular life of the country and to take an active and defining lead in public affairs) differ markedly from earlier prevailing models. Classic statements of various elements of this view include, in addition to Lowi and Milkis cited above, James Ceaser, *Presidential Selection: Theory and Development* (Princeton, NJ: Princeton University Press, 1979); Fred I. Greenstein, "Change and Continuity in the Modern Presidency," *The New American Political System*, ed. Anthony King (Washing-

ton, DC: American Enterprise Institute, 1978), 45–86; Samuel Kernell, *Going Public: New Strategies of Presidential Leadership*, 3rd ed. (Washington, DC: Congressional Quarterly Press, 1997); Richard E. Neustadt, *Presidential Power: The Politics of Leadership* (New York: John Wiley & Sons, 1960); Jeffrey Tulis, *The Rhetorical Presidency* (Princeton, NJ: Princeton University Press, 1987). For challenges to the claim that the modern presidency differs categorically from the office envisioned by the drafters of the Constitution and familiar to nineteenth-century Americans, see, e.g., Ellis, introduction, *Speaking to the People*, 1–15; Harvey C. Mansfield. *Taming the Prince: The Ambivalence of Modern Executive Power* (New York: Free Press, 1989); David K. Nichols, *The Myth of the Modern Presidency* (University Park, PA: Pennsylvania State University Press, 1994). Recently political scientists have suggested that rather than a two-stage history, the development of the American presidency has been defined by three overlapping constitutional regimes: a period of "Constitutional statesmanship" (roughly 1789–1832), in which presidents were expected to aspire to nonpartisanship and to emphasize the restraints placed upon them by the Constitution; a "party period" (roughly 1836–92) in which presidents were mainly understood to represent popular preferences as defined by party organization; and, finally, a "plebiscitary" regime (the twentieth century), in which charismatic leadership was increasingly understood to derive its authority directly from popular opinion, independent of discredited party organizations. See, e.g., Michael J. Korzi, *A Seat of Popular Leadership: The Presidency, Parties, and Democratic Government* (Amherst: University of Massachusetts Press, 2004).

21. Rossiter, *The American Presidency* (New York: Harcourt Brace, 1956), 16.

22. Randolph, quoted at Sidney M. Milkis and Michael Nelson, *The American Presidency*, 27; Hamilton, as Publius, Federalist 70, *The Federalist Papers*, ed. Clinton Rossiter (New York: Signet Classic, 2003), 421. For fuller accounts of the complex deliberations over the role of the presidency during the Constitutional Convention and ratification debates, see Ralph Ketcham, *Presidents Above Party: The First American Presidency, 1789–1829* (Chapel Hill: University of North Carolina Press, 1986), 69–76 and *passim*; Nicholls, *Myth of the Modern Presidency*; and Charles C. Thach, *The Creation of the Presidency, 1775–1789: A Study of Constitutional History* (Baltimore: Johns Hopkins University Press, 1970).

23. Mansfield, *Taming the Prince*, 2–19 and *passim*.

24. Robert A. Dahl, "The Myth of the Presidential Mandate," *Political Science Quarterly* 105 (1990), 355–72; Dahl notes that even on those occasions where presidents like Jackson or Polk sought to establish the popular legitimacy of the president, they cast the presidency as at most a constitutional equal of Congress. The description of the president as "clerk" is from Neustadt's renowned suggestion that the distinctive problem of the modern president is to be endlessly confronted by the question "Leader or Clerk?" *Presidential Power*, 1–8. Mansfield suggests that these alternative views were built into the U.S. constitution from the first.

25. On popular discontent with representative democracy in the nineteenth century and a corrective to the view that the era of party competition was a high-point in the history of civic participation, see Glenn C. Altschuler and Stuart M. Blumin, *Rude Republic: Americans and their Politics in the Nineteenth Century* (Princeton, NJ: Princeton University Press, 2000).

26. Stephen M. Griffin, *American Constitutionalism: From Theory to Politics* (Princeton, NJ: Princeton University Press, 1996), 25–26; Morone, *Democratic Wish*, 66–68 and *passim*.

27. Vidal, *Burr* (New York: Random House, 1973), 147.

28. See, e.g., Ketcham, *Presidents Above Party*, 225–35.

29. Wilson, "The Ideals of America," *Atlantic Monthly* 90 (December 1902), 732; the order of the quotations is reversed; on TR's comparable invocations of Hamilton and Washington as models for national leadership, see, e.g., John Milton Cooper, Jr., *The Warrior and the Priest: Woodrow Wilson and Theodore Roosevelt* (Cambridge, MA: Harvard University Press, 1983), 115–17, 324 and John Patrick Diggins, "Republicanism and Progressivism," *American Quarterly* 37, 4 (1985), 572–98.

30. FDR, Address to Young Democratic Clubs of American (8/24/1935), *PPA*, 4:337.

31. Hamilton, *Federalist Papers*, 431.

32. Ketcham, *Presidents Above Parties*, 124–66; McCormick, *Party Period and Public Policy*, 143–76; A. James Reichley, *The Life of the Parties: A History of American Political Parties* (New York: Free Press, 1992), 82–185.

33. Jackson, "Protest" to the Senate, *Age of Jackson* ed. Robert V. Remini (Columbia: University of South Caroline Press, 1972), 115. Melville: "Thou just spirit of Equality, which hast spread one royal mantle of humanity over all my kind! Bear me out in it, thou great democratic God! . . . Thou who didst pick up Andrew Jackson from the pebbles; who didst hurl him upon a war-horse; who didst thunder him higher than a throne . . . bear me out in it, O God!" *Moby Dick, or The Whale* (New York: Penguin, 2001), 127. As Michael T. Gilmore suggests in his illuminating discussion, Melville's novel casts Ahab in this vein as a demagogic tyrant who, in the implicit comparison to Queequeg, is placed in near direct contrast to a rival, and more traditional, impression of presidential leadership—the image of Washington as an aristocratic creator of Constitutional authority. Gilmore, *Surface and Depth: The Quest for Legibility in American Culture* (New York: Oxford University Press, 2003), 87–94.

34. "Public interests," Jackson, first annual message (1829); "Individuals and States," Jackson, veto message (1832), quoted at Ketcham, *Presidents above Parties*, 152, 154.

35. Korzi, *Seat of Popular Leadership*; Morone, *Democratic Wish*, 74–96; Raymond Tatalovich and Thomas Engeman, *The Presidency and Political Science: Two Hundred Years of Constitutional Debate* (Baltimore: Johns Hopkins University Press, 2003), 43–66.

36. Korzi, *Seat of Popular Leadership*, 52.

37. Richard J. Ellis, "The Joy of Power: Changing Conceptions of the Presidential Office," *Presidential Studies Quarterly* 33, 2 (2003): 269–87; Tulis, *Rhetorical Presidency*; Gerald Gamm and Renee M. Smith, "Presidents, Parties, and the Public: Evolving Patterns of Interaction, 1877–1929," *Speaking to The People*, ed. Ellis, 87–111.

38. Forrest McDonald, *The American Presidency: An Intellectual History* (Lawrence: University Press of Kansas, 1994), 320.

39. Tulis, *Rhetorical Presidency*, 186.

40. Whitman, "This Dust Was Once a Man," *CPP*, 468.

41. Whitman, "Song of the Broad-Axe," "Song of the Answerer," *CPP*, 335, 131; see also, "The Prairie Grass Dividing" where Whitman praises democratic citizens as "Those that look carelessly in the faces of Presidents and governors." *CPP*, 281. Similarly in his 1853 antislavery novel *Clotel, or, the President's Daughter* (New York: Carol Publishing Group, 1995), William Wells Brown indicts U.S. democracy by building his narrative around the sufferings of the illegitimate, enslaved child of Thomas Jefferson, whose pursuit of freedom ends in

suicide "within plain sight of the President's house and the capitol of the Union" (219). For Wells, however, Jefferson is most symbolically powerful as the author of the Declaration of Independence. As the pairing of the White House and the Capitol indicates, the presidency is not otherwise more resonant for him than Congress. When Wells invokes presidential candidates (Harrison, Clay, Van Buren), it is thus to refer to the party competition that exemplifies the ugliness of U.S. democracy. When he points to "statesman" caught in the coils of slavery, they are, as in Harriet Beecher Stowe, more likely to be senators or governors than presidents.

42. On the Progressive Era as a crucial moment in the development of new principles of Constitutional law and political philosophy that reshaped U.S. federalism, see Martha Dethrick and John J. Dinan, "Progressivism and Federalism," *Progressivism and the New Democracy*, ed. Milkis and Mileur, 81–102.

43. Wilson, *Constitutional Government in the United States* (1908. New Brunswick, NJ: Transaction, 2002), 69.

44. Wilson, *Constitutional Government*, 58; exaggerated though it may be, Wilson's enthusiasm may point to the unusual nature of political competition during the Civil War—which, according to Altschuler and Blumin, saw both the era's highest levels of popular participation and an indifference to party tickets and platforms exceptional for the nineteenth century. Politics during the Civil War, in other words, were indeed unusually presidential. Altschuler and Blumin, *Rude Republic*, 177.

45. For a concise summary of recent scholarship on Lincoln's relation to nineteenth-century political institutions and expectations, see Landy and Milkis, *Presidential Greatness*, 114–52. For correctives to the view that Lincoln acted as a constitutional dictator during the Civil War and thus established executive powers that trampled the restraints of law and Constitution, see Michael Les Benedict, "The Constitution of the Lincoln Presidency and the Republican Era," *Constitution and the American Presidency*, eds. Fausold and Shank, 45–61 and Daniel Farber, *Lincoln's Constitution* (Chicago: University of Chicago Press, 2003). Farber in particular makes this case while emphasizing that Lincoln "did stretch the power of the presidency to its outer reaches" and for this reason "became something of a paradigm for later presidents" (20, 8).

46. James C. McPherson, *Abraham Lincoln and the Second American Revolution* (New York: Oxford University Press, 1991); George P. Fletcher, *Our Secret Constitution: How Lincoln Redefined American Democracy* (New York: Oxford University Press, 2001).

47. *Emerson's Antislavery Writings*, ed. Gougeon and Myerson, 144; this was a view that led Emerson in particular to drop his initial dissatisfaction with Lincoln and to develop a newly enthusiastic appreciation of presidential leadership. He found in the election of 1864, for example, a sign that "a nation shall be a nation." Emerson, quoted at Morton Keller, *Affairs of State: Public Life in Late Nineteenth Century America* (Cambridge, MA: Harvard University Press, 1977), 4.

48. Merrill D. Peterson, *Lincoln in American Memory* (New York: Oxford University Press, 1994), 155–67; "Operationalism," James MacGregor Burns, *Presidential Government: The Crucible of Leadership* (Boston: Houghton Mifflin, 1965), 37.

49. Lowell, *Collected Prose*, ed. Giroux, 166; *Philadelphia Evening Bulletin* (April 15, 1865), qtd. at Peterson, *Lincoln in American Memory*, 27. For the widely recognized signifi-

cance of this achievement, see also, Peterson, 3–35; John P. Diggins, *The Lost Soul of American Politics: Virtue, Self-Interest, and the Foundations of Liberalism* (New York: Basic, 1984), 296–333; Guelzo, *Redeemer President*, 19, 369–74, 439–63; McPherson, *Second American Revolution*, 93–112; Michael Paul Rogin, *Ronald Reagan, the Movie, and Other Episodes in Political Demonology* (Berkeley: University of California Press, 1987), 81–114; Harry S. Stout, *Upon the Altar of the Nation: A Moral History of the Civil War* (New York: Viking, 2006); Gary Wills, *Lincoln at Gettysburg: The Words that Remade America* (New York: Simon & Schuster, 1992); Edmund Wilson, "Abraham Lincoln: The Union as Religious Mysticism," *Eight Essays* (Garden City, NY: Doubleday, 1954), 181–202. Interestingly, and perhaps appropriately, a number of Lincoln scholars agree on the significance of Lincoln's sacrificial rhetoric, even while disagreeing about his more specific political views. Anderson and Wills, e.g., view Lincoln as a Jeffersonian and quasi-Rousseauian; Guelzo argues that he remained a Whig throughout his career. All agree, however, that in the rhetoric of sacrifice, Lincoln spiritualized American national identity and gave a depth to what could otherwise seem a mere compact of interest and convenience—thus providing, as Anderson says, "a model of presidential action which is quite beyond liberal politics." *Abraham Lincoln: Quest for Immortality*, 219.

50. Whitman, "Death of Abraham Lincoln," *CPP*, 1046.

51. Quoted at Dethrick and Dinan, "Progressivism and Federalism," 82; for the argument that a robust American nationalism was not fully consolidated until many decades after the Civil War and that the period between 1865 and 1919 was thus one of intense conflict over the definitions of American national identity and its symbols, see Cecilia O'Leary, *To Die For: The Paradox of American Patriotism* (Princeton, NJ: Princeton University Press, 1999).

52. Woodrow Wilson, *Congressional Government: A Study in American Politics* (1885. 1900. New Brunswick, NY: Transaction, 2002), 11; Albert Bushnell Hart, "The Speaker as Premier," *The Atlantic Monthly* 67, 401 (March 1891): 386. For a survey of recent scholarship that qualifies but reaffirms the widely accepted picture of late nineteenth-century congressional and party dominance, see Charles W. Calhoun, "Reimagining the 'Lost Men' of the Gilded Age: Perspectives on the Late Nineteenth-Century Presidents," *Journal of the Gilded Age and the Progressive Era* 1, 3 (July 2002) http://www.historycooperative.org/journals/jga/1.3/calhoun.html.

53. Adams, *Democracy: An American Novel* (1880. New York: Penguin, 1994), 182, 30. During this same period, William Dean Howells appropriately compared the president and the hack novelist—as figures of trivial insignificance—in a way that was nearly the inverse of Whitman's elevated vision and of the understanding that would be prominent in the twentieth century: "It is easy to write a thousand words a day, and supposing one of these authors to work steadily, it can be seen that his net earnings during the year would come to some such sum as the President of the United States gets for doing far less work of a much more perishable sort." In this characterization, neither president nor hack represents the sovereign people, but, as in Adams, is viewed as the representative of a commercial society characterized by graft and inequality. They "consort with bank presidents, and railroad officials, and rich tradesman and other flowers of our plutocracy." Howells, "The Man of Letters as Man of Business" (1893), *Criticism and Fiction and Other Essays*, ed. Clara Marburg Kirk and Rudolf Kirk (New York: New York University Press, 1959), 300. Howells's view is in keeping

not only with his political environment, but with a literary ethic doubtful of the collective embodiment that the advocates of presidentialism would value. In *A Hazard of New Fortunes* (1890. New York: Modern Library, 2002), for example, Howells dismisses both a socialist invocation of "the State" and an authoritarian vision of a "central authority" led by an "emperor, duke, [or] president" as examples of extremist responses to social unrest (344). Thus, although the novel invokes "the sovereign people" as an alternative to the "private war" between capital and labor, it does not anticipate the people embodied by any single figure, but at best represented in the competing viewpoints expressed in the marketplace of ideas (here represented, not by an author or leader, but by the formal mechanism of magazine publication)(407). In short, Howells envisions a public formed by representation, aggregation, and competition, rather than as Whitman, or later Woodrow Wilson would suggest, collective identification.

54. Bryce, *The American Commonwealth*, edited, abridged, and introduced by Louis M. Hacker (New York: G. P. Putnam's Sons, 1959), I: 27, 30.

55. Wilson, "Democracy and Efficiency," qtd. at Daniel D. Stid, *The President as Statesman: Woodrow Wilson and the Constitution* (Lawrence: University Press of Kansas, 1998), 43; in the preface to the fifteenth edition of *Congressional Government* (1900), Wilson noted that the apparent rise of presidential power with the Spanish American War "might put this whole volume hopelessly out of date." With "the greatly increased power and opportunity for constructive statesmanship given the President by the plunge into international politics, . . . the President of the United States is now, as of course, at the front of affairs, as no president, except Lincoln, has been since the first quarter of the nineteenth century." Wilson, *Congressional Government*, lxiii, lxi–lxii. Wilson's attitude was anticipated by McKinley, who reportedly said after America's defeat of Spain: "I can no longer be called the President of a party; I am now the President of the whole people." Qtd. at Korzi, *Seat of Popular Leadership*, 84.

56. Wilson, "Leaderless Government," *College and State*, ed. Ray Stannard Baker and William E. Dodd (New York: Harper Brothers, 1925), 1: 339ff; although Wilson wrote this essay in 1897, it articulates concerns about leadership and government that run consistently throughout his writing and that are forcefully expressed in *Congressional Government*.

57. Wilson, *Congressional Government*, 260, 254.

58. Wilson, "Mr. Cleveland as President" (1897), qtd. at Stid, *President as Statesman*, 39; on the development of Wilson's political theory, see in addition to Stid, Henry Wilkinson Bragdon, *Woodrow Wilson: The Academic Years* (Cambridge, MA: Harvard University Press, 1967); Ceaser, *Presidential Selection*, 170–212; Sidney A. Pearson, Jr., introduction to Woodrow Wilson, *Constitutional Government in the United States* (1907. New Brunswick, NJ: Transaction, 2002), ix–lii.

59. Eldon, J. Eisenach, *The Lost Promise of Progressivism* (Lawrence: University Press of Kansas, 1994), 104–37; McCormick, *Party Period*, 228–59; Daniel Stid, "Rhetorical Leadership and 'Common Counsel' in the Presidency of Woodrow Wilson," *Speaking to the People*, 162–81.

60. Wilson, *Congressional Government*, 92, 61, 203, 205, 218, 279,.

61. Wilson, qtd. at Ceaser, *Presidential Selection*, 180–81.

62. Wilson, *Congressional Government*, 188.

63. Ibid., 56.

64. Ibid., 204; Roosevelt, *Autobiography*, 357.

65. See, Griffin, *American Constitutionalism*, 19–26; Stout, *Upon the Altar of the Nation*, 458; and, especially, Farber, *Lincoln's Constitution*, 26–44.

66. Morone, *The Democratic Wish*. As Danielle Allen notes, a prime experience of democratic life is "the psychic anxiety of being a powerless sovereign." Allen, "Ralph Ellison and the Tragi-Comedy of Citizenship," *Ralph Ellison and the Raft of Hope: A Political Companion to Invisible Man*, ed. Lucas E. Morel (Lexington: University of Kentucky Press, 2004), 38 and for a more complete discussion, Allen, *Talking to Strangers: Anxieties of Citizenship since Brown v. Board of Education* (Chicago: University of Chicago Press, 2004). Interestingly, in counseling against the resentment and diminished citizenship such anxiety might encourage, Allen points approvingly to the counterexample of "the most powerful citizen in the United States" and recommends "a presidential ease and sense of freedom." "Presidents greet everyone and look all citizens in the eye. . . . At one end of the spectrum of styles of democratic citizenship cowers the four-year-old in insecure isolation; at the other, stands the president, strong and self-confident" (162).

67. Wilson, *Congressional Government*, 6; see also, TR's claim, during the 1912 election, in which he ran against Wilson and his own successor Taft, that "the first essential in the Progressive programme is the right of the people to rule. . . . [T]he actions of the Chicago [Republican] Convention, and to only less degree of the Baltimore [Democratic] Convention, have shown in striking fashion how little the people do rule under our present conditions." Roosevelt, "A Confession of Faith," address to Progressive Party convention (August 6, 1912), *Theodore Roosevelt: An American Mind, A Selection from his Writings*, ed. Mario R. DiNunzio (New York: Penguin, 1994), 151.

68. Wilson, *Constitutional Goverrnment*, 109.

69. Quoted at Detrick and Dinan, 85.

70. Cooper, Jr., *The Warrior and the Priest*, 28–29, 69–88; McGerr, *Decline of Popular Politics*, 107–37. On the central role of moral leadership—as opposed, e.g., to policy considerations—to the politics of the modern presidency, see, Bruce Kucklick, *The Good Ruler: From Herbert Hoover to Richard Nixon* (New Brunswick, NJ: Rutgers University Press, 1988).

71. Roosevelt, qtd. at Stephen Graubard, *Command of Office: How War, Secrecy, and Deception Transformed the Presidency, from Theodore Roosevelt to George W. Bush* (New York: Basic Books, 2004), 100.

72. Wilson, *Constitutional Government*, 73, 68.

73. Franklin D. Roosevelt, "Informal Extemporaneous Remarks at Cheyenne, Wyoming" (September 24, 1937), *PPA* 6:382–83; Address to Young Democratic Clubs, 4:337; "Message on the State of the Union" (January 11, 1934), 13:34.

74. John F. Kennedy, *Let the Word Go Forth: The Speeches, Statements, and Writings of John F. Kennedy*, ed. Theodore C. Sorensen (New York: Delacorte Press, 1988), 22; LBJ, qtd. at Burns, *Presidential Government*, xii; Carter, qtd. at Korzi, *Seat of Popular Leadership*, 116.

75. Cf., Wilson's comment to the visiting George V: "You and I, sir—I temporarily—embody the spirit of two great nations." Qtd. at Rogin, *Ronald Reagan, the Movie*, 94.

76. See, in addition to Morone, cited above, Mansfield, who notes that, in the use of representation, the Constitution created "a republican government unlike all previous

republics—one in which the people choose not to be sovereign," Mansfield, *Taming the Prince*, 264.

77. Wilson, *The New Freedom: A Call for the Emancipation of the Generous Energies of a People* (1913. New York: Doubleday, Page & Co., 1918), 50, 82, 76.

78. Wilson, *The New Freedom*, 286–87, 288.

79. As many observers, beginning with William Leuchtenburg's classic treatment of "The New Deal and the Analogy of War," have noted, apart from the heavy emphasis on the executive's responsibility for national security—stressed by every president since World War II—each expansion of the executive's domestic powers has been justified by the rhetoric of war. The pattern begins at least as early as TR's promise, in the wake of McKinley's assassination, to wage war on anarchism and his description of the anthracite coal strike as akin to "the invasion of a hostile army of overwhelming force." Roosevelt, *Autobiography*, 456. It continues, e.g., through the more celebrated examples of FDR's threat to request war powers to fight the Depression and LBJ's war on poverty.

80. Roosevelt, Commonwealth Club Address *PPA*, 1:753; the predominant role of these two features of presidential power can be seen in the fact that the classic treatments of the rise of the modern presidency tend to emphasize one or the other. Compare, e.g., Schlesinger's *Imperial Presidency*, which sees war powers as the engine of presidential aggrandizement, to Tulis's highly influential *Rhetorical Presidency*, which, as its title indicates, sees the creation of a new, plebiscitary presidency beginning with a new freedom for presidents to engage in public rhetoric.

81. Wilson (September 11, 1919), qtd. at John Judis, *The Folly of Empire: What George W. Bush Could Learn from Theodore Roosevelt and Woodrow Wilson* (New York: Scribner, 2004), 114. The contrast was central to Wilson's thinking about the relation between democratic government and national sovereignty. See, e.g., his early comments in *The State*: "Government . . . consist[s] of authority resting on force. . . . [M]any governments seldom coerce their subjects. They in a sense operate without the exercise of force. But there is a force behind them none the less because it never shows itself. . . . The force which they embody is not the force of a dominant dynasty nor of a prevalent minority, but of an agreeing majority. . . . It is latent just because it is understood to be omnipotent." *Woodrow Wilson: The Essential Political Writings*, ed. Ronald J. Pestritto (Lanham, MD: Lexington Books, 2005), 50.

82. Whitman, "By Blue Ontario's Shore," *CPP*, 474. Allen Grossman explores the parallel between Whitman and Lincoln in a classic essay that, while characterizing the symmetry in strongly critical terms, accurately describes its implications. "Both bend the world, with totalitarian immediacy, to the implications of the central sentences of a cultural instrument"— in Lincoln's case the Constitution, as reformed via Lincoln's own transformative leadership, in Whitman's, *Leaves of Grass*, which, by Grossman's analysis, similarly depends on the self-presence of the authorial persona. Grossman, "The Poetics of Union in Whitman and Lincoln: An Inquiry toward the Relation between Art and Policy," *The American Renaissance Reconsidered*, ed. Walter Benn Michaels and Donald Pease (1985. Baltimore, MD: Johns Hopkins University Press, 1989).

83. Ginsberg, *Howl*, 21. Placing himself in San Francisco, Ginsberg addresses Solomons, who as an institutionalized patient is importantly a victim of abusive state power, making, in

the poem's concluding lines, the poet's sympathetic connection to the martyr a means to imagine national cohesion: "I'm with you in Rockland / where we hug and kiss the United States under / our bedsheets the United States that coughs all / night and won't let us sleep . . . . I'm with you in Rockland / in my dreams you walk dripping from a sea- / journey on the highway across America in tears / to the door of my cottage in the Western night" (26). As in the Whitman's elegy for Lincoln "When Lilacs Last in the Dooryard Bloom'd," to which Ginsberg here alludes, but also as in the Gettysburg Address, "Howl" thus imagines a cruel and inadequate political order ("the United States") replaced by a unified nation ("America") through the celebration of popular martyrdom. Like Whitman and Lincoln, too, Ginsberg appears to need the context of civil war to refound the nation. Between the lines quoted above, Ginsberg exults: "we wake up electrified out of the coma / by our own souls' airplanes roaring over / the roof they've come to drop angelic bombs the / hospital illuminates itself imaginary walls col / lapse . . . O starry / spangled shock of mercy the eternal war is / here O victory forget your underwear we're / free" (26).

84. Wright, "On Literature," typescript, n.d. JWJ, box 6, folder 128. Though it is undated, internal evidence indicates that this document was composed in 1939 or early 1940 and suggests that it may be the text of a lecture Wright gave to the Writer's School of the Party-affiliated League of American Writers. See Michel Fabre, *The Unfinished Quest of Richard Wright*, trans. Isabel Barzun (New York: William Morrow & Co., 1973), 193. Unfortunately the Wright estate declines to grant permission to quote from this important document or from Wright's other unpublished critical writings.

85. The demands of "On Literature" were variations on ideas that Wright first expressed programmatically in the unpublished 1935 ars poetica "Personalism"—an essay in which Wright defined an unorthodox literary program for writers on the left and suggested that American writing could be most politically resonant, not in exploring the conditions of the workers or rising class conflict, but in fully plumbing the psychological torments that accompanied the crisis of bourgeois individualism. That manifesto was inspired in part by the influence of Barbusse, who in turn, almost certainly got his own version of "Personalism" by way of the French assimilation of Whitman's *Democratic Vistas*, which originated the term. On Wright's connections with Barbusse, see, Eugene E. Miller, "Richard Wright, Community, and the French Connection," *Twentieth Century Literature* 41.3 (1995), 265–80.

86. Whitman, *Democratic Vistas*, 86 *CPP*, 949, 953, 935, 944, 953, 934, 937, 953, 932. Indeed Whitman specifically casts the role of national literature as surpassing the many factional "voices, pens, minds, in the press, lecture rooms, in our Congress" that take up various piecemeal matters of implicitly parochial interest—"legislative problems, the suffrage, tariff and labor questions, and the various business and benevolent needs of America" (932). Against that confusion he repeatedly describes democratic literature as a form of sovereign imperative: "sternly taking command, dissolving the old, . . . and from its own interior and vital principles, reconstructing, democratizing society" (977).

87. Whitman, preface, 1872, to *As a Strong Bird on Pinions Free*, *CPP*, 1002.

88. Wright, "How Bigger Was Born" (1940), *Native Son* and How *"Bigger" was Born*, 521, emphasis added.

89. Wright, *Black Boy (American Hunger): A Record of Childhood and Youth*, restored text (1944. 1945. New York: HarperPerennial, 1993), 279.

90. Wright, "How Bigger Was Born," 540.

91. Wright, "Are We Solving America's Race Problems?" radio lecture delivered as part of "America's Town Meeting of the Air," May 24, 1945, JWJ MSS 33, box 2, folder 6. See also, Wright's claim in 1943 that he viewed "the Negro question" as a means to make "a constructive criticism upon the culture of the nation as a whole" and his wish that the United States in addressing the issue might make "the first step toward a unified culture." Qtd. at Fabre, *Unfinished Quest*, 258, 260.

92. Wright to Stein (March 15, 1946), qtd. at Fabre, *Unfinished Quest*, 592n36. It is worth noting in this context that among the early influences on Wright was not just Marxism and Chicago sociology, but the Progressive Era cultural nationalism of Van Wyck Brooks and Waldo Frank, social critics who, as Barbara Foley has recently explained with particular clarity, sometimes adopted the rhetoric of socialist revolution toward a more therapeutic program of cultural nationalism. Foley, *Spectres of 1919: Class and Nation in the Making of the New Negro* (Urbana: University of Illinois Press, 2003), 159–97. Wright used epigraphs from Brooks and Frank to frame his first unpublished novel, *Lawd Today*, a depiction of the destruction of a benighted black post office worker. Wright emphasizes the limitations of Jake (who tellingly, singles out for distrust FDR, TR, Wilson, and Lenin) and the racism of modern Chicago by setting the action of the novel entirely on Lincoln's birthday and making the martyred president's legacy an empty media occasion. Jake in particular is deaf to the rhetoric of Lincoln's first inaugural address ("mystic chords of memory, stretching from every battlefield and patriot grave"). The point here and throughout the novel seems to be that the world depicted is a "cesspool" (the book's original title) precisely because it lacks both the vital cultural heritage that Brooks and Frank celebrated and the national leadership represented by Lincoln and the Progressive presidents. Wright, *Lawd Today* (1963. Boston: Northeastern University Press, 1983), 59.

93. Wright, "Towards the Conquest of Ourselves," draft, corrected typescript, n.d., (1943–45?), JWJ box 6, folder 148.

94. Capetti, *Writing Chicago: Modernism, Ethnography, and the Novel* (New York: Columbia University Press, 1993), 210.

95. Wright, "Adventure and Discovery: A Personal Statement," Acceptance Speech for the Springarn medal, draft, corrected typescript (September 1941), Wright Papers, JWJ.

96. Wright to Antonio Frasconi (November 1944), qtd. at Michel Fabre, "Beyond Naturalism?" *Richard Wright: Modern Critical Views*, ed. Harold Bloom (New York: Chelsea House, 1987), 48.

97. Wright, unpublished letter to Mike Gold (May? 1940), qtd. at Fabre, *Unfinished Quest*, 185.

98. Wright, "Can We Depend upon Youth to Follow the American Way?" *Town Meeting: Bulletin of America's Town Meeting of the Air* 4, 24 (April 24, 1939), 16. Wright papers, JWJ, box 3, folder 26.

99. Merriam, *The New Democracy and the New Despotism*, 255–56, 262; Merriam's two examples of such executive leadership were Woodrow Wilson and FDR.

100. Sinclair Lewis, *It Can't Happen Here* (1935. New York: Signet, 2005), 366. The difference between these two parallel conditions in Lewis's telling is that the tyranny of the Corporate State results from its proponents' illegitimate, foreign, and, especially, petty desire for

power, while the new American State which the novel envisions in its final pages will emerge from "the people's war against tyranny" (370). The former condition is typified by a militarized society reliant at base on the concentration camp; the latter is exemplified by the willing service of civilian soldiers who are prepared to sacrifice their lives for "Holy America" (358). As in Whitman and Lincoln, in short, the prospect of state coercion is banished by martyrdom for the nation.

101. Giorgio Agamben, *Homo Sacer: Sovereign Power and Bare Life*, trans. Daniel Heller-Roazen (Stanford, CA: Stanford University Press, 1998).

102. Joseph T. Skerrett, Jr., "Composing Bigger: Wright and the Making of *Native Son*," *Richard Wright's Native Son*: Modern Critical Interpretations, ed. Harold Bloom (New York: Chelsea House, 1988), 138–42.

103. This is all the more striking in that, as Cheryl Higashida has explained, Wright's first book, the collection of stories *Uncle Tom's Children*, written during the height of his radicalism, is built on a "dialectical" model that moves via its major stories through several stages of political development, culminating in both a defense of the Communist Party and a recognition of the suffering and heroism of its women members and fellow travelers. Higashida, "Aunt Sue's Children: Re-viewing the Gender(ed) Politics of Richard Wright's Radicalism, *American Literature* 75, 2 (2003), 395–425. See also, Barbara Foley on the dialectical transcendence of black nationalism implicit in Wright's "Blueprint on Negro Writing." Foley, *Radical Representations: Politics and Form in U. S. Proletarian Fiction, 1929–1941* (Durham, NC: Duke University Press, 1993), 190, 205–12. Both Foley and William J. Maxwell, *New Negro, Old Left: African-American Writing and Communism between the Wars* (New York: Columbia University Press, 1999), 179–202, make the important point that Wright himself and many of his critics confuse the chronology of his break with the Communist Party and possibly overestimate its significance to *Native Son*. Wright did not publicly break with the party until the mid-forties and later gave mistaken dates and locations for some of his clashes with the party, implying that he had acted earlier and more definitively than was the case. He remained associated with party affiliated organizations and positions up through 1940, and in fact still spoke of himself as "a Communist writer" until at least that time. But, if it is possible to overdramatize Wright's dissatisfaction with the party and its importance to *Native Son*, neither should his frustration, or the party's own mixed attitude toward Wright and his work be downplayed. Maxwell claims, for instance, that Mike Gold, the party's literary arbiter, "jumped to the novel's defense" (186); but, as Fabre points out, Gold in fact first waited a month before making a noncommittal reference to *Native Son* and then waited a full additional month before ending a series of party criticisms with a stronger defense. As Fabre notes, the delay itself suggested the party's ambivalence, and Wright responded by remarking on his disappointment with the party, his distaste for the literary restraints imposed by "many Party officials," and his sense of the limits of the party's "political theory" when it came to racism and African Americans. More significantly, as Fabre also notes, Wright's dissatisfaction with the party had been brewing over several years in the later thirties—"a period of definite evolution" away from the Communist Party when Wright was repeatedly frustrated by party discipline and surveillance. Fabre, *Unfinished Quest*, 185, 137. In the pivotal years when he worked on *Native Son*, too, Wright developed a new friendship with the outspoken anti-Stalinist C.L.R. James. In this context, there seems little reason to doubt that Wright's

own memory of his growing dissatisfaction in "I Tried To Be a Communist" was substantially accurate, even if shaped for dramatic effect and distorted by his later, stronger feelings, and that this dissatisfaction contributed the development of his major novel. In particular, *Native Son* appears to reject the party, the developmental schema, and the protofeminist sensibility Higashida points out in *Uncle Tom's Children* all at once. Interestingly Wright's claim that he intended to surpass that collection of stories because he had discovered that it was "a book which even bankers' daughters could read and weep over and feel good about" is often cited to underline his more radical agenda with *Native Son* (HBWB 531). But this may be a misleading impression. The banker's daughter Wright knew best was Jane Newton, a member of the Communist Party, who attempted earnestly but unsuccessfully to keep Wright from including the murder of Bessie Mears in *Native Son*. See, Rowley, *Richard Wright*, 155.

104. Ted Ward to Wright, May 23, 1940; qtd. at Rowley, *Richard Wright: The Life and Times*, 201.

105. Wright, "Can We Depend upon Youth to Follow the American Way?" 17.

106. Wright, qtd. in *PM* (April 4, 1945), qtd. at Fabre, *Unfinished Quest*, 252.

Chapter One: "Masters of Their Constitution"

1. Stein, "Composition as Explanation," *Look at Me Now and Here I Am: Writings and Lectures, 1909–45*, ed. Patricia Meyerowitz (Baltimore, MD: Penguin Books, 1971), 21, 25, *subsequent citations to this volume given as WL*; Stein, *Four in America* (New Haven, CT: Yale University Press, 1947), 169, 175, *subsequent citations given parenthetically as FIA*. My understanding of Stein's biography is informed by Leon Katz, *The First Making of The Making of Americans* diss. Columbia University, 1963; James R. Mellow, *Charmed Circle: Gertrude Stein & Company* (Boston: Houghton Mifflin, 1974); and, especially, Brenda Wineapple, *Sister Brother: Gertrude Stein and Leo Stein* (New York: G. P. Putnam's Sons, 1996).

2. Stein, "English and American Language in Literature," *Life and Letters* (September 10, 1935), 20.

3. Stein, *Everybody's Autobiography* (1937. Cambridge, MA: Exact Change, 1993), 224–25, *subsequent citations given parenthetically as EA*.

4. Ulla E. Dydo, with William Rice, *Gertrude Stein: The Language that Rises, 1923–1934* (Evanston, IL: Northwestern University Press, 2003), 623.

5. On the way Stein's first major writing rejected genealogy for a formal, atemporal, and ultimately antiempirical effort to know and represent character, see Wendy Steiner, *Exact Resemblance to Exact Resemblance: The Literary Portraiture of Gertrude Stein* (New Haven, CT: Yale University Press, 1978). For an account of Stein's refusal of genealogy and its possible roots in Stein's interest in contemporary biological science, see Maria Farland, "Gertrude Stein's Brain Work," *American Literature* 76, 1 (2004), 117–48. For the most careful study of Stein's effort to write "literally" but not "mimetically, representationally," see Dydo, *Gertrude Stein: The Language that Rises*, 6 and *passim*; for a thorough consideration of Stein's anti-empiricism, and the argument that it reflects in fact a more radical empiricism, see, Steven Meyer, *Irresistible Dictation: Gertrude Stein and the Correlations of Writing and Science* (Palo Alto, CA: Stanford University Press, 2001) and, for an important clarification of this argument,

see, Robert Chodat, "Sense, Science and the Interpretations of Gertrude Stein," *Modernism/ modernity* 12, 4 (2005), 581–605; Leon Katz points out the similarity between Stein's concerns in the period that culminated in *Making of Americans* and the attitudes expressed in the work she did during the thirties. Katz, *The First Making*, 241n1. In a thoughtful introduction to *Four in America*—a manuscript written by Stein during the thirties, though not published until 1947—Thornton Wilder argues that Stein engages in various "spiritual exercises" to contend with the problem of audience, including a "buffoonery" that makes her resemble Kierkegaard. Wilder, introduction, *Four in America*, xiv.

6. FDR, Commonwealth Club Address, *PPA* 1:753.

7. E.g., "There is too much fathering gong on just now . . . . [T]here is father Mussolini and father Hitler and father Roosevelt and father Stalin" (EA 137).

8. Stein, "English and American Language in Literature," 20.

9. Stein, *The Autobiography of Alice B. Toklas* (1933. New York: Vintage, 1990), 152, *subsequent citations given parenthetically as ABT.*

10. For thoughtful discussion of James's influence on Stein, see, especially, Meyers, *Irresistible Dictation*, 207–89; Lisa Ruddick, *Reading Gertrude Stein: Body, Text, Gnosis* (Ithaca, NY: Cornell University Press, 1990), 12–54; Liesl M. Olson, "Gertrude Stein, William James, and Habit in the Shadow of War," *Twentieth-Century Literature* 49, 3 (2003): 328–60; Lisi Schoenback, " 'Peaceful and Exciting': Habit, Shock, and Gertrude Stein's Pragmatic Modernism," *Modernism/Modernity* 11, 2 (2004): 239–59. On the significance of Stein's medical education, see Farland, "Stein's Brain Work," 117–48; Meyer, *Irresistible Dictation*, 51–117; and Gene Nakajima, "Gertrude Stein's Medical Education and Her Evolving Feminism," unpublished manuscript, 1986, Chesney Archives, Johns Hopkins Medical Institutions.

11. A rare effort to situate Stein in the context of political movements of her contemporaries can be found in Marianne DeKoven, " 'Excellent Not a Hull House: Gertrude Stein, Jane Addams, and Feminist-Modernist Political Cultures," *Rereading Modernism: New Directions in Feminist Criticism* (New York: Garland, 1994), 321–50. DeKoven's essay makes a valuable comparison between the life trajectories of Stein and Jane Addams, noting that each revised the conventions of the separate spheres to establish public careers and mediatory institutions that aided in transforming gender roles in politics and the arts. But, taking for granted the existence of a "mutuality of progressive politics and avant-garde art," DeKoven neither investigates Stein's connections with actual reform activists and Progressive intellectuals, nor attends to Stein's avowed political views, declining to credit, for instance, Stein's own remarks dismissing feminism and reformism (321). In his comparison of Stein to Henry Adams and William James, Clive Bush makes an unusual and compellingly argued effort to situate Stein's reactions to the political crises of the Gilded Age. But Bush, too, does not discuss Stein's connections to her contemporaries in the turn-of-the-century reform movement. Bush, *Halfway to Revolution: Investigation and Crisis in the Work of Henry Adams, William James, and Gertrude Stein* (New Haven, CT: Yale University Press, 1991), 263–408.

12. Stein, *Wars I Have Seen* (New York: Random House, 1945), 62, *subsequent citations given parenthetically as WIHS.*

13. For a carefully constructed profile of the Progressive intellectuals, see Eldon J. Eisenach, *The Lost Promise of Progressivism* (Lawrence: University of Kansas Press, 1994), 8–47; see also, Dorothy Ross, *The Origins of American Social Science* (New York: Cambridge

University Press, 1991). The Stein family wealth came from Stein's father Daniel's success at unifying the San Francisco streetcar system under his control in the Omnibus Cable Company, which was operated on the elder Stein's death by his son Michael until labor conflict in 1903 encouraged the family to sell the firm and live on their investments. A "stock report" from Michael to Gertrude, when he was still managing his sister's finances, shows that Stein's holdings where almost entirely in banking and rail—"all gilt edge securities paying 4 1/2 to 5% at present market prices." Michael Stein to Gertrude Stein, December 21, 1900, YCAL 76, box 125, folder 2716.

14. See Wineapple, *Sister Brother*, 48–154.

15. Munsterberg to Stein (June 10, 1895), *The Flowers of Friendship: Letters Written to Gertrude Stein*. (1953. New York: Farrar, Strauss and Giroux, 1979), 4; Munsterberg, *The Americans*, trans. Edwin B. Holt (New York: McClure, Phillips & Co, 1904), 600, 603, 604.

16. In other contexts she related it to the awareness that she and her brother Leo had been conceived and born only because two older siblings died in infancy. See, e.g., *Everybody's Autobiography*, 118. Compare, though, the remark by Walter Lippmann, Stein's near contemporary as a student of Royce and James, made in the course of his explanation of the appeal of a pragmatist view of the alliance of science and democratic progress. "There is a terrible loneliness that comes to men when they realize their feebleness before a brutally uninterested universe." Lippman's answer to this condition was the "common discipline" that could be found in the commitment to science and democratic solidarity. A renewal of "the old sense of cosmic wonder" could be created by "devotion to impersonal ends." Lippmann, *Drift and Mastery: An Attempt to Diagnose the Current Unrest* (1914. Madison: University of Wisconsin Press, 1985), 152, 154.

17. On Stein's knowledge of Henry George, see *Everybody's Autobiography*, 158; on the prominent role of the anxiety about civic decline and the loss of American exceptionalism in the development of Progressive Era social science, see Ross, *Origins of American Social Science*, 53–97, 143–72, and *passim*. Interestingly while George emphasized the threat of decline that plagued all corrupt republics, he was the rare turn-of-the-century figure who had little fondness for the language of evolution. Perhaps consequently, he had little influence over the combination of academic social science and middle-class reformism that characterized the discourse of Progressivism. Compare, Bellamy's *Looking Backward*—a book that had vastly greater influence on Progressive Era intellectuals and reformers and which explicitly dismisses traditional republicanism's "cyclical" model of "human history" by embracing the "process of Industrial Evolution." Edward Bellamy, *Looking Backward, 2000–1887* (1888. New York: Signet, 2000), 12, 32, 50.

18. Peter J. Bowler, *The Eclipse of Darwinism: Anti-Darwinian Evolution Theories in the Decades Around 1900* (Baltimore: Johns Hopkins University Press, 1983), 75 and *passim*.

19. Ward, "Transmission of Culture," 319.

20. Stocking, *Race, Culture, and Evolution: Essays in the History of Anthropology* (1968. Chicago: University of Chicago Press, 1982), ch. 10; Robert C. Bannister, *Social Darwinism: Science and Myth in Anglo-American Social Thought* (Philadelphia: Temple University Press, 1979); William F. Fine, *Progressive Evolutionism and American Sociology, 1890–1920* (Ann Arbor, MI: UMI Research Press, 1979).

21. William I. Thomas, "The Significance of the Orient for the Occident," *PPASS* 2 (1907), 729.

22. Small, "The Bonds of Nationality," *American Journal of Sociology* 20 (1915), 635. As Eisenach explains, Small's essay "can stand as a fair copy of the larger intellectual framework of Progressive discussion of American nationality"—both because of Small's personal prominence among reform intellectuals and because his essay synthesized the writings that fellow sociologists and political scientists had published over the previous two and half decades (Eisenach, *Lost Promise*, 54). On the central role of nationalism as the core element of Progressive social, economic, and political theory and the linchpin that related those theories to a program of action, see ibid., 49–73 and *passim*.

23. Leon Fink has recently described this as the central dilemma of Progressive Era reform. Fink, *Progressive Intellectuals and the Dilemmas of Democratic Commitment* (Cambridge, MA: Harvard University Press, 1997).

24. Small, "Bonds of Nationality," 679.

25. Munsterberg, *The Americans*, 10, 23, 24, 604, 605; Munsterberg's book was a significant influence on the definitive statement of Progressive ambitions, Herbert Croly's *The Promise of American Life*; Croly begins his discussion by referring to Munsterberg on page 3.

26. James demonstrates how widely accepted the Lamarckian framework was at the turn of the century precisely because, as possibly its least enthusiastic defender, he nevertheless shared some of its interests. When Stein recalled the influence of Darwin during her time at Radcliffe, she referred specifically to *The Expression of Emotions in Man and Animals*, one of the several places in his writing where Darwin looks close to Lamarck. Here Darwin considered that emotional expressions could become habits by repetition and then be passed on by inheritance to descendants. This was the aspect of Darwin's writing (along with the similar work of Romanes and Bagehot) that James drew on in *The Principles of Psychology* in order to defend his teleological definition of instincts and habits. See Hamilton Cravens, *The Triumph of Evolution*, 73–74 and Jacques Barzun, *A Stroll with William James* (New York: Harper & Row, 1983), 209–14. On the central role of Jamesian pragmatism to the development of Progressive social theory, see James Kloppenberg, *Uncertain Victory: Social Democracy and Progressivism in European and American Thought, 1870–1920* (New York: Oxford University Press, 1986), 298–348 and *passim*.

27. For Royce's assimilation of evolution to Idealism, see *The Spirit of Modern Philosophy: An Essay in the Form of Lectures* (Boston: Houghtpon Mifflin, 1892), 265–340; Stein oversaw invitations to speak at the philosophical club to Royce, G. Stanley Hall, and C. Lloyd Morgan, among others. Stein papers, Yale Collection of American Literature, Beinecke Library, MSS 76, box 118, folder 2547, *further citation of Stein papers given as YCAL*. Hall was in the midst of developing his Lamarckian theory of adolescence, in which the development of the individual recapitulated the evolutionary history of the race. Morgan was pioneering comparative psychology and would later develop a highly spiritualized vision of evolution. Letters from Stein's close friends in Cambridge suggest that she was conversant with the developing social sciences, including Franklin Giddings's widely influential, Lamarckian sociology. See Francis Pollack to Stein (March 13, 1897), YCAL MSS 76, box 119, folder 2562.

28. In the thirties, Stein told Robert Bartlett Haas that while at Radcliffe she had been much concerned with "constitutional history" (Stein quoted at Bush, *Halfway to Revolution*, 268). Hart was a particular favorite of Leo Stein, whose tutelage at that time Gertrude still valued (Wineapple, *Sister Brother*, 50). Hart was also a close friend of Woodrow Wilson and an important influence on W.E.B. DuBois and on Mary Follett, whose paradigmatic work of Progressive political theory, *The New State*, Hart reportedly helped compose. Viewing Darwin as "the great historical master of the age," Hart found in evolution reason to claim that the "United States of today is not a miracle, but a steady and measurable growth, still enlarging, still to put forth new branches for the world's advantage" (Hart, *National Ideals Historically Traced, 1607–1907, The American Nation: A History* 26 [New York: Harper and Brothers, 1907] xiii–xiv).

29. On Stein's interest in Gilman, see Wineapple, *Sister Brother*, 117; on Gilman's reliance on Lamarckian social theory, see Gail Bederman, *Manliness and Civilization: A Cultural History of Gender and Race in the United States, 1880–1917* (Chicago: University of Chicago Press, 1995), 121–69; and for a broader account of the racialist thinking Gilman shared with other Progressive economists, see Thomas C. Leonard, " 'More Merciful and Not Less Effective': Eugenics and American Economics in the Progressive Era," *History of Political Economy* 35, 4 (2003): 687–712.

30. Stein's favored professor at Hopkins was Franklin Paine Mall, renowned for his emphasis on laboratory training and ultimately for work submitting racialist and Lamarckian claims about the size of the brains of women and African Americans to tests that ultimately discredited them. She worked still more closely with Lewellys Barker, who would become a leader of the U.S. eugenics movement that emerged following the decline of reformist Lamarckism. At Radcliffe and Cold Spring Harbor she had studied with Charles Davenport, another future leader of the eugenics movement.

31. Peter Bowler, *The Mendelian Revolution: The Emergence of Hereditarian Concepts in Modern Science and Society* (Baltimore: Johns Hopkins University Press, 1989), 110–27.

32. Patten, "Types of Men," *Popular Science Monthly* 80 (1912): 275.

33. Gerstle, *American Crucible: Race and Nation in the Twentieth Century* (Princeton, NJ: Princeton University Press. 2001), 14–80; Thomas G. Dyer, *Theodore Roosevelt and the Idea of Race* (Baton Rouge: Louisiana State University Press, 1980), 14–16, 37–44, and *passim*.

34. Wilson, "The Ideals of America," *Atlantic Monthly* 90 (December 1902): 725, 732.

35. Wilson, *Constitutional Government*, 54, 57. Elsewhere, Wilson made it clear that evolutionary theory both justified the pride of the "stronger and nobler races" and provided a reassuring answer to the threat of political conflict. "The law of coherence and continuity in political development has suffered no serious breach. . . . The evolutions of politics have been scarcely less orderly and coherent than those in the physical world" (Wilson, *The State: Elements of Historical and Practical Politics* [1889], qtd. at Bragdon, *Woodrow Wilson: The Academic Years*, 175).

36. Hodder, *The Adversaries of the Skeptic, or The Specious Present, a New Inquiry into Human Knowledge* (London: George Allen & Co, 1901), 296, 290.

37. A portrait of Hodder can be found in Hutchins Hapgood, *A Victorian in the Modern World* (New York: Harcourt, Brace, 1939), 150–51, 163–65, 221–22; see also Wineapple, *Sister Brother*, 135–39, 151–68, 172–85.

38. Hodder, *The New Americans* (New York: Macmillan, 1901), 195; Herbert Croly himself made reference to Hodder's novel in *The Promise of American Life*, suggesting briefly, in the course of criticizing the localism and limitation of Hodder's mentor—the New York reform lawyer William Travers Jerome—that Hodder's novel provided an appropriate framework for highlighting the interests of Progressives.

39. Hodder makes the connection between his critique of conventional marriage and his distaste for party loyalty explicit. The novel's villain—the corrupt senator, adulterer, and murderer Howard Lidcott announces that "a man and wife must stick together. A man or woman marries as he joins a party" (389).

40. The force of Hodder's dissent from Progressive visions of national leadership can be clarified by noting how closely his novel resembles Edith Wharton's *The Age of Innocence*—another tale of young love and talent crushed by the provincial customs of marriage, but one where the promise of generational development inspired by the executive leadership, exemplified in the novel by the sudden appearance of Teddy Roosevelt, promises to resolve those problems.

41. Brenda Wineapple has recently discovered a lecture, "Degeneration in American Women," most likely written by Stein in the fall of 1901. The lecture directly reverses the arguments made in the Gilman-inspired "The Value of College Education for Women" that Stein had delivered when beginning medical school only three years earlier and argues that women should dedicate themselves to the biologically destined task of motherhood (Wineapple, *Sister Brother*, 151–54, 411–14).

42. See Katz, *The First Making*, 67; and Arthur Lachman, "Gertrude Stein As I Knew Her," YCAL, MSS 77, box 17, folder 291.

43. Stein, YCAL, MSS 76, box 37, folder 773.

44. Stein, *Fernhurst, Q. E. D., and Other Early Writings* (New York: Liveright, 1973), 7–8.

45. Stein, *Three Lives* (1909. New York: Penguin, 1990), 108.

46. Leon Katz, introduction, *Fernhurst, Q. E. D., and Other Early Writings*, xvi.

47. Addams, *Twenty Years at Hull House*, 89; Patten, *The Theory of Social Forces* (1896); Gilman, *The Man-Made World, of Our Androcentric Culture* (1911), qtd. at Eisenach, *Lost Promise*, 89, 82; Louis Menand offers a particularly vivid account of the Progressive tendency to discount conflict in a discussion of Jane Addams and John Dewey. Menand, *The Metaphysical Club: A Story of Ideas in America* (New York: Farrar, Strauss & Giroux, 2000), 312–15; Eisenach shows it to have been widely shared among Progressive intellectuals and central to their political theory (*Lost Promise*, 74–103).

48. For a thorough reconstruction of the event, see Helen Lefkowitz Horowitz, *The Power and Passion of M. Carey Thomas* (New York: Knopf, 1994), 292–96, 355–60, 366–72, and passim.

49. Stein, *Fernhurst, Q. E. D.*, 47; Leon Katz learned from Alice B. Toklas that Redfern was modeled on Hodder and Wilson, who had earlier been involved in a widely acknowledged conflict with M. Carey Thomas (Katz, introduction, xxxiv). It is also worth noting that

Stein titled her novella and her fictional college with the name, "Fernhurst," of the English country manor of the Pearsall Smith family—a social center of Fabian reform where Leo and Gertrude Stein made a brief discontented visit.

50. DeKoven makes the illuminating observation that Stein's depiction of the educated New Woman resembles Addams's complaint against the effects of higher education for women in her renowned critique of "the snare of preparation" (DeKoven, " 'Excellent Not a Hull House," 321–50). But the comparison obscures a more significant difference. For Addams, higher education is dangerous because its emphasis on refinement threatens to cut women off from useful labor. For Stein, by contrast, it is delusional because it gives women an unrealistic estimate of their power.

51. James, *The Principles of Psychology* (Cambridge, MA: Harvard University Press, 1983), 424; see Gerald E. Myers, *William James: His Life and Thought* (New Haven, CT: Yale University Press, 1986), 181–88. On James's effort to stake out a "via media" more generally, see Kloppenberg, *Uncertain Victory*, 15–63 and *passim*.

52. Stein's reference here was to her brother Leo's efforts to build on James, and Hodder, to develop a pragmatist theory of art, which Stein suggested was "an idealism built on pragmatism. Attention exists—but pragmatically so does consciousness. Attention is a condition of consciousness, some organism doing something with binocular vision is the condition of the existence of attention. The moment you abstract attention beyond that you make the emotional leap into idealism. . . . [T]he minute you make it transcendence it has no meaning, it is no longer conditioned." But, Stein went on to suggest that, while Leo's misguided vision of transcendence reflected his own need to compensate for personal failings, it was also an inevitable outgrowth of James's theory—"a perfectly natural result, bound to come as Spencer's cosmic philosophy sprang out of evolution." The comparison was particularly cruel, given James's antagonism to Spencer. Stein notebooks, YCAL 76, box 39, folders 814–15.

53. On this feature of pragmatism and its importance to Progressive intellectuals, see, e.g., Kloppenberg, *Uncertain victory*, 79–94 and *passim* and Adolph L. Reed, Jr., *W. E. B. DuBois and American Political Thought: Fabianism and the Color Line* (New York: Oxford University Press, 1997), 15–26, 93–126.

54. "The conception with which we handle a bit of sensible experience is really nothing but a teleological instrument. *The whole function of conceiving, of fixing, and holding fast to meanings, has no significance apart from the fact that the conceiver is a creature with partial purposes and private ends*" (James, *Principles*, 456; emphasis in original).

55. Stein, notebooks, YCAL 76, box 38, folder 797.

56. The distinction Stein marks here—between genius and mere intelligence—is one that she aligns with an anti-Semitic strain running through the notebooks. "Jews naturally run themselves by their minds, now they have good minds but not great minds and if you have a good mind and not a great mind your mind ought to be no more than a purveyor to you . . . That is the secret of the inevitable mediocrity" of "the pure intelligent yid." Fittingly, given these terms, she renders James an honorary Jew, and associates him with the prime target of her contempt, her brother—at the same time distinguishing herself and Picasso as more creative thinkers. "Leo and James run themselves by their minds but they have pretty great

minds . . . . Pablo and I recognize the danger and refuse to run ourselves by our minds" (Stein, YCAL 76, box 38, folder 788).

57. Stein, *The Making of Americans: Being the History of a Family's Progress* (1925. Normal, IL: Dalkey Archive Press, 1995), 221, *subsequent citations given parenthetically as MOA.*

58. Stein, notebooks, qtd. at Katz, *First Making*, 161.

59. "Reform side": YCAL, MSS 77, box 17, folder 283; "rouse up": Stein, qtd. at Katz, *First Making*, 193.

60. Stein's first complete design for *The Making of Americans* was reconstructed by Katz, in consultation with Alice B. Toklas, from Stein's notebooks for the novel. For a complete description, see Katz, *The First Making*, 159–94. Even apart from that illuminating narrative framework, however, Stein's anti-Progressive views are evident all through the notebooks— in, e.g., her remarks about a college friend, whose "characteristic attitude toward woman's suffrage and trusts" she criticized; in her description of the "striking credulity" of the rising scientific elite, "even in its reform movements"; and in her angry dismissal of the "Mrs. Charlotte Perkins Stetson type": "the purest fanatics, . . . they have absolute self-righteousness and no self-consciousness . . . their intellect is very genuine but unoriginal, it is personal and intensive but runs into theoretical general grooves mixed with moral purpose" (YCAL, 76 box 37, folder 757; 76 box 37, folder 760; 76 box 37, folder 779).

61. See, e.g., the comment made of an early group of minor characters: "religion . . . was a part of them, it was to all of them a part of their being, it was not a belief in them, it was of them like eating and sleeping and washing" (MOA 109).

62. Stein, *Lectures in America* (New York: Random House, 1935), 104, *subsequent citations given parenthetically as LIA.*

63. For a full consideration of Weininger and his relation to his Viennese context, see Chandak Sengoopta, *Otto Weininger: Sex, Science, and Self in Imperial Vienna* (Chicago: University of Chicago Press, 2000); see also, Allan Janik, *Essays on Wittgenstein and Weininger* (Amsterdam: Rodopi, 1985). Sengoopta points out how rare Weininger's radical neo-Kantianism was in the philosophical circles of turn-of-the-century Vienna (27–29); Steven Beller relates that stance to Weininger's ultraliberal opposition to the rise of social democratic politics in Vienna. Beller, "Otto Weininger as Liberal?" *Jews and Gender: Responses to Otto Weininger*, ed. Nancy A. Harrowitz and Barbara Hyams (Philadelphia: Temple University Press, 1995), 91–102. Weininger's readers among U.S. Progressive intellectuals did not fail to note his significance in this respect. Charlotte Perkins Gilman and Lester Ward each regarded him as a serious threat.

64. Weininger, *Sex and Character*, authorized translation from the Sixth German Edition (New York: A. L. Burt Co., n.d.), 161.

65. Stein, YCAL MSS 76, box 37, folder 761, folder 774.

66. Priscilla Wald, *Constituting Americans: Cultural Anxiety and Narrative Form* (Durham, NC: Duke University Press, 1995), 274–75.

67. The most illuminating account of the transition can be found in Jennifer Ashton, *From Modernism to Postmodernism: American Poetry and Theory in the Twentieth Century* (New York: Cambridge University Press, 2005).

68. Hodder to Gwinn (February 26, 1902) qtd. at Wineapple, *Sister Brother*, 154.

69. Stein, notebooks, as quoted in Katz, *First Making*, 190, 180, 190; Stein's notebooks, which emphasize that David is to be a combination of "Leon & me," mention that in creating his "feeling strong of death," she would "use that time in the J. H. U. gardens when I got sick and faced flunking out of exams." (Stein, YCAL MSS 76, box 38, folder 783).

70. Josiah Flynt and Francis Walton [Hodder], *The Powers that Prey* (London: Ward, Lock & Co., n.d. [1900]), 245; in the amateur ethnography of the underworld Hodder composed with his friend Josiah Flynt (reportedly their effort to find an alternative to academic sociology), "a dead one" is the final chapter (245–60) and, like the conclusion to *The New Americans*, marks the inescapable cruelty of a competitive world. A "dead one" is a criminal "used up, . . . his nerve gone. . . . [W]hen you look at him you keep thinkin' that p'r'aps it'll be your turn next" (255–56).

71. Qtd. at Bannister, *Social Darwinism*, 46.

72. "Associative habits"; "disembodiment": Stein qtd. at Dydo, *The Language that Rises*, 15, 25 respectively. Dydo's thorough reconstruction of Stein's career and compositional process gives a fine overview of Stein's aesthetic principles. Although, she differs with Dydo on one point (whether Stein should be regarded as a "literalist" writer"), Jennifer Ashton largely confirms Dydo's claim that Stein's ambitions centered on the effort to escape the confusions and constraints of ordinary language use in favor of what Ashton describes as a determinist or stipulative account of meaning. Ashton, *From Modernism*, 67–94. For a comparable argument focusing on Stein's view of audience, see Lisa Siraginian, "Out of Air: Theorizing the Art Object in Gertrude Stein and Wyndham Lewis," *Modernism/Modernity* 10, 4 (2003), 657–76.

73. Stein, LIA, 105; "What Are Master-Pieces and Why Are There So Few of Them," *WL*, 148–56, *subsequent citations to this essay given as WMP*; see also, Stein, *The Geographical History of America or the Relation of Human Nature to the Human Mind* (1936. Baltimore: Johns Hopkins University Press, 1995).

74. On these developments in the social sciences, see Ross, *Origins*, 303–470.

75. For an explanation of Stein's libertarian aesthetics and their relation to Stein's hostility to the New Deal, see Szalay, *New Deal Modernism*, 87–93, 117–19.

76. Stein, YCAL MSS 76, box 37, folder 757. Stein's model for such manipulation was her cousin Bird Sternberger, later Gans, on whom Julia Dehning of MOA was based. Stein's angry break with Bird, who she had once greatly admired, was the basis for the later part of the novel and apparently a spur to Stein's creative development generally. Along with her second husband, Howard Gans, a Progressive lawyer, Bird was associated with elite reform circles in New York Jewish society.

77. Stein, qtd. in Rosalind S. Miller *Gertrude Stein: Form and Intelligibility* (New York: Exposition Press, 1949), 146–47.

78. Stein, YCAL MSS 76, box 38, folder 788; on Stein's view of Picasso, see Katz, *First Making*, 137.

79. On Wilson as the elided figure of "patriarchal poetry," see Dydo, *Language that Rises*, 135.

80. Stein YCAL MSS 76, box 37, folder 774; box 37, folder 773.

81. Patten, "The Organic Concept of Society, *Annals of the American Academy*, 405.

82. Stein, "A Long Gay Book," *Matisse, Picasso, and Gertrude Stein with Two Shorter Stories* (Barton: Something Else Press, 1972), 24.

83. Clive Bush is rare among her critics in noting this important feature of Stein's work. See, Bush, *Halfway to Revolution*, 360–61 and *passim*.

84. Milkis, "Franklin D. Roosevelt, the Economic Constitutional Order, and the New Politics of Presidential Leadership," 36–40 and *passim*.

Chapter Two: Governable Beasts

1. Roosevelt, radio address on Brotherhood Day (February 23, 1936), *Public Papers and Addresses* 5:86; Hurston to Charles S. Johnson (12/5/1950), *Zora Neale Hurston: A Life in Letters*, ed. Carla Kaplan (New York: Doubleday, 2002), 634, *subsequent citations given parenthetically in the text as ZNH.*

2. Roth, *Call It Sleep* (1934. New York: Noonday Press, 1991), 398.

3. Brain McHale has explored the parallels between Roth and Joyce here—and the way Roth might be said to depart from and to "contain" the energies of Joyce's text. "Henry Roth in Nighttown, or, Containing *Ulysses*," *New Essays on* Call It Sleep, ed. Hana Wirth-Nesher (New York: Cambridge University Press, 1996), 75–126; see also, for an interesting discussion of the way Roth adopts the metropolitan topos of Joyce and Eliot, Mark Schoening, "T. S. Eliot Meets Michael Gold: Modernism and Radicalism in Depression-Era America," *Modernism/Modernity* 3, 3 (1996), 51–68.

4. Hurston, *Jonah's Gourd Vine* in *Novels and Stories* (New York: Library of America, 1995), 5; *subsequent citations given as JGV.*

5. This was the name given to Hurston's father by his congregation. Valerie Boyd, *Wrapped in Rainbows: The Life of Zora Neale Hurston* (New York: Scribner, 2003). Lucy Pearson mentions the name in *Jonah's Gourd Vine* and underlines the connection between violence and virility emphasized throughout the novel: "She loved to hear him spoken of as 'The Battle-Axe.' She even loved his primitive poetry and his magnificent pulpit gestures, but, even so, a little cold feeling impinged upon her antennae. There was another woman" (98).

6. Walter Benn Michaels, *Our America: Nativism, Modernism, Pluralism* (Durham, N.C.: Duke University Press, 1995).

7. For an excellent discussion, see Szalay, *New Deal Modernism*, 162–200.

8. John Steinbeck, *The Grapes of Wrath* (1939. New York: Penguin, 1992), 525.

9. On Steinbeck's elision of social and natural forces, see Denning, *The Cultural Front*, 266.

10. Lewisohn, *The Island Within* (New York: Harper & Bros., 1928), 346.

11. In a particularly nice touch, Lewisohn highlights the central contradiction of Progressivism—the way its claim to reinvigorate "government by the people" coincided with an attack on partisan corruption that included efforts to narrow the franchise. "In that past government was corrupt. But one still hastened to naturalize the alien in order to buy his vote, and by that very act to reaffirm the theory that government depends upon the consent of the governed" (4).

12. Creel, qtd. at David M. Kennedy, *Over Here: The First World War and American Society* (New York: Oxford University Press, 1980), 145.

13. Qtd. at Milkis and Nelson, *The American Presidency*, 242–43.

14. Karl, *The Uneasy State : The United States from 1915 to 1945* (Chicago: University of Chicago Press, 1983), 65.

15. In addition to Michaels, *Our America*, see, especially, Barbara Foley's *Spectres of 1919*.

16. Williams, *In the American Grain* (1925. New York: New Directions, 1956), 128, 234; see also Williams's vision of George Washington—imagined as a figure of "resistance . . . encitadeled," who concealed within himself "wild paths he alone knew and explored in secret" (141). In keeping with the rendition of the father of the nation as a hero of privacy, Williams remarks, "the presidency could not have meant anything to Washington" (143).

17. "The state must be no external authority which restrains and regulates me, but it must be myself acting as the state in every smallest detail of life" (Mary Parker Follett, *The New State: Group Organization the Solution of Popular Government* [1918. University Park: Pennsylvania State University Press, 1998], 137, 138).

18. Horace Kallen, "Democracy Versus the Melting Pot: A Study of American Nationality" (1915), repr. in *Theories of Ethnicity: A Classical Reader*, ed. Werner Sollors (New York: New York University Press, 1996), 92. The more influential expression of these ideas came in Kallen, *Culture and Democracy in the United States: Studies in the Group Psychology of the American Peoples* (New York: Boni & Liveright, 1924). The avant-garde house of Boni & Liveright also published both Lewisohn and Williams's *In the American Grain* and a number of the major works of the Harlem Renaissance, including Jean Toomer's *Cane* and Alain Locke's seminal collection, *The New Negro*.

19. Locke, "The Contribution of Race to Culture" (1930), *The Philosophy of Alain Locke: Harlem Renaissance and Beyond*, ed. Leonard Harris (Philadelphia: Temple University press, 1989), 202, 203. Both Louis Menand and Ross Posnock point to differences between Kallen and his sometime colleague Locke. They note that Kallen relied on biological theories of race and that he displayed racist condescension to Locke and African Americans in general. By contrast, they point out, Locke was doubtful about such theories and preferred dynamic and functional models of group differentiation. Menand, *Metaphysical Club*, 388–406; Posnock, *Color & Culture: Black Writers and the Making of the Modern Intellectual* (Cambridge, MA: Harvard University Press, 1998), 195–200. Foley shows in her careful reconstruction of Locke's development, however, that during his most influential years in the twenties, he increasingly stressed his attraction to racial essentialism (Foley, *Spectres of 1919*, 198–249).

20. Malcolm Cowley, "My Countryside, Then and Now: A Study in American Evolution," *Harper's Magazine* 299, 1791 (August 1999) (originally published in *Harper's* Jan. 1929), 73, 75; Hemingway, *A Farewell to Arms* (1929. New York: Macmillan, 1986), 185.

21. Cather: "One must know the world *so well* before one can know the parish." Quoting Sarah Orne Jewett, Preface (1922), *Alexander's Bridge* (1912. Mineola, NY: Dover Publications, 2002), viii. Cowley, *Exile's Return: A Literary Odyssey of the Twenties* (1934. New York: Penguin, 1976), 206–45, 245, *subsequent citations given as ER*.

22. Lewisohn, qtd. at Ralph Melnick, *The Life and Work of Ludwig Lewisohn*, vol. 1 (Detroit, MI: Wayne State University Press, 1998), 12.

23. Lewisohn's hospital is in this respect a direct analogue to the school in Anzia Yezierska's *Bread Givers*, where Sarah Smolinksi likewise stumbles across Hugo Seelig, the "landsleute" who emphasizes her genealogical connections to Eastern Europe. Both are ghetto institutions that emphasize not merely ethnic connections, but the ethnic obligations that educated Jews owe to their less wealthy and educated brethren. In both novels, as less emphatically in Sidney L. Nyburg's *The Chosen People*, "the tie of a common race" promises to transcend the difference "between employing Jews and laboring Jews" (Nyburg, *The Chosen People* [1917. New York: Markus Wiener, 1986], 69, 38).

24. H. D., *HERmione* (New York: New Directions, 1981), 78, emphasis in original.

25. Locke, *Race Contacts and Interracial Relations: Lectures on the Theory and Practice of Race*, ed. Jeffrey C. Stewart (Washington, DC: Howard University Press, 1992), 98; Kallen, "Democracy versus the Melting Pot," 84.

26. Lofton Mitchel, "Harlem Reconsidered," *Freedomways* (Fall 1964), 469.

27. Larsen, *Quicksand and* Passing (New Brunswick, NJ: Rutgers University Press, 1986), 186. Both Lewisohn and Larsen highlight this question by using tales of marriage and adultery to foreground the conflict between personal desire and racial obligation. Arthur Levy loves, but must leave, in order to preserve his son's patrimony, his wife Elizabeth. The protagonist of *Passing*, Irene Redfield, kills her rival Claire Kendry—who as the passing figure of the title chooses personal desire over racial identity—in order to preserve her loveless marriage and thus ensure that her husband remains a father to his children and perforce a responsible figure in his community.

28. Walton, *The City Day: an Anthology of Recent American Poetry* (New York: Ronald Press, 1929). Against the impersonality of urban society, Walton celebrated, as many of her contemporaries did, the era's prime symbol of "tribal desire," the Indian. Walton, *Dawn Boy: Blackfeet and Navajo Songs* (New York: E. P. Dutton, 1926), xi and *passim*. On Roth's romance with Walton, see Stephen G. Kellman, *Redemption: The Life of Henry Roth* (New York: Norton, 2005), 73–98.

29. See Roth, *From Bondage* (New York: St. Martin's Press, 1996), 290.

30. Lizabeth Cohen, *Making a New Deal: Industrial Workers in Chicago, 1919–1939* (New York: Cambridge University Press, 1991), chs 2 and 6; Cheryl Lynn Greenberg, *"Or Does it Explode?" Black Harlem in the Great Depression* (New York: Oxford University Press, 1991).

31. Hurston, *Letters*, 413; Hurston's comments on doubting "Race Solidarity" from her childhood are in *Dust Tracks on a Road*: "It does not exist . . . . Personal benefits run counter to race lines too often for it to hold" (*Folklore, Memoirs, and Other Writing* [New York: Library of America, 1995], *subsequent citations given as DTR*).

32. Hurston, *Tell My Horse*, in *Folklore, Memoirs, and Other Writing*, 341, *subsequent citations given as TMH*.

33. Locke, *Survey [Graphic]* 53 (March 1, 1925), 629–30; Locke, "Who and What is 'Negro'?" (1942) and "Frontiers of Culture" (1950), *Philosophy of Alain Locke*, 210, 234; Posnock sees this shift in Locke's thinking beginning in the late 1920s. *Color and Culture*, 200.

34. Horace M. Kallen, *Individualism: An American Way of Life* (New York: Liveright, 1933), 206.

35. Hughes, *The Big Sea* (1940. New York: Hill & Wang, 1993), 223; Roth, *Shifting Landscape: A Composite, 1925–1987*, ed. Mario Materassi (Philadelphia: The Jewish Publication Society, 1987), 63, 111.

36. Roth, *From Bondage*, vol. 3 of *Mercy of a Rude Stream* (New York: St. Martin's 1996), 28.

37. Eda Lou Walton and George K. Anderson, *This Generation: A Selection of British and American Literature from 1914 to the Present with Historical and Critical Essays* (Chicago: Scott, Foresman and Company, 1939), 16.

38. Marcus Klein, *Foreigners: The Making of American Literature, 1900–1940* (Chicago: University of Chicago Press, 1981), 89–226.

39. Roosevelt, *PPA*, 1: 14–15, 752, 754, 747, 751; 2:413 ff.

40. Roosevelt, *PPA*, 2:14; Harold James, *The End of Globalization: Lessons from the Great Depression* (Cambridge, MA: Harvard University Press, 2001), shows this to have been an international pattern. Throughout the international trading system a widely shared enthusiasm for internationalism and international institutions, which peaked in the twenties, gave way to economic nationalism and protectionism during the thirties.

41. Steinbeck, *Grapes of Wrath*, 456; Wheeler, qtd. at James McGregor Burns, *Roosevelt: The Lion and the Fox* (New York: Harcourt Brace, 1956), 341–42; FDR, *PPA*, V: 568–69, I: 752.

42. Theodore Roosevelt, "The New Nationalism" (1910), *Theodore Roosevelt: An American Mind*, ed. Mario DiNunzio (New York: Penguin, 1994), 145, 139. Though less drawn than TR to the martial virtues, Wilson and his supporters assumed, too, that executive leadership depended on the president's ability to educate the nation to "the spirit of civic duty" and to "form it to his own views." Wilson, *Constitutional Government*, 68.

43. TR, "The New Nationalism," 148.

44. Milkis, "Franklin D. Roosevelt . . . and the New Politics of Presidential Leadership"; Jerome M. Mileur, "The Boss: Franklin Roosevelt, The Democratic Party and the Reconstitution of American Politics," *The New Deal and the Triumph of Liberalism*, 86–134.

45. Theodore J. Lowi, *The Personal President: Power Invested, Promise Unfulfilled* (Ithaca, NY: Cornell University Press, 1985), 62, 115; Roosevelt, Acceptance of the Renomination for the Presidency (June 27, 1936), *PPA* 5:235.

46. Louis Howe, qtd. at T. H. Watkins, *The Hungry Years: A Narrative History of the Great Depression* (New York: Henry Holt, 1999), 150; see also Robert S. McElvaine, *Down and Out in the Great Depression: Letters from the Forgotten Man* (Chapel Hill: University of North Carolina Press, 1983).

47. Bonny Lyons, *Henry Roth: The Man and His Work* (New York: Cooper Square Publishers, 1976), 172.

48. Roth, *From Bondage*, 69.

49. Roth, *Shifting Landscape: A Composite, 1925–1987*, ed. Mario Materassi (Philadelphia: Jewish Publication Society, 1987), 114.

50. *Moses, Man of the Mountain* (1939), in *Novels and Stories*, 359, 337, 586, 591, *subsequent citations given as MMM*.

51. In his notes for the novel, Roth left little doubt of Albert's malevolence. Initially he seems to have planned to have Albert directly strike his father and to do so in anger at his

father's domination over his mother. See notebook marked "NOTES Additions VI," Roth Papers, Berg Collection, New York Public Library. For an illuminating account of the novel's oedipal dynamics, see Thomas J. Ferraro, *Ethnic Passages: Literary Immigrants in Twentieth-Century America* (Chicago: University of Chicago Press, 1993), 87–122.

52. Notebook marked "3?B," Roth Papers, Berg Collection, New York Public Library.

53. The connection between violence and religious observation is further emphasized in Roth's notes—where, for example, Roth reminds himself: "On the night of D's beating, don't forget lighted candles. The day is Friday." Notebook marked "3?B," Roth Papers.

54. Hurston, *Novels & Stories*, 877.

55. Hurston, *Their Eyes Were Watching God* (1937) in *Novels and Stories*, 180, 244, *subsequent citations given as TEWWG*.

56. Book "2?H," Roth papers, Berg collection.

57. See, e.g., Michael Awkward, *Inspiriting Influences: Tradition, Revision, and Afro-American Women's Novels* (New York: Columbia University Press, 1991), 15–56; Nellie McKay, " 'Crayon Enlargements of Life': Zora Neale Hurston's *Their Eyes Were Watching God* as Autobiography," *New Essays on* Their Eyes Were Watching God, ed. Michael Awkward (New York: Cambridge University Press, 1990), 51–70. For a dissenting view, taking up Richard Wright's strongly critical view of Hurston's romanticization of a southern black folk, see Hazel V. Carby, "The Politics of Fiction, Anthropology, and the Folk: Zora Neale Hurston," *New Essays on* Their Eyes, ed. Awkward, 71–94; and, for a similar argument, contesting the critical overemphasis on the centrality of Hurston to the canon of black women writers and pointing out her significant idiosyncrasy in a number of important respects, see Ann duCille, *The Coupling Convention: Sex, Text, and Tradition in Black Women's Fiction* (New York: Oxford University Press, 1993), 80–85.

58. Adam Gussow, *Seems Like Murder Here: Southern Violence and the Blues Tradition* (Chicago: University of Chicago Press, 2002), 233–71; Missy Dehn Kubitschek, " 'Tuh De Horizon and Back': The Female Quest in *Their Eyes Were Watching God*," *Modern Critical Interpretations: Zora Neale Hurston's Their Eyes Were Watching God*, ed. Harold Bloom (New York: Chelsea House, 1987), 27–28.

59. Hurston, "Characteristics of Negro Expression," *Folklore, Memoirs, and Other Writings*, 840.

60. Compare Hurston's claim that "you got what your strengths would give you," to the sentiment expressed in *Uncle Tom's Children* and repeated often by Wright: "Freedom belongs t the strong!" Wright, *Uncle Tom's Children* (1938. New York: HarperPerennial, 1993), 220. On the notion that Wright and Hurston resemble each other in a number of significant ways—e.g. in personal careers that, almost uniquely among African American writers at the time, took them from the rural south to the urban north, and in their efforts to use variants of modernization theory (anthropology, Chicago School sociology) to conceive a dialectical relation between southern African American culture and urban industrial society, see William Maxwell, *New Negro, Old Left*, 153–78 and Werner Sollors, "Anthropological and Sociological Tendencies in American Literature of the 1930s and 1940s: Richard Wright, Zora Neale Hurston, and American Culture," *Looking Inward, Looking Outward: From the 1930s through the 1940s*, ed. Steve Ickringill (Amsterdam: VU University Press, 1990), 22–75.

61. See, Gussow, *Seems Like Murder Here*, 268 and *passim*.

62. "[N]ot a Christian," Hurston, "Characteristics of Negro Expression," 836; "barbaric poetry" and "Congo gods," Hurston, *JGV*, 76.

63. Here again, the notes Roth made while working on the novel emphasize the design of the book, stressing not just the fear and vulnerability that are evident in the novel's portrayal of David but the "horrible rage [that] convulsed him" and explicitly linking David to the symbolic figure of the wolf in the children's game played on the street as he flees his home (Book 58, Roth Papers, Berg collection).

64. As Mary Esteve notes, "where the era's preferred metaphors would associate aggregated immigrants with a wave or herd mentality, Roth's immigrants manage to come across, despite his representation of their voices as disembodied, as competent individuals making decisions on the spot. In effect, they are not a wave, but a public" (Esteve, *The Aesthetics and Politics of the Crowd in American Literature* [New York: Cambridge University Press, 2003], 188).

65. Carla Kaplan, *The Erotics of Talk: Women's Writing and Feminist Paradigms* (New York: Oxford University Press, 1996), 107.

66. James Joyce, *Ulysses: The Corrected Text*, ed. Hans Walter Gabler (New York: Random House, 1986), 644.

67. Walton was a student of Alfred Kroeber and Benjamin Putnam Kurtz, among the most prominent "neo-Freudians" in U.S. anthropology. While she worked with them, Kroeber was systematically reviewing the limits of Freud's social theory.

68. Carl E. Schorske, *Fin-de-siècle Vienna: Politics and Culture* (New York: Knopf, 1980), 181–207; Ernest Gellner, *Anthropology and Politics: Revolutions in the Sacred Grove* (Cambridge, MA: Blackwell, 1995), 62–93; see also David Rieff, *Freud: The Mind of the Moralist* (New York: Viking, 1959), 247–56.

69. Freud, *Moses and Monotheism*, trans. Katherine Jones (1939. New York: Vintage, 1967), 104.

70. Gellner, *Anthropology and Politics*, 76.

71. Freud, *Civilization and its Discontents*, trans. Joan Riviere, ed. James Strachey (1930. London: Hogarth Press, 1969), 32, emphasis added.

72. See Marthe Robert, *From Oedipus to Moses: Freud's Jewish Identity*, trans. Ralph Manheim (Garden City, NY: Anchor Books, 1976) and, for a less sympathetic view, Daniel Boyarin, *Unheroic Conduct: The Rise of Heterosexuality and the Invention of the Jewish Man* (Berekely: University of California Press, 1997), 244 ff.

73. Roth, *Shifting Landscape*, 20; in a letter he sent to Eda Lou Walton from Vermont during the composition of novel, Roth enthused about the fact that the family he was staying with did not realize he was a Jew and referred to "our conception of true religious intuition—by that I mean belief in benign significance" (Roth to Walton [August 1932], Roth Papers, Berg collection). Leslie Fiedler's observation—that Roth's use of the Oedipus narrative "seems more Jungian than Freudian"—seems both plausible and resonant in this context (Leslie Fielder, "The Many Myths of Henry Roth," *New Essays on* Call It Sleep, ed. Hana Wirth-Nesher).

74. Freud, *Group Psychology and the Analysis of the Ego*, 101.

75. Rieff, *Freud*, 240.

76. Hurston, "Characteristics of Negro Expression"; "Court Order Can't Make Races Mix," *Folklore, Memoirs, and Other Writings*, 830, 958.

77. Harvard Sitkoff, *A New Deal for Blacks: The Emergence of Civil Rights as a National Issue* (New York: Oxford, 1978); Nancy J. Weiss, *Farewell to the Party of Lincoln: Black Politics in the Age of FDR* (Princeton, NJ: Princeton University Press, 1983).

78. See, e.g., *Dust Tracks*, ch. 12.

79. Hurston, "How it Feels to Be Colored Me," *Folklore, Memoirs, and Other Writings* 827.

80. The onset of Tea Cake's illness immediately follows the passage explaining that Janie has become a better shot than her teacher and that "Tea Cake was a little jealous, but proud of his pupil." The next sentence: "About the middle of the fourth week Tea Cake came home early one afternoon complaining of his head" (316).

81. Leslie Fielder, "Henry Roth's Neglected Masterpiece," *The New Fiedler Reader* (Amherst, NY: Prometheus Books, 1999), 211–19; Tom Samet, "Henry Roth's Bull Story: Guilt and Betrayal in *Call It Sleep*," *Studies in the Novel* 7 (1975): 569–83; Gary Epstein, "Auto-Obituary: The Death of the Artist in Henry Roth's *Call It Sleep*," *Studies in American Jewish Literature* 5.1 (1979): 37–45.

82. Qtd. at Lyons, 170.

83. DuCille, *Coupling Convention*, 123; DuCille suggests that novel's narrative voice, which defends Tea Cake's violence and celebrates Janie's romance, is "parodic" and meant to reveal the way women "expect, accept, condone their own brutalization" (122). My slightly different view is that Hurston accepts brutality as the price of a romance she celebrates.

Chapter Three: The Myth of the Public Interest

1. Lowell to W. F. van Leeuwen (November 16, 1952), *The Letters of Robert Lowell*, ed. Saskia Sassen (New York: Farrar, Strauss & Giroux, 2005), 196; Ellison, introduction, *Shadow and Act* (1964), *The Collected Essays of Ralph Ellison*, ed. John F. Callahan (New York: Modern Library, 1995), 58, *subsequent citations given as CE.*

2. Salinger, *The Catcher in the Rye* (1951. Little, Brown, 2001), 244, 256; on the literary influence of the "new liberalism" that developed during the Cold War, see Thomas Hill Schaub, *American Fiction in the Cold War* (Madison: University of Wisconsin Press, 1991), 3–24 and *passim*; on the intellectual history of Cold War liberalism more generally, see Richard Pells, *The Liberal Mind in a Conservative Age: American Intellectuals in the 1940s and 1950s* (Middletown, CT: Wesleyan University Press, 1989).

3. Mary McCarthy to Hannah Arendt (January 17, 1961), *Between Friends: The Correspondence of Hannah Arendt and Mary McCarthy, 1949–1975*, ed. Carol Brightman (New York: Harcourt, 1995), 110; McCarthy, *The Groves of Academe* (New York: Harcourt Brace, 1952), 98, 205.

4. Trilling, "Manners, Morals, and the Novel," *The Liberal Imagination* (1950. New York: Anchor, 1953), 215.

5. Carol Ohmann and Richard Ohmann, "A Case Study in Canon Formation: Reviewers, Critics, and *The Catcher in the Rye*," *The Politics of Letters* (Middletown, CT: Wesleyan University Press, 1987), 45–67.

6. See, e.g., Peter Shaw, "Love and Death in *The Catcher in the Rye*," *New Essays on the* The Catcher in the Rye, ed. Jack Salzman (New York, Cambridge University Press 1991), 97–114.

7. Garry Wills, quoting Arthur Schlesinger, Jr., *Nixon Agonistes: The Crisis of the Self-Made Man* (1970. New York: Houghton Mifflin, 2002), 335–55.

8. As Ohmann and Ohmann note, the affect of the novel focuses above all on "ceremony" or "mores and conventions." *Politics of Letters*, 58, 59.

9. Arendt, *On Violence* (New York: Harcourt Brace, 1970), 97.

10. Arthur Mizener, "The Love Song of J. D. Salinger," *Harper's Monthly* 218 (February 1959): 83.

11. Updike, *Conversations with John Updike*, ed. James Plath (Jackson: University of Mississippi Press), 43; on the obsessive interest in "form and authority" among the young writers of the fifties, see Schaub, *American Fiction in the Cold War*, 50–67; see also Morris Dickstein, *Leopards in the Temple: The Transformation of American Fiction, 1945–1970* (Cambridge, MA: Harvard University Press, 2002), 83–141.

12. Bellow, qtd. at Schaub, *American Fiction in the Cold War*, 52.

13. Bellow, *The Adventures of Augie March* (1953. New York: Penguin, 1984), 12, 67, 194, 402.

14. Vladimir Nabokov, *Strong Opinions* (New York: McGraw-Hill, 1973), 57.

15. Nabokov, "On a Book Entitled *Lolita*," *Lolita*, 316.

16. Vladimir Nabokov, *Lolita* (1955. New York: Vintage, 1997), 305, 299, 307–8.

17. Appel, ed., *The Annotated* Lolita (1970. New York: Vintage, 1991), 389, see also 451; this is an interpretation in keeping with the view of the novel suggested in Richard Rorty's important account. For Rorty, the passage quoted above is the culmination, formally and thematically, of a series of intimations throughout the narrative reminding us of the moral limits of an aesthetic ecstasy that fails to take account of the suffering of others. The climactic moment, then, states directly Humbert's sudden perception of the truth of his story. Rorty, *Contingency, Irony, and Solidarity* (New York: Cambridge University Press, 1989), 141–68; for an illuminating discussion of the prominent role played by bargaining in *Lolita* and its association with predation, see Rachel Bowlby, *Shopping with Freud* (New York: Routledge, 1993), 50–71.

18. That this aesthetic immortality is inimical to the other ways Lolita might have hoped to be remembered by future generations is emphasized by Nabokov's frame. As John Ray, Jr. points out in his preface, "Mrs. 'Richard F. Schiller' died in childbed, giving birth to a stillborn girl, on Christmas Day 1952" (4). My understanding of Nabokov's novel throughout, and of the possible limits of Humbert's moral recognition, is especially influenced by Michael Wood, *The Magician's Doubts: Nabokov and the Risks of Fiction* (Princeton, NJ: Princeton University Press, 1997), 103–42 and *passim*. Brian Boyd points out that Humbert's epiphany amounts to "a very selective insight" and a "rhetorical strategy" that obscures Humbert's "overriding quest for self-satisfaction" (Boyd, *Vladimir Nabokov: The American Years* [Princeton, NJ: Princeton University Press, 1991], 254). For an analogous discussion of the way Nabokov foregrounds the inadequacies of Humbert's aesthetic and moral formalism, see also Frederick Whiting, " 'The Strange Particularity of the Lover's Preference': Pedophilia,

Pornography, and the Anatomy of Monstrosity in *Lolita*," *American Literature* 70, 4 (December 1998), 832–62.

19. James M. Buchanan and Gordon Tullock, *The Calculus of Consent: Logical Foundations of Constitutional Democracy* (Ann Arbor: University of Michigan Press, 1962), 14, 120, 297. While Arendt's thinking differed sharply from the dominant strains of American political science in the fifties, in certain respects there were points of commonality that Buchanan and Tullock themselves noted in a brief remark comparing their own vision of constitutional agreement to Arendt's view of civic action. See *Calculus of Consent*, 348n4.

20. Buchanan and Tullock, quoting British philosopher T. D. Weldon, who argued that Lockean premises led toward an absence of collective agreement, *Calculus of Consent*, 4; Riesman, "Individualism Reconsidered," 36.

21. The *New Republic* (March 8, 1943), qtd. at Richard Pells, *The Liberal Mind in a Conservative Age* (1985. Middletown, CT: Wesleyan University Press, 1989), 13; on the "cult of leadership" among liberal intellectuals during and after the war, see Pells, *Liberal Mind*, 8–26 and Schlesinger, *Imperial Presidency*, 100–26; on the war as occasioning an expansion in and ultimately a transformation of New Deal planning, see Jytte Klausen, "Did World War II End the New Deal? A Comparative Perspective on Postwar Planning Initiatives," *The New Deal and the Triumph of Liberalism*, ed. Milkis and Mileur, 193–231.

22. Milkis, *The President and the Parties*, 161.

23. Carter, qtd. at Leuchtenurg, *In the Shadow of FDR*, 56.

24. Trilling, *The Middle of the Journey* (1947. New York: New York Review of Books, 2002), 350; Wilson, *Patriotic Gore: Studies in the Literature of the American Civil War* (New York: Farrar, Strauss & Giroux, 1962), 125 and Wilson, "Abraham Lincoln: The Union as Religious Mysticism," *Eight Essays* (1954); Lowell, "Inauguration Day: January 1953," *Life Studies* (New York: Farrar, Strauss & Giroux, 1961), 7.

25. Updike, *The Poorhouse Fair* (1958. New York: Ballantine, 2004), xi, 77, 54, 55, 14, 19, 120, 118.

26. Neustadt, *Presidential Power*, 3rd ed., 120; Hughes, qtd. at Leuchtenburg, *Shadow of FDR*, 52.

27. Eisenhower, qtd. at Robert Griffith, "Dwight D. Eisenhower and the Corporate Commonwealth," AHR 87 (1982), 90.

28. Eisenhower, qtd. at Stanley Karnower, *Vietnam*, 214.

29. Edward S. Corwin, *President: Office and Powers*, 4th ed. (New York: New York University Press, 1957), 271; Corwin specifically singled out TR, Woodrow Wilson, and especially FDR as the most significant actors in the aggrandizement of the presidency. In the era's other most prominent account of the presidency, Clinton Rossiter answered Corwin's view, tellingly by contending that executive power never had the capacity that the advocates of presidential government had envisioned and was restrained less by constitutional structures than by the pluralistic social and institutional relations emphasized in the era's political science. "The power of the Presidency moves as a mighty host only *with* the grain of liberty and morality" (Rossiter, *The American Presidency* [New York: Harcourt Brace, 1956], 52).

30. Robert A. Dahl, *A Preface to Democratic Theory: How Does Popular Sovereignty Function in America* (Chicago: University of Chicago Press, 1963), 150.

31. Earl Latham, "The Group Basis of Politics," *American Political Science Review* 46 (1952): 382; Robert A. Dahl and Charles E. Lindblom, *Politics, Economics, and Welfare* (New York: Harper & Row, 1953), 333 ff.

32. C. E. Lindblom, *The Intelligence of Democracy* (New York: Free Press, 1965), 3.

33. Riesman, "Individualism Reconsidered," 36.

34. Latham, "Group Basis of Politics," 379, 396, 397, *emphasis in original*. Such views were especially prominent in political science, but Thomas Cochran's seminal appeal for a new social history to displace the "presidential synthesis" made an analogous argument. Like his contemporaries in political science and sociology Cochran asked for less attention to the "important unique acts" of history and more to "basic social conditioning" or to "shifting ideas, folkways, and mores." He likewise emphasized that abandoning the presidential synthesis would involve moving away from the nationalist emphasis of earlier historical writing—with greater attention in the United States to the roles of states, regions, and nonnational social institutions and to patterns of cross-national development. From this perspective, he noted, "the Civil War shrinks in magnitude" (Thomas C. Cochran, "The 'Presidential Synthesis' in American History," *American Historical Review* 53, 4 [1948], 748–59, 753, 756, 759).

35. Norberto Bobbio, "Contracts and Contractarianism," *The Future of Democracy: A Defence of the Rules of the Game*, trans. Roger Griffin, ed. Richard Bellamy (Minneapolis: University of Minnesota Press, 1987), 135.

36. Eisenhower, qtd. at Griffith, "Corporate Commonwealth," 92 and *passim*.

37. Dulles qtd. at Stephen J. Whitfield, *The Culture of the Cold War*, 2nd ed. (Baltimore: Johns Hopkins University Press, 1996), 7; X [George Kennan], "The Sources of Soviet Conduct," *Foreign Affair* 26, 2 (1947), 582; see also John K. Jessup et al., *The National Purpose* (New York: Holt, Rinehart, 1960).

38. Republican National Committee 1955, qtd. at Will Herberg, *Protestant—Catholic—Jew*, 281.

39. Dahl, *Preface to Democratic Theory*, 150.

40. Latham, "Group Basis of Politics," 390, 382; E. Pendelton Herring, *The Politics of Democracy* (New York: Norton, 1940), 424.

41. Dahl, *Preface to Democractic Theory*, 132–33.

42. Nabokov, *Strong Opinions*, 63.

43. See, e.g., Hannah Arendt, *On Revolution* (1963. New York: Penguin, 1990); Daniel Boorstin, *The Genius of American Politics* (Chicago: University of Chicago Press, 1953); Catherine Drinker Bowen, *Miracle at Philadelphia: The Story of the Constitutional Convention, May–September 1787* (Boston: Little, Brown, 1966); Clinton Rossiter, *Seedtime of the Republic: The Origins of the American Tradition of Political Liberty* (New York: Harcourt, Brace, 1953).

44. Fittingly April's weak husband, Frank Wheeler, finds his own solution to the problem stressed by Bellow, Salinger, Highsmith, and Nabokov in his memory of the war: "I just felt this terrific sense of life. I felt full of blood. Everything looked realer than real; the snow on the fields, the road, the trees, the terrific blue sky . . . and the way the guys were walking; I sort of loved them, even the guys I didn't like" (Yates, *Revolutionary Road*, 130).

45. Rivers, qtd. at Marjorie Perloff, *Frank O'Hara: Poet among Painters* (Chicago: University of Chicago Press, 1977), 84.

46. O'Hara, "On Seeing Larry Rivers's *Washington Crossing the Delaware* at the Museum of Modern Art," *Selected Poems*, ed. Donald Allen (New York: Vintage, 1974), 101.

47. National Book Award citation, qtd. at Lawrence Jackson, *Ralph Ellison: The Emergence of Genius* (New York: John Wiley & Sons, 2002), 442; "fluid, pluralistic turbulence" and "random assemblies," Ellison, "The Little Man at the Chehaw Station," *Collected Essays*, 500; "near allegory" Ellison, qtd. at Jackson, *Emergence of Genius*, 370.

48. Ellison's "Working Notes for *Invisible Man*," composed shortly after he began working on the novel in 1945, can be found in *Ralph Ellison's* Invisible Man: A Casebook, ed. John F. Callahan (New York: Oxford, 2004), 24–30. On Ellison's attraction to modernist techniques of novelistic construction, see, e.g., Robert N. List, *Dedalus in Harlem: The Joyce-Ellison Connection* (New York: Rowan and Littlefield, 1982). Barbara Foley, "From Communism to Brotherhood: The Drafts of *Invisible Man*," *Left of the Color Line: Race, Radicalism, and Twentieth-Century Literature of the United States*, ed. Bill V. Mullen and James Smethurst (Chapel Hill: University of North Carolina Press, 2003), 163–82, also shows how in the process of composition and revision, Ellison gave increasing weight, along with his developing anti-communism, to the structure of motifs and symbolic parallels that gives a strong organizational plan to *Invisible Man*'s narrative.

49. Ellison, *Invisible Man* (1952. New York: Vintage, 1995), 7.

50. For an especially illuminating account of Ellison's unresolved attitudes toward this problem, see Kenneth Warren, *So Black and Blue: Ralph Ellison and the Occasion of Criticism* (Chicago: University of Chicago Press, 2003); on the limits to Ellison's defense of pluralism, see also Nathan A. Scott, Jr., "Ellison's Vision of *Communitas*," *Ralph Ellison's* Invisible Man: A Casebook, 109–24; Ellison remarked often that his frustration with African American leadership was the inspiration and main theme of his novel. See, e.g., *Collected Essays*, 524–25. His "Working Notes" also show the theme to have been a main concern since early in conception of the novel.

51. For Ellison's appreciation of Locke, see *Collected Essays*, 441–47; see also Ross Posnock, *Color and Culture: Black Writers and the Making of the Modern Intellectual* (Cambridge, MA: Harvard University Press, 2000), 184–219.

52. Schaub offers a particularly illuminating account of the novel's ranter-to-writer structure, *American Fiction*, 91–115; Ellison's notes show it to have been a central part of his design from the beginning. Interestingly, however, it was not until he combined that narrative with the climactic riot-to-epilogue transition that Ellison found a satisfying conclusion to the novel. In his initial plans, the riot was not to be the climax of the novel and the narrator was to discover no great wisdom in its wake, settling in rather to a condition of disenchantment and anomie. Relatedly, in the original outline for the book, during the riot *Invisible Man* was to be pursued not by white racists, but by his own disappointed followers—a bitter culmination, in short, of the novel's depiction of the failure of black leadership. It was not, then, until he found a means of aligning his narrator's growth with the revolutionary foundations of the American republic—and that he envisioned their redemption as the only means to counter the prospect of race war—that Ellison found both a reason for optimism and a form to resolve his novel. See "Working Notes for Invisible Man," *A Casebook*, 24–30.

53. See e.g., Ellison, "Tell it Like it Is, Baby" and "Introduction to the Thirtieth Anniversary Edition of *Invisible Man*, *Collected Essays*, 29–46, 471–85; on the significance of war to

Invisible Man, see John S. Wright, "The Conscious Hero and the Rites of Man: Ellison's War," *Casebook*, 221–52.

54. For a brilliant treatment of the role of sacrifice in *Invisible Man*, see Allen, "Ralph Ellison and the Tragi-Comedy of Citizenship," *Ralph Ellison and the Raft of Hope*, 37–57.

55. "I had known . . . [the Gettysburg Address] most of my life, had been moved by it even before its implications had become meaningful; . . . had pondered its themes of sectional reconciliation and national rebirth many times long since, as the awareness grew that there was little about it that was simple and that it was profoundly implicated both in my life and in the failure of my promised freedom" (Ellison, "Tell it Like It Is, Baby," *Collected Essays*, 44).

56. See, e.g., in addition to Allen, "Tragi-comedy of Citizenship," noted above, the important essay by Gregg Crane, "Ralph Ellison's Constitutional Faith," *Cambridge Companion to Ralph Ellison*, 104–20; Martha C. Nussbaum, "Invisibility and Recognition: Sophocles' Philoctetes and Ellison's Invisible Man," *Philosophy and Literature* 23, 2 (1999): 257–83.

57. Ellison's intense American nationalism has curiously gone mainly unremarked. Many critics who are sensitive to the exclusivity of ethnic nationalism nevertheless follow Ellison in eliding universality and Americanism. See, e.g., Danielle Allen's striking insertion: "how, then, did Ellison think it was possible for an author to get from descriptions of an individual life and its psychic struggles to the 'total American [read: democratic] experience?" ("Tragi-comedy of Citizenship," 39). See also, the elision in Gregg Crane's otherwise acute observation about Ellison's constitutional theory: "As 'covenant,' the nation's charter is a kind of contract—a diverse assembly's binding exchange of promises and reciprocal obligations, but it is also something more than any mere quid pro quo. It represents, however imperfectly, a sacred agreement about the ethical basis of American law and society, deriving its ultimate authority from a plausibly universal moral consensus about the terms of justice and citizenship. This consensus becomes *plausibly* universal when it becomes hard to imagine any sentient being not agreeing to such basic values of coexistence" ("Ellison's Constitutional Faith," 112–13, original emphasis). As will be stressed more fully below, however, Ellison pointedly does not draw either authority or plausibility from a universal moral consensus, stressing rather the nationally distinctive obligations created by U.S. history and ancestry.

58. For the definitive account of *Invisible Man*'s use of "black American folk art," see Robert G. O'Meally, *The Craft of Ralph Ellison* (Cambridge, MA: Harvard University Press, 1980), 74–108; for the view of Ellison as proto–black–nationalist, see Larry Neal, "Ellison's Zoot Suit," *Ralph Ellison's* Invisible Man: *A Casebook*, ed. Callahan, 81–108; while there is much to recommend Neal's view, Jerry Gafio Watts seems to me to best define the consistent view in Ellison's various, complex statements about the relation between black vernacular culture and U.S. democracy: "Ellison has often been misinterpreted by black nationalists as a kindred spirit. . . . [B]ut Ellison is not a black nationalist. He is a Negro nationalist and insofar as he believes that Negro culture is an American phenomenon and occupies a centrality within American culture, Ellison is an American nationalist" (Watts, *Heroism and the Black Intellectual: Ralph Ellison, Politics, and Afro-American Intellectual Life* [Chapel Hill: University of North Carolina Press, 1994], 107).

59. Ellison, "Working Notes for *Invisible Man*," 29.

60. As Barbara Foley points out, the language Jack speaks—an "unknown tongue, the language of the future" (476)—is presumably Russian, as Jack appears to be modeled on

the Russian-born American Communist Party operative Golos depicted in Elizabeth Bentley's 1947 anti-Communist confession *Out of Bondage* (Foley, "The Rhetoric of Anticommunism in *Invisible Man*," *College English* 59, 5 [1997], 542, 530–47). Foley's important essay rightly emphasizes the significance of the "demonization of the left" to *Invisible Man* but does not note the fact that, while he gives it far more credibility, Ellison is almost equally hostile to Garveyite nationalism.

61. In fact, it is Ellison's investment in American nationalism—viewed as an alternative to white racism, black nationalism, and revolutionary socialism—that best explains Ellison's generally unfavorable depictions of sexuality. That unfavorable attitude first crops up in the depiction of the stripper in the Battle Royal scene, extends through the representation of incest in the Trueblood episode and the depictions of prostitution at the Golden Day and culminates in the narrator's distasteful affair with Sybil and his exclamation that "between us and everything we wanted to change in the world they placed a woman . . . debasing both us and them" and "all human motives" (418). The narrator's contrast here—between sexuality and "human motives"—might be better conceived as a version of the classic contrast between heterosexuality and political citizenship, one that again highlights Ellison's resemblance to Arendt. Understood in this light, what Ellison's narrator objects to is the way appetite and desire allegedly interfere with volitional association. Hence, the humiliation the narrator mentions in one boy's undesired erection during the Battle Royal scene and the connection Ellison draws there to a vulgarly bejeweled "merchant who followed her hungrily, his lips loose and drooling" (20). The link made there is between sexual appetite and the desire of the market, each viewed as a debasing alternative to political membership or as a degraded form of merely biological integration (i.e., precisely what Updike envisioned in his future dystopia). The mirror image of such interracial sexual assimilation, Ellison suggests, is the incestuous appetite that is created by segregation, a point dramatized in the meeting of Trueblood and Norton. Though in different ways, both men represent the effect of racism's denial of citizenship and the elevation above it of the familial, private, and sexual. Like many another nationalist, Ellison suggested that in contrast to the impermanence of biological reproduction, a civic immortality could be found in the life of the nation. Thus the narrator's symbolic castration leads to his ultimate recognition of "principle" in the epilogue. Similarly in the riot scene, when Dupre and his fellows prepare to burn down the Harlem tenement, they do so in opposition to a pregnant woman who pleads, "You know my time's almost here" (546). The revolutionary action they represent ("they organized it and carried through alone . . . their own action") is thus specifically opposed to sexual reproduction (548). Interestingly Yates makes a similar implication in *Revolutionary Road*. There, the cowardice of the protagonist is evident in his willingness to accept, without joy, the pregnancy of his wife. Her heroism by contrast is apparent in the self-induced abortion that kills her. For an illuminating, argument similar in some ways to the one made here, but quite different in others, see Nicole A. Waligora-Davis, "Riotous Discontent: Ralph Ellison's 'Birth of a Nation.' " *Modern Fiction Studies* 50, 2 (2004), 385–410.

62. On the importance of paternalism to Ellison's imagination, see Warren, *So Black and Blue*, 25–41 and *passim*.

63. Schattschneider, *The Semi-sovereign People: A Realist's View of Democracy in America* (New York: Holt, Rinehart & Winston, 1960).

NOTES TO CHAPTER THREE

Chapter Four: Come Home, America

1. Ward Just, *A Soldier of the Revolution* (New York: Knopf, 1970), 37; David Harris, *Our War: What We Did in Vietnam and What it Did to Us* (New York: Times Books, 1996), 18.

2. "Housing projects," Mailer, *The Presidential Papers* (1963. New York: Dell, 1982), 35; "center of America," Mailer, *The Armies of the Night: History as a Novel, The Novel as History* (1968. New York: Plume, 1994), 188.

3. Ginsberg, *Writers Take Sides on Vietnam*, ed. Cecil Woolf and John Bagguley (New York: Simon & Schuster, 1967), 36.

4. For the seminal argument that the difference between epistemological and ontological concerns defines the distinction between modernist and postmodernist fiction, see Brian McHale, *Postmodernist Fiction* (New York: Methuen, 1987), 3–25 and *passim*.

5. Mailer, *Advertisements for Myself* (New York: G. P. Putnam's Sons, 1959), 17.

6. Mailer, *Presidential Papers*, 35, 9.

7. John F. Kennedy, *Let the Word Go Forth: The Speeches, Statements, and Writings of John F. Kennedy*, ed. Theodore C. Sorensen (New York: Delacorte Press, 1988), 17–20; see also the description offered by his speechwriter—that JFK aimed to reassert "the primacy of the White House within the Executive Branch and of the Executive Branch within the Federal Government, the leadership of the Federal Government within the United States and of the United States within the community of nations" (Theodore Sorensen, *Kennedy* [New York: Harper & Row, 1965], 389). On Kennedy's emulation of FDR's administrative style, see Leuchtenburg, *In the Shadow of FDR*, 63–120; on Kennedy's executive-centered vision of politics more generally, see Bruce Miroff, *Pragmatic Illusions: The Presidential Politics of John F. Kennedy* (New York: David McKay, 1976) and Gary Wills, *The Kennedy Imprisonment* (Boston: Little Brown, 1982); for a similar, but less critical view, see W. J. Rorabaugh, *Kennedy and the Promise of the Sixties* (New York: Cambridge University Press, 2002).

8. Tad Szulc, qtd. at Miroff, *Pragmatic Illusions*, 120.

9. Arthur M. Schlesinger, Jr., *The Politics of Hope* (Boston: Houghton Mifflin, 1962), 8; see also Richard E. Neustadt, *Presidential Power: The Politics of Leadership* (New York: Wiley, 1960), which in its emphasis on concentrating personal power in executive hands, remarks that "what is good for the country is good for the President and *vice versa*" (189); and for perhaps the most influential statement of such views, see James MacGregor Burns, *The Deadlock of Democracy: Four-Party Politics in America* (Englewood Cliffs, NJ: Prentice Hall, 1963).

10. Mailer, *Presidential Papers*, 50, 46.

11. Ibid., 9.

12. Mailer, *An American Dream* (1965. New York: Henry Holt, 1987), 9.

13. In this respect, of course, Mailer and his contemporaries were drawing on a tradition in political thought by which marriage, especially in the marginal status accorded women, symbolized both the epitome of and the outer boundary of liberal citizenship. See, especially, Carol Pateman, *The Sexual Contract* (Stanford, CA: Stanford University Press, 1988). In the film and literature of the Vietnam War, marriage is used consistently to figure the relations between U.S. soldiers and citizenry and in this way to represent the problems of national

membership and obligation. For an illuminating discussion, see Rachel Adams, "Going to Canada: The Politics and Poetics of Northern Exodus," *Yale Journal of Criticism* 18, 2 (2005) 409–33.

14. Updike, "Bech Meets Me" (1971), *Picked-Up Pieces* (New York: Knopf, 1975), 10–13.

15. Updike, quoting the September 1967 letter to the *New York Times* in which he announced his recent decision to abandon his support of the Johnson administration and advocate "peace at any price," *Self-Consciousness: Memoirs* (New York: Knopf, 1989), 113–14.

16. Seymour Melman, *Teach-Ins: U. S. A., Reports, Opinions, Documents*, ed. Louis Menashe and Ronald Radosh (New York: Frederick A. Praeger, 1967), 30.

17. Interestingly this perspective led both Coover and Vidal to preserve, even as they derided, the mythology of presidential leadership. In *The Public Burning* (1977. New York: Grove Press, 1998), for example, Coover brilliantly parodies the notion that the president acts as the "incarnation" of the American people (8). Effectively following Richard Wright's advice to the novelist, Coover tracks Richard Nixon's aspirations for the presidency, a process whose pivotal steps come, first, when Nixon arranges for the public execution of the Rosenbergs and, second, when, immediately following the executive, he is forcibly sodomized by Uncle Sam (8). The novel thus inverts the presidential symbolism that descends from the Gettysburg Address. (The execution scene, which Coover depicts as a ritual answer to the desperation of the American public, is said to result in "a new birth of freedom" [493].) In Nixon's progress, as in the rhetoric of presidential power and martyrdom, we witness first the coercive exercise of state power (the execution) and then an answer to that coercion in the suffering of the president beneath the will of the sovereign people (the rape of Nixon by Uncle Sam) (493). Coover thus fashions a story that inverts the presidential drama, but that still uses it to define a vision of now malevolent national sovereignty. Vidal has John Hay muse that Lincoln "had willed his own murder as a form of atonement for the great and terrible thing that he had done by giving so bloody and absolute a rebirth to his nation" (Vidal, *Lincoln* [1984. New York: Modern Library, 1993], 712). And see also the revised portrait Robert Lowell offered in his poem "Abraham Lincoln," in one version of which Lincoln is likened to Bismarck and cast as a tyrannical figure who treats war as "the continuation of politics" and thus "politics" as "the continuation of murder." Much like Vidal, Lowell here casts Lincoln as the founder of a grotesque imperial nationalism. He created "the new God/ who breathes-in fire and dies with cooling faith" (Lowell, "Abraham Lincoln," *Notebook*, 3rd ed. [New York: Farrar, Strauss & Giroux, 1970], 171). Only a short time earlier, however, Lowell had celebrated Lincoln for a comparable achievement. In his remarks on the Gettysburg Address delivered at the Library of Congress in 1964, Lowell praised Lincoln for authoring "our one great prose poem." The Gettysburg Address joined "Jefferson's ideals of freedom and equality . . . to the Christian sacrificial act of death and rebirth" and in so doing creating a "symbolic significance" that "goes beyond sect or religion and beyond peace and war and is now part of our lives." The difference between Lowell's two views of Lincoln reflects the way his attitudes, like those of many liberals, changed between 1964 and those of 1970. But equally importantly perhaps, each offers a variation on the central symbolic drama of the presidency—the contrast between the president as arm of coercive force and the president

as martyr and, here, poet. As a commander, Lincoln appears in Lowell's poem as "our one genius in politics" and as the inventor of a malevolent sacrificial ritual that swallows him as it did the nation's soldiers. He "followed the bull to the altar." As the elegist of the Gettysburg Address, by contrast, Lincoln is the author of a virtuous collective poetry that depends not on his exercise but on his symbolic surrender of power. "In his words, Lincoln symbolically died," but for that reason remains "part of our lives" (Lowell, *Collected Prose*, 193).

18. Stone, *A Flag for Sunrise* (1981. New York: Vintage, 1992), 110; in a subsequent interview, Stone endorsed this notion and notably traced the condition he diagnosed to the fact that the United States had created "more a commercial than a military or cultural empire, so it was our appetites that we exported, along with the relevant parts of our popular culture. . . . The point is that so much that is best in America is a state of mind that you can't export" (Stone, "The Art of Fiction XC," *The Paris Review* 98 [Winter 1985]: 56).

19. David Halberstam, *The Best and the Brightest* (1972. New York: Modern Library, 2001), 67; Goodman, *Like a Conquered Province*, 141.

20. Johnson, "Peace without Conquest," address at Johns Hopkins University (April 7, 1965), qtd. at Loren Baritz, *Backfire: A History of How American Culture Led Us into Vietnam and Made Us Fight the Way We Did* (New York: William Morrow, 1985), 38.

21. Kennan in *The Vietnam Hearings*, ed. J. William Fullbright. (New York: Random House, 1966), 115.

22. Charles S. Maier, *Among Empires: American Ascendancy and Its Predecessors* (Cambridge, MA: Harvard University Press, 2006), 110–11.

23. Frances FitzGerald. *Fire in the Lake: The Vietnamese and the Americans in Vietnam* (Boston: Little Brown, 1972), 7; Fulbright, qtd. at Frank Ninkovich, "Anti-Imperialism in U.S. Foreign Relations," *Vietnam and the American Political Tradition: The Politics of Dissent*, ed. Randall B. Woods (New York: Cambridge University Press, 2003), 38.

24. "We Are Choking with Shame and Anger," *Teach-Ins*, ed. Menashe and Radosh, 345, 346; Sontag, *Styles of Radical Will* (New York: Farrar, Strauss & Giroux, 1969), 267.

25. Baritz, *Backfire*, 322, 325–26.

26. For recent uses of the phrase by historians and literary critics, see Keith Beattie, *The Scar the Binds: American Culture and the Vietnam War* (New York: New York University Press, 1998), 106–50; Robert D. Schulzinger, *A Time for War: The United States and Vietnam, 1941–1975* (New York: Oxford University Press, 1997), 215–45.

27. Bill Ayers, address to Weatherman conference, Cleveland, August 1969, originally published in *New Left Notes* (Sept. 1969), repr. as Appendix 1 to *Diana: The Making of a Terrorist* by Thomas Powers (Boston: Houghton Mifflin, 1971), 198–99.

28. Stanley Cavell, *Themes Out of School: Effects and Causes* (San Francisco: North Point Press, 1984), 104; on the prominent role played by the idea of "dissociation" in the antiwar movement, see Howard Brick, *Age of Contradiction: American Thought and Culture in the 1960s* (New York: Twayne, 1998), 156–57.

29. Slater, *The Pursuit of Loneliness* (Boston: Beacon Press, 1970), 15.

30. George McGovern, quoted at Thomas Knock, "'Come Home America': The Story of George McGovern," *Vietnam and the American Political Tradition*, 118.

31. Robert Putnam, *Bowling Along: The Collapse and Revival of American Community* (New York: Simon & Schuster, 2000), 18. On the consensus in support of the war that existed

among most Americans into the late sixties, even among groups that would become prominent opponents of the war, see Rhodri Jeffreys-Jones, *Peace Now! American Society and
the Ending of the Vietnam War* (New Haven, CT: Yale University Press, 2001), 13–41.

32. Slater, *Pursuit of Loneliness*, 45.

33. Slater, *The Pursuit of Loneliness*, revised ed. (Boston: Beacon, 1976), 2; Hacker,
The End of the American Era (New York: Atheneum, 1970), 7; Goodman, *Like a Conquered
Province*, 12.

34. Kennan, *Memoirs, 1950–1963* (Boston: Houghton Mifflin, 1972), 320, 322, emphasis
in original.

35. Hans J. Morgenthau, *Truth and Power: Essays of a Decade, 1960–1970* (New York:
Praeger, 1970), 34, 29.

36. Hacker, *End of the American Era*, 33, 6, 216; Michael Walzer, *Obligations: Essays on
Disobedience, War, and Citizenship* (Cambridge, MA: Harvard University Press, 1970), 237,
204, 237, 217, 210; Baritz, *Backfire*, 338.

37. Baritz, *Backfire*, 37, 42.

38. Walzer, *Obligations*, 9–10, 5.

39. Ibid., 220; it might be said of all these thinkers what Judith N. Shklar notes in her
consideration of Walzer—that his investment in the virtues of membership betrays "a confusion of loyalty and obligation" and that it combines "an extremely individualistic theory of
consent" with a "communitarian view of obligation" (Shklar, "The Work of Michael Walzer,"
Political Thought and Political Thinkers, ed. Stanley Hoffman [Chicago: University of Chicago
Press, 1998], 380, 381).

40. Schlesinger, *The Imperial Presidency*, 418.

41. Ibid., 497, 417.

42. Hans J. Morgenthau, *Truth and Power: Essays of a Decade, 1960–1970* (New York:
Praeger, 1970), 34, 35.

43. McGovern, Speech to Senate, September 1, 1970, qtd. at Thomas J. Knock, "Come
Home, America," 116.

44. McGovern, qtd. at Thomas Knock, "Come Home American," 118.

45. Caputo, postscript (1996), *A Rumor of War* (1977. New York: Henry Holt, 1996), 353.

46. Herr, *Dispatches* (New York: Knopf, 1977), 251, 226.

47. Paul Tillich quoted as epigraph to John Updike, *Couples* (1968. New York: Fawcett
Columbine, 1996).

48. Updike, *Rabbit Redux* (New York: Knopf, 1971), 50, 84.

49. Updike himself pointed to the similarity in the year *Rabbit Redux* was published, noting
that both his novel and Mailer's autobiographical work reflected "a willingness to accept your
personal experience as an adequate metaphor for national experience." *Conversations with
John Updike*, ed. James Plath (Jackson: University of Mississippi Press, 1994), 64.

50. Updike, *Conversations*, 61.

51. Wilfred Sheed noted the parallels Updike established between Piet and JFK in his
original review of the novel: "two men who offer Life and surprise to these dead cells of
American life, these play-churches, and are rejected. Two scapegoats" (Sheed, "Couples,"
New York Times, April 7, 1968). The connection, which is emphasized in the prominence
given to Kennedy's assassination and its similarity to Piet's fall, is also explored in an allegorical set piece in which Piet and Kennedy are each likened to a hamster let out of its cage by

Piet's daughter—so that it can explore "undreamed of continents" and thus become the prey of a predatory house cat ("claws sprang from a sudden heaven") (77). Juxtaposed to an appropriate newspaper headline ("Kennedy praises steel restraint") the set piece implicitly compares Piet's erotic adventures to America's imperial excursions and, laying the blame for each on the solicitations of a feminized public, warns that these wanderings promise to provoke divine retribution (77). Piet will later sense that retribution when the Tarbox Congregational church is struck by lighting.

52. Updike, *Conversations*, 61.

53. The significance of this discovery is deliberately understated, but Stone himself claimed both that the reference to "just us" was meant to include more than "just the two of them" and that it was significant to the resolution of his novel. "Marge and Converse, even in their extreme condition, have an insight. They do come out at the other end of all that [the events of Stone's narrative, but also implicitly the war it allegorizes] having—at least it's imminent—a kind of realization. . . . It's deliberately made inarticulate and kind of nonsensical, but that's what the positive dimension is" (Maureen Karaguezian, "Interview with Robert Stone," *TriQuarterly* 53 [Winter 1982]: 250). As in the work of his contemporaries, Stone's novel hinges on a conflict between two versions of executive power: the coercive violence exerted by the corrupt representatives of an imperial bureaucracy (here, the "regulatory agent" Antheil and his accomplices, who are engaged in the international drug trade) and the alternative represented by the redeemed Hicks. The latter's significance to this antiimperial romance is underscored by the fact that elsewhere Stone describes him as a representative of "true virtue, the old Roman *virtus*" (Stone interview in *Vietnam, We've All Been There: Interviews with American Writers*, ed. Eric James Schroeder [Westport, CT: Praeger, 1992], 115).

54. Stone, "We Are Not Excused," *Paths of Resistance: The Art and Craft of the Political Novel*, ed. William Zinsser (Boston: Houghton Mifflin, 1989), 32–33.

55. Herr interview in *Vietnam, We've all Been There*, 36.

56. Ibid., 37, 48.

57. Harris, *Our War*, 11; in fact, Harris claimed that his book was inspired by outrage over the way Bill Clinton (who "slithered, dithered, mumbled, jumbled, slid, hid, deferred, conferred, allowed, disallowed, invented, and reinvented") failed to live up to the role (21). Harris also shares with Updike, Herr, and others the expressive theory that fits well with his view of collective identity. Because the war is to be understood as "behavior," "intention is meaningless" and it is a moral outrage to speak of it in terms of "mistake" rather than a form of collective embodiment (9). "I have never know the war at arm's length. I remember it on my skin and in my bones" (4).

58. DeLillo, *Libra* (1988. New York: Penguin, 1989), 181.

59. See John J. McClure, *Late Imperial Romance* (London: Verso, 1994), 118–51 and *passim* and McClure, "Postmodern/Post-Secular: Contemporary Fiction and Spirituality." *Modern Fiction Studies* 41 (1995): 141–63 and, for a related argument, Sean McCann and Michael Szalay, "Do you Believe in Magic? Literary Thinking after the New Left," *Yale Journal of Criticism* 18, 2 (2005): 435–68.

60. For especially illuminating discussion, see in addition to McClure above, Jeremy Green, "Disaster Footage: Spectacles of Violence in DeLillo's Fiction," *Modern Fiction Studies* 45, 3 (1999): 571–99; Frank Lentricchia, "*Libra* as Postmodern Critique," *South Atlantic*

Quarterly 89, 2 (1990): 431–53; Skip Willman, "Art after Dealey Plaza: DeLillo's Libra," *Modern Fiction Studies* 45, 3 (1999) 621–40; and all the essays collected in Lentricchia, ed., *Introducing Don DeLillo* (Durham, NC: Duke University Press, 1991).

61. " 'An Outsider in this Society': An Interview with Don DeLillo," by Anthony DeCurtis, *South Atlantic Quarterly* 89 (1990): 289.

62. Address of Senator John F. Kennedy Accepting the Democratic Nomination for the Presidency of the United States (July 15, 1960), *Let the Word Go Forth*, 101, 102.

63. DeLillo, "The Power of History," *New York Times Magazine* (September 7, 1997), 60–63.

Epilogue

1. Anonymous (Joe Klein), *Primary Colors: A Novel of Politics* (New York: Random House, 1996), 24; Leonard Garment, qtd. at H. W. Brands, *The Strange Death of American Liberalism* (New Haven, CT: Yale University Press, 2001), 113; George W. Bush, "President Reiterates Goals on Home Ownership" (June 18, 2002), Office of the Press Secretary, The White House. Available at: http://www.whitehouse.gov/news/releases/2002/06/20020618–1.html.

2. See, e.g., William K. Muir, Jr., "The Primacy of Rhetoric," *Leadership in the Modern Presidency*, ed. Fred I. Greenstein (Cambridge, MA: Harvard University Press, 1988), 260–96.

3. See, e.g., Michael A. Genovese, *The Presidency in an Age of Limits* (New York: Greenwood Press, 1993).

4. In the program's pilot, for example, Jed Bartlett breaks up a squabble between his advisers and a group of religious conservatives, by loudly quoting the first commandment: "I am the Lord your God. Thou shalt worship no other God before me" (Pilot, *The West Wing*, written by Aaron Sorkin, directed by Thomas Schlamme, original air date, September 22, 1999).

5. "A Proportional Response," *The West Wing*, NBC Television, written by Aaron Sorkin, directed by Marc Buckland, original air date, October 6, 1999.

6. This transition is underscored in several ways—in the fact that Charlie, whose initial status of political immaturity is indicated by his last name (Young), will implicitly grow to manhood in his new responsibility; that before he has takes on this new work, he had been orphaned by inner-city violence and, left responsible for the care of a younger sister, is implicitly friendless until he enters the White House; and that his new position will give him the opportunity to rebuke political officials who once treated him with racist condescension. In all respects, *The West Wing* uses the presidency to symbolize the hope that the injustice and instability of liberal society might be overcome by the grandeur of national identity. Another character underscores the point by responding to Charlie's statement with the comment, "It doesn't go away"—thus implying that the charisma of the presidency supplants both the impermanence of private life and the incoherence of daily politics.

7. "What Kind of Day Has it Been," *The West Wing*, written by Aaron Sorkin, directed by Thomas Schlamme, original air date, May 19, 2000.

8. Terry Eastland, *Energy in the Executive: The Case for the Strong Presidency* (New York: Free Press, 1992), 505, emphasis in original. These developments have been widely dis-

cussed, of course. For a good contextualization of the recent Bush administration's aggrandizement of presidential power in the larger context of the history of presidential government, see Andrew Rudalevige, *The New Imperial Presidency: Renewing Presidential Power After Watergate* (Ann Arbor: University of Michigan Press, 2005), and for a more detailed account of the strategy and tactics used by the Bush administration in renewing executive power, see Charlie Savage, *Takeover: The Return of the Imperial Presidency and the Subversion of Democracy* (New York: Little, Brown, 2007).

9. Stephen Skowronek, *The Politics Presidents Make: Leadership form John Adams to George Bush* (Cambridge, MA: Harvard University Press, 1993), 444, 43, 445.

10. See the illuminating survey of journalistic commentary summarized in the most recent edition of Schlesinger, *Imperial Presidency*, ix.

11. Skowronek, *The Politics Presidents Make*, 20, 414, 27, emphasis in original.

12. Ibid., 37.

13. Ibid., 442, 30, 442.

14. David Herbert Donald, *Lincoln* (New York: Simon & Schuster, 1995).

15. Morrison, Nobel lecture (December 7, 1993). Available at http://nobelprize.org/nobel_prizes/literature/laureates/1993/morrison-lecture.html.

16. Richard Slotkin, *Abe: A Novel of the Young Lincoln* (New York: Henry Holt, 2000), 474. In imagining an extraordinarily gifted and ambitious young man with a heroic destiny, Slotkin's novel offers a remarkable restatement of the mythology of presidential leadership. His young Lincoln is particularly concerned to understand the relations among law, force, and eloquence. (From his earliest years, he is concerned with great leaders like King David and whether their authority comes from their "singing" or from the "gift of the man of war" [73].) That problem is made apparent to him, in one respect, by the cruelty and arbitrariness of patriarchal rule ("the Kingdom of Pap"), symbolized by Lincoln's father and his Indian killer Uncle Mordecai (109). It is more importantly dramatized by the defining issue of slavery. Slotkin's narrative hinges on a fictionalized account of the young Lincoln's journey by flatboat down the Mississippi—a journey that forces Abe to confront the darkest underside of American democracy and that gives him the spiritual warrant to become the leader who will reform the national compact. ("I been to the bottom of the River and come back to tell the tale" [474].) As in the classic tales of presidential leadership, that warrant hinges not solely on ambition or determination but on the legitimation the leader receives by virtue of his indebtedness to a martyr whose death establishes ethical demands and sanctifies the recognition of mutuality and shared membership in a national community. In this case, that martyr is the fictional slave Sephus, who when he has a chance to escape surrenders his life rather than kill the young Abe and who thus effectively charges Lincoln with heroic responsibility. "It was on him how Sephus died . . . . It was the dead weight of the man Sephus that give his argument leaden heft in his mind. It was almost more than he could carry—almost" (460). In this manner, Slotkin suggests that Lincoln's eloquence (his singing) will achieve a legitimate authority that surpasses the mere arbitrary assertion of force because it will be used in the service of a mission to reestablish a more just and inclusive republic. But, at the same time that he recreates that mythic vision of presidential leadership, Slotkin ends on reminders that undercut its grandeur—that Lincoln will be first a Whig politician concerned with the state support of commercial development and, more importantly, that his rise will depend on the

continuation of the wars of national conquest. "This was how all of them started," Abe thinks as he sets out for the Black Hawk war, "Columbus and Boone and Washington, Mordecai and Moses, they all went out after Injuns" (472). The inclusion of Mordecai in this list is particularly striking. The young Lincoln has been especially concerned to understand the difference between "the impossible of Washington and Moses" and "the low-down skunk-eating meanness of . . . Uncle Mordecai. And Pap" (455). His final remarks are thus a reminder that presidential power cannot be ultimately fully separated from patriarchal rule and violent conquest. In effect, Slotkin's novel gives us both a heroic portrait of presidential leadership and a reminder of the less appealing corollaries beneath its mythic grandeur.

17. Banks, *Cloudsplitter* (New York: HarperCollins, 1998), 738. For another striking example, see, Thomas Mallon's historical novel *Henry and Clara*, which imagines the lives of the actual persons Henry Rathbone and Clara Harris, the young couple who shared a box at Ford's Theatre with Lincoln on the night of his assassination. Building his narrative around the only other known facts about Rathbone and Harris (that they were step-siblings who later married and that in 1883 Rathbone stabbed Harris to death in Germany and was subsequently committed to an insane asylum), Mallon imagines their story as an effective repudiation of the mythology of the redeemer president whose death, in sanctifying the national compact that would emerge out of the Civil War, would thereby justify its slaughter. In Mallon's telling, Henry Rathbone not only witnessed Lincoln's assassination, but in doing nothing to stop Booth, effectively conspired in the murder out of his fury at the ideological zealousness and waste of the war. For Mallon's Henry Rathbone, in short, the Civil War looks much as the Vietnam War would to later young men. And for him, somewhat as for Slotkin's Abe, presidential power does not look fundamentally opposed to patriarchal power or aggressive force. Most importantly, for Henry Rathbone, there is no redemptive martyrdom that effectively resolves the problem of coercion and thus brings an end to killing. With Henry's murder of Clara, Mallon implies, a cycle of violence that reaches back to the Civil War merely continues. Mallon, *Henry and Clara* (New York: Picador, 1994), 339.

18. For an illuminating discussion of this aspect of Roth's novel, see Anthony Hutchinson, " 'Purity is Petrefaction': Liberalism and Betrayal in Philip Roth's *I Married a Communist*," *Rethinking History* 9, 2–3 (2005), 315–27.

19. Philip Roth, *I Married a Communist* (1998. New York: Vintage, 1999), 301.

20. Roth, *American Pastoral* (1997. New York: Vintage, 1998), 412.

21. Roth, *The Human Stain* (Boston: Houghton Mifflin, 2000), 108.

22. For an especially lucid account of the ways the late Roth's parochialism is evident not just in his paeans to Weequahic, but in his narrative devices and in his implicit theory of personhood, see Robert Chodat, "Fictions Public and Private: On Philip Roth," *Contemporary Literature* 46, 4 (2005): 688–719. See also, Ross Posnock's perceptive discussion of *The Human Stain*, which notes that Coleman Silk displays "the fatal simplicity of all romantic individualists, he imagines his will is sovereign" (Posnock, "Purity and Danger : On Philip Roth," *Raritan* 21, 2 [2001], 96). Though she appears to judge Coleman Silk less harshly, Amy Hungerford makes a similar point when she notes that Roth's novel hinges on a contrast between the combination of artful concealment and deception practiced by the writer, on the one hand, and the pure self-invention of the radically individual protagonist on the other

(Hungerford, *The Holocaust of Texts: Genocide, Literature, and Personification* [Chicago: University of Chicago Press, 2003], 136–46).

23. Roth, *Reading Myself and Others* (New York: Farrar, Strauss & Giroux, 1975), 121, 193, emphasis in original.

24. Ibid., quoting Benjamin DeMott and Edmund Wilson respectively, 121.

25. Ibid., 12, 11, emphasis in original.

26. For a convincing argument that *The Human Stain* in particular rewrites *Invisible Man*, see Timothy L. Parrish, "Ralph Ellison: The Invisible Man in Philip Roth's *The Human Stain*," *Contemporary Literature* 45, 3 (2004) 421–59.

27. Roth, *Portnoy's Complaint* (1969. New York: Vintage, 1994), 8.

28. Roth, "The Story Behind *The Plot Against America*," *New York Times Book Review* (September 19, 2004).

29. Philip Roth, interviewed by Kurt Anderson, *Studio 360*, National Public Radio, November 6, 2004. Available at http://www.studio360.org/yore/show110604.html.

30. Roth, "The Story Behind *The Plot Against America*," 10.

31. See, e.g., Jacob S. Hacker, *The Great Risk Shift: The Assault on American Jobs, Families, Health Care, and Retirement—And How You Can Fight Back* (New York: Oxford University Press, 2006) and Hacker and Pierson, *Off Center: The Republican Revolution and the Erosion of American Democracy*.

32. Transcript of Presidential Press Conference, November 4, 2004, released by Office of the Press Secretary, The White House. Available at http://www.whitehouse.gov/news/releases/2004/11/20041104–5.html.

33. This is the account of presidential government most powerfully articulated by Sidney Milkis in *The President and the Parties*.

34. See, John B. Judis, *The Paradox of American Democracy: Elites, Special Interests, and the Betrayal of the Public Trust* (New York: Random House, 2000) and Thomas Byrnes Edsall, *Building Red America: The New Conservative Coalition and the Drive for Permanent Power* (New York: Basic Books, 2006).

35. Eastland, *Energy in the Executive*, 4.

36. Roth, *The Plot Against America* (Boston: Houghton Mifflin, 2004), 28.

37. Roth disavows the "epic," of course, and claims to replace it with disaster. But it's difficult to find a more appropriate description for the heroic cross-country journey taken by Herman Roth in *The Plot Against America*.

38. For an especially eloquent example of Obama's campaign rhetoric, see, Full Text of Senator Barack Obama's Announcement for President (February 10, 2007), available at: http://www.barackobama.com/2007/02/10/remarks_of_senator_barack_obam_11.php. On the assassination rumors that followed his victory in the Iowa Democratic Caucus, see "'Wash Times' Looks at Fears of Obama Assassination," *Editor and Publisher* (January 7, 2008), available at: http://www.editorandpublisher.com/eandp/news/article_display.jsp?vnu_content_id=1003692434.

INDEX